LONDON ASSOCIATION OF CLASSICAL TEACHERS

LACTOR 21

SPARTA

EDITED BY M.G.L. COOLEY

WITH CONTRIBUTIONS BY
  W. G. CAVANAGH
  T. EDWARDS
  A. HARKER
  S. HODKINSON
  K. R. HUGHES
  M. PRETZLER
  B.W.J.G. WILSON

SPARTA

ISBN: 978-0-903625-40-1

PREFACE

This is, to my knowledge, the first ever full-scale sourcebook on Sparta.[1] By filling that considerable and long-standing gap the LACTOR committee hopes to make easier the teaching of topics on Sparta on school and university syllabuses. This volume has long been promised, and does now finally appear in time for the latest change to UK A-levels.

As an absolute *neodamodes* in studying Sparta I have been greatly dependent on the help offered to me by the two kings and some of the ephors of Spartan studies, (if they will excuse my referring to them in this way!). Professor Paul Cartledge saved me from a huge number of errors, small and great, by his careful reading of a draft, and his comments have greatly improved the text and notes at many points. Stephen Hodkinson's advice was instrumental in forming the structure of the volume; he provided comments on several sections and wrote the introduction to Spartan Epigraphy; I have also reused, with his kind permission, some of the notes he has previously written for schoolteachers. Maria Pretzler will also recognize many of her notes written for JACT incorporated into this volume. Bill Cavanagh provided the notes on Spartan Archaeology (an area which goes way beyond my understanding) and two of the maps. Paul Christesen has generously shared some of his current research on Sparta, even to the point of allowing a new interpretation of an important text to appear here in advance of its full publication. Naturally, though, none of these experts are to be held in any way responsible for the errors and faults that remain.

I am also very grateful to a number of people who have helped translate the texts included here. Brian Wilson translated all the main prose texts: Herodotus, Thucydides, Xenophon's *Constitution of the Lakedaimonians*, and Plutarch's *Life of Lykourgos*. It has been a great pleasure working with him on various LACTORs over the years. Ken Hughes translated Tyrtaios, Alkman and Aristophanes. Both these gentlemen will have wondered if their superb work would ever appear in print, and I thank them for their patience as well as their skill. Terence Edwards translated a good deal of Plutarch, not all of which appears here (some will be on the LACTOR website) and meticulously checked the text. Andrew Harker translated several passages of Xenophon. Other translations are mine.

Most of the photos are from the wonderful British Museum non-commercial images service. I am grateful to Matthew Nicholson, Polly Low, and the Ashmolean Museum Cast Gallery for assistance with other photos.

I dedicate this book to a great friend and former colleague, Jeremy Thomas.

M.G.L. Cooley
Head of Scholars, Warwick School

---

[1] Talbert's 'Penguin' volume translates Plutarch's most important works on Sparta, as well as Xenophon's *Constitution*. Rhodes, *Greek City States* has an excellent section on Sparta. Cartledge, *Sparta and Lakonia* has a very useful appendix, giving all the texts relating to helots.

4

TABLE OF CONTENTS

6

LIST OF FIGURES, MAPS, ILLUSTRATIONS AND TABLES

Illustrations

Tables

8

NOTES AND ABBREVIATIONS

Dates are BC unless otherwise indicated.

'Archaic period' is used to refer to the years 800–500 BC; 'Classical period' for the years 500–323 BC; 'Hellenistic period' for the years 323–100 BC; '(Roman) Imperial Period' for the years 31 BC – AD 200.

Square brackets enclose editorial material inserted into the texts. This includes chapter and section numbers, references to the texts, explanatory glosses, and supplements to fragmentary literary or epigraphic texts. In some cases I have used square brackets part of the way through a word or name to indicate roughly how much of the original Greek word survives.

Like almost all modern editors I have been inconsistent in transliteration of names. In principle I have converted *kappa* to 'k' and *chi* to 'ch'. But some names are so familiar in Latinised or Anglicised versions that a consistent rendering would be pedantic and confusing. So Thucydides and Sicily appear (not 'Thoukudides' and 'Sikelia').

I have tried to be more consistent in translating to refer to the 'Lakedaimonians' as Greek authors always do. They are less consistent in referring to their town as 'Sparta' or 'Lakedaimon', but I have replicated whichever name they used. 'Spartiate' translates that particular term by which a Greek author designated a full citizen. I do of course use the term 'Spartan' in notes to refer to the people and their culture.

BM	The British Museum, London
BSA	The British School at Athens
Cartledge, *SL*	P. Cartledge, *Sparta and Lakonia, A Regional History 1300 – 362 BC* (Routledge 2002)
Cartledge, *Agesilaos*	P. Cartledge, *Agesilaos and the Crisis of Sparta* (Baltimore 1987)
CQ	*The Classical Quarterly* (Oxford University Press)
Diels-Kranz	H. Diels & W. Kranz, *Fragmente der Vorsokratiker* (Fragments of the Pre-Socratic philosophers), 6th ed. Berlin 1952
FGrH	F. Jacoby, *Die Fragmente der griechischen Historiker,* Berlin 1923–58
Hodkinson, *PWCS*	S. Hodkinson, *Property and Wealth in Classical Sparta* (Classical Press of Wales 2000)
Hodkinson, NSW	S. Hodkinson, '*Transforming Sparta: new approaches to the study of Spartan society*' in Ancient History: Resources for Teachers Vol 41–44 (2011–2014) Macquarie University, NSW, Australia
Hornblower, *Commentary*	S. Hornblower, *A Commentary on Thucydides* (3 vols, Oxford, 1991, 1996, 2008)
IG	*Inscriptiones Graecae,* Berlin 1873–
JHS	*Journal of Hellenic Studies*
LSAG	L. Jeffery, *Local Scripts of Ancient Greece* (rev. A. Johnston, Oxford 1990). Numbers refer to the Lakonia section unless otherwise stated.
LSJ	Liddell & Scott, *Greek-English Lexicon,* 9th ed., rev, H. Stuart Jones (Oxford 1925–40)
ML	R. Meiggs & D.M. Lewis, *Greek Historical Inscriptions to the End of the Fifth Century,* (rev. ed., Oxford 1988)
OCD	S. Hornblower & A. Spawforth (eds) *The Oxford Classical Dictionary,* 3rd ed., Oxford 1996
RO	P. Rhodes & R. Osborne, *Greek Historical Inscriptions* 404–323 BC, Oxford 2003
OR	R. Osborne & P. Rhodes, *Greek Historical Inscriptions* 478–404 BC, Oxford 2017
SEG	*Supplementum Epigraphicum Graecum,* Leiden 1923–

GLOSSARY

agathoergoi: men on state missions: see **D22**.

agoge: a term used by post-classical sources to refer to the education of a Spartan boy (cf. *paideia*).

agora: the religious, commercial and political centre of a Greek *polis*.

apella: a feast of Apollo, celebrated on the seventh day of each month. As the Spartan assembly (*ekklesia*) was also held on this day it is sometimes wrongly used to mean the assembly-meeting itself.

dekarchy: literally 'rule by ten', set up in many parts of Athens' former empire by Lysander in 404 BC. The rulers were military despots; their rule unpopular and mostly short. **E130–1**.

eiren (pl. *eirenes,* anglicised to *eirens*): a Spartan man in his twenties.

ekklesia: general Greek name for a voting assembly of all full citizens. See note before **D23**.

enomotia: small group of Spartiate soldiers.

ephor: one of five, annually elected chief magistrates.

gerousia: council of elders (*gerontes*): see note before **D12**.

hebon (pl. **hebontes**): a Spartan man in his twenties.

homoioi ('equals'): the name the Spartiates gave to themselves.

krypteia: group of young Spartans sent out on night-time training exercise of unclear purpose (**D42–D44**).

Lakedaimonians: the Greek term always used to describe 'Spartans'.

Lakedaimon: alternative name for the town 'Sparta' and for the state territory.

lochos: 'unit', led by a *lochagos* (**D85**).

m(i)na (pl. *minai*): unit of currency.

mora (pl. *morai*) a division of the army comprising 500 or 700 or 900 men (**D87**).

mothakes: those adopted as children by wealthy Spartan families: see **D30–D31**.

navarch (Gk. *nauarchos*): commander of the Spartan navy (a regular office only from 409 BC).

neodamodeis: helots probably set free to serve in the army (**D45**).

oliganthropia: shortage of Spartiate manpower.

paidagogos: usually a slave, in charge of a child's education throughout Greece.

paideia: the usual term used by classical authors to describe the education of a boy (*pais*, pl. *paides*) in Sparta and elsewhere in Greece.

paidonomos: a senior Spartan, responsible for supervising boys' education (**D74**).

pentekostys: group of Spartan soldiers.

phidition: the mess-meal, see **E77**.

polemarch: 'war-leader'.

polis (pl. *poleis*): the Greek 'city-state' with its own laws and systems of government. Often translated 'city', but much more the population of a modern town, and including some land and villages around it.

politeia: how a *polis* operated, its constitution, but also customs and general ideas about behaviour of its citizens (*politai*).

proxenos: representative of one Greek state in another (**B1** note).

Pythia: the priestess of Apollo at Delphi (**D8**).

rhetra: a generic term for set of rules forming the basis of the Spartan constitution: the main one attributed to Lykourgos is the 'Great Rhetra': see **D48** *skytale*: secret message stick: see **D21**

stele (pl. *stelai*): a slab of stone or bronze on which inscriptions were carved/incised.

syssition: mess-meal (also known as *phidition, syskania*).

xenos: 'guest-friend', the friendship being between men from different states and including their descendants.

INTRODUCTION TO THE LITERARY SOURCES

Source criticism is a crucial aspect of any study of ancient Sparta. Many literary texts from the fifth century BC onwards reflect an idealisation and distortion of traditions about Spartan society, a concept now generally referred to as the Spartan 'mirage' (see introduction to Section F). It is important to understand that there is no ancient text that can serve as a 'main source', especially because the most extensive accounts, e.g. Plutarch's works on Sparta, were written in the Roman period. Moreover, the information about Sparta's history and culture which is recorded in the surviving literary sources was not recorded by Spartans. Apart from two poets of the seventh century BC, namely Tyrtaios and Alkman, we do not have any literary sources that originate from Sparta. In the classical period, Sparta was not easily accessible to strangers, and therefore many accounts of this period were probably written without personal knowledge of the place, and with little access to primary evidence. Xenophon is a noteworthy exception, but this does not mean that his account is without difficulties. Sparta changed considerably after Messenia was liberated (370/69 BC), and all ancient sources written after the mid-fourth century are either dealing with very different circumstances, or they were actually describing a historical situation which was no longer accurate. Many later sources probably represent a mixture of both failings, combined with Spartan stereotypes.

Since Sparta played a central role in Greek history, especially in the Archaic and Classical periods, its foreign policy and military campaigns are prominent in the historical texts that provide the main narrative for these periods, especially Herodotus, Thucydides and Xenophon's *Hellenika*. The goings-on behind the scenes are more difficult to reconstruct, usually by combining the few details about events in Sparta reported by outsiders with our general knowledge of the Spartan constitution and careful analysis of Sparta's activities abroad.

Alkman: poet of the late-seventh century, BC, probably Spartan. See intro to **A13–A20**.

Aristophanes: Aristophanes' comedies were written between 427 and 386 BC to entertain an Athenian audience at a particular religious festival. They are topical and engage with the political situation of the day, but, since playwrights were competing for the audience's favour, they were probably careful not to present political opinions which would antagonise a large part of the audience. The *Lysistrata* (performed 411 BC) is among a number of Aristophanes' comedies which advocate peace with Sparta, and although there are references to some points of contention in the conflict (chosen for double entendre as much as for topicality), the debate about war and peace is mostly conducted in very general (and of course comical) terms. Aristophanes offers us a number of comedy Spartans, both male and female; the *Lysistrata* is particularly useful as a guide to Athenian stereotypes of Sparta in this period.

Aristotle: (384–322 BC) philosopher and polymath from Chalkidike, but based in Athens for much of his adult life. One of his many interests was in the different constitutions of Greek states. His students researched and described 158 constitutions, among them that of Sparta. This does not survive, but was used extensively by later authors, including Plutarch. Aristotle also used this research for his theoretical work in the *Politics*. He offers valuable criticism of the Spartan system, informed by Sparta's decline in the fourth century.

Athenaios: (flourished *c.* AD 200). From Naukratis in Egypt. His *Deipnosophistai – 'Scholars at Dinner'* presents, in 15 books, the lengthy discussion of a wide variety of subjects, citing some 1,250 authors and quoting over 10,000 lines of verse. Athenaios thus offers a treasure-trove of extracts from authors whose works do not survive, but he does not offer historical criticism himself.

Diodoros: (active 60–36 BC). A native of Sicily, Diodoros wrote a *Library of History* in 40 books, attempting to set events in Greece alongside those in Rome. For much of his account of fifth-century Greece he seems to have followed Ephoros (see below), but his attempts to convert Ephoros' topical treatment into the year-by-year accounts he wanted can result in mistakes in his apparently certain chronological framework (e.g. **H64**). At his best he conveys the virtues as well as the vices of his sources, at his worst he garbles even the accounts he has before him.

Ephoros: (*c.* 405–330 BC), from Kyme (Greek city on the Aegean coast of modern Turkey). His large-scale *History* from early times to his own day was important in antiquity but now lost, except where quoted directly or used as a major source by other writers (e.g. Strabo, Plutarch and Diodoros). Thought to have been pro-Athenian and inaccurate in military descriptions.

Herodotus: wrote *c.* 450s–420s BC. Herodotus was from Halikarnassos in Asia Minor, and is therefore one of the few Greek authors of the classical period who were not Athenian. He did, however, know Athens well and, some of his views are influenced by the growing conflict between Athens and Sparta in the mid-fifth century. Most of his work is based on original research and inquiries, and is therefore informed by the views of his own time. He often refers to (unnamed) informants, "the Spartans say", "the Corinthians have a different version", and it is a characteristic feature of his method that he presents different points of view on many issues. In some instances he also claims to have based his account on Spartan sources which clearly add a different point of view, although we have no way of telling how much of this information is indeed authentic. Herodotus generally admires Sparta's laws and the virtue and courage they inspired in individual Spartans. His narrative of the Persian Wars, especially the account of the battle of Thermopylai (**F9–F26**), had a lasting influence on ancient as well as modern perceptions of Sparta. Herodotus does, however, also present a less admirable side of Sparta: her imperialist tendencies, for example the episode of early attempts to conquer Tegea (and all of Arkadia), and the activities of Kleomenes I.

Kritias: (*c.* 460–403 BC). Most famous from Xenophon's portrayal (*Hell.* 2.3–4) as the extremist leader among the Thirty Tyrants of Athens (404–3). He was also a well-known cultural and intellectual figure (friend of Socrates, related to Plato) who wrote plays and works showing his admiration of contemporary Sparta, which survive in occasional quotations. He seems to have started the Spartan 'mirage' (see section F).

Oxyrhynchos Historian: the name usually given to the Athenian author of a narrative history of Greece found in quite substantial papyrus fragments at Oxyrhynchos. He cannot be identified for certain, but appears to be reliable and a near-contemporary of the events he describes. It is clear that Ephoros and Diodoros followed his account rather than Xenophon's.

Pausanias: (2nd century AD, from Asia Minor) wrote a detailed *Description of Greece*, based on his own visits, and divided into 10 books, by regions. Pausanias was particularly interested in ancient monuments, cults and traditions, and offers many useful details on these, often confirmed by archaeology. Book III deals with Sparta and Lakonia, but little of the information provided can be firmly linked to the classical period, offering instead a detailed insight into perceptions of Sparta in the Roman period. Book IV, on Messenia, offers a lengthy history of the Messenian Wars now regarded as an invention of the fourth century BC.

Plato: (*c.* 429–347 BC) the great Athenian philosopher. Grew up during the Peloponnesian War and with family members split pro- (e.g. Kritias) and anti-Sparta. Not surprisingly his philosophical dialogues sometimes refer to contemporary Sparta.

Plutarch: (before AD 50– after AD 120, from Chaironeia in Boiotia), author of biographical and philosophical writings. Plutarch was a very prolific writer and diligent researcher: often preserving information that is otherwise lost. The *Life of Lykourgos* illustrates this very well: Plutarch cites dozens of earlier works, and assembles a narrative from divergent opinions. But much of his material also dates from after Sparta's decline in the fourth century, and any information in his text that is not explicitly identified as taken from a genuinely archaic or classical source should be considered as secondary material. Moreover, while Plutarch was interested in historical detail, he insisted that his *Parallel Lives* of Greeks and Romans were not history – his main aim was to draw characters which could be instructive as moral examples (see Plutarch, *Life of Alexander* 1), not to provide historical analysis. This explains why for Plutarch the vague and contradictory traditions about a 'historical' Lykourgos were not an obstacle to writing his biography. Plutarch produced a number of works which deal with Sparta or individual Spartans: *Lives* of Lysander, Agesilaos, Agis and Cleomenes III; and in preparation for writing these he compiled *Sayings of Spartans and Spartan Women* and *Lakedaimonian Institutions* later included as part of his *Moralia*.

Simonides: (poet from Keos, flourished around Persian Wars, see on **A21** and **F20**).

Strabo: (64 BC – after AD 21). Wrote a *Geography* in 17 books, a rich source of information about the whole of the Roman Empire, but only occasionally informative about classical Greece.

Theopompos: historian from Chios, lived 378/7–*c.* 320. His summary of Herodotus and continuation of Thucydides survive only in later quotations. His erudition and strong invectives were famous in antiquity and he was known to have been critical of Athens.

Thucydides: (*c.* 455–400 BC). 'Thucydides the Athenian wrote the war of the Peloponnesians and the Athenians' as he tells us in the first words of what we call the *History of the Peloponnesian War.* Later he explains something of his sources of information:

> "I lived through it all while being old enough to understand it, and applied my attention so as to understand it accurately. In addition it happened that I was exiled from my own country for twenty years after my command at Amphipolis (424 BC) and became familiar with affairs on both sides, especially the Peloponnesians', because of my exile, and getting a better understanding of them through my leisure." (5.26.5).

The work does indeed seem to draw on information about the goings-on within the Peloponnesian League, although it is difficult to tell how much he really knew about exact details, for example speeches delivered at league assemblies (see Thuc. 1.22.1). Sparta herself remains a somewhat mysterious place (e.g. Thuc. 5.68.2; cf. 4.80.3). Thucydides does not present the Spartans in a deliberately negative light: both sides receive praise and blame for their actions. However, Thucydides' general view of Sparta seems to be strongly influenced by an Athenian perspective, not so much as an enemy, but rather as a polar opposite, and some of Thucydides' general statements about Sparta can be read as subtle comments on Athens (see 2.5).

Tyrtaios: elegiac poet of mid-seventh century BC, probably Spartan. See intro to **A1–A12**.

Xenophon: (*c.* 430-*c.* 350 BC) writer of various prose works. From a wealthy Athenian family, Xenophon fought in Asia Minor for Cyrus and then Agesilaos II, and again for him at the battle of Koroneia, resulting in his exile from Athens. The Spartans gave him an estate near Olympia, and he may have lived in Sparta and even had his sons participate in the Spartan education system (Plut. *Mor.* 212B). Certainly he had access to first hand information about Sparta and reason to be grateful to Agesilaos and Sparta.

The *Constituton of the Lakedaimonians* (*Lakedaimonion Politeia*) was probably written in the late 390's or 380's BC (chapter 14 is generally considered later). The work offers us the only detailed and well informed information about Sparta before the changes that followed the defeat at Leuktra. Nevertheless, Xenophon's description remains vague in many respects: it was not meant to be a detailed anthropological study, but rather a kind of political pamphlet, defending Sparta against its critics. The text probably depicts a somewhat idealised Sparta, and Xenophon's view of Lykourgos represents an extreme position: he credits more aspects of Spartan society to the lawgiver than any other ancient source, and he expresses a particular admiration. It is impossible to determine how much of this reflects genuine Spartan views, but we can probably assume that this is the perspective of a well-informed sympathiser. Xenophon also used his knowledge about Sparta in his other works. The *Hellenika* (political history covering 411–362 BC) includes many details on Peloponnesian history. Xenophon's biography of *Agesilaos* develops the image of the ideal, noble Spartan. Various comments on Sparta can also be found in Xenophon's philosophical writings.

INTRODUCTION TO THE EPIGRAPHY OF LAKONIA AND MESSENIA

The evidence of epigraphy has been a comparatively neglected aspect of Spartan studies: a neglect that this sourcebook aims to redress. The sources presented include a range of inscriptions displaying the thoughts and actions of a variety of individuals (mostly Spartiate men, but also a sprinkling of others) and collective groups (not just the Spartan *polis*, but also its enemies, including rebel Messenians). These inscriptions are far from complete or fully representative in their coverage. However, their evidence is more diverse and inclusive than the literary texts, providing contemporary 'insider' evidence unmediated by the lens of external or later literary commentators.

The comparative neglect of inscriptions is partly due to the Spartiates' undeserved reputation for illiteracy. Despite Plutarch's claim that their 'reading and writing lessons were restricted to the minimum necessary' (**D76**), recent studies have shown that the Spartiates were far more literate than previously supposed and that the written word was central to the conduct of *polis* affairs. The ephors, whose remit included diplomatic negotiations (**E43, E144**), were elected from the whole citizen body and could include poor citizens (**D18**). Consequently, 'the minimum necessary' was that even ordinary Spartiates needed sufficient literacy to engage with written foreign policy texts, such as the treaties and interim negotiation documents recorded with precision by Thucydides (**B16–22**). These and other official documents, such as records of Delphic oracles and laws such as the 'Great Rhetra' (**D8, D48**), were probably stored in a rudimentary archival system spread across different locations, including the main sanctuaries and the houses of the kings and other citizens engaged in foreign affairs (**E135**).

How many of these official documents were 'monumentalised' as public inscriptions is uncertain. Not secular laws, and probably not oracles either. However, we should not be misled by the small number of public inscriptions surviving today. After antiquity the deserted site of Sparta served as a quarry for lime burners. Also, because the local marble was hard to work, many inscriptions were probably written on bronze plaques, later melted down for their metal content. Diplomatic agreements were often publicly displayed at Sparta itself (**B15, B17, B18**), as were official lists of sporting victors (cf. **C62**). Probable lists of victors in contests at local festivals have been found at both Sparta and the perioikic *polis* of Geronthrai (*LSAG* 195, 201 nos. 44–47). Dedications celebrating military victories were also frequently inscribed at sanctuaries abroad.

These epigraphic practices first become evident in the mid-sixth century, when an agreement with Tegea was displayed on a (now lost) *stele* set up on the banks of the River Alpheios (Aristotle, fr. 592). Around 500 BC the Spartiates dedicated an inscribed bronze cauldron at Olympia (**B3**). They also commemorated their exploits in the Persian Wars with monuments at Thermopylai and Delphi (**B4–5**), and also at home (**F27**). Similar inscribed dedications after military victories continued at Olympia (**B8, 10a–b**) and Delphi (**B23**) for the rest of the fifth century – a practice mirrored by several of Sparta's enemies (**B11, B29, B31–B33**). Among enemy dedications, two examples are especially intriguing: first, the dedications of two spear-butts by the Messenian rebels of the 460s, one at Olympia, the other at the sanctuary of Apollo Korythos at Longa in Messenia itself (**B9a–b**); secondly, the

16

joint dedication by the exiled Messenians and the Naupaktians of the famous winged
Nike of Paionios at Olympia in *c.* 421 BC (**B14**). Around 470, Sparta set up public
inscriptions at Sparta and Olympia listing the multiple athletic victories of one of their
former Olympic victors (**C45–C46**). Public inscriptions at Sparta recording treaties,
alliances and a unique war-fund donation list are not attested until the late fifth century
(**B12, B15, B17–B18**), but we should not assume that it was a new practice. The
late fifth century also sees the first direct epigraphic evidence for the burial abroad
of fallen Lakedaimonian soldiers, the tomb of the war-dead from King Pausanias'
expedition to Athens in 403 (**B25a–b**); but we know from literary evidence that this
practice went back to the sixth century (**E11, H12**).

These public inscriptions are outnumbered by a much greater number of surviving
private inscriptions. The vast majority are formal in character: the main categories
being religious dedications – including sporting and military dedications – and
epitaphs for the deceased. There are just a few examples of informal literacy, most
notably at Amyklai: graffiti inscribed on certain terracotta plaques at the sanctuary of
Agamemnon and Kassandra (G. Salapata, *Heroic Offerings* 55) and masons' names
scratched on architectural blocks from the late-sixth-century throne of Apollo (*LSAG*
200 no. 32). On sixth-century Lakonian black-figure pottery there are a few dipinti
clarifying pictured scenes (*LSAG* 199 no. 8), but no potters' or painters' names;
even the dipinti disappear from classical Lakonian red-figure pottery. There are no
abecedaria and no informal boasts or obscenities.

As indicated, the vast majority of private inscriptions are religious in character,
expressing a dedication made to a god or hero, most commonly as a thank-offering
(**C1–C36**). These dedications were made at diverse sanctuaries, mostly within Spartan
territory, though a significant minority were made at foreign sanctuaries, especially at
Olympia and Delphi but sometimes beyond mainland Greece (**B7, C16**). Some of the
private foreign dedications overlap with official inscriptions: for example, the regent
Pausanias' personal inscription on the tripod and serpent column at Delphi celebrating
his victory at Plataia, which was erased and replaced by an official Spartan inscription
(**B5–6**); or the so-called Navarchs' monument at Delphi, which celebrated the
Lakedaimonians' victory at Aigospotamoi, but also gave centre stage to the personal
achievement of Lysander and his subordinate naval commanders (**B23**). Others
intersect more indirectly with public foreign policy, such as the inscribed marble seats
at Olympia of two Spartiates who acted as *proxenoi* for the *polis* of Elis (**B1–2**), or
the memorial to the deceased King Agesipolis I set up by his father, the exiled former
king Pausanias (**B28**). However, the largest category of private inscriptions at foreign
sanctuaries is those accompanying the dedications of Olympic athletic and equestrian
victors, attested sometimes through the survival of the original inscription (**C49, C55,
C59**), but more frequently through the evidence of Pausanias' *Description of Greece*,
which describes the surviving monuments and inscriptions of Spartiate chariot-race
victors in his account of the sanctuary of Olympia in the second century AD (**C52**).

The private inscriptions within Spartan territory go back to the late seventh century BC
(**C6, C29**) and continue throughout the period covered by this volume. The religious
dedications are inscribed on various kinds of objects and materials. The most common
is diverse types of bronze items, such as figurines and statuettes of humans, gods and

animals (**C3–C4, C17–C19, C27**), mirrors (**C2, C14**), plates or vessels (**C8, C29**) and miniature bells (**C15**). There are a significant number of inscribed dedicatory marble or limestone *stelai* or plaques ((**C7, C11–C12, C28, C31, C34, C36**), including a notable series of hero-reliefs, as well as some dedications on ivory objects (**C6**), pottery (**C21, C32**) and terracotta plaques. Stone or marble *stelai* were also used by athletes listing multiple victories (**C67, C79, C83**), for epitaphs (**B36–B55**) and for a small group of manumission inscriptions (**C20**). The intrinsic value of the materials used and the production costs of the objects bearing the inscriptions, not to mention the costs of the inscriptions themselves, all suggest that the individuals who commissioned them were mostly well-off persons with a fair degree of disposable wealth.

One striking (and perhaps connected) feature, in a society with a reputation for prioritising the collective over the individual, is that the private inscriptions within Spartan territory share the same intensely personal focus as the inscriptions abroad. Many of the dedicatory inscriptions advertise the dedicator's name (**C1, C4–C5, C7–C18, C25, C27–C29, C31**). The athletes' dedications celebrate their individual prowess by listing their victories (**C67, C78, C79, C83, C86, C88, C89**) or by inscribing the dedication on an object – typically a jumping weight or a discus (**C80–C82**) – that they used in the contest. Notably, these sporting dedications are far more numerous than the small number of inscribed dedications with military associations (**C4, C10**). In contrast, most of the inscribed epitaphs are explicit memorials for fallen soldiers (**B36, B40–B43, B47, B49–B53**) or for priests (**B38, B44**); but they too are mostly individual memorials, and the deceased's athletic success is sometimes also mentioned as a supplementary mark of personal esteem (**B53**; cf. **B25a & c**).

Another striking feature is that these various types of inscriptions come not just from Sparta and its environs, but also from elsewhere in Spartan territory, especially in Lakonia. For example, dedications to Artemis and Apollo occur not only at Spartiate sanctuaries like Artemis Orthia and Apollo at Amyklai, but also at sanctuaries in perioikic areas such as the sanctuaries of Artemis at Pleiai (**C9**), Apollo Hyperteleatas at Cotyrta (**C2–C3**), Apollo Maleatas at Prasiai (**C4**) and Apollo Pythaieus at Tyros (**C5**). Dedications by athletes at Amyklai and at Athena Chalkioikos on Sparta's acropolis are matched at perioikic sanctuaries such as that of Apollo at Geronthrai (**C79**) and the hero Timagenes at Aigiai (**C80**). Epitaphs for deceased soldiers or priests are found both at Sparta and at perioikic *poleis* or other settlements such as Pellana (**B49**), Geronthrai (**B43**), Leuktra (**B39**), and Gerenia in Messenia (**B44**). This implies that free Lakedaimonians across Spartan territory shared common religious practices and epigraphic habits: a sign of the cultural homogeneity underpinning the mutual solidarity of Spartiates and *perioikoi* in both peace and war.

A final notable aspect is a small number of dedicatory inscriptions commissioned by women: mostly by Spartiate women, but at least one inscribed mirror dedicated by a woman, a certain Alkido, is known from the perioikic sanctuary of Apollo Hyperteleatas (P.G. Kalligas, *Lakonikai Spoudai* 5, 1980, 21). Though few in number, these inscriptions frequently shed light on wider bodies of archaeological evidence. The bronze figure of Eleuthia (**C27**) – i.e. Eileithyia, goddess of childbirth – dedicated, probably in the fifth century, by a certain Aristomacha, is of unknown provenance; but it plausibly links with two earlier dedications, a bronze pin-head and

18

die, to the same goddess, found at the sanctuary of Artemis Orthia (*LSAG*, rev. edn. 1989, 447 no. A). The die is dedicated jointly to Eleuthia and Orthia, which fits with Pausanias' statement (*Description of Greece* 3.17.1) that Eileithyia's shrine was 'not far' from Artemis Orthia, perhaps within the same *temenos*. Aristomacha's dedication also confirms the presence of female dedicators at the sanctuary, already inferred from the large number of bronze jewellery votives and numerous lead figurines depicting model looms and female figures with elaborately patterned dresses. Equally significant is the prominence of female dedicators to Sparta's patron goddess Athena on the Spartan acropolis. Of the four inscribed bronze offerings found on the acropolis that bear the dedicator's name, three were dedicated by women: a mirror dedicated by a certain Euonyma (**C14**) and two bells dedicated, respectively, by Kalikratia and Eirana (for the first of these, **C15**). The bells, which date between *c.* 475 and the early fourth century, were not associated exclusively with women: the dedicator of a third inscribed bell was male. However, the fact that two of the three known dedicators of the bronze bells were women makes it probable that women also dedicated many of the surviving 34 bronze and 102 terracotta bells from the sanctuary that are uninscribed or whose inscription omits the dedicator's name (cf. A. Villing, *BSA* 97, 2002, 223–295). Bells made in the same workshop also occur outside Sparta: at the Menelaion, at Aigiai in Lakonia and the sanctuary of Apollo Korythos at Longa in Messenia: further evidence, along with the inscribed mirrors, that Spartiate and perioikic women, like their menfolk, shared common religious practices.

Of course, the most dramatic piece of female epigraphic evidence comes from outside Spartan territory: Kyniska's epigram on her statue-base at Olympia, celebrating her four-horse chariot-race success in 396 or 392 (**C55**), which not only emulated but exceeded the inscriptions of male Spartiate chariot-racing victors by boasting about her royal breeding and her unique position as the only female victor at the Olympic games. Unlike her Spartiate male counterparts, Kyniska's epigraphic victory celebrations continued inside Lakonikē, to judge from a small inscribed Doric capital and abacus that she dedicated to Helen at the sanctuary of the Menelaion (*IG* 5.1.235): a fitting dedication for someone whose hero-shrine (**C56**) was later placed close to the sanctuary of Helen, the role-model for all female Spartiates. Thus the epigraphic texts provide precious evidence for the voices of a few, largely wealthy, women speaking in their own words. Sadly, this inclusivity does not extend to the enslaved populations of Lakonikē, especially the helots, whose voices or condition are revealed only at the moment of their self-liberation (**B9**) or manumission (**C20**) from slavery.

Stephen Hodkinson
Nottingham University

INTRODUCTION TO LAKONIAN ARCHAEOLOGY

The archaeological evidence for the Spartan state is, like the written evidence, fragmentary, biased and open to interpretation. Lakonia and Messenia, the regions dominated by Sparta in the Classical period, are among the better researched parts of Greece, but even so archaeological exploration has barely scratched the surface. Sparta's sanctuaries, such as those of Apollo and Hyakinthos at Amyklai or of Orthia by the R. Eurotas, have been extensively explored, but much of the town is known only from scattered remains and excavations in advance of modern development; furthermore, the Archaic and Classical levels are often masked or destroyed by Roman building. With a few notable exceptions, such as Geronthrai and Messene, other towns are even less well-known. Happily, a long tradition of archaeological exploration recording the location and surface remains of ancient sites has mapped the main centres in Lakonia and Messenia, and intensive survey has, in recent years, revealed a pattern of small farmsteads and villages. Recording of ancient quarries and road systems adds to our understanding of ancient topography. All the same there are large gaps in our knowledge, and the database of archaeological information, in contrast with the historical sources, is constantly increasing. Careful study of pottery and other artefacts has improved the precision of archaeological chronology, but dates can seldom be refined even as closely as to a generation or two, so archaeological evidence can only rarely be tied in with historical events but serves better to distinguish broad trends in social and economic history.

Archaeological Background to the Rise of the Spartan State
The Late Bronze Age period (roughly 1700–1100 BC) saw the rise, dominance and fall of Mycenaean kingdoms. Each was ruled from a palace whose king (*wanax*) exercised military control over its territory, harnessed its economic resources, directed large numbers of skilled and unskilled workers, controlled officials in subsidiary towns, patronised local leaders, oversaw religious festivals, priests and priestesses. All these transactions are recorded on clay tablets (in the script known as Linear B). The palace in Messenia, the area later annexed by Sparta, was at Pylos. In Lakonia, Linear B tablets have recently been found and excavated in another imposing palace at Ayios Vasilios, 13 km south of Sparta. The palatial system declined and disappeared – the palace at Pylos was destroyed around 1200 BC, that at Ayios Vasilios perhaps 100 years earlier. The later centuries of the 2nd Millennium saw the fall of major powers over much of the east Mediterranean, as well as Greece. For the period 1100–800 BC archaeology indicates widespread and catastrophic depopulation, as severe in Lakonia and Messenia as anywhere. Around 900 BC graves around Sparta indicate an early sign of the scattered 'villages' from which the later city grew. Pottery of the same period has been found at sanctuaries which were to be the focus of Sparta's calendar of festivals: of Apollo and Hyakinthos at Amyklai, of Athena on the acropolis, of Orthia by the R. Eurotas. Sparta is not alone: sites elsewhere produce similar pottery, some later to be perioikic towns. Over the next two centuries the offerings become richer, and site-numbers slowly increase. But still both Lakonia and Messenia were thinly populated, and archaeology alone, if we did not have the testimony of Tyrtaios, would not indicate that by then Sparta was well on the way to dominating Lakonia and Messenia. A few warrior graves in Sparta and Messenia are our only hint of unsettled times. Modern scholarship indicates a

gulf between the Mycenaean kingdoms and the city states of historical times. The Greeks of the 8th and 7th centuries BC, if in very different terms, recognised that the age of heroes described in the epic tradition was remote from their own world; the Spartans bridged the gap by reference to myth, notably that the Spartan kings as the descendants of Herakles had a right to the land which they and their followers, after moving down from central Greece, had reconquered (A3). How much, if any, historical truth lay behind the myths we cannot say.

Early Archaic (8th–7th centuries BC)

The increasing prosperity of Sparta is witnessed mainly through finds from the sanctuaries: bronze tripods, elaborate pottery, iron weapons, jewellery, carved ivories.

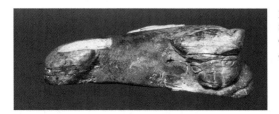

Figure 1. Ivory Lion of 7th century BC, from Sanctuary of Artemis Orthia. The lion is 7.5 cm long. BM 1923,0212: photo © Trustees of the British Museum.

Small temples were built, such as the early one at Pellana (20 km north of Sparta); by the mid-7th century distinctive terracotta roof-decorations (disc *akroteria* [finials], antefixes, *simas* [gutters]) characterised Spartan temples. They are found not only at the major sanctuaries such as Orthia and Amyklai, but throughout Sparta and its environs (e.g. the sanctuaries of Zeus Messapeus, Athena Chalkioikos, Agamemnon and Alexandra, Helen and Menelaos) and elsewhere in Lakonia (at Aigai and Kastraki – 35–50 km south of Sparta); the style was imitated widely in the Peloponnese. Even for their time, these are modest buildings – the temple of Orthia measured about 16 x 7 m (roughly one eighth of the size of the peripteral temple of Hera at Olympia, with its great akroterion). Already the Spartans avoid excessive monumentality at home, but the skill and grace of these artefacts serve to undermine the notion of a grim austerity. Little lead figurines, humbler votives, celebrate the participants in festivals: hoplite warriors, female celebrants – perhaps members of choruses (A14) and processions, flute and lyre players, gods and goddesses and the animals sacred to them, token imitations of rich offerings, and the wreath-crowns worn at festivals.

The earliest inscriptions found in Lakonia belong to the later 7th century (C6, C29), but the alphabet was first introduced to Greece over a century earlier and almost certainly to Lakonia too; writing will already have formed part of a Spartan's education.

Figure 2. 6th-century bronze statuette, 10 cm. tall of warrior, found at Sparta. BM 1929,1016.6: photo © Trustees of the British Museum.

Later Archaic (6th–early 5th centuries BC)

The artistic trends observed in the preceding period continued with increasing sophistication. Lakonian pottery includes vessels for *symposia*, some painted with scenes of luxury, others with images of heroes, but also the unexpected, such as the cup with king Arkesilas of Kyrene in Libya weighing out silphium; great storage jars had elaborate scenes impressed from moulds. This period saw the stone hero reliefs, which have been found both in Sparta and in perioikic Lakonia; however, as in much of the Peloponnese (in contrast to Attica and other regions), free standing *kouroi/korai* are not attested. Bronze working reached a high point with massive vessels *intricately* decorated like the famous Vix krater. The Spartans were *au fait* with the latest developments in architecture, as witnessed by a few Doric capitals (from near Sparta and from Geronthrai and Kalamai), a triglyph from the Menelaion, and the famous 'Throne of Apollo' at Amyklai; but evidence for large temples is hard to identify. The Spartans seem to have had a taste for unusual monuments, often finely worked in valuable materials, such as the 'Bronze House' of Athena Chalkioikos.

Lakonian pottery of the mid-sixth century BC.

Figure 3 (left): Hydria, 39.37 cm tall, found at Vulci in Italy as prized grave-goods. BM 1849,0518.14.

Figure 4 (above): Kylix by 'the Rider Painter', diameter 17.75 cm. BM 1842,0407.7

Photos © Trustees of the British Museum.

For the 6th and 5th centuries intensive archaeological survey has revealed a major change in rural settlement and the development of a dense network of small farmsteads and hamlets. A similar process has been recognised in other parts of Greece, though sometimes starting earlier than in Lakonia. Close to Sparta a mixture of sites ranging from the modest to larger and more prosperous ones has been distinguished; on Kythera sites in the interior were given over mainly to production, those on the coast were larger and more prosperous. A scatter of small sites has also been observed in southern Lakonia, for example around the town of Helos. Intensive survey in Messenia, however, has revealed a completely different configuration made up of larger village communities; these evidently housed the helots who worked the land for the Spartans. A large building excavated at Kopanaki in Messenia contained storage jars and loom weights and other finds indicating agricultural activity. These discoveries indicate changing responses to agricultural production; to a degree Sparta and Lakonia followed a trend recognisable elsewhere in the Peloponnese and central Greece, but at the same time its peculiar social and economic organisation influenced the patterns of rural exploitation.

In Lakonia, as elsewhere in Greece, pairs of grooves spaced an axle width of 1.4 m apart have traced a network of roads; they were carved to prevent carts from slipping. Our best guess dates them, from the settlements they connected, to the 6th century and later. They are found widely, even high in the mountains, and served for both military traffic and the transport of heavy goods, crops and even people.

Classical (5th–4th centuries BC)

The picture of Sparta as no more than a collection of villages is an overstatement by Thucydides (**H1**); like many classical cities it had much open space given over not only to public buildings, but to squares, hippodromes and *palaistrai*. Unfortunately, archaeology has not provided clear evidence for much of its layout, and we are more reliant on written sources. The agora was a hub from which roads led out to the NE, to the Orthia sanctuary and to the main routes northwards, and the Aphetaïs was the processional road leading south to Amyklai; the agora's exact location is disputed. Pausanias, writing in the 2nd century AD, lists shrines and temples dedicated to gods and heroes many of which must have gone back to Archaic and Classical times, and there were tombs within the city, some evidently the locus for cult. The royal cemeteries of Sparta's kings have not, alas, yet been located; they were the most noteworthy but not the only examples of cult dedicated to contemporaries not just to heroes of the mythical past.

Public buildings included the Skias, built to shelter the assembly, the Persian Stoa, promoting Sparta's victory at Plataia, the Spartan messes, and the areas where, much to the shock of other Greeks, not only boys but also girls exercised. Public performances were grand occasions. There is mention of a 'theatre' as a site of religious ceremonial, and clay masks imitating original performance masks were dedicated at the sanctuary of Orthia by players of a series of stock characters. The religious processions also saw display in particular, special carriages (*kannathra*) were decorated with griffins and other beasts while the horses were richly caparisoned. All the same, monumentality was generally muted; though they were kept in repair and re-roofed every so often, evidence for large-scale stone reconstruction of temples is hard to identify.

Some perioikic towns (maps 3–4), to judge from surface remains or the area enclosed by their fortifications, were relatively small, no more extensive than some of the Attic demes: Sellasia 3 ha, Epidauros Limera 4 ha, Zarax 3.7 ha, Geronthrai 3.8 ha, Akriai may have reached 7–8 ha. Others such as Gytheion and Boia, for which we do not have data, may well have been much larger. Some of the identifications on maps 3–4 are secure, but uncertainty surrounds both the location and the status of others, while some of the more obscure towns cannot be placed on the map even approximately. Fortifications, such as those of Epidauros Limera, are thought to belong to the classical period, but are not dated precisely. The Athenian attacks during the Peloponnesian War (and earlier, Thuc. 1.108) on towns near the coast no doubt led to the construction of some defences; we know that Gytheion was fortified at least by 370 BC and excavations at Geronthrai have revealed a late classical phase of construction. The town of Sparta remained open until the Hellenistic period.

The port of Gytheion must have been important from early on and was the site of shipyards for the Spartan fleet. Boia also has a harbour and was important for its mineral resources: traces of iron workings are common there, and the more general area has deposits of lead and copper which may well have been tapped in antiquity. In addition to the agricultural commodities (corn, oil, wine), in particular of Messenia, timber may well have been another significant economic resource; the area around Kythera was famous for producing the prized purple dye.

Evidence from intensive survey close to Sparta has been used to argue for a gradual transformation in rural settlement. The smaller, possibly more marginal, sites become fewer and their holdings perhaps were swallowed up by the larger, more dominant sites. The location of sites also hints at both more investment in farming and perhaps greater diversification in the exploitation of the landscape.

Conclusion

In this brief review some of the contributions to our understanding of early Sparta have been summarised. As in the interpretation of the written sources so in understanding archaeological material there is much that is controversial; for example, some argue that it is possible to recognise the onset of Spartan austerity through an apparent decline in artistic creativity in the later Archaic period, whilst others argue that in this respect the Spartans were no different from other contemporaries elsewhere in the Peloponnese and the decline in arts such as vase painting or the making of bronze vessels does not reflect a political or social reform. These and other debates continue. Furthermore, every year there are fresh archaeological discoveries and new evidence leads to new interpretations. Such uncertainties make the study of archaeology both frustrating and stimulating – this section, perhaps more than any other in this book, will certainly need to be rewritten in the future.

W. G. Cavanagh
Professor Emeritus of Aegean Archaeology, Nottingham University

24

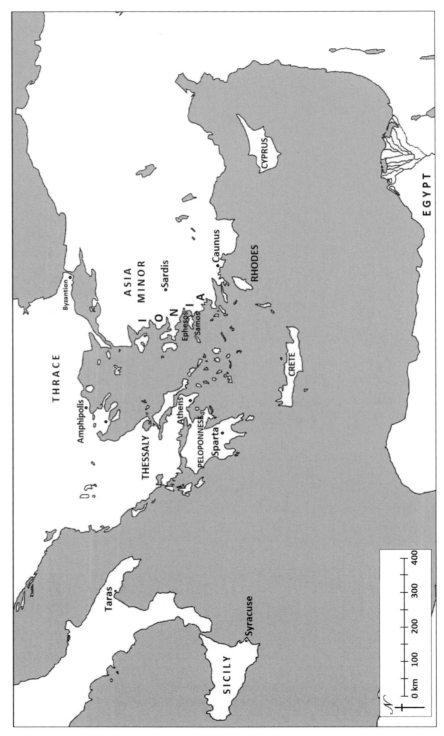

Map 1: Central and Eastern Mediterranean

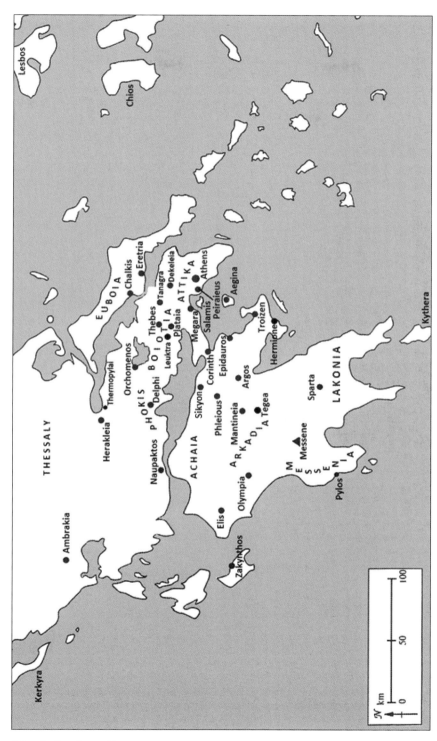

Map 2: Southern Greece

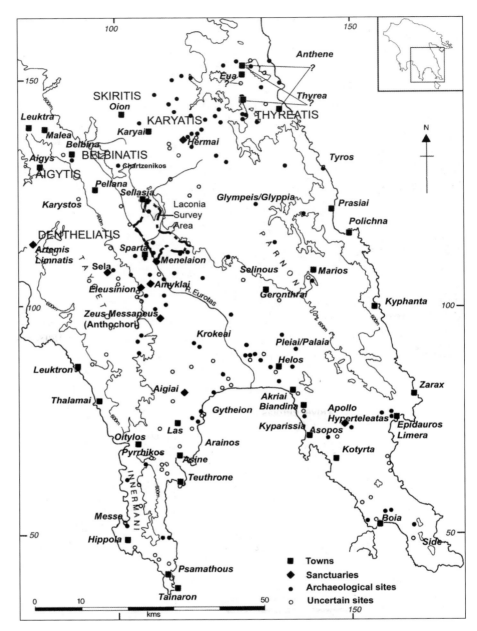

Map 3: Perioikic towns and other sites in Classical Lakonia

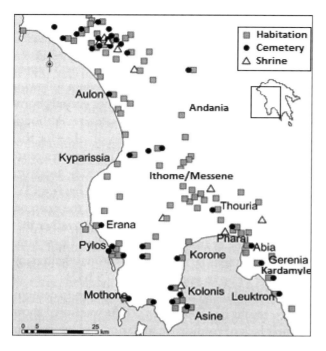

Map 4: Perioikic towns and other sites in Classical Messenia

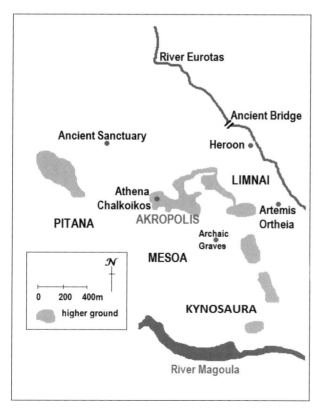

Map 5: The Town of Sparta

SECTION A
SPARTA FROM CONTEMPORARY SPARTAN POETRY

INTRODUCTION: THE EVIDENCE OF POETRY

Our best, and arguably only reliable literary evidence for Sparta comes from the works of two early poets, Tyrtaios and Alkman. But both pose a variety of problems for the historians. Firstly, of course, they were writing poetry not history, whatever the original intentions or the purposes to which they were later put. Then of course 'poetry is what gets lost in translation': the translations here are presented in short lines and verses where appropriate, to remind the reader of the original form, but they are certainly not poetry in English, nor is there any attempt to represent the difference between Tyrtaios' elegies written in traditional Ionic dialect (as used by Homer) and Alkman's lyric poetry, written in Doric dialect. A further difficulty is the way in which the poems survive. They were considered classics in later Greek and even Roman times, and were copied by hand for private and public libraries, but do not survive in anything like book or codex form: instead Tyrtaios, Alkman and Simonides survive either on original papyrus copies preserved in inevitably fragmentary condition in the sands of Egypt, or by being selectively quoted by writers, sometimes as historical evidence, sometimes to illustrate a word or literary feature, or sometimes in anthology. Finally we have no direct evidence about the authors themselves: the anecdotes and even mini-biographies that survive are sometimes by authors writing a thousand years later. All ancient *Lives* of poets tend to treat anything in the poems as autobiographical, and in addition the non-contemporary authors have potentially fallen victim to the reputation of the Spartans; or the irony, surely too good to be true, of Sparta's poet being a crippled Athenian schoolmaster. For more from these poets, see M. L. West, *Greek Lyric Poetry* (Oxford University Press, 1993).

TYRTAIOS: A1–A12

Tyrtaios seems to have lived in the mid-seventh century BC, and had a lasting influence not only on later sources but also on Spartan culture. His poetry continued to be recited in public and private contexts in Sparta, and it illustrates some of the ideals for which the Spartans were so famous. Today Tyrtaios' poetry is considered an invaluable primary source for early Sparta which gives us some insight into a time when momentous changes such as the earliest constitutional laws and the conquest of Messene were still a matter of living memory, and some aspects of Spartan life had not yet reached their 'final' form. Tyrtaios' poems therefore allow us to question some later ideas about the development of Spartan society, especially the 'Lykourgan reforms'. Later authors (e.g. Plutarch) also realised that Tyrtaios was a crucial authentic source for early Sparta, and therefore quoted passages to illustrate arguments about early Spartan history. Apart from a few lines of Tyrtaios that were discovered on papyrus, these quotations ensured the survival of the few poems which are known today. Plutarch, *Lykourgos* 6.5 (**D48** and **A4**) offers an excellent example, which can be used to compare ancient authors' use of earlier texts with modern approaches.

A1   The Suda encyclopaedia on Tyrtaios

Tyrtaios: son of Archembrotos, Lakonian or Milesian, elegiac poet and piper; it is said that by means of his lyric poetry he encouraged the Lakedaimonians when they were at war with the Messenians and thus gave them the upper hand. He is of very ancient date, contemporary with the so-called Seven Sages, or even older. At any rate, he flourished in the 35th Olympiad (640–637 BC). He wrote 'Constitution' for the Lakedaimonians, and 'Advice' in elegiac verse, and 'Martial Songs'; five books.

Tyrtaios: the Lakedaimonians vowed that they would either take Messene or die. When the god's oracular response told them to get a general from the Athenians, they got the poet Tyrtaios, who was lame; he inspired them to courage and captured Messene in the twentieth year of the war. They razed it to the ground and drafted the prisoners into the helots.

[Suda, *Lexicon*, "Tyrtaios"]

The Suda (meaning Fortress) is the name of a tenth-century AD lexicon or encyclopaedia compiled from earlier reference works. Pausanias (4.15.6) has the Athenians deliberately choosing someone likely to be a bad general for the Spartans.

A2   Spartan use of Tyrtaios' poetry

(Of the Pyrrhic Dance) The martial character of the dance makes it clearly an invention of the Lakedaimonians. The Lakonians are warlike, and their sons actually learn by heart these marching songs, which are also called 'Songs-in-Arms'. The Lakonians themselves, too, in their wars march rhythmically while reciting the poems of Tyrtaios from memory. Philochoros says that after the Lakedaimonians had defeated the Messenians through the generalship of Tyrtaios they established the custom on their campaigns that, when they had finished their dinner and sung the Song of Thanksgiving, one by one they should sing the songs of Tyrtaios; and the Commanding Officer should be the judge and give a prize of meat to the winner.

[Athenaios, *Scholars at Dinner* 14.29 = Philochoros, *FGrH* 328 F216]

A3   Tyrtaios 2: 'Eunomia' (Rule of Law)

[...] let us obey [the kings who are]   10
Nearer to the race [of the gods?]
For Zeus himself, the son of Kronos and husband of fair-crowned Hera,
Has given this city to the sons of Herakles;
Together with them we forsook windy Erineos
And arrived in the wide island of Pelops.   15

[Tyrtaios 2, *Rule of Law* = Strabo, *Geography* 8.4.10]

Part of a longer poem, found on Papyrus Oxyrhynchos 38.2824, with traces of several previous and one subsequent line visible. Lines 12–15, also fragmentary on the papyrus, are quoted by Strabo who wrote, 'Tyrtaios indeed says he is from that place in the elegiac poem which is entitled 'Eunomia''.

A4   Tyrtaios 4: Delphi's advice on governing Sparta

Having listened to Phoibos, they brought home from Delphi
God's oracles with their verses of certainty;
The leaders in counsel are the kings, honoured of the gods,
For they look after the lovely city of Sparta,
Together with the eldest-born; and after them the men of the People,   5
Responding in their turn with straight ordinances
Are to say the right things and do everything justly
And not give the city any crooked counsel,
And so victory and power go with the mass of the People.
This was the revelation of Phoibos to the city on these matters.   10

[Tyrtaios 4 = Plutarch, *Lykourgos* 6 + Diodoros 7.12.5–6]

The text is a combination of passages from Plutarch and Diodoros, see **D48** and **F5**.

A5 **Tyrtaios 5: The capture of Messene**
[...] to our king, dear to the gods, Theopompos,
Through whom we captured spacious Messene,
Messene good to plough and good to plant.
For it they fought ceaselessly for nineteen years
With their spears, our fathers' fathers 5
With ever long-suffering hearts;
And in the twentieth they abandoned their rich tilled fields
And fled the great ranges of Ithome.

[Tyrtaios 5]

These verses on the conquest of Messenia are actually put together from three separate quotations of Tyrtaios in later authors: lines 1–2 are from Pausanias 4.6.5; lines 3–4 from an ancient commentator on Plato, *Laws* 629a; lines 5–8 from Strabo 6.3.3.

A6 **Tyrtaios 6&7: The fate of the captured Messenians**
Like asses distressed by great burdens,
Bringing to their masters from grievous necessity
Half of all the produce the ploughland bears.

Lamenting for their masters, both they themselves and their wives,
Whenever the baneful fate of death overtook one.

[Tyrtaios 6&7 = Pausanias, *Description of Greece* 4.14.4–5]

Pausanias in his (largely invented) history of Messenia quotes Tyrtaios for how the captured Messenians were maltreated (lines 1–3) and that they were even forced to mourn their masters (4–5). Hdt. 6.58 (**D10**) notes the compulsion for some *perioikoi* to mourn a Spartan king.

A7 **Tyrtaios 10: '*Dulce et decorum est ...*'**
[106] For everyone in Greece knows that they got Tyrtaios from our city as the general with whom they overpowered their enemies and also set up the way they look after their young; thus they made fine decisions not only in face of the present danger but also for the whole of their future. For he composed elegiac poems which he bequeathed them, which they listen to and are taught to be courageous. [107] And though they have no regard for the other poets, they have valued this one so highly that they passed a law, that whenever they have taken the field under arms they summon everyone to the king's tent to hear the poems of Tyrtaios, in the belief that this would make them especially willing to die for their country. It is useful actually to hear these elegiac poems, in order to understand what sort of deeds made men famous among them.

For it is a noble thing for a good man to fall in the front line
And die fighting for his country.
But to abandon his city and its fertile fields
And be a beggar is most wretched of all,
Wandering about with his dear mother and aged father, 5
Together with his little children and wedded wife,
For he will be hated among all those whom he approaches
For surrendering himself to need and hateful poverty.
He shames his birth and belies his splendid appearance,

And is dogged by all evil and dishonour.   10
So since no one cares about a man who wanders like this,
Or feels respect or pity and the gods do not favour him,
Let us fight passionately for this land and die
For our children, no longer sparing our lives.
But come on, young men, stand firm beside each other and fight,   15
And do not start shameful flight or panic,
But make the spirit in your hearts great and valiant,
And when you fight against men, do not cling to life;
Do not abandon and run away from your fallen
Elders, who no longer have nimble knees,   20
For it is indeed disgraceful, when an older man fighting
In the front line lies fallen in front of young men,
And now with his white hair and grey beard
He breathes out his stout heart in the dust,
With private parts all bloody in his dear hands –   25
A sight for the eyes that brings shame and wrath –
And his skin is laid bare; but for a young man everything is all right,
As long as he keeps the glorious bloom of his lovely youth;
Wonderful for men to behold and lovely to women,
When he is alive, but also fine when fallen in the front line.   30
But let a man stand steadfast with both legs astride
Set firm on the ground, biting his lips with his teeth.

[Tyrtaios 10 = Lykourgos, *Against Leokrates* 106–7]

Lykourgos, *c. 390 – c. 325* BC was an important Athenian statesman, one of whose speeches, against a
political opponent, survives, and includes disproportionately long (but useful!) quotation of poets.

A8   Tyrtaios 11: Fight bravely!
But be confident, for you are descended from invincible Herakles;
Zeus is not yet averting his head from you;
And do not feel fear and terror at the host of men,
But let a man hold his shield straight in the face of their front line,
Thinking life hateful and the black fates of death   5
Dear as the rays of the sun.
For you know the destructive works of Ares who brings many tears,
And you have learnt well the temper of grievous war,
And often you have tasted both flight and pursuit,
You young men, and have had more than your fill of both.   10
For of those who are brave enough to stand beside each other
And go and fight hand to hand in the front line,
Fewer die, and they save the host behind them;
But when men tremble their valour is completely lost;
No one could ever finish recounting all   15
The evils that befall a man if he is dishonoured.
For in blazing war when a man runs away
You seize the chance to stab him in the shoulder-blades,
And it is a disgrace if a corpse is lying in the dust

Pierced behind by a spearpoint in the back.   20
But let a man stand steadfast with both legs astride
Set firm on the ground, biting his lips with his teeth,
Covering his thighs and shins below and chest and shoulders
With the belly of his broad shield;
In his tight hand let him brandish his mighty spear,   25
And shake the fearsome crest above his head;
By doing mighty deeds let him learn how to make war,
And not stand with his shield beyond missile range.
But let a man go near and wound his enemy with his long spear
Or sword at close quarters and kill him;   30
Putting foot beside foot and pushing shield against shield,
And even bringing crest to crest, helmet to helmet,
Chest to chest let him fight with a man,
Seizing the hilt of his sword or his long spear.
And you lightly armed men, crouch behind shields in various places   35
And hurl your great stones,
And fire your smooth javelins at them,
Standing close by the men in full armour.

[Tyrtaios 11 = Stobaeus, *Anthology* 4.9.16 (on war)]

Stobaeus or John of Stobi put together, probably in the early fifth century AD, an anthology from earlier writers arranged by topic to educate his son.

A9   **Tyrtaios 12: Excellence in war**
I would neither mention nor have any regard for a man
For his prowess in running or wrestling,
Not even if he had the size and power of the Cyclopes,
And defeated Thrace's North Wind in running;
Not if he were more handsome in stature than Tithonos,   5
And richer than Midas and Kinyras;
Not even if he were more kingly than Pelops, son of Tantalos,
And had the soft-tongued voice of Adrastos;
Nor even if he was renowned for everything except impetuous courage;
For a man is not good in war,   10
If he could not bear to see bloody slaughter
And lunge at his enemies close at hand.
This excellence, this prize is the best and finest
In the world for a young man to win.
This is a general benefaction for the city and all its people,   15
Whenever a man stands foursquare in the front line and abides
Unceasingly, and completely forgets shameful flight,
Steadfastly risking his life and spirit,
And standing beside the next man gives verbal encouragement.
This man is good in war.   20
All of a sudden he turns and routs the jagged ranks
Of the enemy, and stems the tide of battle with his heroic effort;
And moreover if he falls in the front line and loses his dear life

Stabbed from in front many times through the chest,
Through bossed shield and breastplate,   25
Bringing glory to his city and its people and his father,
This man is bewailed by young and old alike,
The whole city is distressed by a grievous sense of loss;
His tomb and his children and their children,
And all his line thereafter are renowned among men;   30
Never does his good fame perish nor his name,
But though he is beneath the earth, he is immortal,
Since raging Ares laid him low when he was standing firm,
Excelling while fighting for his land and his children;
And if he escapes the long fate of woeful death,   35
And his victory maintains the proud boast of his spear,
Everyone honours him, young and old alike:
He goes down to Hades only after many delights;
As he grows old he is pre-eminent among his citizens, and no one
Wants to cheat him of his respect or his rights,   40
But both the young and his peers and the elders,
All alike give up their place for him on the benches.
So now let every man aim to reach this peak
Of excellence with all his heart, not coasting in the battle.

[Tyrtaios 12 = Stobaeus, *Anthology* 4.10.1 and 6 (on war)]

A10   Tyrtaios 19: In battle

[…] and [pouches?] of stones and […]
Like hosts of [swarming flies?].
[Some were taken] by Ares, bane of mortal men, […]
[In open battle?], while others [he hurled] over [crags].   5
[So let us] like [locusts or cranes?]
[Advance] behind the protective fence of our concave shields,
Pamphyloi and Hylleis and [Dymanes] independently
[Holding up] our ash spears in our hands.
[In this way, entrusting] everything to the immortal gods   10
We shall give obedience to our [sacrosanct] leader.
But in a trice, one and all [together], we shall be thrashing away,
[Standing firm] at close quarters with spearmen;
And awesome will be the clashing of both sides
As rounded shields strike shields,   15
And terrifying will be their war-cries as they fall upon each other,
[Impaling] men's breasts on their [spear];
And they will give no ground though pounded [with missiles];
Battered with [great] slingstones
[Helmets] will ring out with the clatter of war [unflinchingly].   20

[Tyrtaios 19 = Berlin Papyrus 11675]

Pamphyloi, Hylleis and Dymanes were Dorian tribal names (see Hdt. 5.68 and cf. Plut. *Lykourgos* 6 = **D48**).

A11 **Fighting the Argives**

[... (*9 lines unintelligible*) ...]
[...] fierce missiles [...]   10
The grey-eyed daughter of Zeus who bears the aegis.
Many men with javelins [...]
Sharp points [...]
Lightly-armed men running forwards [...]
[Ar]kadians [...] of the Argives [...]   15
[...] by the wall [...]
[...] water [...]
[...] from [grey-eyed] Athena
[...] ditch [...]
They will kill all [...]   20
Of the Spartiates who [...]
Flee back [...]

[Tyrtaios 23a = Oxyrhynchos Papyrus 3316]

A12 **Tyrtaios on Argive and Arkadian alliance with Messenia**

They fought several wars because of Messenian revolts. Tyrtaios says in his poems that
the initial annexation of the Messenians took place in the time of their fathers' fathers;
and the second, when they revolted after making alliance with Argives, [Arkadians]
and Pisatans; the Arkadians provided King Aristokrates the son of Orchomenos as
their general, and the Pisatans Pantaleon the son of Omphalion, and in this war he says
that he himself was the Spartan general.

[Tyrtaios 8 = Strabo, *Geography* 8.4.10]

Fragments from a papyrus from Oxyrhynchos (**A11**) seem to mention Arkadians and Argives fighting
against the Spartiates. This may be the poem Strabo refers to above. The text actually mentions Argives,
Elians and Pisatans, but then an *Arkadian* general. As Pisa was a region of Elis and the terms tend to be
used interchangeably to refer to the people living around Olympia, it is very likely that an explanation of
one or the other term accidentally replaced the name 'Arkadians' in the process of copying the manuscripts.

ALKMAN: A13–A20
Alkman lived perhaps one generation later than Tyrtaios, but wrote poetry different in all respects. It was
lyric poetry, i.e. to be accompanied on the lyre; composed in a range of different metres; written in Doric
(i.e. Spartan) dialect; most significantly, his subject-matter was startlingly different. The two longest
fragments to survive of his poetry were written for girls' choruses, and show 'a pronounced homoerotic
tenor' (*OCD³* under 'Alkman': the entry on Sappho – *the* Lesbian poetess – describes Alkman as an
important and contemporary parallel for Sappho's love poetry). Other fragments suggest a considerable
range to his poetry.

A13 **An ancient potted biography of Alkman**

Alkman: a Lakonian from Messoa: *pace* Krates who mistakenly says he was a Lydian
from Sardis. A lyric poet, son of Damas or Titaros. He lived at the time of the 27th
Olympiad (672 BC) when Ardys, the father of Alyattes was King of Lydia. Being a
great lover he was the founder of love-poetry. He was born of household slaves. He
wrote six books of lyric poetry and the *Diving Women.* He first introduced poetry sung
not in hexameter. He used the Dorian dialect as Lakedaimonians do.

[Suda, *Lexicon* "Alkman"]

For Suda, see **A1**. Messoa was one of the villages that made up Sparta. Alkman's birthplace was widely
disputed, as shown by the alternative attributed here to Krates (second-century BC scholar): as a Hellenistic
epigram on Alkman put it (Antipater of Thessalonica 12 (Gow-Page) = *Palatine Anthology* 7.18), he was
fought over by two continents: 'Poets have many mothers'. Ardys ruled Lydia *c.* 652–619 BC and was the
grandfather of Alyattes. The dating to Ardys' reign is probably about right. The statement that he was a
great lover is typical of the tendency of ancient biographies to draw conclusions about poets from their
subject matter.

A14   Alkman 1: 'Maiden-song'
[…] Polydeukes;
[…] I do not rate Lykaithos among the dead
Nor Enarsphoros and fast-footed Sebros
[…] and the violent […]
[…] and helmeted […]   5
[And Euteiches] and lord Areios
[…] and […] mightiest of demigods;
And […] great leader
[Of the host] and Eurytos
In the turmoil of [Ares'] misery,   10
And [Alkon], mighty warriors,
We shall [not?] pass them over:
All of them [were overpowered] by Fate
[And Device], most ancient powers,
And their strength, being unshod, [was loosed].   15
[Let no] mortal man fly up to heaven
[Or at]tempt to marry Aphrodite
[The Cyprian] queen or some
[…] or a child of Porkos,
[The sea-god]; but the Graces [look after]   20
The house of Zeus, with eyes full of love.

[…] most […]
[…] of gods […]
[…] to friends […]
[…] gave gifts […]   25
[… *(unintelligible)* …]
[…] youth lost […]
[…] time […]
[…] vain […]
[…] went; one of them by an arrow   30
[…] by a marble millstone
[…] Hades […]
[… *(unintelligible)* …]
[…] and unforgettable
Were their sufferings, as they plotted evil deeds.   35

There is vengeance from gods;
And blessed is the man who, sound in mind,
Weaves life's web to the day's end
Unweeping; and so I sing
The radiance of Agido;   40
I see her like the sun, which
Agido summons to shine on us;
But our renowned chorus leader
In no way allows me either to praise,
Or to find fault with her; for she herself   45
Seems to be supreme, just as if
One were to put a horse among cattle,
A strong prize-winner with thundering hooves
That one dreams about from the shade of a cave.

Why, don't you see? The racehorse is   50
Venetian; but the mane
Of my cousin
Hagesichora has a bloom
Like pure gold;
And her silvery countenance –   55
But why am I telling you face to face?
This is Hagesichora here;
And the next in beauty after Agido
Will be a Scythian horse up against an Ibenian;
For as we bring our plough,   60
The Pleiades fight against us,
Rising through ambrosial night,
To dawn like the star Sirius.

For an abundance of purple
Is not enough to give any protection,   65
Nor an intricate snake of solid gold,
Nor yet a headband
From Lydia, the glory
Of dark-eyed girls,
Nor the hair of Nanno,   70
Nor again godlike Areta,
Nor Thylakis and Kleeisisera;
Nor if you go to Ainesimbrota's and say:
'If only Astaphis were with me
And Philylla were to look towards me   75
And Damareta and lovely Vianthemis'.
But no, Hagesichora keeps her eye on me.

For is not Hagesichora
With her pretty ankles present here,
And does she not stay near Agido   80
And praise our festival?
But accept, you gods, their
[Prayers]; for fulfilment and completion
Belong to gods. Chorus leader,
I would like to speak: as for myself,   85
I'm just a girl, vainly screeching from a beam,
An owl; but even so, most of all I long
To please Aotis; for she it was
Who cured our troubles;
But thanks to Hagesichora, the girls   90
Have trodden the path of lovely peace.

For just like the trace-horse
[… *(one line lost)* …]
In a ship too you must
Listen above all to the helmsman;   95
And she is admittedly not
More musical than the Sirens,
For they are goddesses, but this ten of ours
Sings as well as [eleven] girls;
And gives voice like a swan on the streams   100
Of Xanthos; and she with her lovely golden hair.

[… *(the last four lines of the poem are lost)* …]

[Alkman, fragment 1 = Louvre Papyrus E3320]

This poem was found on a first-century AD papyrus in Egypt in 1855 and known as the Louvre Papyrus from where it was taken to. The papyrus was clearly part of a scholarly edition of Alkman, since it also has editorial comments which sometimes elucidate the poem (though the commentary too is fragmentary and sometimes confuses the issue!). The text proclaims itself to have been sung by a chorus of ten girls (98–99: the use of first person singular forms, e.g. line 2, seems to be traditional). This fits the genre of *partheniai* ('maiden-songs') attributed to Alkman by several ancient writers on Alkman (*Testimonia* 8, 9, 15 in Campbell, *Greek Lyric II*). It is in Doric dialect. The first part of the poem as we have it relates to a Spartan myth, in which Hippocöon and his ten sons exiled his younger brother Tyndareos, but were punished by Herakles (see Paus. 3.15.3 on a statue of Herakles in Sparta, connected to this myth), helped by the sons of Tyndareos (Kastor and Polydeukes). The chorus draws appropriate moral lessons (lines 1–39), which are appropriate to the apparent context of a religious ceremony (81–84). The girls then turn to praise of their own chorus-leader, their clothes, and themselves, and with some suggestion of a (Lesbian) love element.

Several elements (besides the gaps in the papyrus) remain obscure: it is not certain whether the chorus is part of a competition – it has been suggested that the reference to the Pleiades (61), normally the star-group, is actually to a rival choir; while the fragmentary commentary seems to suggest that the Pleiades represent Hagesichora (whose name means 'Leader of the chorus' and Agido). Ainesimbrota and Aotis are unknown, perhaps some purveyor of love-spells and a goddess, respectively.

A15   **Alkman 2: fragment on the Dioskouroi**
Most revered by all gods and men
They dwell in a home built by the gods [...]
Kastor – skilled horsemen, tamers of
Swift horses – and glorious Polydeukes.

> [Alkman, fragment 2 = P.Oxy.2389 with Herodian, *Figures of Speech* 61]

This fragment was found on a papyrus from Oxyrhynchos, and identified as being by Alkman by an ancient literary manual explaining as 'Alkmanic' the use of a plural phrase placed between the two singular names it describes – 'as in the second ode: Kastor ... glorious.' Praise for the Dioskouroi would be a natural subject for a choir at a Spartan religious festival (compare Alkman 1.1 and note).

A16   **Alkman 3: Maiden-song with verses on Astymeloisa**
[Muses] of Olympos, [fill] my spirits
[with desire for new] songs:
I [wish] to hear
The [...] voice of girls
Singing a lovely song [to the heav]ens   5
... *(line lost)* ...
It will scatter sweet [sleep] from my eyes,
And lead me to go to the meeting-place,
[Where] I shall rapidly loosen my yellow hair.

   (Gap of 51 lines)

[...] with desire that makes limbs dissolve,   61
And she gazes more meltingly than sleep or death.
And she is sweet quite deliberately.
But Astymeloisa gives me no answer,
But holding her garland,   65
Like a bright star
Of the open heaven
Or a golden shoot, or light eiderdown,
... *(line lost)* ...
[...] she moves away on her long legs.   70
Moist perfume, sitting on the maiden's locks
Graces her lovely hair.

[Truly] Astymeloisa [goes] through the crowd
As the delight of the people
... *(several lines very fragmentary)*...
[...] I might see if somehow [...] she might love me.
She might come close and take my soft hand,   80
And I would immediately do whatever she wanted.

> [Alkman, fragment 3 = P. Oxy. 2387]

Another fragment from a papyrus of Oxyrhynchos. The state of the papyrus suggests that each stanza was nine lines in length, and that about fifty lines are lost after the first stanza, and another 35 lines at the end, where the very starts of lines can be seen, thus making the poem 14 stanzas (or more). Here we have the first stanza, introducing the song: several opening invocations to the Muses from Alkman are quoted by later writers, e.g. fragments 8, 14, 27. By stanzas 7–9 (lines 64–81) we have moved to the theme of unrequited Lesbian love for Astymeloisa (meaning 'cared-for by the city' – line 74).

A17   Alkman 4A
[…] Poseidon […]
I went up from Trygeai
To the lovely precinct of the White Goddesses
With two sweet pomegranates.

The girls, when they had prayed
To the fair-flowing river to ensure
Lovely marriage, and to experience
What is dearest to men and women,
A lawful marriage-bed.

[Alkman, fragment 4A = P.Oxy. 2443 fr 1 + 3213]

A18   Alkman 7
Come, Muse, Kalliope, daughter of Zeus,
Begin the lovely words; set desire on the song,
And make the dance graceful.

[Alkman, fragment 7 = Hephaistion, *Handbook on Metres* 7.4]

A19   Alkman 45
May our chorus please Zeus' house and you too, Lord (Apollo).

[Alkman, fragment 45 = Apollonios Dyskolos, *Pronouns* 105a]

A20   Alkman 81
Alkman changed a line by bringing forward the maidens to say, "Father Zeus, if only that man were my husband."

[Alkman, fragment 81 = Scholiast on Homer's *Odyssey* 6.244]

The (unknown) ancient commentator here cites the views of Aristarchos, the most famous ancient literary critic. He clearly implies that the line he quotes was from a 'maiden-song'.

SIMONIDES: A21–A22

Simonides is a less shadowy figure than Tyrtaios and Alkman. He was from Keos and throughout a long life (*c.* 556–466 BC) was greatly in a demand as a professional poet, working for a great variety of city-states, rulers and private individuals. He wrote a wide variety of poetry, but was most celebrated for his epigrams, though this resulted in many later epigrams being attributed to him. A substantial fragment of a poem was discovered on an Oxyrhynchos papyrus in 1992 (published in *The New Simonides*, edd. Boedeker and Sider, OUP 2001). The fragments are of a poem, in elegiac couplets, epic in language which introduces the deeds of the Greeks at Plataia (479 BC, see **E84–E86**) by comparison with the deeds of the Greek heroes at Troy as celebrated in Homer's *Iliad*. The poem was presumably commissioned for public performance at a festival: Rutherford sets out some possibilities in *The New Simonides* (pages 38–41). Sparta (and Pausanias) seem more prominent than in Herodotus' account, but we cannot be sure whether this reflects the acknowledged view of Greece at the time (much closer to the event than Herodotus) or a deliberate Spartan slant. Corinth gets a mention (line 35), as does Megara (founded by Nisos, line 37) while ?Pan]dion, in line 41, an Attic hero, suggests a reference to Athens.

A21   **'The New Simonides' – Epic style poem on Plataia**

[...] a pine-tree in a glen [... which]
[...] woodcutters cut [...]
[...] and much [...]
[...] the massed ranks [...]   5
[...] Patr[oklos ...]
[...] brought [you] down [...]
[...] by the hand of [Apol]lo [...]
[...] being [...]
[...] by the sons of [Pr]iam,   10
[...] of evil-min[de]d Paris [...]
[...] the chariot of divine justice destroyed
[...] after sacking [it] they came to fabled
[...] the Greek war-leaders [...]
[On whom] immortal glory has been poured by the man   15
[Who] received divine [...] from the dark-haired Muses
[...] and made famous for fu[ture gener]ations
[...] the names of the race of demigods
[But] now rejoice, [son] of the glorious goddess,
[Daughter] of Nereus of the sea. But I   20
[Summon] you to help me, [...] Muse,
[If you care for] the prayers of mortals,
[...] this our delightful song,
So that people may [remember the men]
Who ward[ed] from Sparta the day [...]   25
(... *one line lost* ...)
They do [not] forget [their vir]tue which reaches the heavens
[And the fame] of the men [will be] everlasting.
Leaving [... Eu]rotas and the city [of Spart]a
With the horse-taming sons of [...] Zeus,   30
The [Tyndarid]ai heroes, and mighty Menelaos
[...] the leaders of our [an]cestral city.
But the excellent [son of ... Kleo]mbrotos led these men out
[... *most of line lost* ...] Pausanias.
[...] and famous deeds of Corinth   35
[...] of Pelops son of Tantalos
[...] city of Nisos from where
[...] tribes of neighbouring men
[...] confident in [...] who with
[...] the plain [...]   40
[... dri]ving out ... of [Pan?]dion
[...] of godlike [...]
[...] having conquered [...]

[Simonides, *Plataia* = P.Oxy. 3965]

A22   Epigram probably by Simonides on the Spartan dead at Plataia
Immortal fame these men established for their dear land,
Around themselves they cast the dark cloud of death:
They died, yet are not dead, since in the world above their virtue
Exalts them and brings them back from the house of Hades.

[Simonides 9 (Page) = *Palatine Anthology* 7.251]

'There are separate tombs for the fallen Lakedaimonians and for the Athenians with epitaphs by Simonides inscribed on them.' Paus. 9.2.4, describing Plataia. Two epigrams likely to be those mentioned by Pausanias are preserved in the *Palatine Anthology* of Greek epigrams (also 7.253 = Simonides 8 (Page)): 'fine epigrams, worthy of a gifted poet on a great occasion' (Page, *FGE* on 'Simonides' VIII and IX).

SECTION B
SPARTA FROM MAINLY SPARTAN SOURCES

This section contains contemporary historical documents, mostly written or at least partly-commissioned by Spartans, and inscribed for public display. These either still survive, or were quoted by writers who saw them and whose readers could also have seen them. They are not, of course, simply neutral historical record – on the contrary, many were explicitly erected to boast of achievements – but as public documents, inscribed at considerable effort and expense, they were subject to contemporary public scrutiny. For an introduction to Spartan Epigraphy, see pages 15–18.

B1   Marble seat at Olympia I, *c.* 550 BC
Gorgos, *proxenos* of the Eleans

[*SEG* 11.1180a]

Marble seat installed in the stadium at Olympia, *c.* 550 BC. Inscription retrograde and in Lakonian lettering. A *proxenos* would represent the interests of another city-state in his own town: so Gorgos and Euwanios (**B2**) were Spartans who acted in the interests of Elis (which also controlled the Olympic festival). (See Hodkinson, *PWCS* 339–343 (with photo)).

B2   Marble seat at Olympia II, *c.* 500 BC
(The seat) of Euwanios, the Lakedaimonian *proxenos*.

[*SEG* 26.476]

B3   Dedication to Zeus at Olympia
The Spartiates dedi[cated this to Oly]mpian [Zeus].

[*IG* 5.1.1563 = *IvO* 244]

This inscription is on the rim of a *lebes* (large bronze vessel) and is thought to date to the late sixth or early fifth century BC. It is not known what prompted this dedication.

B4   Epitaph for the dead of Thermopylai, after 480
        Tell the Lakedaimonians, passer-by,
        We followed orders, and here now we lie.

[Herodotus, *Histories* 7.228.2]

For the context see **F20** (Herodotus actually tells us that this inscription was set up by the Amphiktyons), and for another contemporary epigram, see **A22**.

B5   The Serpent Column (Greek victory monument), after 479
The base remains at Delphi, but the column, formed of three intertwined serpents was moved to Constantinople by Constantine and still stands in the ancient hippodrome, though without the metal serpents' heads (one preserved in Istanbul Museum). It lists 31 sets of citizens, from states which fought in the Second Persian War (480–479 BC), and was dedicated at Delphi, after the battle of Plataia, together with a golden tripod, later melted down (Hdt. 9.81 = **E61** and Paus. 10.13–19).

B5a   Serpent Column inscription

B5b   The Serpent Column

The following
fought
the war:

Lakedaimonians
Athenians
Corinthians

Tegeans
Sikyonians
Aiginetans

[Another 25 names follow, mostly in groups of three]

[ML 27]

B6   Pausanias' tripod inscription
The Greek leader, when he destroyed the Persian army,
Pausanias, dedicated this memorial to Phoibos.

[Thucydides, *History of the Peloponnesian War* 1.132 (see **E26**)]

No trace remains of this inscription which Thucydides says Pausanias had inscribed on the golden tripod set up at Delphi together with the Serpent Column (**B5**) but which was erased immediately: see ML 27 for doubts about where (or even whether) this inscription was written.

B7   Pausanias' Black Sea inscription
A memorial of his virtue, dedicated to Lord Poseidon
By Pausanias, ruler of spacious Greece,
At the Black Sea: a Lakedaimonian by race, the son
Of Kleombrotos, of the ancient family of Herakles.

[Nymphis of Herakleia, *FGrH* 432 F 9 = Athenaios, *Scholars at Dinner* 12.50]

Herodotus (4.81) mentions the dedication by Pausanias at the entrance to the Black Sea (i.e. Byzantium). Nymphis came from Herakleia in Byzantium and wrote *A History of My Fatherland* in the third century BC, quoting this poem as evidence of Pausanias' luxury and arrongance and saying that he had the poem inscribed on an existing dedication.

B8   Thank-offering to Zeus at Olympia
Receive, o Lord Olympian Zeus, son of Kronos, this statue fine,
With heart propitious to the Lakedaimonians.

[ML 22 = *IG* 5.1.1562 = *IvO* 252]

The inscription still visible on a cylindrical base of stone from Olympia. It was also transcribed accurately with slightly 'modernized' spelling by Pausanias 5.24.3 who described the poem as being on 'a Zeus, twelve feet high, to the right (east) of the Temple of Olympian Zeus, which they say is an offering of the Lakedaimonians, when they put down in war the second Messenian revolt.' Assuming that Pausanias was right (there is nothing in the inscription itself to provide a certain context), this revolt may have been the famous Helot Revolt of 465 BC, or far less well-attested unrest in Messenia around 490 BC, if such a thing actually happened (see **E60**).

B9 **Messenian dedications of bronze spear-butts from their revolt, *c.* 460 BC**
a) The Messenians (Methanians) from the Lakedaimonians
b) The Messenians (Methanians) dedicated this from spoils from the Athenians

[a) *IvO* 247; b) *LSAG* Messenia no.3]

Two bronze spear-butts, a) inscribed in a single line on one side, found at Olympia; b) on four sides, found at the sanctuary of Apollo Korythos at perioikic Longa in Messenia. They have only recently been identified as Messenian spoils of the basis of the Erxadieis treaty (**B15**) which shows that Lakonian dialect allowed *theta* to stand for double *sigma* in standard classical Greek, hence 'Methanians' = 'Messenians'. The only, and entirely plausible occasion for such dedications was the Messenian revolt of 464 BC in which the Athenians initially helped the Spartans (see Thuc. 1–101–3 = **E62**). See Bauslaugh, R. A. (1990) "Messenian dialect and dedications of the 'Methanioi,'" *Hesperia* 59: 661–8, with illustrations, including of the Erxadieis treaty.

B10a **Thank-offering at Olympia for victory at Tanagra, 458/7 BC**
[The temple] has [a golden dish] from [Tanagra],
[The Lakedaimonians and their] allies put [up the gift].
[One tenth from the Argives and the Ath]enians
And [the Ionians] for [the victory] in the war.
[…] Cor[inthians …]
[… *(all but one letter lost)*…]

[ML 36 = OR 112]

B10b **Pausanias' description**
(*Pausanias is describing the Temple of Zeus at Olympia and a statue of Victory at the top of its eastern pediment* ...) Under the statue of Victory (*Nike*) a golden shield has been set up with the Gorgon Medusa engraved on it. The epigram on the shield shows who dedicated it and the reason they dedicated it: it reads as follows:
The temple has a golden dish from Tanagra,
The Lakedaimonians and their allies put up the gift.
One tenth from the Argives and the Athenians
And the Ionians for the victory in the war.

[Pausanias, *Description of Greece* 5.10.4]

Three marble fragments have been found at the site of the temple of an inscription which matches that quoted by Pausanias (with minor dialect differences, not represented here), but which originally contained a third couplet. Most probably the golden shield, described in the inscription as a dish (*phiale*) because of its shape, was the main dedication, but the Corinthians added a separate dedication. For the battle of Tanagra, see Thucydides 1.107.5 = **H23**, mentioning that the Athenians had Argive and other allies.

B11 **Argive spoils from Sparta**
a) The Argives dedicated this to Apollo.
b) [The Argives to Apollo] a tenth (of the spoils) from Lakedaimon.

[FD 3.1.90 and FD 3.1.573]

These inscriptions from Delphi, taken together, may represent what Pausanias described in **H24b**. For the historical puzzle of the Battle of Oinoe, see **H24**.

B12   The Spartan War Fund, *c.* 427 BC or later?

Front   *Side*

    Given by the [...], who are friends of the Lakedaimonians,
    for the war, four hundred *darics* [*(a few words unintelligible)*]
    Given by the Aiginetans to the Lakedaimonians for the
    war, fourteen *mnas* and [ten *staters*]
5   [Given by ...]s to the Lakedaimonians [*(number)*] *darics.*

    Given by Som[...]ophon from Olenos in Achaia [and ?]
    to the Lakedaimonians for the war trireme[...]   Given by the
    [...] and thirty-two *mnas* of silver.   Melians to
10 Given by those exiled from Chios who are friends   the Lakedai-
    of the Lakedaimonians, one thousand Aiginetan *staters.*   monians
                                                                       twenty
    [Given by ...]non to the Lakedaimonians for the   *mnas*
    war, four thousand and a further   of silver.
15 [...] thousand and of raisins   Given by Mo-
    [...] talents.   lokros to the
    [Given by the ... *(a few words unintelligible)*]   Lakedaimo-
    [...] many [...] and eight hundred *darics*   nians, a talent
    [and ... *(some letters unintelligible)*] talents.   silver.
20 [Given by ... to the Lakedaimonians] for the war   Given by
    [...] thirty *mnas*   the Melians
    [and ... two or three] thousand *medimnoi* and   to the
    [...]ty [...] and [*(some letters unintelligible)* six-   Lakedai-
    ty [...]. [Given] by the Ephesians to the Lakedaim-   monians
25 [onians for the] war, one thousand *darics.*   *(lost)*

        [W. T. Loomis, *The Spartan War Fund, IG V 1,1* (Stuttgart 1992) = OR 151]

The inscriptions was laid out on two sides of a rectangular block, as represented in the translation above which also tries to represent the Greek word order, with the word 'given' emphatically placed first.

Nothing about the text of the inscription provides us with a certain date. This has given rise to much controversy, exemplified by Meiggs & Lewis having to agree to disagree (ML page 184)! Lettering forms can provide a very approximate date: more accurate attempts rely on working out when all the donors mentioned might have been willing and able to contribute to Sparta. Loomis (see above) surveys views of previous scholars (pp. 56–60) and arguments from letter-forms and historical factors before coming down in favour of 427 BC. Osborne-Rhodes (forthcoming, no. 151), suggest 427–412 BC.

For *darics* – the gold coin of the Persian Achaemenid empire, see **E155b**.

B13   Athenian dedication for victory at Pylos, *c.* 425 BC

The Athenians from [spoils from] the Lakedaimonians at Pylos.

                    [*IG* 1³.522 = *SEG* 10.325]

Bronze shield-facing found in a cistern in the agora at Athens (*JHS* 66 (1936), pages 138/9 with line drawing, fig. 2). Pausanias reports seeing shields taken from Spartans captured on Sphakteria in the Painted Stoa in the agora (Paus. 1.15.4). See M. Lippman, D. Scahill, P. Schultz, *AJA* 110 (2006) 551–563, for the suggestion that shields were at some point displayed on the temple of Athena Nike on the akropolis, as in Aristophanes, *Knights* 847–859. For the Pylos episode, see **E87–E96**.

STATUE OF WINGED NIKE (VICTORY) AT OLYMPIA BY PAIONIOS, *c.* **423 BC: B14 A–D**
Monument, inscription and a literary account all survive for this work, with the impressive 10m triangular base still prominent at the site of Olympia and the statue itself in the Olympia Museum. Pausanias' own view notwithstanding, the Messenian version he reports for the context of the dedication must be right (**B14d** – for Sphakteria see **E87–E96**). And despite their reported dread of the Spartans the commissioning of this work must have been deliberate and provocative.

B14a   The inscription
The Messenians and Naupaktians dedicated (this) to Olympian Zeus as a tenth of what they took from their enemies. Paionios from Mende made it and won the competition for making the *akroteria* on the temple.

[*IG* 5.1.1568 = ML 74 = OR 164]

B14b   Photograph of Winged Nike *(Cast Gallery, Ashmolean Museum)*

B14c   Photograph of the statue base *in situ*

B14d   Pausanias explains Paionios' *Nike*
The Dorian Messenians who once took over Naupaktos from the Athenians dedicated a statue of Victory (*Nike*) on a column at Olympia. This is the work of Paionios of Mende, made from enemy spoils, when, I think, they fought the people of Akarnania and Oiniadai. The Messenians themselves say their offering came from their achievement at Sphakteria alongside the Athenians and that the name of their enemy was omitted through dread of the Lakedaimonians, since they have no fear of the people of Akarnania and Oiniadai.

[Pausanias, *Description of Greece* 5.26.1]

B15   Erxadieis treaty – 5th century (date disputed)
[Treat]y with the Aitoloi E[rxadieis].

- To h[ave friendshi]p and peace, [for ever] without [tric]kery, and
- An alli[ance against anyone exc]ept the Man[tineans (?),
- Follow]ing the Lak[edaimonian]s wherever they may lead, b[y land a]nd by sea, having th[e same] friend and [enemy] as [the Lakedaimo]nians. They shall not e[nd (a war)] without the permission of the La[kedaimonians,] send[ing envoys] to the same (states) [as the Lakedaimo]nians.
- [They shall not rece]ive exil[es] who have partici[pated in illegali]ties.
- If anyone should [lead an expedition] with warlike intent [against the] land of the Erxadieis, [the Lakedaimo]nians shall he[lp] with all their streng[th according to their ability.]
- If anyone should le[ad an expedition with warlike in]tent against th[e] land of [the Lakedaimo]nians the E[rxadieis shall help with all their strength according to their ability]…

[Osborne & Rhodes 128 = ML 67 bis]

This inscription was found on the akropolis of Sparta. Estimated dates based on plausible historical context vary from early fifth to early fourth century: see now Osborne & Rhodes for a tentative dating to 450 BC. I place it here merely to aid comparison with the treaties copied by Thucydides below.

This text is very fragmentary, and the exact meaning of some phrases remains unclear, but it offers some authentic insight into the workings of Sparta's alliances. The Aitoloi Erxadieis are not known from any other source: they were presumably a very small community (not a city) in Aetolia (central Greece). Clauses (5) and (6) are the usual mutual pledges of a defensive alliance, but the real nature of the agreement becomes clear in (3), where the Aitoloi Erxadieis agree to follow Sparta wherever she leads (a phrase also echoed in the literary sources, e.g. Xen. *Hell.* 2.2.20) and more or less sign away their freedom in determining their own foreign policy. Clause (2) is very fragmentary and the reconstruction here is in doubt, but if this reading is correct, it may offer the Erxadieis a chance to honour existing relations with other states (Mantineia in this case) by opting out of league campaigns against long-standing friends. Since we are dealing with a very small state, it is difficult to tell whether this part of the treaty was representative: did large *poleis* such as Corinth or Tegea agree to the same restrictive conditions concerning relations with other states? It seems clear, however, that all Peloponnesian allies did agree to follow 'wherever Sparta led', although, as we have seen, they were eventually allowed to have a say in such decisions. Clause (4) is also significant: 'exiles who have participated in illegalities' may refer to fugitive helots. It is generally thought that one crucial aim of Sparta's alliances was to ensure that all neighbouring states would support her against any rebellious activities of the helots, especially those in Messenia: the Aitoloi Erxadieis, however, were not near neighbours of the Spartans.

Note that there is no reference to Sparta's other allies in this treaty. In fact, members of the league did not have to have mutual agreements, and some went to war against each other. In such cases Sparta's promise to defend allies against an attack, as in (5), gave her the right to intervene, but she did not always get involved, presumably leaving her allies a free hand as long as a conflict did not pose a threat to her own interests.

TEXTS OF TREATIES GIVEN BY THUCYDIDES: B16–B22

Thucydides' accuracy in reporting the exact terms of treaties and alliances can be confirmed by the 'quadruple alliance' of 420 BC between Athens, Argos, Mantineia and Elis. Thucydides reports this at 5.47, and by chance a good proportion of the Athenian copy has survived (*IG* 1³ 83), enough to check and confirm that there are only very small discrepancies. Provision was made within the treaties for their public record (**B17** section 10) and Thucydides can be assumed to have had a verbatim copy. One small indication of his precision is that he preserves the Spartan name 'Koryphasion' (**B16**, section 4, **B17** section 7) without giving any explanation to his Athenian readers that this was the place famous to them as Pylos (see **E87–E96**): instead he had carefully pointed out this alternative place name at 4.3.2, presumably to allow for the exact transcription (Hornblower, *Commentary* vol. II page 114).

It is not so clear why Thucydides' *History* includes both texts, **B19–B20** (5.77, 5.79), since the former apparently represents a resolution of the Spartan assembly which Lichas took with him to Argos, the latter the final version of the treaty. One clause remains exactly the same. Both texts are in Lakonian (Spartan) dialect with some Attic features (no attempt is made to reproduce this in the translation). The usual solution is that the doubling refects that Thucydides' *History* remained unfinished overall and that even the completed books were not always finally revised.

Thucydides also gives texts of three agreements between Sparta and Persia in 412/1 BC (*History of the Peloponnesian War* 8.17–18 (**B21**), 8.37 (not included here) and 8.58 (**B22**). These become more precise (Hornblower vol. III.801), only the third one is really a treaty, with far more frequent mention of the Persian king, and therefore probably requiring his explicit approval (Hornblower, *Commentary* vol. III.925).

For all of these documents, see Lane Fox, 'Thucydides and Documentary History' in *CQ* 2010, who gives entirely plausible reconstructions in each case of how Thucydides may have got hold of copies or drafts of these diplomatic documents.

B16   Spartan truce with Athens, 423

[1] As regards the sanctuary and oracle of Pythian Apollo we have resolved that it should be open, without fear of treachery to anyone who wishes in accordance with long-established laws. [2] This has been resolved by the Lakedaimonians and those of their allies present: and they agree to send ambassadors to do all they can to persuade the Boiotians and Phokians. [3] As regards the god's revenues, we have resolved to do our utmost to seek out the guilty parties, fairly and justly, using long-established laws, both you and we and the others who are willing, all using long-established laws. [4] As regards the matters mentioned, this is what the Lakedaimonians and the other allies have resolved.

The following is what the Lakedaimonians and their allies have resolved if the Athenians make a treaty:

- Both sides are to stay in their own territory, owning what we now own; the Athenians at Koryphasion should stay between Bouphras and Tomeus.

- Those in Kythera are to have no contact with our allies, nor we with them, nor they with us.

- Those at Nisaia and Minoa are not to go beyond the road leading from the gates by the shrine of Nisos to the temple of Poseidon, and from the temple of Poseidon straight towards the bridge to Minoa (nor are the Megarians and their allies to go beyond this road); and the Athenians are to keep the island which they captured, but have no contact with people in either direction.

- At Troizen, they are to keep what they now have, just as the people of Troizen have formally agreed with the Athenians.

- [5] In using the sea, the Lakedaimonians and their allies are to sail in their own waters and their allies', not in warships, but in oared ships up to a capacity of five hundred talents.

- [6] Heralds and ambassadors, together with any retinue they wish, are to come and go with safe conduct, by land and sea, to the Peloponnese or Athens, to negotiate an end to the war and to resolve disputes.

- [7] During this period neither you nor we are to take in deserters, whether slave or free.

- [8] You are to be legally accountable to us and we to you, according to long-established practice, and disputes are to be settled by arbitration and without war.

[9] This what the Lakedaimonians and the other allies have resolved. If you think anything would be more fair and more just, come to Lakedaimon and tell us. Neither the Lakedaimonians nor their allies will ignore any just proposals you make. [10] Those who come are to do so with full authority, just as you insisted with us. The truce shall be for one year.

[Thucydides now gives the Athenian resolution]

[119.1] These matters the Lakedaimonians and their allies have formally agreed with the Athenians and their allies on the twelfth day of the Lakedaimonian month of Gerastios. The following made and swore to formal agreement: for the Lakedaimonians, Tauros, son of Echetimidas; Athenaios, son of Perikleidas; Philocharidas, son of Eryxilaidas *(other names follow, two from Corinth, two from Sikyon, two from Megara, one from Epidauros, three Athenian strategoi).*

[Thucydides, History of the Peloponnesian War 4.118–19]

B17   Text of the 'Fifty Years Peace', 421 BC

[18.1] "The Athenians and the Lakedaimonians and their allies made a treaty in the following terms, and swore to it city by city.

- [2] Concerning the common sanctuaries, that anyone who wishes is to be free to sacrifice there and to go there and to consult the oracles as individuals or state representatives, according to tradition, by both land and sea.

- That the sanctuary and temple of Apollo at Delphi, and the people of Delphi should determine their own governance and their own taxes and their own laws for themselves and their territory, according to tradition.

- [3] That the treaty shall last for fifty years between the Athenians and allies of the Athenians, and the Lakedaimonians and the allies of the Lakedaimonians, without any deceit or malfeasance, by both land and sea.

- [4] Let it not be permitted to bear hostile arms for the Lakedaimonians and the allies of the Lakedaimonians against the Athenians and the allies of the Athenians, nor for the Athenians and the allies of the Athenians against the Lakedaimonians and the allies of the Lakedaimonians, not by any trickery or plot. If any disagreement arises between the sides, legal process and oaths should be used, in accordance with whatever is agreed.

- [5] Let the Lakedaimonians and their allies return Amphipolis to the Athenians. With regard to all the cities surrendered to Athens by the Lakedaimonians, their inhabitants shall be allowed to go where they wish with all they possess; the cities are to pay the tribute as assessed by Aristeides and are to be independent. Neither the Athenians nor their allies shall begin any fighting with harm in mind, so long as the cities go on paying the tribute, now that the treaty has been agreed. These cities are Argilos, Stageira, Akanthos, Skolos, Olynthos, Spartolos. They are to be allies of neither side, the Athenians or the Lakedaimonians. If the Athenians convince these cities it is permitted that these cities should willingly make themselves allies of the Athenians.

- [6] That the inhabitants of Mekyberna, Sane, and Singos should live in their own cities, just like the people of Olynthos and Akanthos.

- [7] Let the Lakedaimonians and their allies give back to the Athenians Panakton.

- Let the Athenians give back to the Lakedaimonians Koryphasion, Kythera, Methana, Pteleon, and Atalante; and any Lakedaimonian men who are in the public prison at Athens or anywhere else in a public prison under Athenian control. And that they should release the Peloponnesians besieged in Skione and any other allies of the Lakedaimonians in Skione, and any people sent in by Brasidas, and any Lakedaimonian allies who are in the public prison at Athens or anywhere else in a public prison under Athenian control. Let the Lakedaimonians and their allies likewise give back any Athenians they hold.

- [8] Regarding Skione, Torone and Sermylies, and any other city which the Athenians hold, that the Athenians should decide about these and other cities just as they see fit.

- [9] That the Athenians should swear oaths to the Lakedaimonians and their allies city by city. Let seventeen men from each city swear whatever oath is most sacred in each place. Let the oath be as follows, "I shall abide by this treaty and formal agreement honestly and without trickery." Let the oath sworn by the Lakedaimonians and their allies to the Athenians be in the same terms, and let both sides renew the oath each year.

- [10] That *stelai* should be set up at Olympia, Delphi and the Isthmos, at Athens on the akropolis and in Lakedaimon at Amyklai.

- [11] If they have omitted anything of any sort, the oath shall still be valid if both sides employ fair discussions to make changes to it, as both sides think fit, the Athenians and the Lakedaimonians.

[19.1] The beginning of the treaty shall be: in Lakedaimon, when Pleistolas is ephor, on the fourth day before the end of the month of Artemision; at Athens, when Alkaios is archon, six days before the end of the month Elaphebolion. [2] The following swore the oaths and formalised the agreement: the Lakedaimonians, Pleistoanax, Agis, Pleistolas, Damagetos, Chionis, Metagenes, Akanthos, Daithos, Ischagoras, Philocharidas, Zeuxidas, Anthippos, Tellis, Alkinadas, Empedias, Menas, Laphilos. The Athenians, Lampon, Isthmionikos, Nikias, Laches, Euthydemos, Prokles, Pythodoros, Hagnon, Myrtilos, Thrasykles, Theagenes, Aristokrates, Iolkios, Timokrates, Leon, Lamachos, Demosthenes.

[Thucydides, *History of the Peloponnesian War* 5.18–19]

B18   The Alliance between Sparta and Athens, 421 BC
[5.23.1] The Lakedaimonians and Athenians shall be allies for fifty years on the following terms:

* If any enemies come to Lakedaimonian territory and do damage to the Lakedaimonians, the Athenians should help the Lakedaimonians by the strongest means they can, to the best of their ability. If they ravage the land and then leave, their city shall be regarded as at war with the Lakedaimonians and the Athenians, and shall be punished by both until both cities jointly break off hostilities. These actions shall be taken honestly, promptly, and openly.

* [2] And if any enemies come to Athenian territory and do damage to the Athenians, the Lakedaimonians should help the Athenians by the strongest means they can, to the best of their ability. If they ravage the land and then leave, their city shall be regarded as at war with the Lakedaimonians and the Athenians, and shall be punished by both until both cities jointly break off hostilities. These actions shall be taken honestly, promptly, and openly.

* [3] In the event of an uprising of the slave-body, the Athenians shall to the best of their abilities come to the aid of the Lakedaimonians with all their forces.

* [4] The same people on both sides who have sworn to the other treaty shall swear to these terms too. The oath shall be renewed each year by the Lakedaimonians going to Athens for the Dionysia festival, and by the Athenians going to Lakedaimon for the Hyakinthia. Each side shall set up a *stele*; the one at Lakedaimon next to the statue of Apollo at Amyklai, the one at Athens on the akropolis next to the statue of Athena. If the Lakedaimonians and the Athenians decide to add to or remove anything from this alliance, whatever they see fit, the oath shall still be valid for both. (*Thucydides gives the names of those who swore the oath, exactly the same people who swore to the treaty at 5.19, above.*)

[Thucydides, *History of the Peloponnesian War* 5.23]

B19   Decision of the Spartan assembly on a treaty with Argos, 418 BC
[1] The Assembly of the Lakedaimonians has decided on the following terms to make an agreement with the people of Argos:

* The Argives shall give back to the people of Orchomenos their children, to the people of Mainalia their menfolk, and to the Lakedaimonians those held as hostages in Mantineia.

- The Argives shall leave Epidauros and demolish its walls; [2] if the Athenians refuse to do likewise, they shall be deemed enemies of Argos and of the Lakedaimonians and of the allies of the Lakedaimonians and of the allies of Argos.

- [3] The Lakedaimonians, if they hold the children of any city, shall return them to all such cities severally.

- [4] With regard to the sacrifice due to the two gods, the Argives shall if they wish impose an oath upon the Epidaurians; if not, they shall swear it themselves.

- [5] All the cities of the Peloponnese, whether great or small, shall enjoy independence in accordance with their ancestral customs.

- [6] If any city outside of the Peloponnese shall invade their land with hostile intent, all those subject to this agreement shall together resist such assault in whatsoever manner is deemed most appropriate by the peoples of the Peloponnese.

- [7] All such people outside of the Peloponnese as are allies of the Lakedaimonians shall be parties to this treaty on the same terms as the Lakedaimonians, and all such as are allies of the Argives shall likewise be parties to this treaty on the same terms; all shall keep what is their own.

- [8] These terms shall be declared to the allies and shall be ratified by them if they think fit, subject only to reference to their home governments, if they so decide it to be necessary.

[Thucydides, *History of the Peloponnesian War* 5.77]

B20   Text of the formal alliance between Sparta and Argos, 418/7 BC

[78.1] This document was agreed by the Argives first of all, and then the Lakedaimonian army left Tegea and went home, after which normal relations were restored between the two cities. Soon after that the same men as before contrived to persuade the Argives to abandon their alliance with the Mantineians, the Athenians, and the Eleans and to forge an alliance with the Lakedaimonians. The terms were these:

[79.1] The Lakedaimonians and Argives have decided on the following terms that there should be a treaty and alliance for fifty years:

- To be dealt with on fair and equal terms in accordance with their ancestral customs;

- The other cities in the Peloponnese may join in the treaty and alliance in their own right as independent cities, keeping what is their own and being dealt with on fair and equal terms in accordance with their ancestral customs;

- [2] All such people outside of the Peloponnese as are allies of the Lakedaimonians shall be parties to this treaty on the same terms as the Lakedaimonians, and all such as are allies of the Argives shall likewise be parties to this treaty on the same terms; all shall keep what is their own.

- [3] If there is any need for joint military action, the Lakedaimonians and Argives should make decisions as fairly as possible with regard to their allies.

- [4] If there is any disagreement amongst cities inside or outside the Peloponnese, whether about boundaries or anything else, the decision shall be made <as follows>: if there is a quarrel between one allied city and another, it should be taken to another city which is thought fair by both cities.

- Private individuals are to follow legal procedures in accordance with ancestral customs.

[Thucydides, *History of the Peloponnesian War* 5.78–79]

B21   First agreement between Sparta and Persia, 412 BC

[1] On the following terms the Lakedaimonians and their allies made an alliance with the King and with Tissaphernes.

- Whatever land and cities the King possesses, and the King's forefathers possessed, let the King own.

- And whatever monies or other things used to be paid from these cities to the Athenians, let the King and the Lakedaimonians and their allies take joint action to prevent the Athenians getting these monies or anything else.

- [2] And let the King and the Lakedaimonians and their allies jointly wage war on the Athenians.

- And let the war against the Athenians not be ended unless both sides agree – the King and the Lakedaimonians and their allies.

- [3] If any people revolt from the King, let them be declared enemies of the Lakedaimonians and their allies; and likewise if any people revolt from the Lakedaimonians and their allies, let them be declared enemies of the King.

[Thucydides, *History of the Peloponnesian War* 8.18]

B22   Treaty between Sparta and Persia, 412/1 BC

[1] "In the thirteenth year of Darius' rule, when Alexippidas was ephor in Lakedaimon, an agreement was made on the plain of the river Maiandros between the Lakedaimonians and their allies and Tissaphernes and Hieramenes and the sons of Pharnakes, concerning the affairs of the King and of the Lakedaimonians and their allies.

- [2] The land of the King – all that is in Asia – is to be the King's; and he may decide about his own land as he wishes.

- [3] The Lakedaimonians and their allies are not to go against the King's land to create any trouble, nor is the King to go against the land of the Lakedaimonians or their allies to create any trouble.

- [4] If any of the Lakedaimonians or their allies goes against the King's land to create trouble, the Lakedaimonians and their allies are to prevent it; and if any of the King's subjects goes against the land of the Lakedaimonians or their allies to create trouble, the King is to prevent it.

- [5] Tissaphernes is to provide for the upkeep of the ships now in existence according to the agreement until the ships of the King come.

- [6] When the King's ships arrive, the Lakedaimonians and their allies are to provide for the upkeep of their own ships themselves, if they wish. But if they wish to receive the upkeep from Tissaphernes, he is to provide it, but once the war has ended, they are to pay Tissaphernes for whatever they have received.

- [7] When the King's ships arrive, the ships of the Lakedaimonians and those of their allies and those of the King are to fight the war jointly as Tissaphernes and the Lakedaimonians and their allies see fit. If they wish to end the war against the Athenians, they are to end it under the same terms.

[Thucydides, *History of the Peloponnesian War* 8.58]

THANK-OFFERINGS AT DELPHI FOR VICTORY AT AIGOSPOTAMOI, 405 BC: B23A–J
This is usually, though not certainly identified with the remains of a two-storey rectangular building just within the sanctuary of Apollo at the start of the Sacred Way. Plutarch, *Lysander* 18.1 mentions his statue and dedications; Pausanias gives a description, while many fragments of the inscriptions have been found. The monument was deliberately built next to the Marathon monument of the Athenians, before itself being trumped by a vainglorious Arkadian monument placed opposite (**B33**). Plutarch commented that such displays made him ashamed of his fellow Greeks.

B23a   **Lysander**
He set up a statue on this monument, when he won
With swift ships and sacked the power of Kekrops –
Lysander, having crowned unravaged Lakedaimon, the akropolis
Of Greece, country of fine dances.
He of sea-girt Samos composed this poem: Ion.

[Osborne & Rhodes 192c]

Kekrops was a mythical king of Athens. Ion of Samos also composed **B23b** but is otherwise unknown.

B23b   **Polydeukes**
[Son of Zeus], Polydeukes, Ion also in these verses
Has crowned your [marble] base
Since you stood, even before the naval commander,
As first of the leaders of spacious Greece.

[Osborne & Rhodes 192b]

Various Spartan allies at Aigospotamoi
B23c   […]thios, son of [Lysi]machides, [naval commander of the Boio]tians
B23d   K[imm]erios, son of Pelasgos, from Ephesos.
B23e   Aiantides, son of Parthenios, from Miletos. Teisander made this.
B23f   Theopompos, son of Lapompos, from Malea. Alypos made this.
B23g   A[ut]onomos, son of Samios, from Eretria.
B23h   Apollodoros, son of Kalliphon, from Troizen.
B23i   [Kom]on, son of […] from Megara.

[Osborne & Rhodes 192d–h]

B23j   Pausanias' description of monuments celebrating Aigospotamoi

[7] Opposite stand the dedications of the Lakedaimonians of spoils from the Athenians: the Dioskouroi, Zeus, Apollo, and Artemis; then Poseidon and Lysander, son of Aristokrites, being crowned by Poseidon; Agias who acted as Lysander's soothsayer, and Hermon, helmsman of Lysander's flagship. [8] [*In section 8, omitted here, Pausanias lists the artists of the other statues mentioned, including Antiphanes, see **B33b** note.*]

[9] Behind those just mentioned were set up the statues of those who assisted Lysander at Aigospotamoi, whether Spartiate or allied forces, namely: Arakos and Erianthes, one of them Spartan, the other (Erianthes) Boiotian … the Chians Kephisokles and Hermophantos and Hikesios; Timarchos and Diagoras from Rhodes; Theodamos of Knidos; Kimmerios from Ephesos, and the Milesian Aiantides. [10] Tisander made those statues, while Alypos of Sikyon made the next ones – Theopompos of Myndos and Kleomedes of Samos … (Pausanias goes on to mention 15 others, from Karystos, Eretria, Corinth, Troizen, Epidauros in the Argolid, Pellene, Hermione, Phokis, Megara, Sikyon, Ambrakia, Leukas, and Sparta)

[Pausanias, *Description of Greece* 10.9.7–10]

B24   The decree of the ephors on Athens, 404 BC

[4] One still hears Lakedaimonians say that Lysander wrote the following to the ephors: 'Athens has been conquered.' But the ephors wrote back, " 'Conquered' is enough." But this story was made up to sound plausible. The real decree of the ephors was this: 'The authorities in Lacedaimon have decided. If you (Athenians) destroy the Peiraieus and the long walls, leave all the cities, holding only your own land, and if you take back your exiles, if you do this, you may have peace. Concerning the number of ships, [5] do whatever is decided there.'

[Plutarch, *Lysander* 14.4–5]

The final word 'tenei' is given in LSJ as Doric for '*there* ... or perhaps equivalent to *here*', the second of which might make better sense, unless they were delegating responsibility to Lysander.

B25a   Remains of the Lakedaimonian soldiers' tomb in Athens, 403 BC

The still quite substantial remains (12.4m wide) of a tomb built of large stone blocks, in the Athenian Kerameikos (main cemetery). 24 male skeletons were found, all wrapped in decayed cloth, perhaps the *phoinikis* (red Spartan warrior's cloak). Several still had weapons lodged in their fronts. The central part of the building, which was later extended on either side, housed 9 bodies, laid side by side, with an inner wall separating skeletons 1–6 from 7–9. Skeleton 7 was slightly separated from 8 and 9 by an extra stone: it has thus been suggested that this was Lakrates, the Olympic victor, with the two polemarchs being also slightly distinguished in their burial. The inscription was written retrograde, with the L and A of 'Lakedaimonians' much larger with each letter after each of the two names preserved. It is interesting to note that Xenophon changes the order of the two polemarchs, and gives a different spelling of Thibrak/chos.

B25b   The inscription
Thibrakos polemarch L Chairon polemarch A […]

[*IG* 2² 11678]

B25c   Xenophon on Lakedaimonians killed at Peiraieus, 403 BC
In this fighting two polemarchs, Chairon and Thibrachos, were killed; also Lakrates, a victor at Olympia; and other Lakedaimonians who now lie buried in the Kerameikos outside the gates of Athens.

[Xenophon, *Hellenika* 2.4.33]

B26   Lysander dedicates a gold crown at Athens, 403 BC
A golden crown which Lysander the Lakedaimonian, son of Aristokritos, dedicated; its weight, 66 5/6.

[*IG* 2² 1388, lines 32–34]

This item is one of many listed in an inventory of treasures of Athena. The weight is given in *drachmai* converting to 288g.

B27   Sparta liberates Delos, 403–399 BC
(Fragment a)
God.
The dues of the Lakedaimonians went sent to Delos, in accordance with the agreements just as in accordance with the other reciprocal arrangements.
(Fragment b)
[…of the precincts] and the sacrifices and temples and property of the god. The kings were Agis, Pausanias. The ephors were Thyionidas, Aristogenidas, Archistas, Sologas, Phedilas. At Delos the *archon* was [A]nd[rodik?]os.

[*IG* 5.1.1564 = Rhodes & Osborne 3]

The two fragments can be dated to 403–400, since King Agis died *c.* 400, but none of these ephors appear on Xenophon's list of the 28 eponymous ephors during the Peloponnesian War (431–404), at *Hellenika* 2.3.10 (**E32**). Delos, important sanctuary of Apollo, had been the centre of the Delian League, and under fairly direct Athenian control. The Spartans after their victory in the Peloponnesian War here recorded sending what they had promised to Delian Apollo and presumably freed Delos from her previous obligations to Athens under the Delian League.

Damonon *stele*: see C83

B28   Memorial to Agesipolis, 380 BC
As a memorial for his beloved son Agesipolis,
Pausanias dedicated me. Hellas sings his excellence in unison.
Kleon of Sikyon made [me].

[M.N. Tod, *A Selection of Greek Historical Inscriptions*, vol. II, no. 120]

Agesipolis I was Agiad king of Sparta from 395–380. He reigned as a minor for some of his reign (Xen. *Hell.* 4.2.9, of 394) after his father, King Pausanias, was condemned to death for poor leadership but fled to Tegea (**E136**, Xen. *Hell.* 3.5.25) and then Mantineia. Agesipolis died of illness while on campaign and received a royal burial at Sparta (Xen. *Hell.* 5.3.19). His father, Pausanias, would presumably not have been able to attend, hence this unusual memorial, on two fragments of a black limestone base at Delphi. Though it is not surprising for Pausanias to praise his son as universally admired, Xenophon (*Hell.* 5.3.20) suggests that Agesipolis at least got on very well with the other Spartan king, Agesilaos.

B29   Athenians dedicate spoils from Lakedaimonians at Delphi, 375/4
When Leochares was *archon* at Delphi and Hippodamas was *archon* at Athens, the Athenians and their allies, after capturing spoils from the Lakedaimonians, dedicated to Pythian Apollo this tripod and statues of girls.

[*SEG* 33.440a]

This inscription from Delphi can be dated by mention of Hippodamas, archon at Athens in 375/4. The occasion for Athens capturing Spartan spoils could have been a failed attack on the Peiraieus in 378 (Xen. *Hell.* 5.4.20) or more likely their naval victory off Naxos in 376 (Xen. *Hell.* 5.4.61).

B30   Theban monument after Leuktra, 371
Xenokrates,
Theopompos,
Mnasilaus
When the spear of Sparta ruled, then Xenokrates took by lot the task of offering a trophy to Zeus, not fearing the host from the Eurotas or the Lakonian shield. "Thebans are superior in war", announces the trophy won through victory by the spear at Leuktra; nor did we run second to Epaminondas.

[*IG* 7.2462 = Rhodes & Osborne 30]

Limestone block found at Thebes. The verse inscription is complete in three elegiac couplets and mentions no dedication, nor does it seem to have been the base for any object, so it was probably a gravestone for the men named. No explanation can be found for the monument naming three men but only writing about one, but Xenokrates is known as one of the Boiotian senior officials who supported Epaminondas at the battle of Leuktra and was chosen by lot to carry something into battle (Paus. 9.13.6–7 and 4.32.6: for the battle, **E106–E112**).

B31   Tegean/Arkadian dedication of Lakonian sails and arms at Delphi
After capturing the sails/the weapons of the Lakonians, the peoples of Tegea, Arkadia (gave a tenth part) to Apollo.

[*SEG* 31.558 and 559]

Two similar inscriptions found at Delphi, one mentioning 'sails', the other 'weapons'. The context should have been the foundation, after Leuktra in 371 BC, of an anti-Spartan 'Arkadian League' led by Mantineia and Tegea, and including most Arkadian states by 369 (compare Xen. *Hell.* 6.5.6), but which had already broken down by the second battle of Mantineia.

B32 Thessalians honour Pelopidas, *c.* 363 BC

Sparta he made desolate – the Boio[tian leader] who [came] very many times to [save our cities] with fine words one could trust: The Thessalians dedicated this statue of Pelopidas […]. Lysippos made [it].

[*SEG* 22.460 = *SEG* 35.480]

Statue base, from Delphi. Various restorations to the text have been made, but the key words which start the text about him 'making Sparta desolate' are certain. For Pelopidas, see Plutarch, *Life of Pelopidas* especially 33 on the desire of the Thessalians to honour him after his death in 364 BC.

B33a Arkadians celebrate their ancestry and ravaging Sparta

Pythian Apollo, Lord, the native people from holy Arkadia gave these statues as first-fruits: Zeus once slept with Kallisto, Lykaon's daughter and begot a son, Arkas, of sacred race. Elatos and Apheidas and Azan were born to him by his wife Erato in Arkadia. Laodameia, daughter of Amyklas gave birth to Triphylos. From the daughter of Gongylos was Amilous Erasos. Their descendants, the Arkadians, after ravaging Lakedaimon, set this up for you, a memorial for their posterity.

[FD 3.1.3]

B33b Pausanias' account

Next are the offerings of the Tegeans from Spartan spoils: Apollo and Victory (*Nike*), and the heroes of the region, Kallisto and Lykaon, and Arkas who gave his name to the land, and the sons of Arkas, Elatos, Apheidas, Azan, and after them Triphylos. His mother was not Erato, but Laodameia, daughter of Amyklas the king of Sparta. Erasos, son of Triphylos, also has a statue dedicated to him. Those who made the statues were Pausanias of Apollonia, who made the Apollo and Kallisto; Victory (*Nike*) and the statue of Arkas were by Daidalos of Sikyon; Samolas of Arkadia made Triphylos and Azan; Antiphanes of Argos made Elatos and Apheidas and Erasos. The Tegeans sent these offerings to Delphi when they had taken prisoner Lakedaimonians who were attacking their territory.

[Pausanias, *Description of Greece* 10.9.5–6]

The monument is clearly the same one. Pausanias wrongly attributes it to the Tegeans instead of the Arkadians, but unless he is completely mistaken about the artists, Daidalos and Antiphanes, they can be shown to have been working at Olympia *c.* 400 (Paus. 6.2.8) and at Delphi in 403 (Paus. 10.9.8 = **B23j**). So the monument must have been erected within a working lifetime of these dates, though it could commemorate a much earlier victory. The occasion could have been a plundering raid on Sparta involving Arkadians, Xen. *Hell.* 6.5.27–8

SPARTAN EPITAPHS: B34–B55

B34 Spartan tombs

Their tombs are cheap and the same for all.

[Herakleides Pontikos, *Constitution of the Spartans* 2.8 in *FGH* ed. Müller]

B35   Plutarch on Spartan tombstones

a) He (Lykourgos) did away with inscription on memorials (*mnēmeia*), except for those who had died in war, and also with mourning and lamentations.

[Plutarch, *Instituta Laconica* no.18 = *Moralia* 238d]

b) Those burying the body were not allowed to inscribe the name, unless the man had fallen in battle or the woman was a priestess. Mourning was limited to a brief period of eleven days.

[Plutarch, *Lykourgos* 27.2]

Plutarch collected the Spartan sayings and customs, of which his *Instituta Laconica* forms a part, in preparation for writing his *Lives.* His second version here shows him changing the correct version of a ban on memorials to a less accurate reference to tombstones.

The statements of Herakleides and Plutarch can be borne out from evidence of surviving inscriptions. These are firstly very few in number compared to other places in the classical world. 24 'in war' stones are known in total: in contrast Clairmont's *Classical Athenian Tombstones* (1993) covers 9 volumes, and over 3,000 pages, but describes itself as a supplement to A. Conze's *Die attischen Grabreliefs*! Spartan memorials are also small (on average only just over a foot tall) and plain with at most a simple pediment for decoration, in contrast with any number of Attic stelai from the same period with beautiful figures carved in relief. They have just the name (**B37, B39, B46**), or with the addition of 'in war' (**B36, B40–B43, B47, B49, B50**) or 'priest' (**B38, B44**). **B43** reminds us that the stele are memorials, not strictly tombstones as Spartans were buried where they fell. **B48** shows that Spartans could use the patronymic more usual elsewhere in Greece for a foreigner, and presumably for a Spartan (**B45**). On the memorials, see Low, 'Commemorating the Spartan war-dead' in Hodkinson & Powell 2006, 85–109 with images.

A couple of inscriptions from Lakonia name women with the (Laconic) description, 'in bed' presumably meaning in childbirth. Of these **B55** is probably Hellenistic; **B54**, being written retrograde should be earlier, *possibly* classical. Matthew Dillon, 'Were Spartan Women who died in childbirth honoured with inscriptions?' in *Hermes*, 135 (2007), pp. 149–165, following Hodkinson, points out that an inscription from the Tainaron peninsula (*IG* 5.1.1277) lists seven women, only three of whom are followed by 'in bed', thus showing that death in childbirth was not the reason for the names being inscribed. Despite this dearth of evidence texts of Plutarch (as for example Talbert's translation for Penguin, *Plutarch on Sparta*) have been changed to read as if he mentioned women dead in childbirth, rather than priestesses.

B36   Ainesias in War

[*IG* 5.1.703, early 4th century]

Reconstructed from drawing and dimensions given in *IG*. The second 'H' in *Ainehias'* name is a *heta*, originally an aitch sound, but often transliterated as an 'S' – compare Age*h*ipolis in **B44** (more conventionally the name Agesipolis). The stele is 39cm high and 22 cm wide. Now in Sparta Museum, SM 377. Photograph in P. Low, 'Commemorating the Spartan war-dead' in *Sparta and War* 2006, alongside photos of memorials of Olbiadas (**B49**) and Euryades/Taskos (**B53**). The monument is extremely plain, without so much as a border, and the lettering goes right to the edge of the stone. At most, the memorial stones of the classical period have a simple pediment, e.g. to Olbiadas. One Hellenistic and one Roman-period monument have simple relief carvings.

B37   Elephas

[*IG* 5.1.699, nr. Menelaion, 6th century]

B38   […]os, priest

[*IG* 5.1.1329, Leuktra, 6th century, see Dillon, p.161]

B39   Aideus

[*IG* 5.1.214, Sparta, 5th century]

B40   Ainetos in war

[*IG* 5.1.701, Magoula, 5th century]

B41   Haire*h*[ippos] in w[ar]

[*IG* 5.1.702, unknown location, 5th century]

B42   Bastias in war

[*IG* 5.1.707, Amyklai, 5th century?]

B43   Eualkes in war at Mantineia

[*IG* 5.1.1124, Geronthrai, 418 BC]

For the battle of Mantineia, see Thuc. 5.70–73 (**E103**) and 74.2 (**E104**) stating that the dead were buried at Tegea, whereas this stone, back in Geronthrai was a memorial. See P. Low in Sparta & War (2006), esp. 88–89 and maps 1 & 2.

B44   Age*h*ipolis, sacred official

[*IG* 5.1.1338, Gerenia, 5th century, see Dillon, p.162]

B45   Desposios (son) of Palamon

[*IG* 5.1.1590, Sparta, 5th century]

B46   Hubrion

[*SEG* 47.352, nr. Sellasia, late 5th century?]

B47   Telephanes in war

[*IG* 5.1.1125, Geraki, early 4th century]

B48   Cheiris, son of Thegeitos, a Megarian

                      [*IG* 5.1.718, Sparta, 4th century BC]

B49   Olbiadas in war

                      [*IG* 5.1.1591, Pellana, late 4th century]

B50   Nika*h*ikles in war

                      [*IG* 5.1.704, Kefala, nr. Sparta, late 4th century]

B51   Gorgopas in war

                      [*SEG* 56.460, Sparta, late 4th century]

B52   Ona*h*imos in war

                      [*SEG* 46.390, Marios, Lakonia, late 4th century]

B53   Euryades, Olympic victor, in war; Taskos in war

                      [*IG* 5.1.708, 3rd century]

B54   [*(name lost)*] in childbirth.

                      [*IG* 5.1.713 (written retrograde)]

B55   Agippia in childbirth.

                      [*IG* 5.1.714]

SECTION C
SPARTA IN RELIGION AND
RELIGIOUS FESTIVALS⁵

INTRODUCTION:

Spartans had a reputation for piety. This was retrojected onto Lykourgos' law being given religious approval (**D19, D48, D49, F3, F5**), and to Lysander apparently wishing for the same for his proposed changes (**E133, E134**). Even in the military sphere, it was religious concerns that were offered for Spartans coming late to Marathon (**H16**) and to a military reversal a century later (**C70**): many further examples are given by Parker, (*Spartan Religion* in Powell (1989)) who describes Spartans as 'almost uniquely willing to ascribe national misfortunes to collective religious guilt' (p.161, noting various examples reported by Herodotus and Thucydides. Oracles feature prominently in Spartan history (e.g. **H9, H10, F18**, and see index 'oracles'). In part this reflects the Greek world of the time: sanctuaries are the first item in the Spartan-Athenian truce of 424 and treaty of 421 (**B16, B17**); in part it reflects the interest of some of our sources (Herodotus and Plutarch); but the sources in this chapter show that it reflects a wide range of society, from personal dedications (**C1–C38**) to major state festivals (**C61–C94**), and including how Sparta projected herself onto the Panhellenic stage of the Olympic Games (**C39–C60**).

SPARTAN RELIGIOUS DEDICATIONS: C1–C38

This section collects together some of the texts accompanying religious dedications within Lakonia in the Archaic and Classical periods. In doing so it gives an impression of the range of religious worship within this area and period. Dedications were generally made as thank-offerings at a sacred site, sometimes in fulfilment of a particular vow: they might have been an object prized by the owner; a representation of an object appropriate to the deity or to the dedicator's situation; and in a substance appropriate to the dedicator's wealth; some were accompanied by an inscription, which sometimes survives, while the object itself may have been melted down or reused. For Spartan Epigraphy in general, see pages 15–18. Dedications are arranged here by Olympian Gods in alphabetical order, followed by those to minor gods and heroes.

APOLLO: C1–C5

Apollo was regarded, from the very first lines of Homer's *Iliad,* as one of the most powerful of the Greek gods, with responsibilities including the arts, the sun, prophecy, medicine and archery. In Sparta his name appears in an earlier form, Apelon. He was worshipped in Lakonia is a variety of different guises. The three most important festivals in Sparta (see **C61–C77**) all honoured Apollo, and his worship at the Hyakinthia was sufficiently important at least for the men of Amyklai to be released from campaign in 390 BC, with disastrous results (**C70**). The importance of the Amyklaion is also confirmed by the fact that it was next to Apollo's statue, and on the Athens akropolis, that copies of the 'Fifty Years' Peace' were placed (**B18**).

C1   Early dedication to Apollo at Amyklaion

Dorkonidas/Dorkoilidas dedicated (this) to Apelo.

[SEG 11.689 = LSAG 5]

Bronze handle with archaic lion's head, from the sanctuary at Amyklaion, late 7th-early 6th century.

C2   Dedication to Apollo Hyperteleatas

To Apelo (Apollo) Hyperteleatas

[SEG 11.989]

Bronze handle, perhaps from a mirror, found at the shrine of Apollo Hyperteleatas at Kotyrta in S. Lakonia. The epithet seems to mean 'beyond perfection', 'leaping above' or 'superachieving'. Existence of priest of Apollo is attested through to the Roman period. A date in the second half of the sixth century is suggested by the writing.

C3   Bronze goat dedicated to Apollo Hyperteleatas
Apelo (Apollo) Hyperteliatas

[*SEG* 11.905 = *LSAG* 35]

Found at the shrine of Apollo Hyperteleatas (above), now in the Louvre, Paris. Jeffery dated to 6th C, *SEG* to 5th.

C4   Bronze soldier dedicated to Apollo Maleatas *c.* 525 BC
Charil{l}os dedicated this to Maleatas

[*LSAG* 37 = *IG* 5.1.927]

Found at modern Kosmas, high up Mt Parnon. The precinct of Apollo Maleatas was at Prasiai, on the coast (see Map 3).

C5   Dedication to Pythian Apollo
Menoitios dedicated (this) to Pythian (Apollo).

[*IG* 5.1.928 = *LSAG* 36]

Bronze handle, from dedication by Menoitios to Apollo Pythaieus, Tyros, 6th century

ARTEMIS: C6–C9
Artemis (Artamis in the Doric dialect), had an important place in Spartan religion, like her twin brother, Apollo. The twins and their mother, Leto, each had statues in Sparta's agora (Paus. 3.11.9 = **C73**). The original goddess Ϝορθαία 'Worthaia' was assimilated to Artemis and the sanctuary of Artemis Ortheia, just outside the town of Sparta, was one of the most important in Lakonia, especially famous as the site of the boys' contests (**C84–C90**, to which notorious 'whipping-contests' were added in the Roman period (**C91–C94**). Very many dedications to her were unearthed here (**C6–C8** and for the contests, see **C86–C94**). Artemis was also worshipped as Artemis Limnatis in Dentheleatis (see map 3) on the borders of Lakonia and Messenia, (Strabo, 8.4.9, Pausanias, 3.2.6). It was Spartan custom to sacrifice a goat to Artemis Agrotera (the Huntress) just before the battle charge (Xen. *Hell.* 4.2.20 – (Nemea, 394 BC)).

C6   Ivory plaque showing ship
Wor(th)aia

[Lakonian letters, retrograde: *IG* 5.1.252b = *LSAG* 1]

Ivory plaque showing departure of ship and crew. Ship and lettering clumsily carved, using the *digamma* (Ϝορ<θ>αία). The offering found in the lowest archaeological layer of the sanctuary of Artemis Orthia, suggesting a date possibly as early as the late 7th century BC.

C7   Limestone horse dedicated to Ortheia, 6th century
Panidas from Tarra? dedicated me to Wortheia

[*IG* 5.1.252 = Woodward 169.1 in Dawkins p.367 and Plate LXVII.28]

Sparta, sanctuary of Artemis Orthia. Relief of horse, carved on limestone, now broken, with inscribed dedication, written 'boustrophedon'. This form of writing, the lettering and the archaeological context all suggest a date in 6th century BC. This may be the earliest of many horses dedicated to Artemis.

C8   *phiale* dedicated to Artemis Limnatis

Prianthis dedicated this to Limnatis.

> [*IG* 5.1.226 = *LSAG* 39 = Robert, *Collection Froehner* i.27, plate 14]

One of the better preserved inscriptions to Artemis Limnatis, found at Limnai, one of the villages of Sparta. It is inscribed on a bronze *phiale* (shallow dish) with the name of the dedicator, and seems to date to the sixth century BC. Other similar objects have been found, some with just the name Limnatis (*IG* 5.1.225, others giving the name of the dedicator, *IG* 5.1.1497 = *LSAG* 18).

C9   Dedication to Artemis at Pleiai, 5th century

Pei*h*ipis dedicated (this) to Artamis.

> [*IG* 5.1.1107a]

Pleiai was 25 miles south-east of Sparta. Use of the letter *heta* (for sigma) suggests a fifth-century date.

ATHENA: C10–C15

Notwithstanding their later enmity towards Athens in the Peloponnesian War, Athens' patron goddess was also the patron goddess of Sparta. Pausanias mentions several sanctuaries of Athena in Sparta (3.11.9 = **C73**, 3.12.4, 3.15.6) and describes the most important, on the Spartan akropolis, to Athena Poliachos ('Guardian of the City') or Athena of the Bronze House at 3.17.1–4: the former name is known from the Damonon inscription **C83**, the latter from Thuc. 1.134 = **E26**.

C10   Miniature breastplate

To Athanaia

> [W.W. Lamb, 'Bronzes from the Acropolis, 1924–27', *BSA* 28, 82–95, no.22 pl. VIII]

4.4 cm tall, bronze, with Athena's name written retrograde. Also illustrated in Hodkinson, *PWCS* p. 292.

C11   Stele of Wanaxibios with relief of a *kore.*

Wanaxibios

> [*LSAG* 27 = *IG* 5.1.215]

Stele found in precinct of Athena Chalkioikos, inscribed 'Wanaxibios' (with initial digamma) and with relief of *kore* (girl) holding a lotos-flower. Jeffery dates this to 525–500 BC and judges from the subject of the picture and its location, that this must be a dedication by the man named.

C12   Stele dedicated by Eteoi(tas) to Athena, *c.* 510–500

Eteoi[tas] dedicated (this) to Athena.

> [*SEG* 11.653 = *LSAG* 30]

C13   Dedication to Athena 'Zosteria', fifth century

To Athena [Zos]teria ('of the Warrior's Belt'?), [Kal]litelidas dedicated (this).

> [*IG* 5.1.1116]

C14   Bronze mirror dedicated by a Spartan woman, mid 5th century

Euonyma dedicated (this) to Athena

> [*SEG 11.662* = Woodward I 271/3, n. 5 c. del. fig. 6, Wo. IV 252, n. 6.]

C15   Bronze bell dedicated by a Spartan woman, 5ᵗʰ century BC

Kalikratia dedicated (this) to Athene

[*SEG* 11.664 = *JHS* 44, 1924 page 259, fig 3]

Bronze bells were popular dedications to Athena: about 50 in all have been found in excavations and dated to the fifth century BC, see Hodkinson, *PWCS* 277 and note on page 18.

HERA: C16–C17
Hera was worshipped in Sparta as 'Argive Hera' and as the goddess of marriage (Paus. 3.13.8).

C16   Bronze lion dedicated to Hera

Eumnastas, a Spartiate, to Hera

[*LSAG²* 16a (page 446) = *SEG* 48.1151]

Inscribed figurine of a (cute) bronze lion from the Heraion on Samos, *c.* 550 BC, once an attachment to a drinking vessel. The lion is couchant and is 10 cm high and 16 cm long, (though his hind part is cut off). The inscription is around his mane. Now in Vathy Museum. Picture in Hodkinson, *PWCS* 343.

C17   Bronze cow in British Museum

Lakos dedicated me to Hera

[BM 1909,0522.1]

Bronze figurine, just over 8cm in length, from about 530 BC, with inscription on the cow's back.

POSEIDON: C18–C20
For Spartans, living inland but in a part of Greece especially prone to earthquakes, the chief importance of Poseidon ('Pohoidan' in Lakonian), and one celebrated in games (see **C83**), was as 'Earth-holder', i.e. protecting against earthquakes. For helots, his sanctuary at Tainaron could provide a refuge for helots (**C20**), hence the Spartan view that their impiety there caused the earthquake of 465 BC, a view prevalent 50 years later (see Thuc. 1.128 (**E62b**)). Poseidon's precinct in Sparta was to Poseidon of Tainaron (Paus. 3.12.5); he was also worshipped in Sparta as 'Safe-guarder' 'Horse-tending' and 'of the Home' (Paus. 3.11.9, 3.14.2, 3.14.8).

C18   Bronze bull dedicated to Poseidon

Anphimenidas dedicated (this) to Pohoidan (Poseidon)

[*SEG* 11.955 = *LSAG* 33]

Now in Paris, *Cabinet des Médailles.* Ed. L. Robert, *Collection Froehner* I 1936, n. 23 with photo, plate IX. The lettering is on the back and the left hind leg. Jeffery described this as a bull, *SEG* as a ram: it is not dissimilar in appearance from **C19**, see Jeffery's sketch in the Poinikastas website, http://poinikastas.csad. ox.ac.uk. Late 6th century?

C19   Bronze ram dedicated to Poseidon the charioteer

Xenoklees dedicated (this) to Pohoidan the driver

[Fitzwilliam Museum GR.4.1933]

In the Fitzwilliam Museum, Cambridge – 34mm high, 51 mm long. Published by Cartledge, ' "To Poseidon the Driver": an Arkado-Lakonian ram dedication' in *Periplous: Papers on Classical Art and Archaeology Presented to Sir John Boardman,* edd. G.R.Tsetskhladze et. al. (London 2000). Cartledge, *Spartan Reflections*, 181, describes it as an example of cultural interaction between Sparta and Arkadia, *c.* 525 BC.

C20   Manumission stele, *c.* 450–432 BC

Theares dedicated Kleogenes to Pohoidan. The ephor was Daiochos; the witnesses Arion, Lyon.

[Marble stele, *IG* 5.1.1228 = BM 1880,0917.1]

This marble stele, 57.15 cm high and 29.21 cm wide, but sadly not on display in the British Museum, is one of four similar objects (*IG* 5.1.1228–1231) found at Tainaron in the ruins of the temple of Poseidon in the nineteenth century. All four follow the same formula: *name* (slave owner) dedicates *name* (slave) to Poseidon, ephor and two witnesses named. The inscriptions do not tell us whether the owners were Spartiates or *perioikoi,* but the slave's name sounds very Greek (comprising two Greek stems very common as name-elements: '*kleos*'– glory + '*gen-*'– birth). So the slave was probably a (Greek) helot. For late sources stating that helots were state-owned and modern doubts that this was true in the classical period see note on helot ownership, page 106).

ZEUS: C21–C24

Spartan kings were priests of Zeus of Lakedaimon and Zeus, Lord of Heaven (**D5**) and sacrificed to him before going on campaign (**D7**). Pausanias mentions a site sacred to Zeus in Lakonia, near Hermai (3.10.6) and a sanctuary of Messapian Zeus (3.20.3); the title linked to the name of a people/place (**C21**). Zeus was very prominent for the Messenians, as Zeus of Mt Ithome. For an official Spartan dedication to Olympian Zeus, see **B3**.

C21   Cup dedicated to Messapian Zeus, early 6th century

[…,] Mesapian [Zeus?]

[Catling & Shipley, *BSA* 84, 1989, 187–200]

Several fragments of a black-glazed cup were found in excavations in 1987 near the modern town of Aphyssou, just east of Sparta, and near a small sanctuary of Zeus Messapeus. See Catling, 'A sanctuary of Zeus Messapeus: Excavations at Aphyssou, Tsakona, 1989', *BSA* 85, 1990, 15–35 and Catling & Shipley, 'Messapian Zeus: an early sixth-century inscribed cup from Lakonia', *BSA* 84, 1989, 187–200 for details and pictures of this cup.

C22   Messapean Zeus

Messapeai, area of Lakonia. The local name Messapeus: since Zeus is honoured there. Theopompos (book) 57.

[Stephanus, *Lexicon* 'Messapeai' = Theopompos, *FGrH* 115 F245]

Stephanus was a Byzantine lexicographer possibly of the fifth century AD. Theopompos wrote in the fourth century BC.

C23   Eurystratidas dedicates weapons possibly at Olympia

[To Zeus, son of Kronos], Eurystratidas the Lakedaimonian [dedica]ted these weapons: [may you] always be gracious to him.

[*SEG* 11.1214 = *LSAG* 19]

This inscription is on a strip of bronze, probably from Olympia, *c.* 550–525 BC. Plutarch suggests (*Spartan Sayings*, 18) that the Spartans did not follow the usual Greek custom of dedicating weapons of defeated enemies. If so, the weapons dedicated could have been Eurystratidas' own, on ceasing to be of military age, or even winning the 'race-in-armour'.

C24   The Lightning God

Of Zeus 'Katabas' (Descending in Lightning). In the fifth year. Sacrifice. Meal. Gaihulos.

[*IG* 5.1.1316]

Zeus might be worshipped in any place struck by lightning. This inscription was from Thalamai in Messenia and seems to date from the early fifth century BC. Katabas is explained in LSJ as equivalent to Kataibates (coming down in thunder and lightning). 'Meal' here translates a rare word connected with 'grinding' – presumably ground barley.

OTHER GODS: C25–C28

C25   Offering to the gods
Chalqodamans offered me to the gods, a most beautiful dedication.

[*IG* 5.1.231]

From Sparta. Shown to be early (6th century?) by being retrograde and using the letter koppa, rendered here by 'q'.

C26   Spring to Herakles
This eternal (?) spring besides Epandris is dedicated to Herakles, being given as a thank-offering for healing. Hail, mighty Herakles; in return for gifts, send perfect health on Epandris and its children.

[*IG* 5.1.1119, Geronthrai, fourth century BC]

Herakles had a special relevance to Sparta as mythical founder of the line of its twin kings (Hdt 6.52).

C27   Bronze figure of Eileithyia in British Museum
Aristomacha dedicated (me) to the Eleuthia.

[*SEG* 11.953 = *IG* 5.1.1345 = BM 1814,0704.1284]

Eileithyia was the usual Greek name for the goddess of childbirth, known in Doric as Eleuthia. This bronze figure, 12.2 cm tall, of a woman holding a flower, is of unknown provenance, but probably 5th century. Eleuthia is also thought to have been worshipped alongside Artemis Orthia (Paus. 3.17.1), and a bronze *tessera* was found there in 1908 with Eleuthia's name in the genitive case. (*SEG* 2.81).

C28   Relief-stele to Tyndaridai
Plestiadas d[edicated] me to the Dioskouroi, a statue of the twin sons of Tyndareos, dreading their wrath.

[*IG* 5.1.919 = *LSAG* 24]

The Dioskouroi (= 'sons of Zeus') or Tyndaridai (= 'children of Tyndareos' were the twin sons of Leda. Worshipped throughout Greece (and Rome), they had a particular place in Spartan religion, since Kastor's mortal father was Tyndareos, King of Sparta (with Pollux or Polydeukes being the son of Zeus). Kastor's tomb was in Sparta (Paus. 3.13.1).

The relief stele was found at Sellasia north of Sparta and depicted the twins facing each other. The entire top half is lost, but the inscription, turned sideways, and fitting between the legs of the twins is largely preserved (see line drawing from Tod & Wace, *A Catalogue of the Sparta Museum*, no. 447). It dates from *c.* 525 BC.

HERO-WORSHIP: C29–C38

This is a peculiarity of Greek worship in general, a 'deceased person who exerts from his grave a power for good or evil and who demands appropriate honour' (Burkert, *Greek Religion* 203). The honours given involved setting apart one particular grave, a *heroon* and bringing there sacrifices and votive gifts. The key difference from the worship of gods is that hero-worship relates to a specific location, usually a burial-place. The practice may stem from the rediscovery in the eighth century of old graves (e.g. **C31, C32**), but it continued with the same status being provided for founders of colonies, and of people well within living memory, such as athletes, political leaders and generals. Examples include Orestes (**H10**), Chilon (**C34, C35**), Chionis (**C45, C46**), Hipposthenes (**C48**), Leonidas (**F27**), Kyniska (**C56**), Brasidas (**E38**), and perhaps paving the way for the divine worship at Samos of the living Lysander (**C37, C38**).

THE MENELAION: C29–C31

A few miles south-east of Sparta, above the River Eurotas is the Menelaion or shrine of Menelaus, husband of Helen. Mycenean remains of 15th–13th centuries have been found here alongside a shrine from *c.* 700 BC, and the obvious guess is that the shrine was established at the site where Menelaus and Helen were thought to have lived at the time of the Trojan War (and see Paus. 3.19.9). Excavations in the 1970s found inscriptions dedicated to the couple: H.W. Catling, 'Excavations at the Menelaion, Sparta, 1973–1976' in *Archaeological Reports* No.23 (1976–1977), pp. 24–42 now in http://www.jstor.org/stable/581107.

C29   Small bronze *aryballos* dedicated to Helen

Deinis dedicated these to [Helen, wife of] Menelaos.

[Catling, *Excavations at the Menelaion, Sparta*, figs. 25, 26]

Inscribed bronze *aryballos* (small vessel/flask), dated to the mid seventh century BC.

C30   Claw-like object dedicated to Helen

To Helen

[Catling, *Excavations at the Menelaion, Sparta*, fig. 27]

Inscribed retrograde with heta *c.* 570 BC on a bronze *harpax* (claw-like object of presumed sacrificial use).

C31   Limestone *stele* for Menelaos

Euthykrenes dedicated this to Menelaos.

[Catling, *Excavations at the Menelaion, Sparta*, fig. 28]

Small blue limestone *stele* the lettering of which suggests a date early in the fifth century. Traces at the top of the *stele* indicate that the dedication was probably a large bronze statuette (lost).

SANCTUARY OF ALEXANDRA/KASSANDRA: C32–C33

Two separate sets of thousands of votive offerings have been discovered at Amyklai near the sanctuary of Apollo. The offerings, mainly terracotta plaques with figures, range in date from early seventh to late fourth century BC. Dedicatory inscriptions on vases to Agamemnon and Alexandra show that this area must be the sanctuary mentioned by Pausanias. Full analysis by G. Salapatas, *Heroic Offerings: the terracotta plaques from the Spartan sanctuary of Agamemnon and Kassandra*. (Michigan 2014).

C32   Various vase fragments
Agamemn[…]; Alexa[…];[…]ndra

[Sparta Museum 14662, 6052, 6053]

C33   Sanctuary of Alexandra/Kassandra
Amyklai was destroyed by the Dorians and has thereafter remained a village. The sanctuary and statue of Alexandra are worth seeing. The Amyklaians say that this Alexandra is Kassandra, the daughter of Priam. There is also there a statue of Klytaimnestra and a tomb thought to be Agamemnon's.

[Pausanias, *Description of Greece* 3.19.6]

C34   Chilon relief found near Sparta
[Ch]ilon

[*IG* 5.1.1 = *LSAG* 26 = Wace, *archaiologike ephemeris* 1937, 217ff fig 1]

Relief of a figure from near Sparta, *c.* 525 BC, labelled, albeit the first letter is missing, as Chilon (Spartan ephor and 'sage'), and presumably showing Chilon being treated as a hero (see **C35** below for his sanctuary).

C35   Pausanias on Chilon's *heroon*
As one goes towards the gates from Chiton, there is the *heroon* of Chilon who was regarded as a sage and who, together with Dorieus, son of Anaxandridas, went on an expedition to Sicily.

[Pausanias, *Description of Greece* 3.16.4]

For Dorieus' royal birth, failure to be made king, and expeditions, see **E8, E9, H13, H14.**

C36   Relief from Magoula in Berlin museum
'The young men (*koroi*) [put up] (a statue of) me, Thiokles […]

[*LSAG* 29 = *IG* 5.1.457 = Tod & Wace, 104, fig.4]

A large snake opposite the young man suggests a heroized person, and the artistic style can be dated by experts to the 'Leagros period', 510–500 BC. [Picture from Tod & Wace, A Catalogue of the Sparta Museum, OUP 1906, digitized by Google.]

C37   Divine honours for Lysander, before 395 BC

For, as Douris observes, he was the first Greek to whom cities set up altars as if a god, and they made sacrifices, and he was the first to whom they sang hymns of praise. One which is recorded has the following beginning:

> *We sing a hymn to the general of blessed Greece coming from spacious Sparta, "o, aie, paian!"*

[4] The Samians also voted to call their festival to Hera the Lysandreia. Of the poets, he always kept with him Choirilos so that he might celebrate his achievements in poetry. Once, pleased with Antilochos who composed some verses for him, he gave him a cap filled with silver. When Antimachos of Kolophon and a certain Nikeratos from Herakleia competed with poems in celebration of him at the Lysandreia, he awarded the crown to Nikeratos, so Antimachos in his anger destroyed his poem.

[Plutarch, *Lysander* 18.3–4]

C38   A pankration winner at the Lysandreia

Victor in the pankration for the fourth time at the Lysandreia

[Deutsches Archaeologisches Institut, *Archaeologischer Anzeiger* 1965, p.400]

Part of a statue base found at the sanctuary of Hera on Samos bearing a fragmentary inscription honouring an athlete.

OLYMPIC GAMES: C39–C60

It was said that Chilon watched his son compete and win at boxing at the Olympic Games, and then died, a happy man (Pliny, *Natural History* 7.119 and 7.180). The interest in this story is not its veracity (a variety of considerations make it highly improbable), but what it shows later generations thought appropriate. Athletics was prized; especially at the Olympics; especially in Sparta; perhaps especially at a combat event. We are very well-informed about the Olympic Games, which provided a common chronological framework for Greek history (e.g. **E7**). But we do not now have anything like a full list of winners for every event, though they did exist (**C41**). Instead we have a patchwork of information including anecdotes in literary sources and inscriptions from Olympia and elsewhere, mainly surviving through being recorded by Pausanias. The results are perhaps surprising: after early dominance in the stade race, Sparta's best event, especially in the fifth century, is the one for which, in any age, great wealth is a prerequisite – horse-racing – or in an Olympic context, the four-horse chariot race, for which the owner, not the charioteer, was crowned. It is worth noting that there was often a clear relationship between victories at Panhellenic games and political success in archaic and classical Greece. Amongst the prime examples of how this was done are the epinician odes of Pindar and Bacchylides – poems commissioned to celebrate a victory. It is striking that despite the wide geographical range of commissions for these poets in the first half of the fifth century, no surviving poems celebrate Spartan victories at festivals (see Hodkinson, *PWCS* 317–9).

C39   Table of Olympic victors in the stade race by states

Olympics	Dates	City state of victors in the stade race				
Olympics	Dates (BC)	Messenia	Sparta	Athens	Kroton	Elis
1–10	776–740	6				3
11–20	736–700	1	5			
21–30	696–660		6	2		
31–40	656–620		8	1		
41–50	616–580		5		2	
51–60	576–540		1		4	2
61–70	536–500				1	
71–80	496–460				5	
81–90	456–420	2		1		
91–100	416–380					2
101–110	376–340			3		
111–120	336–300		1			
Totals /120		**9**	**26**	**7**	**12**	**7**

[Eusebius, *Chronicle*]

Eusebius' *Chronicle* records names and states of all the Olympic stade race victors, and Olympic victor lists were widely available and even a sub-genre of literature, widely used by universal historians such as Diodoros and other authors. See P. Christesen, *Olympic Victor Lists and Ancient Greek History*, Cambridge 2007; and **C41** for a fragment. According to Eusebius' list, Messenia and Sparta dominated the early stade races, before declining to the status of the great majority of the hundreds of city-states in producing an occasional winner. The table above includes, by way of comparison, the most successful states outside Lakonia. Christesen (above, e.g. chapter 2.6 and appendix 10) regards the pattern of Messenian prominence ending abruptly and Spartan dominance fading away as too good to be true and pointing to the winners having been later invented to fit with Greek history. Most scholars though accept the general reliability of the victor lists, and Hodkinson discusses various reasons for Sparta's declining success 'An Agonistic Culture' in *Sparta: New Perspectives* (London 1999) 147–87.

C40   Table of Olympic events and the origins of the inaugural victors

Event	First held in ...	Winner's origin	Source
Stade-race	1st Olympics, 776	Elis	
Two-stade race (*diaulos*)	14th Olympics, 724	Elis	
Dolichos	15th Olympics, 720	Lakonia	= Paus. 5.8.6, DH 7.72.3
Wrestling	18th Olympics, 708	Lakonia	= Paus. 5.8.7
Pentathlon	18th Olympics, 708	Lakonia	= Paus. 5.8.7
Boxing	23rd Olympics, 688	Smyrna	
4-horse chariot	25th Olympics, 680	Thebes	
Pankration	33rd Olympics, 648	Syracuse	
Horse race	33rd Olympics, 648	Thessaly	
Boys' wrestling	37th Olympics, 632	Lakonia	= Paus. 5.8.9
Boys' stade race	37th Olympics, 632	Elis	
Boys' pankration	38th Olympics, 628	Lakonia	= Paus. 5.9.1
Boys' boxing	41st Olympics, 616	Sybaris	
Race in armour	65th Olympics, 520	Heraia	
Cart-race	70th Olympics, 500	Thessaly	= Paus. 5.9.1
Kalpe	71st Olympics, 496	Achaia	= Paus. 5.9.1
2-horse chariot	93rd Olympics, 408	Elis	
4-foal chariot	99th Olympics, 384	Lakonia	= Paus. 5.8.10 = *IG* 2² 2326

[Eusebius, *Chronicle*]

Eusebius' *Chronicle* also notes when different Olympic contests were first held and who won. Again the table shows the prominence of Spartan competitors, mostly in the relatively early stages of the games. The same information is also given in an inscription *IG* 2² 2326 and in Paus. 5.8.9–10. The boys' *pankration* was discontinued immediately, the cart-race and the *kalpe* from 440 BC.

C41   List of Olympic Victors in the 78th Olympic Games, 468 BC

[P]armeneides of Poseidonia, the stade race
[Par]meneides, the same, the two-stade race (*diaulos*)
[…]medes the Lakonian, the *dolichos*
[..]tion of Taras, the pentathlon
[Epha]rmostos of Opous, the wrestling
[Me]nalkes of Opous, the boxing
[..]titimadas of Argos, the *pankration*
[Lyk]ophron of Athens, the boys' stade race
[..]emos of Parrhasia, the boys' wrestling
[…]os of Athens, the race in armour.
[..]nymos of Syracuse, the chariot race.

[P.Oxy II 222]

A papyrus from Oxyrhynchos preserves a list of Olympic victors 480–468, giving names of the victors, their hometown and the events, always in the same order. Overall 42 victors are listed from 23 different places. Argos won six victories, including two with 'public horses'; Syracuse won five times (three different athletes); Sparta's three victories were in two of the three long distance races whose results are preserved, and in the boys' stade race.

C42   Lakedaimonians the first to exercise naked

The Lakedaimonians were the first to strip naked, to take off their clothes in public and rub themselves with oil after exercising. Before that, even at the Olympics athletes competed with loin-cloths around their genitals, and it is not many years since this custom died out.

[Thucydides, *History of the Peloponnesian War* 1.6.5]

A much earlier date than Thucydides implies is given by **C43** and Paus. 1.44.1 (Orsippos of Megara in 720 BC). Plato, *Republic* 452c credits the Cretans (often thought to have inspired Spartan reforms – **F3, D63**). See Hodkinson, *PWCS* 220–1.

C43   A Spartan 'invents' running naked

The first person to try taking off his clothes and running naked at the Olympics, in the fifteenth games (720 BC) was Akanthos the Lakedaimonian.

[Dionysius of Halicarnassus, *Roman Antiquities* 7.72.3]

C44   Other notable Spartan Olympic successes

26th Olympics (676 BC): Philombrotos of Lakonia won the pentathlon at three Olympics.

29th Olympics (664 BC) Chionis of Lakonia, whose jump was 33 feet, (won) the stade race.

37th Olympics (632 BC): A wrestling contest for boys was added, and the winner was Hipposthenes of Lakonia, who leaving out the next Olympics, won five times in a row, at the men's wrestling.

[Eusebius, *Chronicle*]

As well as a complete list of stade race winners (**C39**) and winners of inaugural events (**C41**), Eusebius also recorded other notable 'Olympic records'. Those involving Spartans in the Archaic and Classical periods are excerpted above. Other even longer figures exist in the manuscript for Chionis' jump, but even this figure is clearly impossible for a single, standing jump. Nor is it clear whether he actually won the overall pentathlon, the only Olympic event involving the long-jump. Eusebius records him also winning the next two stade races, and see also **C45–C46**. For Hipposthenes and his son, see **C47** and **C48**.

C45   Chionis monument at Sparta

Very close to the monuments erected to the Agiads you will see a *stele* on which are inscribed the victories won on the track by Chionis, a Lakedaimonian man at various games including the Olympics, where he won seven victories, four at the stade race, the others at the two-stade race (*diaulos*): the race with the shield at the close of the games did not yet exist. Chionis is said to have taken part, with Battos of Thera in founding Kyrene, and in subduing the neighbouring peoples.

[Pausanias, *Description of Greece* 3.14.3]

C46   Chionis monument at Olympia

A *stele* has been dedicated in Olympia listing the victories of Chionis the Lakedaimonian. Those who think that Chionis put up the *stele* himself, rather than the Lakedaimonian people are guilty of foolishness. For given that on the *stele* it says that there was not yet a race in armour, how on earth could Chionis know that the Eleans would add it to the programme later? But even more foolish are those who say that the statue erected beside the *stele* is a real portrait of Chionis – actually it is a work of the Athenian Myron.

[Pausanias, *Description of Greece* 6.13.2]

Chionis won multiple Olympic victories in the seventh century. A long time later (certainly a while after the the race in armour was introduced in 520 BC), the Spartans set up two monuments to him, doubtless at about the same time. The Athenian sculptor Myron (flourished *c.* 470–440 BC) was commissioned to produce a generic statue of a runner, rather than one which could claim to be a real portrait of him. The reference to the race in armour not existing on the Olympic programme in his day only makes sense as an attempt to justify his record of wins as greater than someone with a similar number of wins, but who had another event open to him. An obvious candidate was the multiple Olympic winner of the 480s, Astylos from Kroton who then transferred allegiance to Syracuse: his statue and victories are mentioned by Pausanias just before those of Chionis. P. Christesen, 'Kings playing politics: the heroization of Chionis of Sparta, *Historia* 59, 2010, 26–73. (JSTOR http://www.jstor.org/stable/pdf/27809550.pdf) makes a convincing case for the public promotion of Chionis around 470 BC being in the interests of Sparta vis-à-vis the rising power and prestige of Syracuse; of the Agiads who in allowing his memorial close to their own may have been claiming some kinship with him, and hoping to repair the damage to their family inflicted by Pausanias; and even in the interests of good relations with the Battiad kings of Kyrene.

C47   Spartan father and son with eleven Olympic victories between them, from 632 BC

On the road to the right of the hill there is a statue of Hetoemokles. Hetoemokles himself and Hipposthenes his father had gained Olympic victories at wrestling: eleven in total, with Hipposthenes managing to gain one more win than his son.

[Pausanias, *Description of Greece* 3.13.9]

C48   Olympic victor heroized

Nearby is a temple of Hipposthenes who won many victories at wrestling. They honour him because of an oracle, paying Hipposthenes the same honours as Poseidon.

[Pausanias, *Description of Greece* 3.15.7]

C49   Dedication of long-jump weight by a Spartan at Olympia, c. 500?

Akmatidas the Lakedaimonian, the clear victor in the pentathlon, dedicated this.

[*SEG* 11.1227 = *LSAG* 20]

The inscription is written continuously on both sides of the weight. The last word, here translated as 'clear' is 'ἀσσκονικτεί' which seems to be a strange spelling, or even a mis-copying for ἀκονικτ(ε)ί, meaning 'without dust (from the arena)'. Though possibly a metaphor, it is also some of the best evidence for the theory that if a pentathlete won the first three events (discus, long-jump, javelin) he would have won overall, without even the need for the stade race or for getting dusty while wrestling.

C50   Euagoras of Sparta wins three consecutive Olympic chariot victories

Opposite Kimon were buried the mares which won three Olympic victories. Other horses had previously done the same thing – those of Euagoras the Lakonian, but no others besides these.

[Herodotus, *Histories* 6.103.3–4]

Pausanias 6.10.8 mentions a chariot dedicated by Euagoras at Olympia. Aelian, *Nature of Animals* 12.40 says that Euagoras gave his horses a splendid burial. His victories were probably in the mid-sixth century.

C51   King Demaratos wins a chariot victory (perhaps 504 BC)

Among Demaratos' many good services to the Lakedaimonians was his victory at Olympia in the four-horse chariot race – an achievement unmatched by any of the previous kings of Sparta.

[Herodotus, *Histories* 6.70.3]

C52   Spartan dominance of fifth-century chariot-racing at Olympia

[1.6] Kyniska, daughter of Archidamos, her family, and her Olympic victories have already been mentioned in what I have written about the kings of the Lakedaimonians. At Olympia, next to the statue of Troilos, there stands a stone base with chariot, horses, charioteer and a statue of Kyniska herself. This is the work of Apelles, inscribed with epigrams about Kyniska. [1.7] Next to Kyniska, there are statues of Lakedaimonians dedicated as having won the horse-races. Anaxandros was declared the winner of the chariot race, though the epigram on his statue says that his father's father had previously been crowned in the pentathlon. He is depicted as praying to the god. [1.8] Polykles who was nicknamed 'Poly-Bronze' also won the four-horse chariot race: his statue hold the ribbon in its right hand, and next to him are two boys, one holding a hoop, the other asking for the ribbon. Polykles also won with his horses at Pythian, Isthmian and Nemean games, as his epigram says.

[2.1] The Lakedaimonians after the Persian invasion were of all the Greeks the most eager to make their mark at breeding horses. In addition to those I have already mentioned, the following breeders from Sparta have statues dedicated further on than that of the athlete from Akarnania: Xenarkes, Lykinos, Arkesilaos and Lichas son on Arkesilaos. [2.2] Xenarkes also claimed victories at Delphi, Argos, and Corinth. Lykinos took colts to Olympia, and since one of them failed the test, entered them in the race for fully-grown horses and won with them; he set up two statues at Olympia made by Myron of Athens. As for Arkesilaos and Lichas his son, the former won two Olympic victories, while Lichas, at the time when the Lakedaimonians were banned from the games, entered his chariot in the name of people of Thebes, and tied a ribbon around his winning charioteer; and was whipped for this by the Greek Judges.

[Pausanias, *Description of Greece* 6.1.7–8 and 6.2.1–2]

For **Kyniska**, see **C55–C57**. **Polykles** will have gained his nick-name from having commissioned a number of bronze statues. **Lykinos'** victory is hard to reconcile with Pausanias' text translated above: the race for colts was established only in 384 (Paus. 5.8.10 in **C40**) but **Myron** was a very famous sculptor of the mid-fifth century. The answer is probably that something has gone wrong with Pausanias' text, which should say that one of the two statues was set up by Lykinos and the second, by Myron, was for Arkesilaos' victories, which fits Myron's floruit (see Hodkinson, *PWCS* 330 n.15). Besides the costs of raising and training thoroughbred horses, the costs of having statues made was high and certainly gives the lie to the notion of Spartan lack of money.

C53   Lichas flouts the ban on Sparta at the Olympics and is whipped, 420

But there was very real fear among all those at the Olympic festival that the Lakedaimonians might arrive with an army, especially when the Lakedaimonian, Lichas the son of Arkesilaos, was given a beating on the course by the umpires. His chariot had won the race but it was declared that the Boiotian people were the victors because Lichas had no right to compete. But Lichas had come out onto the course and crowned his charioteer, thus trying to demonstrate that he was the owner of the chariot. As a result, everyone became much more apprehensive that events might take a nasty turn. In fact, however, the Lakedaimonians kept the peace and the festival ran its usual course.

[Thucydides, *History of the Peloponnesian War* 5.50.4]

C54   Table showing Spartan winners of Olympic chariot race, 448–420 BC

Date	Name	Monument at Olympia	Notes	Reference
448 BC	Arkesilaos	Statue		**C52**
444 BC	Arkesilaos	Statue		**C52**
440 BC	Leon			Schol. on Eur. *Hipp.* 231
436 BC				
432 BC	Xenarkes?	Statue	Other 'periodoi' wins	**C52**
428 BC	Anaxandros	Statue		**C52**
424 BC	Polykles	Statue	Complete set of 'periodoi' wins	**C52**
420 BC	Lichas	Statue	Spartans banned	**C52, C53**

Altogether 18 monuments are known to have been put up at Olympia to celebrate victors in the four-horse chariot race between 560 and 364 BC, and of these 11 were for Spartans (Hodkinson, *PWCS* 320–3). So not only did the Spartans dominate the event that demanded the greatest resources but paid to ensure that their wins were noted for posterity. Spartan dominance was ended in 416 by Alkibiades (Thuc. 6.16): it is possible that the Spartans were still banned then.

C55   Kyniska celebrates her Olympic victory, 396 BC

Sparta's [kings are my]
Fathers and brothers; after winning [with a chariot of swift-footed horses]
Kyniska set up this statue. I say that I am the only woman
Out of all Greece to win the crown.
Apelles, son of Kallikles made this.

[*IG* 5.1.1564a = *IvO* 160]

Kyniska was daughter of Archidamos, sister of Agesilaos and half-sister of Agis. The epigram is on the top of a fragmentary circular statue base made of black marble, with the name of the sculptor on the side (see Paus. 6.1.6 = **C52**). The epigram is also preserved in the *Palatine Anthology* 13.16 (thus guaranteeing the words not preserved on the stone).

C56   Kyniska's *heroon*

Also in the Platanistas ('Plane-tree Grove') is the *heroon* (hero-shrine) of Kyniska, daughter of Archidamos, king of the Spartiates. She was the first woman to breed horses and the first to win the chariot race at Olympia.

[Pausanias, *Description of Greece* 3.15.1]

Pausanias first mentions Kyniska and her Olympic victory at 3.8.1–3, noting that it paved the way for other women, especially Lakonian women, and mentioning, but not quoting her verse monument (**C55**). Pausanias mentions the statue-group of Kyniska's smaller-than-life-size bronze horses at Temple of Zeus at Olympia as worth seeing (5.12.5) in addition to the larger statue-group within the Altis (sacred area) of Olympia (6.1.6 = **C52**).

C57   Chariot racing the mark of wealth

Surely Agesilaos did what was seemly and dignified when he adorned his own estates with possessions worthy of a man – keeping hounds and horses for warriors – but persuaded his sister Kyniska to breed chariot horses, and showed by her victory that such a stud is a mark not of manliness but of wealth.

[Xenophon, *Agesilaos* 9.6]

C58   Euryleonis – female winner of chariot race, perhaps 368 BC

By the so-called *Skenoma* (Tent) is a statue of a woman, who the Lakedaimonians say is Euryleonis: she won an Olympic victory in the two-horse chariot race.

[Pausanias, *Description of Greece* 3.17.6]

C59   Deinosthenes' monument gives distances to Lakedaimon, 316 BC

Deinosthenes, son of Deinosthenes, the Lakedaimonian dedicated this to Olympian Zeus after his victory in the stade race. From this stone to Lakedaimon is 630, and from there to the first stone is 30.

[*IvO* 171]

Deinosthenes as appropriate for the winner of the stade race, gives the distance in stades back to, presumably, the edge of his home town and thence to the agora.

C60   Spartan lack of interest in boxing

Boxing was a Lakonian discovery and Polydeukes was best at it (hence poets celebrated his achievements at it). The ancient Lakedaimonians boxed because they did not have helmets and thought it not right for their countrymen to fight in them, but that a shield would act as a helmet for someone practised at wielding it. In order to guard against blows to the face and to endure those they received, they worked at boxing and thus trained at 'covering' their faces. But later on they gave up boxing and *pankration* too, thinking it shameful to compete at events in which one person giving up would sully the reputation of Sparta as lacking courage.

[Philostratos, *On Athletic Training* 9–10]

Polydeukes (the mortal Dioskouros) was celebrated for his boxing by, e.g. Theocritus, *Idyll* 22. The Philostratos who wrote this was probably the best known of the four members of this family, who was a favourite of the wife of Septimius Severus, and wrote in the first half of the third century AD. His works are generally more concerned with rhetoric and style than historical accuracy or plausibility, but he may preserve the traditional Spartan explanation for their apparent lack of interest in 'combat sports' – there is no evidence for Spartan victories at any Panhellenic sites, and their own games do not seem to have had these events.

SPARTAN FESTIVALS: C61–C94
In addition to the Panhellenic festivals, Greek city states usually had their own, annual religious festivals. Three major Spartan festivals celebrated Apollo – the Karneia, Hyakinthia and Gymnopaidiai. As at the Panhellenic festival, the Pythian Games at Delphi, Apollo was honoured with a range of sporting and cultural events and competitions. Inevitably we know far less about these than about the Olympic Games, and there is a particular danger that the festivals of the archaic and classical period may have been very different from those that continued well into the Roman Imperial period from which some of our sources come. In addition the Damonon stele (**C83**) lists many Lakonian equestrian and athletic festivals.

KARNEIA: C61–C68
The Karneia was the most important Spartan festival, celebrated over nine days in late summer by Dorian Greeks elsewhere, but thought to originate in Sparta. The title 'Karneios' is obscure (Paus. 3.13.3–5 and **C63**). Celebration of the festival was the reason given by the Spartans for not being able to help the Athenians at Marathon (**H16**). A variety of events are known over the nine days of the festival, but it was 'above all a choral and musical festival of Panhellenic importance'. (*OCD³*, 'Carnea'). The festival was ancient and of sufficient status for the very important fifth-century historian, Hellanikos to have written a list of winners (**C62**). The festival was still celebrated well into Roman times, with winners and a priestess being attested (*IG* 5.1.82; 5.1.209; *IG* 5.1 page 131).

C61   A contest of lyre-players
The Karneia, a contest for lyre-players, was held for the first time at Lakedaimon.

[Eusebius, *Chronicle,* under 26th Olympiad (676–673 BC)]

C62   Karneian 'Victor-lists'
Terpander was the first ever winner at the Karneia, as Hellanikos records in his poetic 'Karneian Victors' and the version he wrote as a list. The Karneia was instituted in the twenty-sixth Olympiad [676 BC], as Sosibios says in his book *On Time.*

[Athenaios 14.37 = Hellanikos, *FGrH* 4 F85a = Sosibios, *FGrH* 595 F3]

Terpander was a famous musician and poet from Lesbos who seems to have operated mainly in Sparta, and seems to have been regarded as very much a Spartan poet (see Plut. *Lykourgos* 28 = **D44**), apparently responsible for setting Sparta's laws to music (Clement of Alexandria, *Miscellanies* 1.16.78.5). However even the few meagre lines attributed to him, thirteen in all, are quoted by writers no earlier than the first century AD (e.g. Plut. *Lykourgos* 21.4) and are thought to be Hellenistic inventions. An ancient commentator on Aristophanes also refers to Hellanikos' *Karneian Victors* (Scholiast V on Aristophanes, *Birds* 1403 = *FGrH* 4 F86).

C63   The name
The Karnea: Praxilla says the name came from the Karnos, son of Zeus and Europa, who was loved by Apollo, while Alkman says it was from a Trojan called Karneos.

[Scholiast on Theocritus, *Idyll* 5.83]

The shepherd Lakon says in Theocritus' pastoral poem (3rd century BC) that he is saving a ram for (sacrifice at) the forthcoming Karnean festival, which the ancient commentator explains in this note.

C64   Hymns to Apollo
Nor does the chorus celebrate Apollo for just one day:
For there are many songs to him.

[Callimachus, *Hymn to Apollo* 2.30–31]

Callimachus, a third-century BC poet is praising Apollo generally, rather than writing about the Spartan Karneia. Later in the poem (2.85–87) he speaks of Apollo enjoying dancing at the time of the Karneia when Cyrene in N. Africa is being founded (by Dorian Greeks from Sparta *via* Thera).

C65   'Karneatai' fund the festival

Karneatai: unmarried men who are chosen by lot to pay the expenses (*leitourgia*) for the Karneia, five for each festival, they pay the expenses for four years.

[Hesychios, *Lexicon*, 'Karneatai']

Leitourgia ('work for the people') was the ancient Greek system of getting rich people to pay for things of benefit to the state at their own expense – a sort of combination of modern taxation and sponsorship of events. Though a usual feature of democratic Athens, it was unusual at Sparta. Expenses might include training the choruses and certainly provision of animals for sacrifice and then feasting.

C66   The 'Grape-runners'

Staphylodromoi: at the Karneian festival, someone runs, covered in woollen ribbons and praying to the gods for the good of the city. Young men, who are known as *staphylodromoi* ('grape-runners') pursue him, and if they catch him they expect, according to local tradition, good fortune for the city, if not, the opposite.

[Bekker, *Anecdota Graeca* 305.25]

Bekker's *Greek Selections* are from the enormous quantity of Byzantine classical scholarship. There is no way of dating or assessing this definition, but it has been plausibly linked by anthropologists to other traditional cult practices of hunting down something for the good of the community (see Burkert, *Greek Religion* 234–6). *Staphylodromoi* are also explained by Hesychios who says they are some of the Karneatai (see **C65**).

C67   A frequent athletic winner at the Karneia

Aiglatas set up this statue to the Karneian (Apollo), having five times won the long (race) and he also added the *dolichos* three times, and at Athena's [festival …].

[*IG* 5.1.222 = *LSAG* 22 = *SEG* 14.329]

The inscription was found near the temple of Apollo Karneios. A pair of ram's horns (see note to **C63** above) appears above the inscription. Jeffery dates the inscription to the latter part of the sixth century. The letters are very carefully cut *boustrophedon* ('reflecting equally the merits of Sparta's athletes and stone-workers during the period' – Jeffery, p.192). Here the 'long' race was clearly different from the *dolichos*.

C68   A military aspect to the Karneia?

Demetrios of Skepsis says in the 1st book of *Trojan Forces*, 'The Karneian festival is for the Lakedaimonians a representation of military training. For there are nine places numbered, called *skiades*, something like tents; and nine men eat in each, and everything is done by spoken commands. Each *skias* has three *phratriai* and the Karneian festival lasts nine days.'

[Athenaios, *Scholars at Dinner* 4.19]

Demetrios of Skepsis (near Troy) was born *c.* 214 BC and wrote in exceptional detail on the Homer's catalogue of Trojan forces in *Iliad* 2. The emphasis on 'three' and 'nine' seems to reflect the more ancient 'Dorian' division into three tribes (see note on **A10**).

HYAKINTHIA: C69–C71
In Greek mythology Apollo accidentally killed his young male lover, Hyakinthos with a discus throw (Ovid, *Met.* 10.162ff, Apollodoros 1.3.3). The games, held at Apollo's ancient sanctuary at Amyklai (see Paus. 3.18–19), both celebrated and mourned him, and an account survives of two of the three days of this festival. It was at the Hyakinthia in Sparta (and the Dionysia in Athens) that the oath of the fifty years' peace was to be renewed annually (Thuc. 5.23 = **B18**). Another indication of its importance is that Amyklaian Spartans might be specially released from campaign to attend, as in 390 BC – see **C70**.

C69   An account of the first two days of the Hyakinthia
Didymos the grammarian … says that Polykrates writes in his *Lakedaimonian Customs* that the Lakedaimonians celebrate the festival of Hyakinthia over three days. On account of the grief for what happened to Hyakinthos, they do not wear garlands at the dinners, nor bring in cakes or pastries or give things that accompany these; nor do they sing a hymn to the god; nor do they introduce anything of the sort that they do at the other festivals. Instead they dine in a very orderly fashion and then leave.

On the middle day of the three a diverse spectacle takes place, a large and important gathering. Boys play their lyres in formal tunics, sing to the flute, play on all the strings together with the plectrum in a lively rhythm, and sing to the god in a high pitch. Others dressed up and on horseback parade through the theatre. And numerous choruses of young men (*neaniskoi*) enter the theatre and sing some of their national poems, while dancers mingling with them perform an ancient dance accompanied by flute and singing. As for the maidens, some ride in richly decorated wicker carriages, some process in racing-chariots drawn by horses. The whole city is at a pitch of excitement and pleasure at the spectacle. They sacrifice large numbers of victims all through this day, and the citizens put on a banquet for all their friends and their own slaves. No one misses the festival – instead the city tends to be emptied for the spectacle.

[Polykrates, *FGrH* 588 F1 in Athenaios, *Scholars at Dinner* 4.17]

Didymos was an Alexandrian scholar of the first century BC; Polykrates is otherwise unknown (presumably a Lakonian local historian), and it is not clear why he (or Didymos or Athenaios) omitted an account of the third and final day of the festival, though possibly the maidens paraded on day three. We should not imagine a built-up **theatre** but simply a place where people could watch (the original meaning of θέατρον).

C70   The importance of the Hyakinthia
The people of Amyklai always return for the Hyakinthia for the hymn to Apollo, if they happen to be on campaign or abroad for any other reason. So at this time, Agesilaos left behind at Lechaion all the Amyklaians in the army.

[Xenophon, *Hellenika* 4.5.11 (390 BC)]

This episode, which led to a Spartan military reversal in 390 is also mentioned by Paus. 3.10.1.

C71   Agesilaos takes part in the Hyakinthia
He returned home to the Hyakinthia and joined in singing the hymn to the god exactly where the choirmaster placed him.

[Xenophon, *Agesilaos* 2.17]

Xenophon could have been at the festival as a guest of Agesilaos.

GYMNOPAIDIAI: C72–C77

The Gymnopaidiai, though explained by ancient scholars as literally a festival of naked boys (*paides*) more probably referred to naked or unarmed dancing (*paidia*), (see Parker in Powell (1989), 149–151). It may have been instituted after Sparta's defeat by Argos at Hysiai in 669/8 BC, which would fit with crowns later worn to celebrate this defeat being avenged at Thyreai *c.* 546 BC, below, **H11**. If so the purpose would presumably have been to celebrate the skills of training, teamwork, fitness and endurance worked on by boys and men alike to prevent such future defeats.

C72   Not the occasion for the 'whipping contests'

Gymnopaidia/ai: some say this is a Spartan festival in which the ephebes run around the altar at Amyklaion whipping each other on the back. This is wrong: they celebrate the festival in the agora; there is no whipping; instead there are processions of naked choruses.

[Hesychios, *Lexicon* 'Gymnopaidiai']

C73   An important festival

The Spartiates have in their *agora* statues of Apollo, Artemis, and Leto. The whole area is called *Choros* (Dancing) because at the Gymnopaidiai – this is a festival which the Lakedaimonians take as seriously as any other – the ephebes perform dances in honour of Apollo.

[Pausanias, *Description of Greece* 3.11.9]

C74   A mid-summer festival, teaching endurance

In addition, at the Gymnopaidiai, they have to show endurance, competing in the full heat of the summer …

[Plato, *Laws* 633b–c (continuing **C85** and **D42**)]

C75   Special crowns commemorate Thyreai

Thyreatic: this is the name of some Lakedaimonian crowns, as Sosibios says in his *Sacrifices*, adding that they are now called palm crowns from what they are made of. The leaders of the choruses wear them to commemorate the victory at Thyreai at the festival when they celebrate the Gymnopaidiai. There is a chorus of boys before dawn and another of the men in the early afternoon, dancing naked and singing songs by Thaletas and Alkman, and hymns of Dionysodotos the Lakonian.

[Sosibios, *FGrH* 595 F5 = Athenaios, *Scholars at Dinner* 15.22]

The translation here follows Bayliss' brilliant emendation of the text ('Sosibios (595)' in *Brill's New Jacoby*).

C76   An event to entertain foreign visitors

Lichas used to entertain foreign guests who were on a visit to Lakedaimon at the Gymnopaidiai.

[Xenophon, *Memorabilia* 1.2.61]

Xenophon is comparing Socrates' genuine hospitality with Lichas becoming famous throughout Greece for his invitations – something also mentioned by Plutarch, *Kimon* 10.5 as comparable with Kimon of Athens courting democratic support by his generosity. For Lichas at the Olympics, see **C52–C54, H42**.

C77   News of Leuktra brought to the Gymnopaidiai

The man bringing news of the disaster arrived at Lakedaimon on the last day of the Gymnopaidiai while the men's chorus was inside. The ephors when they heard of the disaster were naturally grief-stricken, but they did not take them off stage, but allowed them to complete the competition.

[Xenophon, *Hellenika* 6.4.16 (continued in **E112**)]

Xenophon, resident in Sparta at this period may even have been at the festival in question (see **E112**).

OTHER SPARTAN FESTIVALS: C78–C83

C78   Victory-dedication from Magoula, *c.* 500–475 BC

[…] whole […] he having won … ran (?) the quickest … giving thanks … son of P[…] … [son] of Zeus who holds the aegis.

[*LSAG* 48 = *IG* 5.1.238 = Tod & Wace, no 611]

C79   A runner victorious at all distances

[… won] the stade race [and … the *dolich*]os for the third time, also the two-stade race (*diaulos*) for the fourth time; at the *Hekatombaia* he won the five-*dolichos* in his third year: at another festival he won the stade race and two-stade race and *dolichos* and the five-*dolichos* and the race in armour all on the same occasion.

[*IG* 5.1.1120]

Stele found at the akropolis at (perioikic) Geronthrai, in the sanctuary of Apollo. The *pente dolichos,* presumably five times the length of the *dolichos* may therefore have been roughly equivalent to the modern half-marathon. 'In his third year' presumably means in his third year as a runner in the men's rather than boys' race.

C80   Jumping weight dedicated to a local hero

Tachistolawos dedicated (this) to Timagenes

[*SEG* 38.328]

Jumping weight of just under 2kg, found in 1982/3 in excavations at a sanctuary at (perioikic) Aigiai in southern Lakonia, and dated by letter-forms, including the digamma, to last quarter of 6th century BC. Timagenes, not mentioned in any literary sources, was presumably a local hero, possibly with games in his honour.

C81   Jumping weight dedicated to Athena

Paitiadas to Athena

[*SEG* 11.655]

Early fifth-century stone jumping weight found on Sparta's akropolis. Another weight, probably slightly earlier in date, but on which only the start of a name, Kleocha… is preserved, was also found on the akropolis, in the precinct of Athena Chalkioikos (*IG* 5.1.216 = *LSAG* 21).

C82   Discus dedicated to Apollo or Poseidon of Amyklai
A victory-prize for the Amyklaian

[*SEG* 11.697]

Bronze discus, now in Athens Museum, inv 8618.

C83   Inscription listing the many victories of Damonon and his son, 400 BC?
[1] Damonon put this up for Athena, guardian of the city, having won the following competitions, which none of the current generation has done. These were the victories Damonon achieved with his four-horse chariot, holding the reins himself: four times at the Earth-holder's Games), and four times at Athena's, four times at the Eleusinia Games.

[12] And at the Poseidonia Games at Helos, Damonon won – and his race-horse won on the same occasions – holding the reins himself, in the *kalpe*, seven times, with horses bred from his own mares and his own stallion.

[18] And at the Poseidon's Games at Thouria, Damonon won eight times, holding the reins himself, in the *kalpe*, with horses bred from his own mares and his own stallion [24] And at Arion's Games, Damonon won eight times, holding the reins himself, in the *kalpe*, with horses bred from his own mares and his own stallion and his race-horse also won. [31] And at the Eleusinian Games, Damonon won, holding the reins himself, in the *kalpe*, four times.

[35] The following victories Enymakratidas achieved: first at the Lithesia he won the boys' long-distance race and the horse-race together on a single day. And Enymakratidas won at Arion's festival [… *(line lost)* …] the long-distance race [and the horse race together on a single] day. [43] And at the Games of Mt Parparos, Enymakratidas won the boys' stade race and two-stade race and long distance race and horse-race all together on the same day. And Damonon won the stade race and two-stade race as a boy at the Earth-holder's Games. And Damonon won the stade race and two-stade race as a boy at the Lithesia Games.

[56] And Damonon won the stade race and two-stade race as a boy at the Games at Malea. [59] And Damonon won the stade race and two-stade race as a boy at the Lithesia Games. [62] And Damonon won the stade race and two-stade race as a boy at the festival of Mt Parparos, and the stade race at Athena's Games.

[66] When Echemenes was ephor, Damonon won the following victories: at Athena's Games, in the *kalpe*, holding the reins himself, and in the horse-race, together on the same day, and his son also won the stade race.

[72] When Euippos was ephor, Damonon won the following victories: at Athena's festival, in the *kalpe*, holding the reins himself, and in the horse-race, together on the same day, and his son also won the stade race.

[81] When Aristeus was ephor, Damonon won the following victories: at the Earth-holder's Games, in the *kalpe*, holding the reins himself, and in the horse-race, together

on the same day, and his son also won the stade race and the two-stade race and the long-distance race on the same day. They both won together.

[90] When Echemenes was ephor, Damonon won the following victories: at the Earth-holder's Games, in the *kalpe*, holding the reins himself, and his son also won the stade race [and the two-stade race and the long-distance race together on the same day].

[*IG* 5.1.213]

By very kind permission of the author, I follow the new interpretation of this text by Paul Christesen, 'A New Reading of the Damonon *Stele*' (forthcoming). He convincingly explains the frequently used phrase '*enhebohais hippois* – with young (female) horses' as being a reference to a horse-race where the riders had to run alongside and mount a cantering horse – a race referred to by Greek writers of the Roman period as *kalpe* (see **C40**). The skill was very relevant to Greek cavalry fighting, and the context would therefore be one in which the Spartans, conscious of the need to improve their cavalry fighting, introduced a new category of horse-contest to their local games and allowed Damonon to erect this striking monument on the Spartan akropolis (it is 0.94m high, 0.24m wide, and has a relief, now in poor condition of a four-horse chariot and driver) to show off his victories, and also his considerable prosperity in having the resources and considerable land-holding necessary for breeding, training and maintaining racing horses.

There was clearly a flourishing local circuit of minor games: Helos – 20 miles south of Sparta in the Eurotas valley; Thouria – 20 miles west of Sparta; Parparos – mountain in Kynouria, 30 miles (as the crow flies) north-east of Sparta; Malea, a town 25 miles up the Eurotas valley from Sparta. None of the ephors named in line 66ff matches those given by Xenophon *Hellenika* 2.3.10 (**E32**) as eponymous ephors for the Peloponnesian War. So the inscription can be dated to outside this period, but it cannot be certain whether it was before or after the war. A date around 400 BC would perfectly fit the scenario of encouraging cavalry training suggested above. That was also when Agesilaos was apparently encouraging Kyniska to prove in 396 BC that anyone could win Olympic chariot races (**C57**): Damonon's local *kalpe* victories were *more* impressive.

ARTEMIS ORTHIA: C84–C92
This festival shows above all the dangers of later tradition (and a memorable story) obscuring real history. Hesychios (above **C72**) shows that idea of Spartan boys having to endure a whipping for as long as possible as a contest forming part of their education is as ancient as it is wrong. This did happened in Roman times as the deplorable entertainment for tourists described by Cicero (**C92**) and seem to have been so popular as to merit the building of the semi-circular seating of the third-century AD Roman theatre. Despite claims these represented 'the customs of Lykourgos' with an entirely specious justification (**C93**), the only fourth-century BC sources show a less gruesome contest. Of the great many inscriptions found at the site celebrating victories at the festival, the huge majority are Hellenistic or Roman in period, celebrating victories in contests much more typical of the rest of the Greek world (**C87–88**).

C84   Cheese-stealing competition
Lykourgos made it a special competition to steal cheeses from the altar of Artemis Orthia, while giving others to task of whipping the would-be thieves, thus seeking to demonstrate that a little pain means a long term gain in fame and delight.

[Xenophon, *Constitution of the Lakedaimonians* 2.9]

C85   'Raids' resulting in whippings
I would try to mention a fourth [sc. Spartan institution aimed at promoting war] – the endurance of pain – which is very much a feature of our society, in fighting by hand with each other, and in the 'raids' with many whippings resulting each time.

[Plato, *Laws* 633b–c]

C86 Dedication to Ortheia, fourth century BC.

To Ortheia, Arexippos as victor set these up at the boys' meeting place, clear for all to see.

[*IG* 5.1.255 = Woodward No1, in Dawkins page 296]

A fairly early date, (Wilamowitz suggested early 4th century) is indicated by use of digamma and hetas. The inscription had cuttings for five sickles, the prizes for victory.

C87 Winner of the *moia* (musical contest)

Xenokles, son of Xenokles, in the time of Euetes, after winning the boys' musical contest (*moia*) dedicated (this) to Ortheia. And, similarly, in the time of Hipparchos.

[*IG* 5.1.269 = Woodward no.19 in Dawkins, p. 306]

None of those mentioned can be dated. The text and layout of the inscription show that it was dedicated after Xenocles won his first victory, with mention of the second victory and dedicated sickle being squeezed on later.

C88 Winner of the *kelea* (horse-ride), 1st century BC

Nikippos, son of Kallikratidas, in the time of Pratoles, after winning the boys' *kelea*. To Ortheia.

[*IG* 5.1.263 = Woodward no.17 in Dawkins, p.305]

C89 Winner of the boys' hunt, 1st century AD

Lysikrates son of Charixenos, in the time of Aristokles, after winning the boys' hunt, to Artemis Ortheia.

[*IG* 5.1.274 = Woodward no.26 in Dawkins, p.309–10]

C90 Isopsephic poem celebrating a victory

Leonteus, *bouagos,* dedicated this gift to Ortheia, 2730
After winning the music contest and taking the prize, 2730
And my father crowned me with words equal in numbers. 2730

[*IG* 5.1.257 – Sparta, 1st century AD or later]

A highly unlikely fusion of Spartan tradition with recondite Hellenistic poetry, in which the fact that Greeks used letters also for numbers meant that an expression or line of poetry could be assigned a numerical value ($\alpha = 1$; $\beta = 2$; $\omega = 800$). The challenge was to produce a natural-sounding verse or couplet whose letters, viewed as numbers, added up to exactly the same value as the next line. The technique, known as isopsephic poetry was created by Leonidas of Alexandria in the first century AD and became popular. The numbers are entirely correct.

C91 Winner of the contest of endurance, early 2nd century AD

[*(name lost),* with Alka]stos as his *bouagos*, and when Deximachos was *patronomos*, after winning the contest of endurance, to Ortheia.

[*IG* 5.1.290 = Woodward in Dawkins, p316–7]

This is the only dedication to mention the contest of endurance (*karteria*). The officials named suggest a Trajanic date (AD 98–117). A *bouagos* is defined by Hesychios as a 'pack-leader of boys' while the patronomate was instituted by Kleomenes III (235–222 BC) to supplant the ephorate.

C92   The whipping contest

Certainly at Sparta, boys accept beatings at the altar, so that much blood flows from their wounds, and even, on several occasions as I heard when I was there, with fatalities. But none of them has ever shouted out or even groaned.

[Cicero, *Tuscan Disputations* 2.34]

C93   Introduced by Lykourgos to replace human sacrifice

There was an oracle that the altar should be bloodied with human blood: this used to be someone chosen by lot, but Lykourgos changed this to a whipping of ephebes, so that the altar could get its fill of human blood in this way: the priestess stands by them, holding the wooden statue of the goddess. It is small and therefore normally light, but if the floggers hold back their strokes because of an ephebe's good looks or noble birth, then the statue becomes too heavy for the woman to carry, and she blames the floggers and says that it is their fault that she is struggling.

[Pausanias, *Guide to Greece* 3.16.10–11]

C94   Flogging contests at Artemis Orthia

Throughout the day at the altar of Artemis Orthia, and often to the point of death, they endure it all, cheerful and haughty, competing with each other to win out by being the one who can endure being flogged the most and the longest. The survivor gains very great respect amongst them. The contest is called the flogging and happens every year.

[Plutarch, *Spartan Customs* 40 (*Moralia* 239D)]

The vital point to note is that this revolting practice was not classical but designed for sadistic Roman tourists (Cicero, *Tusculan Disputations* 2.14 (34)).

SECTION D
SPARTAN INSTITUTIONS IN THEORY

Introduction: The political structure of Sparta: kings, *gerousia*, ephors, assembly
The Spartan political system was considered exceptional in the classical period, especially because it retained an hereditary kingship, an aspect of government which in most other Greek cities belonged to the distant, mythical past. At the same time, the unusual dual kingship was embedded in a system that followed the standard Greek pattern, namely a combination of leading magistrates, a council and the assembly of all fully qualified citizens which distributed power and provided checks on the activities of all its constituent parts. The Spartans simply called this system *eunomia*, which means 'good laws', 'good governance' or 'abiding by laws'.

How should we define the Spartan constitution? One could think of the Spartiates as a small wealthy élite with exclusive political rights, which would make Sparta a narrow oligarchy, and it fits this category reasonably well. An oligarchy implies a significant number of citizens who do not enjoy the right to participate in the political process. In Sparta these would be the *perioikoi* who had the right to own land, an exclusive right of citizens in most other cities, but were completely excluded from the political process in Sparta. The helots, albeit that they were Greek males who elsewhere would have counted as part of the populace, are only partly relevant to this argument because all Greek states had large populations of slaves which cannot be taken into account when a constitution is assessed in these terms (note that women were also universally excluded, therefore such discussions generally concern the free, adult male population). When ancient commentators analysed the Spartan *eunomia*, however, they looked only at the Spartiates as full citizens of the Lakedaimonian state and their access to the decision-making process. The system was generally seen as a rare example of a 'mixed constitution', a system which was considered particularly stable because it combined the best aspects of the three main forms of government, namely monarchy, oligarchy and democracy. The Spartan constitution was generally praised, especially by the wealthy intellectual élite of Athens which was dissatisfied with radical democracy. Aristotle's discussion of problematic aspects of the Spartan system in the *Politics* (e.g. **D1**, **D13**, **D18**) is therefore a particularly valuable alternative view.

KINGS: D1–D11
Sparta had two kings at any given time, and these positions were hereditary in two royal families, the Agiads (Agiadai) and the Eurypontids (Eurypontidai). The succession in the two families was not always straightforward and could cause major internal crises. Herodotus maintains that sons born when their father was already king were preferred to older brothers born before his succession (**D3**). It is difficult to tell whether this was indeed ever the case. Succession crises were common in both royal houses, and if there was a doubt about the legitimacy of the heir apparent, or if it was difficult to determine who had the best claim, the matter became a highly political issue, e.g. Kleomenes (**E9**), Demaratos (Hdt. 6.61 = **E20**) or the disputed succession of Agesilaos II in 399 BC (**E45**). Herodotus also took it for granted that the ephors, on behalf of the *polis*, (compare their mutual monthly exchange of oaths) could get involved in royal family matters if a king did not produce an heir (**E8**). The kings had a number of privileges representing their special position (see **D8–D9**). According to Plutarch (**D75**), the heir to the throne did not go through the Spartan education system because (as he implies) the obedience instilled in Spartiate youths was not appropriate for a king who would have to be a commander. The kings enjoyed the revenue of extensive estates and were given a share of public sacrifices (meat, or hides – also a form of material income), and they must have been very wealthy, even if they, too, kept up the appearance of Spartan austerity. The exalted position of the king was particularly emphasised at a royal funeral where they were, as Xenophon says, 'honoured as demigods' (**D9.9**, **D10–D11**).

The most conspicuous function of the Spartan kings was their role as military commanders, with almost unlimited power in the field, e.g. **E97**, which could also include far-reaching decisions about foreign policy. The religious role of the king including carrying out all important sacrifices, especially those at the crossing of the Lakonian border and sacrifices before battles and important actions, and in taking the omens from such sacrifices. Although we should not be too cynical about the possible manipulation of such rituals, we might still assume that such omens were probably likely to support the king's intentions (see Parker in Whitby, *Sparta*, ch. 8).

While the kings could speak in debates in the *gerousia* as well as in the assembly, their influence was limited by the powers of the assembly, the *gerousia* and particularly the ephors. Kings could be put on trial, before a special court, for example on charges of treason following an unsuccessful campaign or controversial foreign policy decisions, and, if convicted, would be fined or even deposed and sent into exile (see **D19**, **E19, E20, E23, E25, E26, E44, E136, H21**, and de Ste Croix, 'Trials at Sparta' in Whitby (2002), 69–77). Moreover, there were often disagreements or even long-term rivalries between the two kings (see **D1, D2**) which could further diminish their individual clout. Nevertheless, some kings managed to assert significant influence on policy decisions: this depended less on actual constitutional power than on an individual's personal authority and ability to draw on his personality and experience to make the most of his position (**E29**.79.2, **E39, E47**). Cartledge notes that all kings had charisma: they were literally untouchable; anyone had to stand in a king's presence (*Spartan Reflections,* 62). Successful and inspiring military commanders had a particular advantage, because their war record would have given them particular clout in the assembly. The most striking examples are Kleomenes I (*c.*520–*c.*490 BC: **E8–E23**) and Agesilaos II (*c.*399–360: **E45–E50**), who each dominated a whole period of Spartan foreign policy and also had significant influence on politics at home (see Cartledge *Spartan Reflections* ch.5). On the other hand, there were Spartan kings whose activities left almost no trace in our sources (e.g. Kleomenes II, 370–309 BC): some were probably content to carry out their duties without seeking to be at the centre of policy making.

D1   The Kings

As for the kingship, whether it is better or not better for states, should be a separate discussion; but certainly it would be better that each should be chosen for his own lifestyle rather than as they are chosen now. It is clear that the lawgiver does not himself think that he can make them great and good – at any rate he mistrusts them as not being sufficiently good men, and therefore they used to send enemies together on embassies and thought that the safety of the state was dependent on the kings being at loggerheads.

[Aristotle, *Politics* 1271a18–26 (continued in **D62**)]

Aristotle's discussion of Spartan institutions in book 2 of his *Politics* can be read continuously in **D47, D27, D69, D54, D28, D19, D13, D1, D62, D98, D84, D55**. It is important to note that it was composed in the 330s/320s by when Sparta was a second-rate power.

D2   Origins of Spartan Kingship

[2] Shortly afterwards, Aristodamos' wife, Argeia, gave birth to twins. Aristodamos, after acknowledging the twins, fell ill and died. [3] So the Lakedaimonians of the time wished to make the older child king, in accordance with the law. But they were not able to tell which one they should choose, since they were so alike and similar. Not being able to decide, or even before trying, they asked the mother. [4] She said that even she could not tell them apart: in fact she certainly did know, but hoped that somehow they might both become kings. The Lakedaimonians were completely puzzled and so sent to Delphi to see what the oracle advised them to do. [5] The Pythia told them to treat both boys as kings, but to give greater preference to the older one. That was what the oracle said, but the Lakedaimonians were no less puzzled as to how to find out which one was older, until a Messenian man whose name was Panites made a suggestion. [6] This was what Panites suggested to the Lakedaimonians, that they should watch the mother to see which of the two she would wash and feed first: if she always seemed to do it in the same order, the Lakedaimonians would have everything

they were looking for and wanting to find, but if she varied and did it alternately, it would be clear that she knew no more that they did and they would have to find some other means. [7] Then, as the man from Messenia suggested, the Spartiates watched the mother of Aristodamos' children always taking them in the same order and giving the older one preference in feeding and washing, since she did not know why they were watching. Taking the baby which was always given preferential treatment by his mother as the older one, they brought him up at public expense. They named him Eurysthenes and the other one Prokles. [8] When they grew up, they say that, though brothers, they were always at loggerheads with each other their whole lives, and this was the case with their descendants.

[Herodotus, *Histories* 6.52]

Besides the intrinsic improbability of this story, the separate lines of kings had separate burial places, suggesting they were different families. Furthermore in the 'junior' line several of the earliest kings have highly dubious names: Soös, Prytanis, Eunomos (Safe, Commander, Law and Order) in the lists of Hdt. 8.131.2 = **E1**, and Paus. 3.2, 3.3, 3.7 = **E4**). These kings were presumably invented to give the Eurypontid kings as many ancestors as the Agiads, and make them appear to have reigned as long. The *dyarchy* or dual kingship is an unparalleled institution which we cannot definitely explain, but perhaps the best guess is that it reflects an early amalgamation of two communities (perhaps the original 'villages' or groups of villages – see Thuc. 1.10.2 = **G2**).

D3   Succession of kings

Even in Sparta, Demaratos suggested, the custom was that if children were born before their father was king, another one, born once he had become king, would be heir to the throne.

[Herodotus, *Histories* 7.3]

D4   Coronation of kings

Eventually the Lakedaimonians were persuaded to bring Pleistoanax back from exile in the nineteenth year, with the same dances and sacrifices as when they first founded Lakedaimon and established the kings.

[Thucydides, *History of the Peloponnesian War* 5.16.3]

D5   Religious and military privileges of the kings

The Spartiates have granted their kings certain special prerogatives. First of all they hold two priesthoods, those of Zeus of Lakedaimon and Zeus, Lord of Heaven. Then, they have the right to declare war on any country they please; in this, no Spartiate can oppose them without incurring the penalty of religious pollution (and consequent exile). On active service, the kings lead the advance and are the last to retreat and are allocated a personal bodyguard of a hundred picked soldiers. On their expeditions they are entitled to the use of as many cattle as they please, and the skins and backs of all sacrificed animals are apportioned to them.

[Herodotus, *Histories* 6.56]

There is no evidence from the historical period to support Herodotus' assertion that the kings on their own could declare war. For the debate in Sparta on the Peloponnesian War in which King Archidamos argues against war, but is opposed by an ephor and by vote of the assembly, see **E29–E30**.

D6   Rules about kings on campaign

[2] As a result of this disagreement [*sc. between Demaratos and Kleomenes I*], a law
was made at Sparta that both kings were not allowed to follow an army when it went
abroad: previously they had both done so. One of them would be released from the
army, and one of the Tyndaridai would also be left behind: previously (images of) both
of these special helpers would follow the army.

[Herodotus, *Histories* 5.75.2 (see **E14** for background)]

D7   The king as army commander

[13.1] I shall now explain the sort of power and status which Lykourgos gave to the
king when he is on active service. First of all, when in the field the state maintains
the king and all his staff. The polemarchs dine with him in the mess, to ensure that
their constant proximity to each other means that they can more readily discuss any
problems, should the need arise. Three other *homoioi* (equals) also mess with them;
their job is to ensure that all the king's requirements are attended to, so that no worries
can distract him from concentrating totally on military matters.

[2] First things first: I shall go back and explain the procedures by which the king launches
a military campaign. He and his accompanying staff begin by making a sacrifice back
home to Zeus the Leader. If that sacrifice appears propitious, the fire-bearer takes a
blazing ember from the altar and leads the way to the frontier. There the king makes a
second sacrifice, to Zeus and Athena. [3] Only when the omens from the sacrifices to
both these gods are seen to be good does he cross the country's frontier. The fire from
these two sacrifices leads the way and is never quenched, and all sorts of sacrificial
animals follow behind. Whenever he makes a sacrifice, the king starts the rituals before
dawn while it is still dark, hoping to win first call on the god's goodwill ahead of the
enemy. [4] All the senior officers attend the sacrifices: the polemarchs, unit-leaders
(*lochagoi*), leaders of 50 men (*pentekonteres*), the commanders of allied forces, the
commanding officers of the logistics companies, and any of the leaders of contingents
from the various cities who chooses to be present. [5] Two ephors also attend, but they
take no part in the proceedings unless requested to do so by the king. But because they
watch what each person does, they ensure that all present conduct themselves with the
appropriate level of decorum. Once these rites have been completed, the king calls them
all together and issues his orders for the day. In fact, anyone watching all this could
well imagine that all other Greeks are mere amateurs in the art of soldiering, while the
Lakedaimonians alone are the true professionals in the overall conduct of war.

[6] When the king is in personal command of the army, unless the enemy suddenly
appears, no one marches in front of him, except the *Skiritai* and the mounted
reconnaissance patrols. But if they ever think that a battle is going to be joined, then
the king takes the first part (*agema*) of the leading regiment (*mora*) and turns to the
right until his own position is between two regiments and their two Commanding
Officers. [7] The troops ordered to act as their escort are marshalled by the senior
member of the king's own staff, who consist of those *homoioi* who share the king's
mess, plus seers, doctors, flute-players, and army commanders, and such allies as
have volunteered their support and happen to be present. So there is no problem with
contingency planning, since nothing is left to chance.

[8] The following arrangements made by Lykourgos also seem to me particularly useful when it comes to the actual fighting. When they are sacrificing a she-goat in full sight of the enemy, the custom is for all the flute-players present to play and every Lakedaimonian to wear a wreath; all weapons are also required to be polished. [9] It is also permitted for young soldiers [to comb their hair so as?] to go into battle looking cheerful and well groomed. They pass on morale-boosting messages for their group-commanders *(enomotarchai)*, because it is impossible for the whole of each section to hear the words from their own individual leader when he is out of earshot. Nevertheless, it is the duty of each polemarch to see that this is all carried out efficiently.

[10] The king alone is responsible for the decision to pitch camp when the time seems right and to indicate the right location. But sending out delegations to friends or foes is not his business. Whenever decisive action is required, all decisions stem from the king. [11] Those seeking arbitration are referred by the king to the Greek judges *(hellanodikai)*, financial disputes to the treasurers, and those with plunder to sell to the official auctioneers. With all this taken out of his hands, the king has no other commitments left to him on active service beyond his priestly obligations to the gods and as general of his army.

[Xenophon, *Constitution of the Lakedaimonians* 13 (continued in **E70**)]

D8   Peacetime privileges of the kings

[57.1] So much for their military prerogatives. Their peacetime privileges are as follows. At all public sacrifices, the kings are the first to take their seat at the subsequent feast; they are the first to be served and they are each given portions of every dish double the size of those served to other guests. Theirs is the right to pour the first libations, and the skins of all sacrificed animals belong to them. [2] On the first and the seventh day of every month the public purse supplies to each of them an unblemished animal to sacrifice at Apollo's temple, plus twelve gallons of barley meal and a Lakonian quart of wine. They preside at all athletic competitions in special seats of honour. They have the right to nominate any citizens they wish as *proxenoi*, including two 'Pythians' each, ambassadors whose duty it is to go on embassies to Delphi and to dine with the kings at public expense. [3] If the kings cannot attend these dinners, three pints of barley and half a pint of wine are sent to them each at home; if they are present, they again receive double helpings. They are honoured in exactly the same way if they are invited to private dinner parties.

[4] They are the official guardians of all oracles, though the 'Pythians' also share the knowledge of their contents. There are also some legal matters over which the kings exercise sole jurisdiction. In the case of a girl inheriting her father's property, if her father has not betrothed her to anyone, then the kings decide who is entitled to marry her. They also control the management of the public roads. [5] If anyone wishes to adopt a child, he must do it in front of the kings. They are entitled to sit in council with the twenty-eight members of the *gerousia*; in their absence their closest relatives among the members exercise the kings' prerogatives, and cast two votes for the kings and a third for themselves.

[Herodotus, *Histories* 6.57 (continued in **D10**)]

proxenoi: see **B1** note; **two votes**: Thuc. flatly contradicts Hdt. here (**H1**).

D9   Privileges of a Spartan king

[15.1] I should like now to explain the constitutional settlement which Lykourgos established between the king and the state. This royal charter, as it were, is the only one which still exists in its original form, whereas all the constitutions of the other Greek states have clearly been modified, and continue to be so, to this day.

[2] He laid it down that the king, by virtue of his divine origin, shall offer all public sacrifice on behalf of the state; that he shall lead the army on all expeditions sent out by the state; [3] that he shall receive a portion of every sacrificial animal as his prerogative; that specified tracts of high quality land in many of the territories of the *perioikoi* shall belong to him, sufficient to sustain the royal household adequately but without excessive wealth. [4] To ensure that even the kings shall mess publicly, Lykourgos designated for them a public mess tent and honoured them with a double portion of rations at each meal, not in order to encourage them to eat double but so that they could use it as a way of paying a similar compliment to anyone they chose. [5] He also gave each king the privilege of choosing two mess-mates, who are called 'Pythians'. They were also entitled to take a tithe of one piglet from every litter of pigs, to ensure that the king should never run short of sacrificial victims, if he felt the need to consult the gods on any matter.

[6] Anyone without access to water knows better than most how useful it is for every sort of purpose. A pool near the kings' houses provides them with ample supplies. Everyone rises from their seats when the king appears, except for the ephors from their official chairs. [7] Kings and ephors exchange oaths with one another once a month, ephors on behalf of the state, the kings on their own behalf. The king's oath declares that he will reign in accordance with the established laws of the state; and for the state the ephors declare that so long as the king keeps his oath, they will maintain the royal prerogatives undiminished.

[8] Such, then, are the domestic honours bestowed upon the king during his lifetime. They are not really significantly greater than those of the individual citizen, because Lykourgos had no desire to encourage in them the characteristic arrogance of tyrants, nor to stimulate in the ordinary citizen resentment at the king's powers. [9] As for the honours heaped upon a king at his death, here the laws of Lykourgos aim to show that the kings of the Lakedaimonians are honoured not as mere mortals but as demigods.

[Xenophon, *Constitution of the Lakedaimonians* 15]

D10   Funerals of Spartan kings

[58.1] These are the normal prerogatives granted by the Spartiates in common to their kings during their lifetimes. Their deaths are marked by the following ceremonies. Riders carry the news across the whole of Lakonia, while the womenfolk go round the city beating metal basins. When this happens, it is the duty of two free citizens per household, one man and one woman, to dress themselves in unwashed garments, as a sign of mourning. The punishment for failure to do so is a heavy fine. [2] There is one custom which the Lakedaimonians have in common with the barbarian nations of Asia to mark the death of their kings; in fact it is a custom common to almost all barbarian nations everywhere when their kings die. When a king of the Lakedaimonians dies, it is a compulsory obligation imposed not just on the Spartiates themselves, but also people from all Lakedaimon, and a number of *perioikoi,* to attend the funeral. [3] As a result, many thousands of them, together with helots and also Lakedaimonians themselves, congregate in one place. They all join the women folk, wildly beating their foreheads in a paroxysm of grief, crying out in lamentation that the king who has just died was the best king they had ever had. If the king has fallen in battle, they make an image of him and carry it to burial on a lavishly decorated bier. After the funeral, all public business and the election of officials are suspended for ten days, all of which are devoted to national mourning.

[59.1] In the following single respect their custom corresponds with that of the Persians. After the death of the old king and the appointment of his successor, the new king cancels the debts of any Spartiate who owes money to the royal or the state treasury. Similarly, the incoming Persian king remits all the taxes owed by all his subject cities.

[Herodotus, *Histories* 6.58–59 (continued in **D24**)]

D11   Mourning for Spartan kings

The *agora* was sprinkled with chaff and all sales ceased for three days.

[Herakleides Lembos 372.11 = Aristotelian *Lak. Pol.* 611.11]

For further details on funerals and mourning for Spartan kings, see Hodkinson *PWCS* 262–3, and Cartledge, *Agesilaos* ch. 16.

THE *GEROUSIA*: D12–D15

The *gerousia*, 'council of elders' consisted of 30 members, namely 28 *gerontes* (literally old men, elders) and the two kings (of any, adult, age). All full citizens over 60 (though in practice only members of the elite) were eligible, and membership was for life. This means that a very small proportion of all citizens (especially compared to the numbers required to serve as ephors) could ever reach this position, and it is likely that most *gerontes* came from the most distinguished families. New members were elected, after campaigning, by acclamation of the assembly (**D13, D15**). The *gerousia* discussed proposals for the assembly and prepared motions for assembly meetings. They also, together with the ephors, formed the most important court of law in Sparta which dealt with most serious criminal cases (see **E44**).

The continuity in a body of officials appointed for life and the collective experience and esteem among the community would have given the *gerousia* a good deal of clout in its dealings with the ephors who were in office for merely a year. The *gerousia* was therefore at the centre of the political process and had considerable influence on policies. This body could also serve as a crucial power base for the kings, since they could probably expect that some close associates or family members would be selected as *gerontes* who would then support them in meetings of the *gerousia* (compare **E50** for Agesilaos' 'block-vote' and **E44**).

D12   Elections to the *gerousia*

[10.1] I think that the law by which Lykourgos contrived to encourage the practice of virtue right into old age was also well conceived. He made election to the *gerousia* take place towards the end of a man's life, thus discouraging any temptation to neglect principled conduct even in old age. [2] The way in which he gave protection to elderly men of good character was wholly admirable. By establishing the elderly as judges for trials of capital offences, he gave to the old a prestige that surpassed that of men in their prime. [3] Inevitably, therefore, this ensured that for everyone election to this body generated the most intense contest of all. Athletic contests are all very well;

but they are only tests of physical prowess. But election to the *gerousia* sets up a judgement of a man's character and moral quality. Just as personal qualities outweigh physical strength, so victory in a contest of moral quality is a far more worthwhile pursuit than any physical success.

[Xenophon, *Constitution of the Lakedaimonians* 10.1–3 (continued in **D51**)]

D13   Aristotle's view of the *gerousia*

In addition their regulations for the office of elders are not good. If they were aristocrats, sufficiently well trained in courage, one could perhaps say that they benefited the state, though whether they should be in charge of important trials for life is debatable (for old age can affect mind as well as body). [1271a] But the way they were trained means the lawgiver himself does not trust them as good men, so the system is unsafe. Men who have held this office have been shown to have betrayed for bribes and to have corruptly given away many public interests. Therefore it would be better if they were not exempt from being held to account as they now are. One might perhaps think it good that the ephors have the power to hold to account all the other offices, but this gives far too much to the ephorate, and we say that this is not the way that accounting should be given. Moreover their way of judging the choice of elders is childish; nor is it right that a man hoping to be thought worthy of the office should have to campaign for it. For a man should hold office whether he wants it or not, if he is worthy of it. But as things stand the lawgiver clearly does the same thing here as for the rest of the constitution in making citizens ambitious, and he uses this in the election of elders. For no one would ask for this office if he were not ambitious. However in human life pretty well the great majority of deliberate wrongdoing comes about through ambition and love of money.

[Aristotle, *Politics* 1270b35–1271a18 (continued in **D1**)]

D14   Lykourgos invents the *gerousia*

[5.6] Lykourgos was responsible for many innovations, but of these the most important was the establishment of the *gerousia*. This Plato describes as a source of safety and moderation for the state, because its equal vote on issues of major importance was blended with the less considered judgement of their kings. Hitherto the constitution had been somewhat unstable, sometimes tending towards the tyrannical rule of kings, at others more inclined towards the democratic tendencies of the common people. [7] But now, with the rule of the *gerousia* established as a source of support and stability at the heart of government, the constitution gained security and good order, because the twenty-eight elders always supported the kings as a counter-weight to democratic tendencies, while reinforcing the common people against any royal inclination to tyranny. Aristotle records that this *gerousia* was originally set up as a body of thirty, but that it was fixed at twenty-eight because two of Lykourgos' original associates in the project lost their nerve and cried off. [8] But Sphairos maintains that twenty-eight was always the number that were party to Lykourgos' plan. There may be something in the proposition that the number twenty-eight is the product of seven times four and also that it is the next 'perfect' number after six, because it is equal to the sum of its own parts. But I find it much more likely that he chose exactly that number, so that the total membership of the council would be thirty when the two kings were added to the twenty-eight elders,

[Plutarch, *Life of Lykourgos* 5.6–8]

For **Sphairos** see **E77** and note.

D15   Elections to the *gerousia*

[26.1] As I have explained, Lykourgos personally appointed the original members of the *gerousia* from those who had been in on his secret plans. But thereafter he ordained that when one of them died he should be replaced by the man judged to have the greatest merit of all those over the age of sixty. Of all the competitions in the world, this seems to have been the most fiercely contested. It was not a question of who was the fastest runner or the strongest wrestler, but in the catalogue of wise and noble men, it was the wisest and the best of them all who was supposed to be elected. For the rest of his life he would enjoy a sort of victor's crown for virtue, in the shape of political power over life and death decisions, rights of citizenship, and all life's other most important matters. [2] This was the method of election. A mass assembly of the people was summoned; the chosen candidates were locked up in a building nearby, where they could neither see nor be seen, and could only hear the shouts of the assembled people. As in other matters, decisions about the candidates were reached by acclaim. One by one, as chosen by lot and not all together, each candidate was introduced and led through the assembly without saying a word. [3] The judges, who were kept apart from the proceedings and equipped with writing tablets, made a note of the level of shouting as each candidate passed through. They had no idea who the shouting was for; only the order of appearance, whether it was for the first, second, third and so on as they were brought in. Whoever got the most and the loudest cheers they declared elected. He was duly crowned and made a circuit of all the temples of the gods, followed by crowds of young men praising and honouring him. Women too joined the celebrations, singing songs in honour of his virtues and celebrating the blessings of his life. [4] Each of his close relatives would serve him a meal, saying that this was an honour accorded to him by his city. But once this circuit was completed, he went off to his usual mess where everything went on in the usual way, except that he was given a second portion, which he accepted and kept for later. Once the mess dinner was over, his female relatives would by now have gathered at the doors of the mess hall. He would invite the lady he most respected to come forward and hand over to her the portion of the meal which he had 'kept for later,' declaring that he had himself received it as a prize for virtue and that he was giving it to her for the same reason. This was followed by cheers from all those present and she was escorted home by the whole company of women.

[Plutarch, *Life of Lykourgos* 26]

Second portion: as regularly given to a king to pass on as a compliment (**D9**.4).

THE EPHORATE: D16–D21

The ephors were the five leading magistrates of Sparta, elected annually by the assembly. It is likely that all Spartiates over 20 who were allowed to vote in the assembly were also eligible for this office. Aristotle (**D18**) suggests that comparatively poor citizens were able to become ephor. In fact as the citizen body shrank, since an ephor could only serve once, ever poorer Spartans had to serve. One of the five was the eponymous ephor, whose name would be attached to the year in the Spartan calendar (**D16**). The ephors held much of the executive power in Sparta and conducted day-to-day political activities. They had control over the education system and they could also impose fines on individual citizens (including kings) for not carrying out their duties, or if they did not satisfy standards of citizen behaviour. The ephors were involved in the judicial process, especially at trials of a political nature (**E50**), and they may have handled appeals against decisions of the *gerousia*. As chief magistrates they also summoned the *gerousia* and the assembly and presided over their meetings. They were probably also able to propose legislation. The ephors received foreign embassies in Sparta and decided which ambassadors would be allowed to speak to *gerousia* or assembly. Finally, they oversaw the organisation of the army, they selected men for élite corps and controlled the *krypteia* (see **D42–D44**). When a war was declared, the ephors decided which sections of the citizen body should be called up for military service. These duties add up to very considerable power with comparatively little control. Ephors were probably accountable to the *gerousia*, but we do not know exact details about any process of scrutiny.

D16   The eponymous ephor

The ephors manage all the most serious business and provide the ephor who gives his name to the year.

[Pausanias, *Description of Greece* 3.11.2]

D17   Introduction of the ephorate

[7.1] Although Lykourgos' constitutional arrangements sought to share power, the oligarchy remained effectively undiluted and the dominant force. His successors saw it as "swollen and arrogant", to quote Plato, "and sought to rein it in by imposing on it the restraining powers of the ephorate." Roughly some 130 years after Lykourgos came the appointment of the first ephors, Elatos and his associates, during the reign of Theopompos. [2] They say that Theopompos was roundly abused by his wife for handing on to his sons a royal power that was less than that which he had inherited. "On the contrary," he replied, "it's greater, because it will last longer." The facts support his contention: by renouncing excessive powers, they avoided the associated dangers which jealousy inspires, and did not suffer the fate meted out by the Messenians and Argives to their kings, who refused in any way to surrender or even loosen the shackles they imposed upon their peoples. This makes a very clear demonstration of the wisdom and foresight of Lykourgos, when we compare it with the internal revolution and sheer bad government of their kinsfolk and neighbours, the kings and peoples of Messenia and Argos. [3] Originally their fortunes had seemed to be very similar to that of the Lakedaimonians – indeed in the allocation of land they might have seemed to have had the advantage. But their prosperity did not last long: their kings became arrogant and overbearing, the common people intransigent, and as a result their established constitutional arrangements were thrown into chaos. This made it all too clear that the Lakedaimonians had truly been divinely blessed in the man who had devised for them such a mixed and balanced form of government. But of course all that still lay in the distant future.

[Plutarch, *Life of Lykourgos* 7 (continued in **D57**)]

D18   Aristotle's criticism of the ephorate

But the rules about the ephorate are also bad. Absolute power over the most important matters is theirs, but the ephors come from the whole population with the result that very frequently extremely poor men stumble into office, who can be bought as a result of their poverty. This has been shown many times previously and just now at Andros, since some were corrupted by money, and ruined the whole state as far as they could. Furthermore, because their power was too great and like a tyrant's, even the kings were forced to curry popular favour. The result was that the constitution was further damaged, since a democracy arose from an aristocracy. So this office holds the constitution together, since the people keep quiet through sharing the supreme power, with the result that it has come about, either due to the lawgiver, or to chance, that it has worked out well in practice. For it is necessary for the future survival of the constitution that all parts of the state should wish it to exist and to continue unchanged. As it is, the kings do so because of the honour given them; the great and the good because of the *gerousia* (this office is a prize for excellence); the people because of the ephorate (for appointments are made from the whole citizenry). And yet though it is right that this office should be chosen from everyone, it should not be chosen as it currently is since the method is too childish. In addition the ephors have authority in important legal cases, though appointed by chance, and therefore it would be better not to make their own minds up, but to judge according to written laws and rules. Furthermore the lifestyle of the ephors is not in keeping with the policy of the state, since it is too relaxed, whereas that of the others goes too far towards harshness so that people cannot endure it but secretly abandon the laws and enjoy bodily pleasures.

[Aristotle, *Politics* 1270b6–35 (continued in **D13**)]

Though some of Aristotle's interpretation is extreme (for example that **a democracy arose from an aristocracy**), the fact that there were no **written laws and rules**, nor any popular judiciary, nor any public scrutiny of outgoing officials, as for example at Athens, did make the ephors hugely powerful.

D19 Spartan obedience to authority and the ephorate

[8.1] It is common knowledge that in Sparta obedience to the officers of state and the laws is an outstanding feature of their society. But it is my impression that Lykourgos made no attempt to promote this level of discipline until he had persuaded all the most powerful men in the state to agree with him. [2] My evidence for this is as follows: in other states the more powerful citizens don't want to appear subservient to the officers of state; they think such deference would not be the mark of a free society. But in Sparta the most powerful citizens are the ones who show the greatest deference towards the magistrates, taking pride in their own humility, and in running instead of walking to obey their summons. They believe that if they themselves set an example of scrupulous obedience, the others will follow their lead. And that is in fact the way it is.

[3] It seems likely that these were the same citizens as the ones who united to establish the power of the ephorate, because they realised that such obedience represents the highest civic, military, and domestic value. They believed that the degree of respectful obedience a magistrate could command would be proportionate to his powers. [4] So the ephors have the right to impose fines on anyone they choose, and to exact immediate payment; they can depose a magistrate from his office even in mid-term, and can also imprison him and put him on trial for his life. Since they possess such extensive powers, by contrast with the practice in other cities, they do not allow elected officials to rule as they like for the whole year of their elective term; instead, rather like tyrants and the presidents of the games, they punish with immediate effect anyone they detect breaking the law in any particular. [5] There were many other excellent ways in which Lykourgos contrived to encourage citizens in their willing obedience to the laws. But I think one of his cleverest schemes was as follows: he did not reveal his constitutional proposals to the common people until he had first gone off to Delphi, accompanied by all his most powerful political allies, and asked the god whether it would be better and more advantageous for Sparta that she should obey the laws which he had devised for them. Once the god had replied that it would be better

for them in every way, only then did he enact them, thus ensuring that it would be not only illegal but also blasphemous to refuse to obey laws which had been sanctioned by the Pythian oracle.

[Xenophon, *Constitution of the Lakedaimonians* 8 (continued in **D96**)]

D20   Physical inspection of young men by the ephors

Concerning the Lakedaimonians, Agatharchides writes in his twenty-seventh book that it is considered a deliberate offence if someone looks rather unmanly or has a body that is overweight. Young men have to present themselves, naked, before the ephors every ten days, while the ephors inspect their clothing and bed-coverings every day. This is quite right; and the Lakedaimonians' cooks see to the preparation of meat and nothing else.

[Agatharchides, *FGrH* 86 F10 = Athenaios, *Scholars at Dinner* 12.74]

Agatharchides wrote histories in mid-second century BC Alexandria. It cannot be ascertained what period Agatharchides is writing about, but Athenaios continues by relating, also from the 27th book, a story of Lysander publicly rebuking a Spartan for being too fat.

D21   Ephors send secret instructions

[5] The message-rod is as follows: when the ephors send out a navarch or a general, they make two round pieces of wood exactly equal in length and thickness so that they match each other in shape and size. The ephors keep one and the other they give to the person sent out. The pieces of wood they call *skytalai* (message-rods). [6] So whenever they want to say something secret and important, they make a document like a long, narrow leather strap and they wind it round the *skytale*, leaving no gaps, covering its entire exposed surface all around with the document. Having done this they write on the document what they want, as it is lying around the *skytale*. When they have written on it, they take the document off and send it without the wood to the general. [7] When he receives it, he cannot in any way read it (since the letters have no connection to each other, but are split-up) unless he takes his own *skytale* and winds the strip of document around it, so that, when the strip is restored to its spiral arrangement, and the letters follow each other in the right order, he can look around the rod and discover the connections between the letters.

[Plutarch, *Life of Lysander* 19.5–7]

For the *skytale* in use, see **E53**.

D22   *Agathoergoi* (men on state missions)

These *agathoërgoi* are the five oldest citizens to graduate from the *Hippeis* each year. Their duty for the year following their graduation is to remain busily engaged on state missions wherever required.

[Herodotus, *Histories* 1.67.5 (for context see **H10**)]

For the *Hippeis,* the 'Royal Guard', comprising 300 *eirens* (men between 20 and 30 years of age) see **D79**.

THE ASSEMBLY: D23

The assembly (*ekklesia*, not '*apella*', see *OCD* under 'Apellai' and **D48** note) included all Spartiates with full political rights, i.e. probably all men over 30 years of age who had not been excluded for some reason (serious crime, cowardice, inability to contribute to the *syssitia*). Its main responsibility were decisions on foreign policy, particularly about war and peace (see **B16**). The *ekklesia* elected elders and ephors, appointed generals (if no king was available to lead a planned campaign), decided disputes over the royal succession and voted on proposed laws (which were not written).

Sessions were held in the open, originally in a place 'between Babyka and Knakion' (see **D48**, 6.2 and 6.4: for Plutarch it was no longer clear where this location was). Votes, at least in elections, were cast by shouting (**D15**, **D23**). There was apparently no open debate in the assembly: officials presented the motions, but we have no evidence that common members of the assembly were allowed to voice their views (compare **D48**). Nevertheless, the assembly could play an important role, especially if there was a serious disagreement between kings, *gerousia* and ephors, and it seems that under such circumstances the opposing positions were indeed presented at meetings and then put to the vote (see **E28–E31**, **E140**, **E142**, **E143**, **H37**).

The Spartan assembly had little power compared to the sovereign Athenian *ekklesia*. It is not clear whether full citizens of Sparta were eligible from the time they were elected to a mess, aged 20, or from *c*.30 when they completed their further military training. In either case the decision making process was carefully controlled and assembly decisions did not carry as much weight as in a fully democratic *polis*. Kings, *gerousia* and ephors prepared the motions, and in the classical period the ephors chaired meetings: they decided how to present a case, whom to call to speak, when to call a vote, and when to end a meeting, which could all have an influence on the outcome (see **E31**). Moreover, Spartans were brought up to be obedient and to respect their elders: such ideals do not foster a lively political debate. Plutarch (**D48**) suggests that the leaders of the state (kings, later ephors?) could also overrule a decision of the assembly, although it is not clear whether this was actually the case in the classical period. It is also likely that officials could make fairly important decisions without consulting the people at all. The Spartan assembly therefore added a democratic element to the constitution, but since the decision making process was mainly in the hands of a very small body of officials, the system nevertheless has a strongly oligarchic character. Xenophon mentions a 'little *ekklesia*' (**E53b**) but we know nothing else about this body.

D23   Spartan voting

Lakedaimonians take decisions by acclamation rather than voting pebbles

[Thucydides, *History of the Peloponnesian War* 1.87.2 (see **E31**)]

SOCIAL STRUCTURE: INTRODUCTION

Spartan society was divided into a very small group of full citizens, the Spartiates (*Spartiatai*), and a large majority of inhabitants (*perioikoi* and helots) who neither participated in political activities nor in the famous Spartan way of life. Together these groups made up the Lakedaimonian state. Other Greek cities also had large populations which were excluded from citizenship (resident aliens, slaves, women), and states with oligarchic regimes admitted only a part of the citizen population to the political process, usually on the basis of a property qualification. In Sparta, however, the group of full citizens was extremely small compared to the rest of the population: the Spartiates were essentially an exclusive, land-owning ruling élite. It is crucial to understand this when discussing Spartan society: although there were wealthy and 'poor' Spartiates, all citizens of Sparta essentially belonged to the same social class, which meant that, unlike in more inclusive societies such as democratic Athens, the political system did not have to accommodate different needs and lifestyles.

The development of Spartan society is best explained in the context of the consolidation of communities (the emerging *polis*) in the ninth to sixth century which went hand in hand with increasing social stratification. While most Greek societies underwent changes that led to a gradual widening of political participation (often catalysed through a period of tyranny), the Spartiates seem to have managed to benefit from aggressive expansion in the eight and seventh century, which eventually allowed them to consolidate their position as political, military and economic élite in an unusually large territorial state. The large size of the Lakedaimonian state meant that even as a very small élite the Spartiates alone represented one of the largest hoplite forces of early classical Greece (8,000 in 480 BC, compared to 9,000 Athenians at Marathon in 490 BC), which could be multiplied by adding the *perioikoi* and Peloponnesian allies. Sparta's military success allowed a few thousand Spartiates to control a subject population of at least a hundred thousand for about three centuries (on demographics see Figueira in Luraghi & Alcock, *Helots*, ch. 9). At the same time, it can be argued that the pressure of keeping such a large territory under control defined Spartan society and helps to explain some of its austere, militaristic features (see below, 'Helots').

SPARTIATES: D24–D29

Full citizens of Sparta (adult males) had the right to participate in the political process, but they were also subject to the laws of Sparta which strictly regulated their lifestyle. Spartiates had to undergo the state regulated education system, followed by purely military education until the age of 30, they were subject to strict laws concerning marriage and family life, and they were obliged to be members of and attend the *syssitia* (also known as *phiditia*, *syskania*), regular evening meals within a specific group of fellow-citizens. Every citizen had to contribute part of his income to the *syssitia*: this was a kind of property qualification, since men who were not able to meet these contributions would lose their full citizen rights. Spartan law also regulated the lives of women and the upbringing of girls (see **D68–D70**).

For Spartiate property and wealth, see **E71–E76**.

D24   Spartan hereditary professions

The Lakedaimonians also resemble the Egyptians in the following respect. Their heralds and flute-players and meat-cooks adopt their father's professions, so the son of a flute-player becomes a flute-player, the son of a meat-cook, a meat-cook, the son of a herald, a herald. No one else can take on the job because they have a clear voice and exclude them but they fulfil the job according to ancestral tradition. That is just how things are.

[Herodotus, *Histories* 6.60]

Meat-cooks: though *mageiros* can just mean a butcher or a cook, it can also be an official at a sacrifice (LSJ) which is probably the specific meaning here.

D25   The only outsiders to become Spartiates

The Spartiates having great need of Teisamenos conceded all that he wanted. And having done so, Teisamenos from Elis became a Spartiate and, acting as seer for them, helped them to win the five great contests. He and his brother were the only people ever to become Spartiate citizens.

[Herodotus, *Histories* 9.35]

See continuation in **H22**. Teisamenos had made it a condition that his brother should also be made a Spartan citizen.

D26   Civil strife

This [civil strife in states ruled by an aristocracy] is bound to happen whenever there is a large number of people who have come to think that they are just as good as the rulers. This was exactly the case with the so-called 'Partheniai' (they were descended from the Spartiates (*homoioi*)) who detected them in a conspiracy and despatched them to colonise Taras. Or when some people who are great and no lesser in ability are given no official recognition by those of higher office, which is how Lysander was treated by the kings. Or when a man of courage gets no share in office, as with Kinadon who in Agesilaos' time contrived an attack on the Spartiates. Or when some people are exceedingly poor and others very rich: this especially happens in time of war, and happened in Lakedaimon after the Messenian War. Evidence for this comes from the poem of Tyrtaios called 'Good Order' (*Eunomia*), [1307a] since some were so afflicted as a result of the war that they thought the land should be redistributed. Or again if one man is pre-eminent and capable of becoming even more so, so as to become a monarch, just as in Lakedaimon, Pausanias seems to have been after leading the war against the Persians.

[Aristotle, *Politics* 1306b22 – 1307a5]

Partheniai and Taras: **H5–H6**. Lysander's treatment: **E132**. Kinadon: **E53**. Tyrtaios' *Eunomia*: **A3**. (Regent) Pausanias' behaviour: **B6–B7** and **E25–E27**.

D27   The importance of a good system of slavery

That it necessary for a state that is to be well governed to provide leisure from drudgery is a matter of common agreement: but how this is to be provided is not as easy to ascertain. The class of serfs in Thessaly often attacked the Thessalians, just as the helots seem continually lying in wait for disasters to befall the Lakedaimonians. With regard to the Cretans nothing of this sort has yet taken place: the reason is probably that the neighbouring states, [1269b] even when at war with one another, never ally themselves with the rebels, because it would not be in their own interests as they also have *perioikoi*; but with the Lakedaimonians their neighbours were all hostile, Argives, Messenians, and Arkadians. With the Thessalians too, the revolts happened initially because there was a war with their neighbours, the Achaians, Perrhaibians, and Magnesians. It seems also, besides anything else, that it is very hard work to keep watch on them and in determining how to deal with them. For if they are given any latitude they become insolent and claim equal treatment to their masters; but if they suffer brutality in their lives, they hate and plot against them. So it is clear that the people in these cases have not found the best way to deal with the helot-system.

[Aristotle, *Politics,* 1269a34–1269b12 (continued in **D69**)]

OLIGANTHROPIA

During the classical period, the number of Spartiates declined rapidly, and a lack of citizen manpower (*oliganthropia*) became a serious problem for Sparta (for a discussion see Cartledge, *Sparta and Lakonia*, ch. 14; Forrest, *History of Sparta*, 131–7). The decline is striking: see **D29**. There are few incidents with casualty figures that would explain such a decline, except the earthquake of *c.* 464 BC, which allegedly claimed twenty thousand lives (**E63**). Casualties in war were comparatively low by classical Greek standards: our sources report few battles with significant numbers of fallen Spartiates in the whole period, notably Thermopylai in 480 BC (299) and Leuktra in 371 BC (400 of out 700 fighting), which were both seen as exceptional. In 425 BC Sparta offered peace to Athens in order to recover 120 Spartiates captured on Sphakteria (**E94**): the loss of a mere 120 men was clearly considered very serious. Spartan family law seems especially concerned with maintaining citizen numbers, which would suggest that manpower was already an issue in the Archaic period. Thus, men who remained unmarried were subjected to various sanctions (**D71**.1–2), and the law allowed Spartiate men to swap wives and women to share husbands in order to produce legitimate children (**D71**.6–10, **D68**), see also intro to **D64–D72**).

Since *oliganthropia* denotes a decline of citizen manpower as opposed to that of the general population, it probably reflects a social-demographic change rather than a purely physiological or genetic one. The main reason is probably best sought in a combination of economic and social factors exacerbated by the Spartan system. Ancient authors generally prefer the idea that Sparta's decline was due to a neglect of her ancient customs (e.g. **E70**). This argument is typical for ancient historiography, but one might suggest that Sparta could not actually halt the decline precisely because she maintained the old laws for too long and did not react to social changes within her society. For example, in a society where status depended on property qualification it cannot not have been in the interest of Spartan families to produce too many children: all sons would inherit equal shares, and in Sparta even daughters could inherit or would have to receive dowries, which means that in a family with too many children the next generation might no longer have enough land to support their citizen status (compare **D54**). Ultimately, some families acquired large amounts of land, which means that there was less to go round for others to achieve the required property qualification. Aristotle offers such a scenario as an explanation for Sparta's decline (**D28**).

D28   Spartan *oliganthropia* (shortage of manpower)

As a result, although the land could support one thousand five hundred cavalry and thirty thousand hoplites, the total number was not even one thousand. What has actually taken place has made it clear that their arrangements in this were at fault, given that the state did not withstand a single blow but was destroyed through its *oliganthropia*. They say that under earlier kings they used to give a share in their citizenship to others so that there was no *oliganthropia* then, although they spent a long time at war, and they say that there were once ten thousand Spartiates. But whether or not this is true, it is better to fill the state with men by levelling out inequalities of wealth. The law on producing children militates against putting this right. [1270b] For the lawgiver, wishing there to be as many Spartiates as possible, gives incentives for citizens to have as many children as possible: they have a law that a man who has had three sons should be exempt from military duty, and the father of four exempt from all taxation. However it is clear that if many sons are born, and the land divided accordingly, there will inevitably be many poor men.

[Aristotle, *Politics* 1270a29–1270b6 (continued in **D18**)]

D29   Table showing decline of Spartiate population

480 BC	8,000	Hdt. 7.234.2 = **F23**
418 BC	3,500	Thuc. 5.68 = **E101**
394 BC	2,500	Xen. *Hell.* 4.2.16 = **E124** note
371 BC	*c.* 1,500	Xen. *Hell.* 6.1.1
370 BC	< 1,000	Aristotle, *Pol* 1270a31 = **D28**

It is possible or even likely that Thucydides has halved the true figure for 418 BC – see note on **E101**.

***MOTHAKES*: D30–D31**

Hodkinson (*PWCS* 355) concludes that the sources, although they are late (Phylarchos, 3rd century BC, Aelian, 3rd century AD, describe a genuine status-type of the classical period: free-born Lakedaimonians from poor or disenfranchised families, adopted by a wealthy 'patron' with the possibility or certainly of citizenship.

D30 *mothakes* as 'foster-brothers'

Those called mothakes amongst the Lakedaimonians are free, but not actually Lakedaimonians. Phylarchos writes the following about them in the twenty-fifth book of his *Histories,* "The mothakes are foster-brothers of the Lakedaimonians. For each of the boy-citizens, as their individual circumstances allow, have one, or two, or in some cases more foster-brothers. So the mothakes are free, though not actually Lakedaimonians, but still share exactly the same education. They say that Lysander who fought the Athenians at sea was one of these, though he became a citizen through his courage."

[Phylarchos, *FGrH* 81 F43 in Athenaios, *Scholars at Dinner* 6.102]

D31 Some famous *mothakes*

Kallikratidas and Gylippos and Lysander were called mothakes at Lakedaimon. This was the name for slaves of the wealthy whom fathers sent along with their sons train alongside them in the gymnasia. Lykourgos having allowed them to mingle in the boys' *agoge* gave them Lakonian citizenship.

[Aelian, *Miscellaneous History* 12.43]

***PERIOIKOI*: A NOTE**

We hear very little about this group, although they made up a significant part of the population in Spartan territory. The *perioikoi* were the inhabitants of at least 50 towns, almost all in Lakonia (with a few in Messenia): their name might be translated as 'those who live in the outskirts', 'those who live around (us)'. They were personally free, but politically their communities were subject to Sparta, and the *perioikoi* did not enjoy any form of citizen rights in Sparta. However, they were ethnically Lakedaimonians and fought with the Spartiates in the Lakedaimonian army. By the time of the Persian Wars they fought as hoplites alongside the Spartiates, and later, during the Peloponnesian War, they were incorporated within the Spartiate contingents.

Exact details about conditions for the *perioikoi* remain a matter of discussion. It seems that their lives were similar to those of Greeks elsewhere: ancient authors sometimes referred to their towns as *poleis* (e.g. Xen. *Lak. Pol.* 15.3 = **D9**, *Hell.* 6.5.21, Thuc. 5.54.1), and they probably had local governments to deal with their own affairs. *Perioikoi* also owned their own land and were free to engage in any economic activity. Xenophon (*Hell.* 5.3.9 = **E57**) refers to wealthy *perioikoi*, and we have to assume that their communities included all social classes, including slaves (see **C20** for possible manumission of a slave of a *perioikos*). The wealthiest *perioikoi* probably had personal connections with leading Spartans, especially the royal families who owned perioikic land. Thus, the main effect of Sparta's rule was essentially that the *perioikoi* did not determine their own foreign policy and had to follow Sparta's command in war. They also acted as a first line of defence against invasion by land or sea.

The *perioikoi* probably handled most of the economic activities that were prohibited to Lakedaimonians, but which clearly must have continued to allow the state to function. All the important harbours of Lakonia, especially Gytheion, which served as chief naval base, were perioikic communities, and we can assume that *perioikoi* were involved in overseas trade and fishery. Lakonia had various natural resources which were presumably exploited by the *perioikoi,* for example iron and lead deposits as well as high quality building stone. Even if crafts and arts declined at Sparta after the mid-sixth century, there were still many goods that were produced locally, for example pottery and of course armour and weapons. The Spartiates clearly had to rely on a variety of goods and services provided by the *perioikoi*, although the mechanism of exchange between the two groups remains unknown.

There is little we know about the attitude of the *perioikoi* towards their Spartan superiors. Cartledge (*Sparta and Lakonia* 155) suggests that they formed a 'territorial reserve against the helots', essentially loyal to the Spartans and involved in keeping the helots under control. 464 BC, when two Messenian periokic communities sided with the helot revolt was the exception before 370/69 BC. Cartledge also stresses that there is very little evidence for the involvement of *perioikoi* in activities against Spartan rule. On the other hand, Xenophon (*Hell.* 3.3.6 = **E53b**) counts *perioikoi* among the malcontents who were claimed to be plotting a revolt in 399 BC, and he reports (Xen. *Hell.* 6.5.25 = **E59**) that in 370/69 BC Theban troops were met by a delegation of *perioikoi* who offered support for an invasion. Not all *perioikoi* shared this enthusiasm, however, because some participated actively in the defence of Lakonia. The situation in Messenia may have taken on its own dynamics once there was an emerging regional identity which gave both *perioikoi* and helots a common cause. Two *perioikic* towns supported the Messenian revolt of 464 BC (Thuc. 1.101.2 = **E62**), and may in fact have played a crucial role in the uprising. Later on, after the foundation of the new urban centre at Messene, their settlements remained intact as towns within the Messenian state (see Luraghi, *Ancient Messenians*, esp. 198–208).

HELOTS

The helots were a part of the population of both Lakonia and Messenia who were subjects of the Spartiates with limited personal freedom. The origins of the helot system should probably be sought in Lakonia, and we have no factual evidence to explain how one section of society there came to gain control over the land and over a significant part of the population. We might assume, however, that an early version of this system was already in place in Lakonia, and the Spartans extended it when they gained control over Messenia. Ancient authors derived εἵλωται (*heilôtai*) from Ἕλος (*Helos*), see **D37**, but a derivation from the stem εἱλ- (*heil-* = captured) is probably more likely (LSJ εἵλως).

Helot conditions of life were somewhat different from those of slaves in most other parts of Greece. Most helots worked the land belonging to individual Spartiates, and on those estates which served as main residence for a Spartiate family they were probably also employed as household servants. They were tied to the land, and chances of gaining freedom were rare (in return for military service). Unlike slaves, helots were able to raise their own families and to expect stability in their lives. While slaves in most Greek cities were a mix of Greeks and non-Greeks, recently enslaved people and those born into slavery, the helots were a relatively homogenous group which reproduced over generations, and which was not only undeniably Greek, but also native to the region. The helots were crucial to maintain the Spartan system: they did most of the agricultural work (in all ancient Greek states agriculture was the basis of economic activity), which gave the Spartiates the resources and free time to maintain their unique society.

HELOT OWNERSHIP: D32–D35

Later sources state that helots were officially owned by the state, which means that no individual Spartan could sell them or free them (Strabo, based on his quotation from Ephoros **D34–D35**). More recent scholars have shown that classical period texts of Xenophon (**D32**) and Aristotle (**D33**) do not bear out this state ownership and that helots are better regarded as 'the private property of their Spartiate holders, but also as subject to various forms of communal intervention.' (Hodkinson, *PWCS* p.115; and for an important contribution to the debate, see D. Lewis, *Greek Slave Systems and their Eastern Neighbours* (Oxford 2017) ch.6).

D32   Use of other people's slaves

It was the same with slaves: where necessary he allowed them to use those that belonged to someone else.

[Xenophon, *Constitution of the Lakedaimonians* 6.3 (see **D50** for context)]

D33 Personal possessions available to others

(In well-run states …) each person has his own possessions but makes some available for his friends to use and others for communal use, just as in Lakedaimon they use each other's slaves practically as their own as well as horses and dogs.

[Aristotle, *Politics* 1263a33–37]

D34 Owners of slaves not allowed to free them

The Heleians who held Helos revolted, were taken by force in a war, and condemned to be slaves with the stipulation that their owner was not allowed to free them, nor sell them abroad.

[Ephoros, *FGrH* 70 F 117 = Strabo, *Geography* 8.5.4 (see **H3**)]

D35 Strabo's summary of the helot-system

For the Lakedaimonians held them as state-slaves in a particular way, assigning certain settlements for them and particular duties.

[Strabo, *Geography* 8.5.4]

HELOTS AND MESSENIANS: D37–D44

Note that the term 'Messenians' is sometimes used almost synonymously with 'helots'. This is incorrect in two respects: firstly, there were helots in large numbers in Lakonia as well as in Messenia, and secondly, a significant number of the inhabitants of Messenia were *perioikoi*. However, the terms are easily confused because the Messenian helots were conspicuously involved in revolts against Sparta, or at least in one particularly memorable uprising in the Classical period (464 BC), and their successful bid for freedom in 370/69 BC reduced Sparta to a middling power of small significance.

In fact, Messenian history is a complicating factor in any discussion of helots: ancient tradition offers many details, including one extensive narrative of Sparta's conquest (Pausanias 4.1–29). However, almost everything postclassical texts can tell us about these matters seems strongly influenced by the Messenians' efforts to 'reconstruct' a history for their region after they gained their freedom in 370/69. Except for the few details we can derive from earlier literary sources and archaeological evidence, all this material should be handled with extreme caution, especially the detailed tradition about the Messenian Wars, which is best regarded as a form of elaborate national myth (see Luraghi in Luraghi & Alcock, *Helots*, ch.5).

Most helots worked for absentee landlords, and they were probably quite independent in organising their activities, as long as they were able to supply their master with a 'rent' in kind, which the Spartiate would use to maintain his own household and to meet his contributions to the syssitia (Plut. *Lyc.* 8.7 = **D57**; *Mor.* 239E = **D36**). It is possible that helots could have private possessions (*de facto*, if not *de iure*). In Messenia there is also evidence that they had their own local cults: some sanctuaries date back to the eighth century, possibly before the Spartans took over, but votive deposits continued, and new sanctuaries were created in the archaic and classical period. The situation was probably similar in Lakonia, but there it is impossible to distinguish between the traces of the cult activities of Spartiates, helots and *perioikoi*, because there was less regional separation.

The community life of helots has been subject to lively scholarly debates, especially in the context of the Messenian revolt. This uprising was the reaction to an earthquake which devastated Sparta in 464 BC, and it saw the rapid development of a large regional movement at very short notice (Thuc. 1.101–3 = **E62**). How were the helots organised? Was there any form of regional solidarity among them? The evidence does not offer a clear picture of helot settlements. Some evidence from Pylos on the west coast of Messenia seems to suggest that they lived in large villages, while evidence from Lakonia seems to point at communities around a large estate. In some areas helots may have lived in scattered farmsteads. It seems likely, therefore, that not all helots in Lakonia and Messenia were settled in the same way. However, the question has a wider significance, since communities living in larger villages would need to organise themselves, which might in turn lead to (quasi-)political activities and a certain degree of social stratification.

The helot revolt of 464 was clearly a memorable event, and at least from that moment on the Greeks were aware of the great danger the Spartans might face from an enemy within. Various texts report measures to emphasise helot status (**D40–D41, D43**), and some may be a reaction to the Messenian Revolt as Plutarch suggests (**D44**), though Tyrtaios (fr. 6–7 = **A6**) already demonstrates a clear notion of helot inferiority. The Spartiates also kept themselves ready to subdue the helots by force. They never sent their whole army abroad, and there was a constant threat of violence against the helots (main source: Plutarch *Lyk.* 28 = **D44** – based on Aristotle) including the mysterious *krypteia*. This institution has been variously interpreted as an initiation rite or a fully organised secret police, but one should avoid making too much of the rather slim evidence. Nevertheless, it probably meant that helots could never feel entirely safe from surveillance or random attacks. (And see the sinister episode reported by Thucydides (4.80 = **E68**)).

Apart from such internal measures, the Spartans were also keen to include a special 'helot clause' in some of the state treaties they concluded, especially those with Peloponnesian neighbours. They usually demanded that the state in question refrain from harbouring fugitive slaves (i.e. helots), e.g. Thuc. 4.118.7 = **B16**; possibly also the Erxadieis Treaty **B15**; while the Sparta-Athens treaty, agreed after the Peace of Nikias of 421 BC, included a provision that the Athenians would come to Sparta's aid if the *douleia* (slave class) revolted (Thuc. 5.23.3 = **B18**).

D36   Fixed rent for helots

The helots worked the land for them, paying a rent established in advance. Charging a higher rent was forbidden, so that the helots might make some profit and be happy to serve, and the masters would not be greedy for more.

[Plutarch, *Lakonian Customs* 41 = *Moralia* 239E]

D37   Helots

Helots are not by birth the slaves of the Lakedaimonians, but the inhabitants of Helos and the first to be defeated by them, as many writers attest, including Hellanikos in his first book.

[Hellanikos, *FGrH* 4 F188]

Hellanikos (*c.* 480–395) was an important ethnographer and chronicler, from Lesbos, a subject-ally of Athens.

D38   Thucydides on the helots and Messenians

The majority of the helots were descendants of the original indigenous population of Messenia, who had been enslaved by the Lakedaimonians. Thus they were all known as Messenians.

[Thucydides, *History of the Peloponnesian War* 1.101.2]

D39   Thucydides on the helots II

As far as the Lakedaimonians were concerned, considerations of security ...
[either] ... were always paramount in matters regarding the helots
[or] ... against the helots were always paramount.

[Thucydides, *History of the Peloponnesian War* 4.80.3 (see **E68**)]

Thucydides' language is capable of being taken in two different ways here. The first alternative above, implies simply that where helots were concerned, Spartans put safety first. The second would imply that fear of the helots was a major factor for all Spartan policy. The first is perhaps to be preferred as a translation (as by Hornblower, *Commentary* vol.II, page 265). See the continuation of the passage (**E68**) for the extreme measures employed on one occasion in Spartan history.

D40   Spartans permanently watchful against helots

The Lakedaimonians have, with regard to the helots, the right of killing first, and Kritias says about them that the most enslaved and the most free are in Lakedaimon. Another thing that Kritias himself says is that because of mistrust towards these helots a Spartiate at home takes out the handle of his shield. Not being able to do this on campaign because of the frequent need for rapid action, he goes about always carrying his spear since this would make him superior to his helot who might revolt but with only a shield. They have also devised locks which they think would be too strong for any helot attempt.

[Kritias, fr.37 (Diels-Kranz 81B37) = Libanius, *On Slavery* 2.87]

Kritias, *c.* 460–403 BC was a friend of Socrates, and leader of the 'thirty tyrants' at Athens installed at the end of the Peloponnesian War. He wrote plays, philosophy and also (favourably) on Sparta both in verse and prose. Some writings of his survive through being quoted by other authors.

D41   Treatment of helots

Myron of Priene writes, in the second book of his *Messenian History,* that the Lakedaimonians treated the helots with the utmost arrogance: they imposed on the helots every demeaning task leading to their complete humiliation. For example they insisted that they must all wear a dog-skin cap; be dressed in animal skins; receive a set number of beatings each year irrespective of any wrongdoing, so that they would never forget that they were slaves. In addition, if any of them overstepped how they thought a slave should appear, they set death as the penalty, while the owners were penalised if they did not take down any who were getting fat. And when they assigned land to them they always set a fixed amount that they must produce for them.

[Myron of Priene, *FGrH* 106 F2 = Athenaios, *Scholars at Dinner* 14.74]

Myron of Priene was a historian, probably of the third century BC. His *Messenian History* was criticised as inaccurate by Pausanias (the writer).

D42   The *krypteia* simply as an endurance exercise

In addition there is the so-called *krypteia* which is amazingly physically demanding as regards endurance: in winter they go without shoes or blankets; they look after themselves without servants, and spend night and day wandering about the countryside.

[Plato, *Laws* 633b–c (continuing **C85**, continued in **C74**)]

The problem with Plato's account is that it does nothing to explain the name, *krypteia* – to do with something secret.

D43   *Krypteia* as a killing exercise

It is said that Lykourgos also introduced the *krypteia*. In accordance with this institution even now they go out by day and conceal themselves, but by night they use weapons to kill as many of the helots as is expedient.

['School of Aristotle' *Spartan Constitution,* excerpted by Herakleides Lembos 373.10 ed. Dilts – trans. Cartledge]

A set of descriptions of how government of various Greek *poleis* developed was attributed to Aristotle (384–322 BC), though more likely they were written by his pupils, or simply under his general influence. Herakleides of Lembos made excerpts from these in 2nd–century BC Alexandria, and Plutarch (**D44**) also uses the Aristotelian account.

D44   Treatment of helots and *krypteia*

[28.1] In all these arrangements, there was no trace of the injustice and arrogance with which some have charged Lykourgos in his legislation. They suggest that it was pretty good at producing brave soldiers, but inadequate in developing any idea of justice and right conduct. The so-called *krypteia*, if this was indeed one of Lykourgos' institutions, as Aristotle records, may be the reason for Plato's having reaching the same conclusion about Lykourgos and his constitution. [2] The *krypteia* functioned as follows: from time to time the magistrates would select from the young men the ones who seemed the most intelligent, and send them out into the countryside at random equipped with daggers and basic rations, but nothing else. By day they would scatter into remote and obscure locations, concealing themselves and simply lying low. But at night they would come down to the roadways and cut the throats of any helot that they caught. [3] They would often also work their way through the fields and murder those with the strongest and most powerful physique. Thucydides has a similar story in his *History of the Peloponnesian War*. He tells how helots whom the Lakedaimonians had identified as being conspicuously brave were crowned with garlands, as if they were going to be granted their freedom, and then taken in procession round the temples of the gods – and a little while later they all disappeared, more than two thousand of them altogether. Nor could anyone tell, either then or afterwards, how they had been wiped out. [4] Significantly, Aristotle reports that the ephors, whenever they first took office, would make a formal declaration of war on the helots, so that their murder would never involve religious pollution.

There were other features of the Lakedaimonians' savage brutality towards them. They would compel them to drink large quantities of undiluted wine and then bring them into the messes, as an example to the young men of the effects of drunkenness. They would compel them to sing songs and dance dances that were vulgar and demeaning, while banning them from those of a more respectable kind. [5] This is the traditional explanation of the story of the Theban expedition into Lakonia, where they captured some helots and commanded them to sing the songs of Terpander, Alkman, and Spendon, the Lakonian. They refused, on the grounds that their masters would not approve. This gives us a very clear perception of the truth of the saying that "in Lakedaimon the free man is more free than anywhere else, and the slave more servile." [6] My own view is that such savage ill treatment by the Lakedaimonians was in fact a later development, consequent upon the great earthquake, when the helots united with the people of Messenia in revolt against them, causing massive devastation to their territory and the greatest threat to their city there had ever been. I certainly could never attribute to Lykourgos a measure as abominable as the *krypteia*, something so utterly alien to his general record of gentleness of character and concern for justice. I would cite the evidence of Delphi in support of this view.

[Plutarch, *Life of Lykourgos* 28]

For **Aristotle**, see note to **D43** above. For the **Thucydides** story (4.80), see **E68**, where in fact Thuc. has the helots putting themselves forward, rather than the Spartans identifying them. For the most free/most servile contrast, made by Kritias, see **D40**.

HELOTS: CONCLUSION

The texts above seem to corroborate the image of significant tension between Spartans and helots which led to constant vigilance on the part of the Spartans. This may however be because peaceful co-existence does not 'make the headlines'. In fact there are also many instances where the Spartans seem to have relied on their helots, for example when they drafted some of them into their armies as hoplites (Thuc. 4.80 = **E68**, Xen. *Hell.* 6.5.28–9) or auxiliary personnel (Hdt. 6.80–1, 9.80.1 = **E61**, 9.85 = **E51**) with seven helot attendants for every Spartan hoplite serving at Plataea (Hdt. 9.28–9 = **E84**). Helots who had served as hoplites also had a chance of manumission (Thuc. 5.34 = **E52**, 7.58), while there were also large numbers of *neodamodeis* – helots almost certainly set free in order to serve in the army (**D45** and Xen. *Hell.* 3.4.2 = **E131**; 396 BC) or as garrisons. Moreover, we also have to appreciate that it took a powerful earthquake (literally!) to instigate a major revolt in Messenia in 464 BC; the decisive defeat at Leuktra 371 BC (**E106–E112**), followed by Theban invasion in 370/69 BC is often assumed to have triggered a revolt, though the sources simply speak of an external liberation (e.g. Diod. 15.66.6). Presumably Spartans would have regarded a helot failure to resist Theban invasion as a 'revolt'. There were clearly times when Spartan worries about the helots were justified, but we should also not over-interpret the relatively few (if impressive) pieces of evidence to draw a picture of constant fear and repression which threatened to consume Spartan society. Though Aristotle and Thucydides portray helots as trouble, Herodotus and for the most part Xenophon portray them simply as part of the scenery.

D45   Freed Spartan slaves

Myron of Priene says in the second book of his *Messenian Wars*, "The Lakedaimonians often freed slaves, and called some 'aphetai' (released), others 'adespotai' (masterless), some 'erykteres' (kept back?), others 'desposionautai' (master sailors) whom they sent on voyages; others were 'neodamodeis' (new members of the citizenry *(damos)*) who were different from the helots.

[Myron of Priene, *FGrH* 106 F1 = Athenaios, *Scholars at Dinner* 6.102]

Myron's history of the Messenians (almost entirely lost) was criticised as inaccurate by Pausanias, whose own account of the Messenians is now thought to be much more national myth than history!

SPARTAN INSTITUTIONS

Spartans seem to have been very proud of their institutions. Something of this admiration was also shared in our sources by certain members of the Athenian élite who had seen some of the failings of democracy and looked to the alternative model of Sparta. Of the four types of *politeia* outlined in Plato's *Republic*, his Spartan-based timarchy lies closest to his ideal *politeia*; but it is described as a mixture of good and evil and includes several negative features such as contentiousness, love of money and a tendency to degenerate into oligarchy (547c–549b). In his *Laws*, although Sparta is regarded as a broadly well-governed polis, there is explicit criticism of several fundamental flaws (e.g. 628e–638b; 688a–c). In particular, Spartan education is criticised for producing men lacking the highest warlike virtues or true mastery over pleasures and women lacking a clear private or public role (548d–549b; 666d–667a; 806a; Patterson 2013). Plato's method in the *Laws*, in which scattered critical comments on Spartan institutions contribute to his construction of an ideal *politeia*, is followed by Aristotle in Book 7 of his *Politics*. In Book 2, moreover, Aristotle adds a new approach, providing independent, systematic discussions of certain noteworthy theoretical and existing states, starting with Sparta, in which his recognition of certain laudable features is outweighed by his severe criticism of a number of fundamental flaws (Schütrumpf, "Aristotle on Sparta" in Powell & Hodkinson 1994). (Hodkinson – NSW notes).

LAWS AND RESPONSIBILITIES: D46–D51
For the Spartan belief, shared by others, that their laws had remained unchanged since the time of Lykourgos, see **F3–F6**.

D46   Demaratos to Xerxes on the Spartans

"So the Lakedaimonians, fighting singly, are the equals of any man, but together they are the best of all. They are free, but not altogether free. For they have a master above them – the law, which they fear much more than your subjects fear you. They do whatever it commands; and it always commands the same thing; not allowing them to run away, no matter what the number of men facing them in battle, but staying in the line of battle to conquer or die."

[Herodotus, *Histories* 7.104.4]

Hdt. here imagines the exiled king Demaratos (see **E20**) offering this (prophetic – see **F23**) advice to Xerxes during his invasion of Greece in 480 BC.

D47   Aristotle's introduction to his criticism of the Spartan constitution

As regards the constitution of the Lakedaimonians and that of Crete, and pretty well the other constitutions too, there are two things to be considered: firstly whether anything has been set in law well or not well in comparison with the best arrangement; secondly whether there is anything that goes against the purpose and tenor of the constitution that was laid out for them.

[Aristotle, *Politics* 1269a29–34 (continued in **D27**)]

D48   Lykourgos and the Great *Rhetra*

[6.1]   Lykourgos was so enthusiastic about his new ruling council that he even got an oracle about it from Delphi. It is known as a *rhetra,* and it goes as follows:

- Set up a temple to Zeus Sullanios and Athena Sullania;
- Tribe the tribes and obe the obes;
- Set up a *gerousia* of thirty, with the founder-leaders (*archagetai*);
- From time to time, have an *Apella* between <the streams of> Babyka and Knakion;
- Thus to propose and rescind;
- For the people, decision and power.

[2] In this document, the reference to "tribing the tribes and obing the obes" covers the method of assigning the general population to small groups, which he designated *phylai* and *obai.* "Founder-leaders" is the archaic name for the kings; to "have an Apella" is to call an assembly of the people, because the source and origin of the constitution is attributed to Pythian Apellon (Apollo). The modern names of the Babyka and Knakion are the Cheimarros and the Oinous respectively, though according to Aristotle the Knakion is a river and the Babyka a bridge. [3] The Lakedaimonians held their assemblies between these two rivers, though the area lacked any form of colonnade or other kind of building, which Lykourgos felt would not be conducive to serious discussion. In fact he thought such things positively harmful, since they encouraged vacuous ideas and empty verbiage in the minds of those who had assembled for serious discussion, as they gazed around at the statues and paintings, theatrical scenery, and the extravagant adornments of their council buildings, when they were supposed to be deliberating. Once the people had been assembled en masse, no one was allowed

to table a proposal; they had the power only to accept or reject the motion laid before them by the members of the *gerousia* and kings. [4] But in time the people managed to distort and mangle his intentions by passing amendments or deletions. So Polydoros and Theopompos, the kings, added the following rider to the *rhetra*.

- But if the people shall adopt a crooked proposal, the elders and founder-leaders shall have the power of dissolution.

This means that they should not ratify the proposal but should withdraw it totally and dissolve the assembly, on the grounds that it was attempting to pervert and distort what was in the state's best interests. [5] They even managed to persuade the city that this was the god's addition to the *rhetra*, and there is a reminder of this in the poems of Tyrtaios.

[*Plutarch here quotes Tyrtaios 4, see* **A4**]

[Plutarch, *Life of Lykourgos* 6 (continued in **D17**)]

Plutarch is generally assumed to have quoted the 'Great *Rhetra*' from Aristotle's *Lakedaimonian Constitution*. The language of the *rhetra* is obscure and archaic, resulting in further corruption of the text. Much therefore remains very unclear, though it's now generally agreed that the 'rider' is part of the original document. Kennell, *Spartans, a New History*, 45–49 gives a translation and line by line commentary. Though Plutarch says the *apella* is an assembly (*ekklesia*), a scholiast (ancient commentator) on Thucydides 1.67 tells us that is was actually a festival of Apollo, held on the 7th day of each month. The *ekklesia* meeting was held on the same day.

D49   Lykourgan laws

[13.1] Lykourgos recorded none of his laws in writing, and indeed one of his laws, known as *rhetrai* or spoken ordinances, expressly forbids it. For he thought that the most powerful and significant forces working for the good of the city and the high moral standards of its citizens would be imbued by the character training and education of its citizens. These, he believed, would remain unchanged and firmly rooted, if reinforced by the free choice imparted in the young by an education which would act as a far more binding force than compulsion, since it played the role of legislator for every one of them individually. [2] As for minor financial issues of contracts and other randomly occurring problems, he believed it was better not to obstruct their operation by imposing masses of red-tape and inflexible regulations, but rather to allow them to be governed by such additional rules and modifications as educated leaders might decide upon as the situation required from time to time. Indeed he totally linked the whole business of legislation to the process of education.

[3] As I have already stated, one of his *rhetrai* forbade the use of written legislation. A second sought to curb extravagance, stipulating that the roof of every house should be constructed with axes and the doors with saws, and with no other tools. Years later Epaminondas is said to have remarked at his own dining table that such a meal would hardly encourage treachery; but it was Lykourgos who first clearly foresaw that a house built with such simplicity could offer no incentive to luxury or extravagant living. [4] No one could be so lacking in good taste or good sense as to introduce into such a simple house, built for ordinary people, things like ornate silver bedsteads and blankets dyed with purple, or golden drinking vessels and such associated luxuries; a man was bound to harmonise and adapt his bed to his house, its coverings to his bed, and the rest of his goods and chattels to that. [5] It was as a result of being used to this, so the story goes, that when Leotychidas I was once a dinner guest in Corinth,

he gazed in amazement at the ceiling of the house with its extravagantly squared and coffered panelling, and asked his host if his country grew square trees.

[*For the alleged existence of a third rhetra forbidding frequent campaigns against the same nation, see* **H69**]

[6] Lykourgos called these ordinances *rhetrai* to give the impression that they were oracles and came from the god.

[Plutarch, *Life of Lykourgos* 13.1–6 (continued in **D70**)]

D50   Shared responsibilities in Spartan society

[6.1] Here is another feature of his reforms which is different from the majority. In the other Greek cities each man has full control of his own children, servants, and finances. But Lykourgos wanted to devise a system whereby, without doing anyone else any harm, the Lakedaimonians would derive benefit from one another. So he made it a rule that everyone should exercise control over his own children and those of everyone else. [2] Once a man realises that all Lakedaimonians alike stand *in loco parentis* to all children, he is bound to control all those over whom he has control in the same way as he would wish his own to be controlled. If a boy confesses to his father that he has been beaten by another parent, it would be rather shocking if his own father did not give him another beating. This all goes to show how much they trust one another to issue appropriate instructions to their children. [3] It was the same with servants: where necessary he allowed them to use those that belonged to someone else. He made the same rule for the use of hunting dogs. Anyone needing the dogs would invite their owner to the hunt; and he would be happy to send them along, even if he himself had not the time to join the hunt. So too with the use of horses: anyone who is incapacitated or needs a vehicle or wants to get somewhere in a hurry will take a horse, if he happens to see one anywhere, make careful use of it, and then put it back where it belongs.

[4] Here is another example of his arrangements which is not to be found in other nations. Whenever a hunting party has been kept out late and gets back with nothing to eat, because by chance they had failed to make previous arrangements, he made it a rule that those who had adequate supplies should leave some of what they had prepared, so that those who needed it could open up the sealed provisions and help themselves to what they required, before re-sealing and leaving what remained. By providing a share of what they had to one another in this way, he ensured that even those with scarce resources received a share of all that the countryside offered, whenever they ran short of something.

[Xenophon, *Constitution of the Lakedaimonians* 6 (continued in **D53**)]

D51   Spartan civic virtue

[10.4] And here is another admirable feature of Lykourgos' legislation. He came to understand that the pursuit of moral qualities does little to benefit the state, when it is left entirely to an individual's good intentions. So in Sparta he made the practice of virtue of every kind compulsory for all, in public as well as private life. Private individuals differ from one another in moral quality, depending on the degree to which they actively practise it; so of course Sparta surpasses all other cities in moral quality, because there alone is morality a matter of public obligation. [5] A significant aspect of Lykourgos' system was that, whereas other states inflict punishment where someone does wrong to someone else in some way, he imposed penalties no less severe on anyone who paraded his indifference about whether or not he lived as uprightly as possible. [6] It would appear that as far as he was concerned, enslavement, embezzlement, and theft are crimes that hurt only the individual victims; but criminals and cowards commit treason against the whole body politic. So in my opinion he was right to impose the harshest penalties of all on such offences. [7] In fact he made it an inescapable obligation to practise every form of political virtue. To all those who carried out those legal obligations to the full he gave full and equal political rights as a personal possession, without reference to any deficiencies of health or lack of financial resources. But if anyone failed to carry them out to the full, he made it clear that such a man was no longer to be regarded as one of the *homoioi* ('Equals').

[Xenophon, *Constitution of the Lakedaimonians* 10.4–7 (continued in **F1**)]

WEALTH AND PROPERTY: D52–D59

The Spartiates called themselves *homoioi*. The Greek term means 'Equals' or 'Similars' and is perhaps best translated as 'Peers', which reflects a sense of equality within an exclusive élite. This name is programmatic: much of the Spartan way of life seems designed to disguise differences in terms of wealth or family background. Typical ways of displaying wealth such as elaborate houses, furniture, clothes and jewellery, or any kind of luxury, were prohibited or frowned upon. In other Greek cities the élite would hold elaborate banquets, but Spartiates were obliged to attend their *syssitia* (see introduction to **D60–D63**). Funerals and funerary monuments – another important way of displaying wealth and family pride – were also severely regulated in Sparta (see **B34–B35**). Moreover, Spartiates were not allowed to own gold or silver, and the iron money used in classical Sparta was only fit to facilitate fairly small everyday transactions. These restrictions on the most common ways of conspicuous consumption meant that the Spartans appeared austere to other wealthy Greeks, but in spite of the modern connotations of the term 'Spartan' we should regard the Spartan lifestyle as comfortable prosperity masked by a display of austerity. The Spartan way of life offered all crucial aspects of a Greek élite lifestyle: landed property, leisure (no need to work for a living); a life dedicated to leisure pursuits, namely socializing, politics, exercise and hunting; and active contribution to the city's defence. The difference is that wealthy Greeks elsewhere could choose how to display their wealth and how to spend their time, while in Sparta citizens were not only restricted to these 'honourable' pursuits, but also to following strict guidelines which regulated their activities within those parameters.

Equality among Spartiates was, however, never more than an ideal. Apparently Tyrtaios (paraphrased in Aristotle *Politics* 1306b36) mentioned demands for a redistribution of land, and late tradition (Plut. *Lyc.* 8 = **D57**) suggests that the land was indeed divided into equal parcels for all Spartiate families. There is, however, no evidence that in reality the land holdings of different Spartiates were, or ever had been, on a similar scale. In the classical period, land was held as private property which was passed down the generations through inheritance and dowries, and that alone would have led to constant, if slow, changes in the distribution of property among individual families. Moreover, Spartiates were not allowed to engage in any form of trade, which means that there was no way of supplementing insufficient income from property by other means. Eventually, this process led to increasing polarization between wealthy and (comparatively) poor: some Spartan families failed to produce their contributions for the *syssitia*, and therefore lost their full citizen rights. Others clearly had the wealth required to succeed (and to flaunt their success) at chariot racing on a Panhellenic stage (see **C50–C58, C83**). See also **E71–E76**.

D52   Spartans' restrained lifestyles
The more restrained style of clothing used to this day was first adopted by the
Lakedaimonians – and the more wealthy among them in other respects made
themselves very much like the people in their style of living.

[Thucydides, *History of the Peloponnesian War* 1.6.4]

D53   No opportunities for wealth creation in Sparta
[7.1] There are still more regulations laid down by Lykourgos which run counter to
the prevailing pattern in other Greek states. Elsewhere, it seems to me, everyone is out
to make as much money as he can. One is a farmer, another a ship's master, another
a merchant, and others make their living as craftsmen. [2] But in Sparta Lykourgos
refused to allow free citizens to have anything to do with money making; only activities
which contributed to the freedom of the state were to be regarded as permissible
occupations for its citizens. [3] The reason is obvious: what would be the attraction
of wealth in a state where he had insisted on equality for all in their contributions
towards the common necessities of life, and the same standard of living for all? The
pursuit of money for the sake of pleasure could only be pointless. After all, they do not
even need to spend money on clothing, since they regard good physical condition as
the finest kind of bodily adornment. [4] Nor do they even need to accumulate wealth
in order to spend it on the fellow members of their messes. Lykourgos had made the
act of helping mess-mates by physical labour more honourable than spending money
to the same end. As he pointed out, hard labour is work for the good of the soul;
expenditure is simply useful work for one's money.

[5] He also enacted the following measures to prevent the dishonest acquisition of
money. First of all he devised a system of currency which made it impossible to bring
into the house even as small a sum as ten *minai* without the knowledge of house owner
or his servants, because it would take up an enormous amount of space and require
a wagon to transport it. [6] Random official searches for gold and silver take place,
and if any is found the owner is fined. So what would be the point of trying to gain
wealth, when its possession would give you more grief than you would get enjoyment
by spending it?

[Xenophon, *Constitution of the Lakedaimonians* 7 (continued in **D19**)]

D54   Spartan inequalities of wealth
In addition to what has been said, one might censure the Lakedaimonians for an
imbalanced distribution of wealth. For some of them have come to attain too much
property, and others a tiny amount. Therefore the land has fallen into the hands of a
small minority, and this through bad regulation of the laws. For the lawgiver made
buying and selling an existing estate dishonourable, and rightly so, but because he
allowed those who wanted to, the right to give away or bequeath their estates, the
end result was, inevitably, exactly the same. And it is the case that almost two-fifths
of the whole country is owned by women, since many women inherit and because of
the giving of large dowries: it would have been better to draw up laws for there to be
no dowry, or a small or moderate one. But as things stand one is permitted to give

an heiress in marriage to whomever one wants; and if someone dies without making arrangements, then whoever he leaves as heir can give her in marriage to whomever he wishes.

[Aristotle, *Politics* 1270a15–29 (continued in **D28**)]

The **large dowries** were a daughter's legal inheritance given to her at the time of her marriage. Hodkinson suggests (*PWCS* 94–103) that a daughter had a right to inherit half as much as her brother, which would mean that a Spartan girl with just one brother would be given one third of the parental property as a dowry.

D55   Public funds

In addition, public finances are badly dealt with by the Spartiates. For there is no common state fund for the large-scale wars they are forced to fight. They are also bad at paying taxes, since most land is owned by the Spartiates and they do not scrutinise each other's tax payments. The result is the opposite of the benefits the lawgiver wanted. For he has created a city without money, but individuals with a love of money. So, concerning the constitution of the Lakedaimonians, enough should have been said, since these are the things that one might especially criticise.

[Aristotle, *Politics* 1271b10–19]

D56   Features of the Spartan system

First, with regard to having land – that no one should have a larger share, but all citizens should have an equal share of the state's land. Second, with regard to having money – since with them it is completely dishonourable, it follows that competition to get more or less of it is totally abolished from the constitution.

[Polybius, *Histories* 6.45]

Polybius, in comparing the Roman republic to other systems of government, criticised authors who compared the Spartan system to that of Crete. His praise here is balanced by what he says later (**E74**).

D57   Distribution of land to Spartiates

[8.1] Lykourgos' second and revolutionary constitutional innovation is to be seen in his redistribution of land. Savage inequalities prevailed and the city was plagued by the large numbers of those who were helpless and poverty stricken, while wealth was entirely concentrated in the hands of the few. He set about eliminating arrogance and resentment, criminality and extravagance, and those yet more significant and powerful sources of disease in the body politic, the extremes of poverty and wealth. [2] He persuaded the Lakedaimonians to deposit all their land into a single common pool, and then to make a brand new distribution of it, such that they would in future all live with one another on a basis of equality and an equal share of the resources needed to make a living. Since in future there would be no difference or inequality between one man and another, high status would depend entirely upon personal qualities, and the only differences between them would be based on criticism for wrongdoing and praise for noble actions.

[3] Having established this principle, he set about putting it into practice. He divided the land of Lakonia into 30,000 allotments, and allocated them to the dwellers-round about, the *perioikoi*. As for the land belonging to the city of Sparta itself, that he divided into 9000 allotments, which would belong to the 9000 Spartiates. Some

say that Lykourgos made only 6000 allotments, and that 3000 were later added by Polydoros; others that Lykourgos allocated half the 9000 allotments, and Polydoros the other half. [4] Each man's allocation was sufficient to produce an annual crop of 70 measures of barley, 12 measures for his wife, and an appropriate amount of other fresh produce. He thought that this should be sufficient to ensure a good state of health and general well-being, for a population that had no need of anything else. Legend has it that some time later he was travelling through the country on his return from a visit abroad, shortly after harvest time, and saw the heaps of grain piled up in lines and all equal to each other. He remarked to those who were present that the whole of Lakonia looked like the property of many brothers who had recently shared out their lands between them.

[Plutarch, *Life of Lykourgos* 8 (continued below)]

D58   Spartan money
[9.1] He then tried to share out all their goods and chattels as well, so as to eliminate totally all forms of inequality or discrimination. But he realised that any form of direct confiscation would prove very unpopular, so he contrived a more roundabout way of achieving his objectives, using a more political method to curb their natural acquisitiveness. He started by banning all forms of gold and silver coinage and making iron the only form of legal tender. This form of coinage was both bulky and heavy, but he gave it minimal value, so that cash worth ten *minai* required a huge granary to hold it and a yoke of oxen to transport it. [2] Ratification of this law rapidly removed a wide variety of crimes from the scene in Lakedaimon. No one was going to steal, offer as a bribe, defraud, or plunder someone of something that could not be concealed or coveted by others once it was possessed. It could not even be profitably cut up. He is even supposed to have used vinegar so that the red-hot iron would not be tempered properly, thus removing its effectiveness or use for any other purpose and robbing it of its strength and malleability.

[3] His next move was to expel all forms of useless or superfluous arts and crafts. The majority would have probably fallen out of use anyhow because of the new common coinage, since there was no longer a market for such skills. For the iron coinage was impossible to transport to the rest of Greece and had no credibility as a currency, since it was treated as a joke. As a result it was impossible to buy foreign goods or to make even small purchases; no mercantile cargoes came to their ports; none of the sophists (teachers of rhetoric) visited Lakonia; no charlatan soothsayer or purveyor of prostitutes came there, nor did any craftsmen working in gold and silver ornaments. There was no recognised coinage with which to pay them. [4] Luxury, gradually deprived of all that promoted or encouraged it, simply died away of it own accord. Those who had great possessions enjoyed no advantages because their wealth could find no opportunity for public display but had to remain stored up at home, serving no useful purpose. For this reason ordinary domestic equipment and essential goods such as couches, chairs, and tables were superbly made there, while Kritias tells us that the Lakonian earthenware cup, or *kothon*, gained a very high reputation among soldiers on active service. [5] The colour of its surface texture masked the unpleasant appearance of the water which they often had to drink, since the muddy ingredients were caught and trapped inside the cup by its lip so that only the more palatable water actually reached the mouth. This, too, was the legacy of their great lawgiver:

craftsmen were freed from useless activity and could display their skills in products of genuine utility.

[Plutarch, *Life of Lykourgos* 9 (continued in **D63**)]

D59   Spartan ban on money

The Lakedaimonians were prevented by their customs from bringing money into Sparta, as Poseidonios writes in his history, or from obtaining silver or gold, but did so nonetheless and deposited it with the neighbouring Arkadians. Later they treated them as enemies rather than friends so that suspicions should go unchecked because of the hostility. Historians say that the gold and silver previously in Lakedaimon was laid up in the Temple of Apollo at Delphi.

[Poseidonios of Apameia, *FGrH* 87 F48 = Athenaios, *Scholars at Dinner* 6.23–25]

COMMON MEALS (*SYSSITIA*): D60–D63
This was one of the defining features of the Spartan system. Election to a *syssition* group provided the ultimate aim of the education system and was subject to a unanimous vote of approval among all members. Continued membership provided a sort of property qualification, since men who were not able to meet these contributions would lose their full citizen rights. In addition messes probably formed a basic grouping within the army. They must have established a sense of (male) community of equal or greater importance than the family unit. They formed an alternative to the *symposion* ('drinking-together') culture found elsewhere in Greece, most notably Athens, which was the preserve of the richest members of the society and might be the venue for philosophical discussion, poetry or simply excess drinking (**D60**). *Syssitia* ('eatings-together') remains the generic name: the Spartans seem to have referred to *syskania* ('tenting-together') or *phiditia* (etymology in **D63**).

D60   Spartan *syssitia* contrasted with Athenian *symposia*

Kritias makes this clear in his poem:

At Sparta it is custom and established practice	1
To drink from the same wine-cup	
And not to name people to drink their health …	
For as a result of such drinking, tongues are loosened	
To shameful stories; bodies grow weak;	10
Cloudy weakness sits on the eye,	
Forgetfulness of mind wastes memory away:	
The mind is deceived: household slaves become	
Undisciplined; ruinous expense descends on the house.	
Lakedaimonian boys drink just enough to bring	15
The minds of all to cheerful optimism,	
Their tongues to friendliness and restrained laughter…	
The Lakedaimonians' lifestyle is ordered on terms of equality	25
To eat and drink as appropriate to making	
Them able to think and work: nor is there a day	
Set aside to soak the body in unrestrained drinking.	

[Kritias fr. 6 (ed. Diels-Kranz 81B6) = Athenaios, *Scholars at Dinner,* 11.41]

For Kritias, see note on **D40**.

D61   Spartan mess-system

[5.1] This gives a reasonable summary of the regulations which Lykourgos established as the appropriate educational regime for each individual age group. I shall now try to explain his arrangements for the lifestyle of the population as a whole. [2] When he came on the scene he found that Lakedaimonians, like all the other Greeks, lived and dined at home. He realised that this was a primary source of disorderly conduct, and so he set out to reduce this indifference to established codes of conduct by setting up the system of open public messes. [3] He laid down a specific level of nutrition designed to ensure that no one over-ate or starved. But hunting can be a source of many dietary supplements; and there are times when rich men provide wheat loaves instead of the usual ones. As a result the tables are never bare of food while the diners are present, yet they are never extravagantly supplied. [4] He put a stop to the custom of compulsory drinking, which is physically debilitating and mentally damaging. He permitted each man to drink when he was thirsty, in the belief that this was the least harmful and most socially pleasant form of consumption. After all, how could anyone do any harm to himself or his household through gluttony or drunkenness under such a system of open public eating together. [5] For of course in other states the usual custom is for men of the same age to socialise together, and that is a sure recipe for the lowest level of self-restraint. But in Sparta Lykourgos mixed the age groups together, so that the younger men could learn as much as possible from the experience of their elders. [6] Indeed the custom is for the conversation at such mess dinners to revolve around the great achievements of the state's heroes, with the result that in such gatherings there is little room for vulgarity, drunken excess, or insulting language and behaviour. [7] This custom of public dining has other beneficial effects as well. They have to walk home after dining and must therefore be careful not to become too drunk to walk, since they are fully aware that they will not be staying at the mess table all night. They will have to be able to do by night anything they would do by day, and anyone still liable for military service is not even allowed to use a torch to help him on his way.

[8] Lykourgos also noted the effect of this standardised diet on the energetic and the idle: the former have clear skin, muscular bodies, and strong limbs; the idle are too clearly puffy, flabby, and weak. He took the implications of this seriously. Recognising that the sort of man who works hard of his own free will usually looks pretty fit physically, he laid it down that whoever happened to be the senior member present at each gymnasium should be careful to ensure that the exercises set for those attending should be appropriately demanding for the rations provided. [9] My own view is that he got this about right. One would be hard put to it to find men who were healthier or more robust than the Lakedaimonians. They exercise their legs, arms and necks equally effectively.

[Xenophon, *Constitution of the Lakedaimonians* 5 (continued in **D50**)]

D62   Aristotle's view of common meals

Also unsatisfactory are the arrangements first established about the commons meals, called the *phiditia*. For it ought to be the case that funds come from public revenue, just as in Crete: but with the Lakedaimonians everybody has to contribute, even those who are very poor and unable to afford this expense, the result being the reverse of the lawgiver's intention. For he wishes the arrangement of the common meals to be a democratic feature, but it becomes utterly undemocratic by being arranged in this way. For it is not easy for the very poor to participate, but the ancient mark of citizenship for them is that anyone who cannot pay this tax cannot belong.

[Aristotle, *Politics* 1271a26–37 (continued in **D98**)]

D63   Lykourgos establishes common messes

[10.1] But Lykourgos wanted to put still greater pressure on luxury and to eliminate the competitive acquisition of wealth: so his third political innovation was his most ingenious. This was the institution of common messes, so that Lakedaimonians met to eat together on a common and standard dietary regimen of boiled meat and cereals. They were thus prevented from spending their time at home, reclining at table on expensive couches and growing fat under cover of darkness like gluttonous animals thanks to the ministrations of their cooks and confectioners. [2] The effect of such a life style would prove morally and physically debilitating by leaving them free to indulge every kind of appetite and excess, long sleeps, hot baths, extreme idleness, and a sort of hypochondriac's need for daily nursing care. This was certainly no mean achievement; but an even greater one was the way he managed to make wealth "an irrelevance," as Theophrastos puts it, and to have created an "un-plutocracy" by his system of common messing and economical diet. [3] There was no use for wealth, nor any enjoyment of it; no one could see or show off their many possessions, when the rich man was compelled to go and dine beside the poor man. Of all the cities under the sun, only in Sparta might one see the proverbial Wealth, lying on the ground, blind and motionless, lifeless as a painting. For it was impossible for a rich man to enjoy a nice dinner at home first, and then go off to the common mess with a full stomach; everyone else kept a close eye on those who did not drink or eat with them, and hurled insults at them for lacking self control and being too soft to share the common diet.

[Section 11 (omitted here) mentions initial opposition to Lykourgos' 'mess system' including a physical attack on him and his saintly response.]

[12.1] Turning now to the system of common messes: Cretans call them "men's clubs" (*andreia*), the Lakedaimonians "comrades' halls" (*phiditia*), on the assumption that they encourage friendship or comradeship (*philitia*), replacing the letter *delta* with a *lamda*; alternatively, as encouraging habits of thrift and economy, making an etymological connection with *pheido* (I am sparing). On the other hand, as some people argue, there is nothing against the proposition that the first letter (*phi*) has been unnecessarily added to *editia*, a word which embraces the idea of way of life (*diaita*) and eating (*edode*). [2] They would meet in groups of about fifteen, give or take a few, and each mess member would contribute every month a bushel of barley-meal, eight gallons of wine, five pounds of cheese, and five half-pounds of figs, plus a very small sum of money for "extras". One particular custom was that anyone who had made a sacrifice of first-fruits or had enjoyed a successful hunt would send a share of it to the mess. The reason was that it was permitted for anyone who had been kept late by sacrificing or hunting to dine at home; but everyone else was required to be present at the mess dinner. [3] For a long time they rigidly preserved this system of "messing". For example, when King Agis had returned from a successful campaign against the Athenians, he wanted to stay at home and dine with his wife. So he sent for his share of rations, but the polemarchs refused to send them over; next day he was so irritated that he failed to make the statutory sacrifices – so they fined him.

[4] Boys also used to come to these messes, rather as if they were attending schools of formal etiquette. There they could listen to political discussions and learn at first hand how free men behaved. In this way they got used to joining in games and general jollity (no dirty stories allowed!), and learned to be the butt of jokes against themselves without taking offence. This business of learning to take a joke against oneself seems to have been a Lakonian speciality, but anyone who felt that he could not stand it had only to ask and the banter ceased. [5] When each of the boys came into the mess, the senior member present would point to the door and declare: "Not a word goes out of that door." The procedure for electing a candidate for the mess is traditionally said to have been as follows: each of the members took a piece of soft bread in his hand and when the servant came round with a bowl on his head he would throw it in without a word, just like casting a vote. If the bread remained exactly as received, it meant "yes"; but a "no" vote was indicated by crushing the bread tightly in one's fingers. [6] The crushed bread has the force of a marked voting-stone in the courts, and even if only one such was found in the bowl, the would-be candidate was rejected, since they wanted all their fellow-members to be congenial. The candidate rejected in this way was said to have been "caddied", because the bowl into which the pieces of bread were thrown was known as a caddy (*kaddichos*).

Of all their dishes, the one they most enjoy is black broth. The older men do not even ask for the bits of meat to be included in their helping, leaving it for the young men to enjoy; the soup simply poured out for them is a feast in itself. [7] It is said that one of the kings of Pontus even bought himself a Lakonian chef for the sake of his black broth. But then when he tasted it, he said it was filthy. To this his cook replied, "Your Majesty, those that would be initiated into this soup must first bathe in the waters of the Eurotas." After drinking in moderation they all go home, without lights of course, since walking with lights is forbidden for this or any other sort of journey. They want to get everyone used to marching confidently on dark nights without any sort of fear. So much for the system of messes.

[Plutarch, *Life of Lykourgos* 10 and 12 (continued in **D49**)]

WOMEN: D64–D72
While Spartan men led a uniquely regulated life, their women were famous (and notorious) for being unusually independent and more ready to appear and speak in public than women elsewhere. Spartan women were also praised for their beauty: an association with the most famous Spartan woman, namely Helen 'of Troy', probably came to mind easily (Cartledge, *The Spartans. An Epic History*, 46–53). For a concise overview of the crucial issues see Cartledge, *Spartan Reflections*, ch.9; S. Pomeroy, *Spartan Women* offers a detailed treatment of the subject. Unlike other Greek *poleis*, the Spartan state took an interest in girls' education. While elsewhere girls usually stayed at home and learned typically 'feminine' tasks such as spinning and weaving, their Spartan counterparts participated in physical exercise and also took part in competitions (Plut. *Lyc.* 14.3 = **D70**, Xen. *Lak. Pol.* 1.4 = **D68**). What was particularly shocking for foreign visitors was that such activities were carried out in public, in full view of men, and girls as well as young women wore clothes that would be seen as extremely immodest elsewhere, e.g. just a short *chiton* (tunic), and on some occasions they even appeared naked (see Plut. *Lyc.* 14.4–7 = **D70**). It seems likely that Spartan women were generally less shy to show themselves outside the house or to appear in public without a veil than upper class women elsewhere (note Aristophanes *Lys.* 79–245, esp.79–84 = **D66**).

Spartan girls and young women also participated in choruses at festivals, which means that they also needed some training in singing and performing poetry, and group rehearsals in preparation for specific occasions. Seventh-century Sparta did not only produce the war poems of Tyrtaios which seem such a perfect fit for the Spartan stereotype, but also the poet Alkman who invented the genre of choral songs for performances of girls or young women (see **A13–A20**).

The main aim of girls' education was apparently to produce healthy mothers for healthy Spartan children; although a public education probably also ensured that the women fully subscribed to the community's values. Spartan mothers reminding their sons of their duty to fight valiantly or die are a commonplace in ancient tradition, and they clearly played an important part in upholding the society's ideals (Pomeroy *Spartan Women* 57–62; with many examples; note especially Plutarch, *Sayings of Spartan Women* **F30, F33, F35**). Spartan women were probably married later than most girls elsewhere in Greece (late teens, rather than early/mid teens), and the unusual customs surrounding marriage at Sparta (**D71**) may mean that they remained in their parents' house for some time even after they were married. Since Spartiates were obliged to spend much time with the other men, especially for dinners with their mess, and were also often involved in warfare, the women probably enjoyed comparative freedom in running their household, and they needed a certain independence and the ability to control an estate (note that the two wives of king Anaxandridas apparently remained in separate households: Hdt. 5.40 = **E8**).

Again, it was unusual in ancient Greece (but not unique to Sparta) that women could own property in their own name: in most places any property that a woman received as inheritance or dowry would be held by her *kyrios* or legal guardian (usually the husband or nearest male relative), but we have no evidence that this was also the case in Sparta. Property could not be bought and sold in Sparta, but it changed hand through inheritance, dowries and gifts. Aristotle suggests that there were many such heiresses, and that the Spartans were also used to give large dowries (*Politics* 1270a23–5 = **D54** with note). In the classical period Spartan women were probably subject to the general restrictions on conspicuous consumption of wealth, e.g. strict rules on dress, jewellery or luxury items. Exceptional women, mostly members of the royal families, engaged in exclusive activities such as the breeding of race horses, most famously Kyniska, see **C55–C57**.

It is difficult to tell how far we should follow our ancient sources in their observations about Spartan women's status and behaviour. The licentiousness of Spartan women was a cliché which scandalised outside observers, and no doubt the idea of girls exercising publicly and in the nude excited fantasies, too – something that Aristophanes (*Lys.* 79–84 = **D66**) clearly found a useful source for laughs when he introduces his Spartan woman on stage. Moreover, outsiders' perceptions of Spartan women were probably shaped by exceptional women, especially members of the royal families. Nevertheless, even if we have to be careful not to overestimate or generalise information about their situation, it seems clear that Spartan women's status within society was indeed different from that in most other Greek states.

D64   Bronze figurine of a woman, British Museum

Bronze figure of a girl. She may be running or, since she glances back, dancing. The bronze rivet surviving in the right foot perhaps suggests that this figure was originally a decorative fixture attached to a vessel or utensil. Produced in Lakonia, 520–500 BC, probably found at Prizren in Kosovo.

Height: 114 millimetres
Width: 90 millimetres
Depth: 22 millimetres
Weight: 167 grammes

[BM 1876,0510.1]

D65   Plain appearance
Adornment has been banned for women in Lakedaimon; nor are they allowed to grow
their hair long or wear gold jewellery.

[Herakleides Pontikos, *Constitution of the Lakedaimonians* 2.8 in *FGH* ed. Muller]

D66   Lysistrata welcomes a stereotypical Spartan woman
LYSISTRATA: Welcome Lakonian Lampito, my darling!
                How beautiful you look, my sweetie!
                And that complexion! And those rippling muscles of yours!   80
                You could even throttle a bull.
LAMPITO: By the twin gods I'm sure I could;
                I work out and do my squat-jumps.
KALONIKE: And your boobs – what a fantastic pair you have!
LAMPITO: Hey! You're feeling me up like a sacrificial victim.

[Aristophanes, *Lysistrata* 79–84 (performed 411 BC)]

D67   Healthy babies
In response to Euripides writing that 'children of a father and mother who have had
to earn a meagre living are better' Kritias writes, "But I would begin from a man's
birth: how could someone be physically best and strongest? If the father takes exercise
and eats healthily and puts his body through hard labour; and the mother of the child
before its birth strengthens her body and exercises.

[Kritias fr.32, (Diels-Kranz 81B32) = Clement of Alexandria, *Miscellanies* 6.9]

D68   Spartan women, marriage and children
[3] To begin at the beginning: let us first consider the question of procreation. In other
countries, young girls, who are the state's future mothers and are thought to have
been properly brought up, are nurtured on the most restricted diet possible and with a
minimum of delicacies. They are forced to abstain from wine completely or else only
to drink it diluted with water. The rest of the Greeks expect their girls to sit quietly
at their spinning, in imitation of the sedentary existence of most craftsmen. But if
women are brought up like that, how could anyone expect them to produce sturdy
children? [4] As far as Lykourgos was concerned, there were enough female slaves to
produce clothing, whereas the most important task for freeborn women was producing
children. So as a first priority he laid it down that physical fitness was as important
for women as for men. So he established women's competitions in both running
and wrestling, in the belief that the offspring of two strong parents would be all the
more robust.

[5] He saw, too, that among other nations generally when a newly married woman
joined her husband's household his initial response was to spend an inordinate amount
of time with her. His policy was the exact reverse. He ordained that it was a disgrace
for a man to be seen going into or leaving his wife's room. With such constraints
imposed upon their association, it was inevitable that the husband's sexual desire
would be all the greater, and any consequent children would be more vigorous than if
their parents had had too much of one another. [6] As well as this, he also put an end
to the practice of men marrying whenever they chose, and instead ordained that they

should marry when at the height of their physical powers, on the assumption that this too was eugenically advantageous. [7] It could happen of course that sometimes an old man married a young wife. He noted that such elderly husbands kept a particularly jealous eye on their younger wives. Here too his policy was the exact reverse of the norm. He made it acceptable for an older man to bring into his household a someone who was physically and morally admirable, for the purpose of siring children for him. [8] However, if a man did not want to live with a wife at all but still had an ambition to beget admirable offspring, Lykourgos introduced a law which gave him the right to beget children with any mother of fine children and noble birth, provided he could persuade her husband to give his consent.

[9] He gave permission for many such arrangements. As a result, women like the idea of running two households, while their husbands are keen to acquire for their own children brothers who will be part of their families and share their status, without making any financial demands upon them. [10] So his policy for procreation was the exact opposite of the prevailing practice in Greece. Whether it resulted in children in Sparta becoming bigger and stronger than children elsewhere is an open question for others to decide.

[Xenophon, *Constitution of the Lakedaimonians* 1.3–10 (continued in **D74**)]

D69   Spartan Women
In addition the freedom given to women is harmful as regards both the purpose of the constitution and the prosperity of the state. For just as man and woman are part of the household, it is obvious that a state, almost equally divided in two, should make regulations both for its male population and for the female: so in any constitutions with bad regulations for its women, half of the state must be deemed to have been ignored in its laws. This is what has happened there, since the lawgiver wanted the whole state to be tough, and in respect of the men, he clearly did so, but neglected matters concerning the women. For they live wantonly in absolutely every way, and luxuriously. As a result it is inevitable that wealth should be honoured in such a constitution, especially if they happen to be ruled by women, as is the case with the majority of military and warlike races, except the Celts and any others who have openly honoured intercourse amongst men. It appears that the first storyteller had good reason to link Ares with Aphrodite, since intercourse with men or with women appears to be characteristic of all such [i.e. military or warlike] people. Since this was the case with the Lakedaimonians, many things were controlled by women in the time of their empire. Yet what difference does it make whether the women rule or the rulers are ruled by women? The result is the same. Now bravery is useful in no everyday activities, but only in war, yet it was in this respect that the Lakonian women were most harmful, as they made clear in the attack by the Thebans. For they were no use, unlike women in other states, but created more panic than the enemy.

It seems that initially the freedom given to Lakonian women came about for good reasons. [1270a] This is because the men went abroad away for their homes for long periods on military campaigns, fighting the war against the Argives and then the one against the Arkadians and Messenians. But when they had gained leisure time they put themselves in the hands of a lawgiver and were prepared to obey him because of their military lifestyle (which has many virtuous elements). But as for the women, they say that Lykourgos tried to bring them under his laws, but gave it up when they resisted. So the women themselves are responsible for what happened, and clearly so for this particular mistake. We are not, however, examining who should be blamed or not blamed, but what has been done that is right or wrong. But as regarding women, a situation that is not right not only makes for a degree of impropriety in the running of the state but contributes in some way to a love of money.

[Aristotle, *Politics* 1269b12–1270a15 (continued in **D54**)]

D70   Lykourgos' rules on upbringing of girls

[14.1] He regarded education as the most important and noble task of a lawgiver. So he started from the earliest possible moment, by laying down rules for births and marriages. Aristotle is wrong when he suggests that in this he was trying to impose a proper discipline on women, but was forced to abandon the attempt because of their emancipated lifestyle and excessive powers derived from the fact that their menfolk were always away on military expeditions. The men had no choice but to leave the women in charge, and for this reason tended to mollycoddle them to an excessive degree and even to address them as "Your Ladyship." The reality is quite different: Lykourgos gave the greatest possible attention to girls' upbringing also. [2] For them, before puberty, he instituted a physically tough curriculum of running, wrestling, discus and javelin throwing, so that the products of their wombs should have a really strong start in a powerful body, and develop all the more strongly. As a result the mothers would also better tolerate childbirth and be able to endure labour pains more easily and successfully. He had no time for the idea of a sheltered upbringing for girls any more than boys, and eliminated all forms of feeble effeminacy, even to the extent of compelling them to take part in processions naked and to dance and sing at certain festivals in the presence of young men as spectators. [3] Sometimes they in turn would poke fun and hurl good-natured abuse at anyone who got out of line; and by contrast they would also write hymns of praise and deliver them in honour of those who deserved it, thus encouraging competitiveness and an eagerness to excel in the young men themselves. Any young man who was praised for his courage and won a high reputation among the girls in this way would go off with a tremendous boost to his morale after winning such high praise, while the sting of even light-hearted mockery or teasing had just as much force as serious criticism, particularly since the kings and elders were all participants in the festival along with the rest of the citizens.

[4] There was nothing embarrassing about the girls being naked – a sense of decency was always present and vulgarity forbidden. Rather it encouraged a simplicity of character and a cult of physical fitness, as well as giving women a sense of their own nobility, since they were seen as sharing in courage and heroic ambition just as much as the men. This whole process led them to think and speak as history relates Leonidas' wife, Gorgo, once did. It seems that, when some foreign woman once remarked to her that Lakonian women were the only ones to rule their men, she replied, "Yes. But then, we are the only women who give birth to real men."

[Plutarch, *Life of Lykourgos* 14]

D71   Lykourgos' rules on marriage

[15.1] Of course there were also in all this certain incentives to marriage. I am referring to those festival processions, along with the scant or non-existent clothing of the girls, and the athletic competitions in full view of the young men, who were of course inevitably attracted by what Plato calls "erotic compulsion" rather than any high minded intellectual or "geometrical" excitement. But as well as this, Lykourgos also ensured a degree of disgrace for those who did not marry. They were banned from being spectators at the Gymnopaidiai. In winter the magistrates would force them to march naked around the *agora*, [2] and as they marched they had to sing a song specifically written against themselves, to the effect that they were getting what they deserved for disobeying the laws. They were denied, also, the courtesies and respect which young men customarily showed towards their elders. No one ever criticised a famous comment made to Derkyllidas, even though he was a distinguished general, when he approached a group of younger men. One of them refused to give up his seat to him, saying that "you have failed to produce a son who will one day offer the same courtesy to me."

[3] Their marriages take the form of a kind of kidnapping. They carry off their wives, not when they are small and as yet unready for marriage, but when they are in the full flower of sexual maturity. Her so-called "bridesmaid" then takes charge of the "captive", shaves her head close to the skin, dresses her in a man's cloak and sandals, lays her on a bed of straw alone in the dark, without a light. Her bridegroom, stone cold sober and therefore far from impotent, having had dinner as usual at the mess, sneaks into her room, undoes her girdle, and then picks her up and carry her off to bed. [4] He will not spend much time with her, but will then depart discreetly to his normal sleeping quarters to spend the night as usual among the other young men. This remains the normal practice subsequently: he spends his days and nights among his contemporaries, but visits his bride secretly and with the utmost care, fearful of the shame that would ensue if anyone catches him in her house – his bride acts as a fellow-conspirator with him, contriving to help him devise opportunities for a tryst without anyone else knowing about it. [5] This normally went on for quite a long time, to the extent that some fathered children before they had even seen their wives in daylight. Such limitations to their sexual intercourse acted as a training in self control and moderation, but also served to bring to their love-making both physical vigour and partners who were fresh and ripe for procreation, rather than with their powers fading and glutted by unrestrained sexual activity. Some lingering spark of desire and delight was always left behind for each of them.

[6] Having attached to the institution of marriage such a quality of modesty and orderliness, he was no less eager to remove the futile, feminine inclination to jealousy. As well as eliminating from marriage all that was shameful and dishonourable, he also made it perfectly acceptable for men of good standing to share children and the privilege of begetting them. He ridiculed those who wanted such rights to be the exclusive preserve of an individual and were prepared to murder and even go to war in defence of their rights. [7] He made it possible for an elderly man with a young wife, who took a liking to some good looking young man and thought well of him, to introduce him to his wife, and when he had bestowed upon her his noble seed, to adopt the offspring as his own. In the same way, if some noble man greatly admired the

mother of fine children and impeccable conduct who was married to another man, he could get the husband's permission to sleep with her – like a farmer planting seed in productive soil – thus creating excellent sons, who would come of aristocratic lineage and have the best of pedigrees. [8] Lykourgos' motives for this were twofold: first, he did not regard children as the private property of their parents so much as the common property of the state; he therefore wanted its citizens to come from the best possible stock rather than as the result of random selection. Secondly, he saw a great deal of stupidity and conceit in the regulations of other states in such matters. They wanted their dogs and horses to be sired by the best quality animals and would go to any lengths of bribery or special favours to persuade their owners to provide them. But when it came to their women, they locked them up and guarded them closely, claiming sole rights of procreation, even if they themselves were idiots, well past their prime or even diseased. [9] Such people failed to realise that children of low quality are the first to reflect the poor breeding of those that possess them or bring them up; and vice versa with good children, if they come from noble stock. These practices, sanctioned for the sake of good breeding and national eugenics, had so little to do with the later reputation of their women for sexual promiscuity that in those days adultery was totally unheard of there. [10] There is a good story told about Geradas, a very old fashioned sort of Spartiate, who was asked by a stranger what punishment was applied to adulterers in their country. "There aren't any adulterers among us," he replied. "Yes," he answered, "but just suppose there was one?" "He would be fined one enormous bull," said Geradas, "so big that it could cover Mount Taygetos and drink from the river Eurotas." "But how," said the flabbergasted stranger, "how could there possibly be a bull as big as that?" "Indeed," laughed Geradas; "and how could there possibly be an adulterer in Sparta?" So much, then, for my account of marriages.

[Plutarch, *Life of Lykourgos* 15]

D72   Spartan women value education
In these states [Sparta and Crete] it is not only the men who think highly of education, but also the women.

[Plato, *Protagoras* 342d]

EDUCATION: D73–D81
Education and values in Sparta; the roles of men and women
Spartan society was held together by a set of very strong values which were instilled into every Spartan boy, and possibly the girls as well, during years of an education controlled by the state. This special Spartan education was a precondition for becoming a citizen, and it created a high degree of conformity within Spartan society, while also separating Spartiates from all others, be they *perioikoi*, helots or Greeks from other cities. Xenophon includes Spartan customs, education and family life in his treatise on the Spartan constitution (*politeia*): while for us, a constitution is the set of laws determining how the institutions of government are organised and controlled, the Greek word *politeia* means much more: *politeia* stands for all aspects of life typical for a particular *polis* – it includes laws and rules that govern public institutions as well as customs, religious traditions and general ideas about proper behaviour in public as well as private contexts. This universal concept of *politeia* is particularly clear in Sparta, where state interference in what we would call a 'private' sphere was more pronounced than in other Greek *poleis*. The Spartans had a particularly comprehensive view of what could be seen as 'public business': this included the raising of new generations of citizens, which in most Greek cities was a matter of private family life.

The Spartan Education System for Boys

The Spartan education system was famous in antiquity, and it was a matter of much discussion. Nevertheless, we have only two fairly comprehensive accounts, one by Xenophon (*Lak. Pol.* 2.1–4.6 = **D74, D77, D79**) and one by Plutarch (*Lyc.* 16–21 = **D73, D76, D78, D80**). But since the Spartan education system became a matter of philosophical discussion and, over the centuries, legend, late sources on the issue, such as Plutarch, have to be treated with caution.

Most fundamentally, research over the last generation has questioned whether a comprehensive and fully-regulated education system existed before the late third century and whether the term *agōgē* traditionally applied to education in the Classical period is a misnomer (N.M. Kennell, *The Gymnasium of Virtue* University of North Carolina Press 1995, 113–14; J. Ducat, *Spartan Education*, Classical Press of Wales 2006, 69–71). The term is never applied by any classical-period source specifically to Sparta's public education. Indeed, it was not a local Spartan term, but a general Greek word. It does not appear in any source in a specifically Spartan context until *c.* 240–230 BC. The consistent ancient term for the Spartan education in the classical period (e.g. in Xenophon's *Constitution*) is simply the general Greek term *paideia*.

Many modern accounts of the boys' education draw on Plutarch as a main source and add information from other sources to create a general picture. However, we cannot deal with the system as if it had been a tradition that remained the same over centuries. As Kennell (*Gymnasium of Virtue,* see especially ch. 1) has shown, we are dealing with a complex process of change over time, and the education system underwent extensive 'reconstruction' work in the Hellenistic and Roman periods. Later forms of the system probably resembled the original one in essentials, but also included many new features. This means that for the classical period, we have to rely mainly on Xenophon who was clearly familiar with the system, but only offers a rough overview. For a full discussion of the classical system on this basis see J. Ducat, *Spartan Education* (2006).

At the age of seven, Spartan boys (*paides*) moved away from their families to live and be educated with the other boys in their age group, see **D74, D76**. At some point during their teenage years (the exact age is disputed), the boys (now referred to as *paidikoi*) moved on to the next stage and began to be introduced to Spartan society. While the boys' life is described as almost feral, the teenagers had to learn proper behaviour in society. One of the young men in their twenties became a kind of mentor who would advise and admonish the boy, and also take him to common meals (compare Plut. *Lyc.* 17 = **D78**). Since the term used for this older boys is *erastes* ('lover' used both sexually and non-sexually), it is usually assumed that these relationships could be (and perhaps mostly were) of a homosexual nature, although Xenophon (*Lak. Pol.* 2.12–14 = **D74**) does his best to deny this. Finally, a contest at the sanctuary of Artemis Orthia marked the transition from boyhood to young man, see **C84–C85**: in classical times this was not the show for sadistic Roman tourists it later became (**C91–C94**). Once their education was completed, the young men had to be elected to a *syssitia* group, which was subject to a unanimous vote of approval among all members. We do not know what happened with young men who did not find a mess willing to admit them. Membership in such a group was a precondition for full citizenship, so we have to assume that very few failed to be selected, especially once the Spartan manpower shortage became a serious problem: it is difficult to imagine that at this point the Spartan state would have risked to exclude many young men who had successfully passed through and were technically qualified for full citizenship.

The details of the Spartan education system have inspired a good deal of scholarly discussion. Apart from the complex arguments about specific details there are three major issues: firstly, what, apart from physical endurance, teamwork and obedience, did the boys actually learn?; secondly, how harsh was the system in reality?; and thirdly, what were the origins of the system? Our sources tell us a lot about the tests of endurance and physical education that the boys at Sparta had to undergo, but they say little about basic skills such as literacy which would have been part of primary education elsewhere. Music, poetry and dance were important aspects of Spartan cultural life, especially as part of festivals. Spartan youths were expected to perform at such occasions, and were clearly trained to do so. Moreover, the Spartans were also proud of their distinctive custom of 'Laconic' speech, and the skill to express a thought concisely and effectively was probably practised at common meals when the boys were expected to answer questions accurately and in the appropriate manner. (Plut. *Lyc.* 19–21). We have no evidence to say for certain, but it seems likely that most Spartiates achieved at least a basic level of literacy (note the need to read military dispatches; use of inscriptions in Sparta). To a modern eye the Spartan education system looks extremely harsh, and it is worth asking whether our sources exaggerate these distinctive features because they were so 'typically Spartan'.

Young Men *(Hebontes, eirens)*
In most Greek cities young men became full adult citizens once they reached military age, usually around the age of twenty. Spartans, however, entered a stage between their education and full adulthood, probably between 20 and *c*.30 years of age, which Xenophon (*Lak. Pol.* 4.1–6 = **D79**) saw as a unique feature of Spartiate life (for an overview see Ducat, *Spartan Education* 101–112). The young men (*hebontes* in Xenophon, *eirens* in Plutarch) participated in the *syssitia* and were liable to military service together with the older Spartiates, but may not yet have been allowed to vote in the assembly. The *hebontes* were involved in musical performances (choruses, dance) at festivals, and they also participated in competitions, which means that training in musical as well as physical disciplines probably remained a regular part of their lives.

D73   Lykourgan rules on Spartan infants

[16.1] It was not the father's decision whether to bring up his offspring. He would first have to bring it in his arms to the place called the Lesche (public meeting place), where the elders of the tribesmen gathered. Having assessed the infant, they instructed him to rear it, if it seemed sturdy and robust, and they assigned to it one of the nine thousand allotments of land. But if it seemed weak or deformed, they sent it to the so-called Apothetai (the place of cast-offs), a great chasm at the foot of Mount Taygetos. [2] They believed that it was neither good for the child itself, nor for the state, that any infant should be born which was not naturally well nourished and robust from the very beginning of its life. For the same reason, women never washed their babies in water, using wine instead as a sort of test of their physical strength. Medical opinion has it that epileptics and sick children react badly to undiluted wine, vomiting or developing seizures, while healthy children have their physique strengthened and tempered by it, like steel. [3] Bringing up babies required considerable expertise also from their nurses. No swaddling bands for babies was the rule, so that their limbs and bodies could develop freely; no complaining, no fussy food fads, no fear of the dark, or anxieties about being left alone; no letting down the family with temper tantrums and tears. No wonder foreigners sometimes bought Lakonian wet-nurses for their children. They say that the Athenian Alkibiades, for example, had a Lakonian nurse called Amykla.

[Plutarch, *Life of Lykourgos* 16.1–3(continued in **D76**)]

D74   Spartan education policy

[2.1] Now that I have explained their policy for procreation, I should like to set out the education policy (*paideia*) of them and others. In other parts of Greece, parents who claim to educate their sons as well as possible put them under the care and control of a *paidagogos* at the very first opportunity, as soon as they are capable of understanding what is said to them. They immediately send them off to school to learn to read and write, study the arts, and improve their physical development in the exercise ground. But as well as that they soften their feet by putting them into sandals, and undermine their physical fitness by varieties of clothing and usually letting them eat as much as they want.

[2] Lykourgos did the opposite. Instead of letting each individual father appoint a slave as *paidagogos*, he gave overall charge of boys' education to the so-called *paidonomos* (boy-herd), who was appointed from one of the members of the highest political class. He gave this official full authority to compel their attendance, to supervise them, and to punish them severely if they misbehaved. He gave him a team of young men (*hebontes*) armed with whips with which to inflict punishment where necessary. As

a result high levels of respect for authority and general discipline are characteristic of their society. [3] And of course, instead of softening their feet with sandals, he insisted on hardening them by compelling them to go barefoot. He believed that this sort of training would make them better at climbing hills and safer when coming down steep slopes, and that a boy who had got used to running about in bare feet would jump, sprint, and run more athletically than one with sandals. [4] And instead of undermining their physical fitness by all sorts of clothing, he thought it best to get them used to wearing one tunic all the year round, since this would get them better prepared to face cold and heat alike. [5] As for their diet, he laid it down that the *eiren* should allow them to have only enough food to ensure that they never felt full, so that they would all have experience of what it felt like to be hungry. He believed that those who had been trained in this way would be better able to keep going on an empty stomach where necessary, and, if so instructed, would be better able to carry out orders without food for longer, since they would not look for luxuries, but would tolerate whatever kind of food they were given, as well as leading healthier lives. [6] He also believed that such a dietary regime would make their bodies more slender, and would thus increase their height more effectively than a richer diet which led to fat.

But he wanted to avoid them becoming too desperate through starvation, without making it too easy for them to get what they wanted. So he did allow them to alleviate their hunger pangs by some stealing. [7] It must be obvious to anyone that it was not because he was unable to supply provisions for them that he encouraged them to supplement their rations by deceit. Obviously anyone planning a robbery must go without sleep at night and practise deviousness by day; he must lay traps and organise surveillance teams, if he wants to make a successful raid. All this makes it self-evident that by means of this sort of education he wanted to make boys (*paides*) more skilful at finding supplies and better soldiers overall. [8] It is a perfectly sensible question to ask why, if he thought theft such a valuable training, he ordered a severe beating for anyone caught in the act. The reason seems obvious to me: in all spheres of life teachers punish their pupils for failing to carry out effectively what they have been taught. So the Lakedaimonians punish those who are caught for being ineffective thieves. [9] He made it a special competition to steal cheeses from the altar of Artemis Orthia, while giving others to task of whipping the would-be thieves, thus seeking to demonstrate that a little pain means a long term gain in fame and delight. In this there was a supplementary lesson also: that where speed is of the essence, idleness brings the least reward and the greatest supply of troubles.

[10] Even when the *paidonomos* was away, Lykourgos did not want the boys (*paides*) to lack supervision. So he made it possible for any citizen who happened to be present to issue to the boys whatever instructions he thought fit and to punish them for any misdemeanour. The effect of this was to make the boys more respectful of authority – and in fact men and boys alike respect authority more than anything else. [11] And if by any chance on some occasion no adult was present, so as to ensure that the boys still had an authority figure, he put the most quick-witted of the *eirens* in charge of each platoon. As a result, the boys are never without someone to give them orders.

[12] I think I need to say something also about love-affairs with boys, since this also has a relevance to education (*paideia*). Elsewhere in Greece, in Boiotia for example, men

and boys (*paides*) live together like a man and wife; elsewhere, in Elis for example, they buy time with young men by doing them favours. In other places, however, it is totally forbidden for would-be lovers even to talk to boys. [13] But Lykourgos was totally opposed to all this sort of thing. If someone of transparently good character admired a boy's character and tried to associate with him and to develop an entirely honourable friendship with him, he gave it his approval, since he regarded this as an ideal form of education (*paideia*). But if it was perfectly obviously a matter of lust for his body, he laid it down that this was wholly abominable, and in this way he brought it about that in Lakedaimon a loving relation with boys (*paidikoi*) was little different from that of parents for children (*paides*) or brothers for siblings, and had nothing to do with sexual attraction. [14] Hardly surprisingly, many people refuse to believe this, because in many other Greek cities the laws do not prohibit such desire among men for boys (*paides*).

I have now completed my survey of the Lakonian education system (*paideia*) and that of the rest of Greece. As to which of them produces men who are the most obedient, respectful, and self-disciplined in all important aspects of their lives, I again leave to the decision of anyone who is sufficiently interested.

[Xenophon, *Constitution of the Lakedaimonians* 2 (continued in **D77**)]

D75   Future kings normally exempt from normal education
The *agoge* was a harsh and painful way of life but one which taught the young boys to be obedient. It was this, they say, that led to Sparta being dubbed 'man-breaking' by Simonides as having customs which made her citizens especially obedient to her laws and submissive, just like horses which are broken in from the very start. The law exempts boys being raised as future kings from this compulsory practice.

[Plutarch, *Life of Agesilaos* 1]

D76   Education of Spartan boys (*paides* – from 7 years)
[16.4] But Plato tells us also that Perikles put Zopyros in charge of Alkibiades as his *paidagogos*, even though he was nothing more than an ordinary slave. Lykourgos, by contrast, refused to allow the sons (*paides*) of Spartiates to be assigned to *paidagogoi*, whether bought or hired, nor would he allow fathers to bring up or educate their children just as they pleased. As soon as they all reached the age of seven, he took over control and enrolled them in *agelai* (herds), thus ensuring that they all shared the same discipline and upbringing, and so got used to playing and studying together. [5] He put in charge as captain of each *agele* someone who was outstanding in good sense and bravest in fighting spirit; the others all looked up to him, obeyed his orders, and accepted his punishments, so that their education became a training in the habit of obedience. The older men would keep an eye on them in their sports and were always encouraging them to fight and compete with one another in many ways, with the deliberate intention of assessing the character of each for courage and aggression in such battles.

[6] Reading and writing lessons were restricted to the minimum necessary. All the rest of their education was directed towards the habit of instant obedience, endurance of pain, and military success. To this end, as they grew older the level of physical

exercise was increased, their heads were shaved, and they learned to go barefoot and usually to exercise naked. From the age of twelve they no longer wore tunics and were issued with one cloak per year. With little exposure to such luxuries as baths or oils, except on a very few days annually, their bodies became dry-skinned. [7] They slept together in companies or packs on pallet-beds stuffed with the tops of reeds that grew beside the River Eurotas, which they collected for themselves, breaking them off with their bare hands and without knives. In winter they inserted into this stuffing what was known as 'lycophon', a material which was thought to offer a degree of extra heat.

[Plutarch, *Life of Lykourgos* 16.4–7 (continued in **D78**)]

D77   Spartan *paidikoi* – late-teenagers

[3.1] When they grow up from boys (*paides*) to being youngsters, other states release them from the control of *paidagogos* and schoolmaster. No one is any longer responsible for their development; they are set free to do as he pleases. Lykourgos, however, saw things entirely differently. [2] He realised that at this age they develop a powerful will of his own, a belief that they knows all the answers becomes very apparent, and appetites for various pleasures overtake them. Lykourgos' answer was to keep them hard at work all the time and to find ways of never giving them a moment to themselves. [3] He laid it down that anyone who tried to avoid these tasks should be denied all forms of reward, thus ensuring that not only the state authorities but also all those who cared for them made it their business to prevent them from being disgraced in front of all their fellow citizens through dereliction of duty. [4] In addition to this, he was very keen to instil firmly in them a sense of decency and decorum. So when they were out on the streets he required them to keep their hands firmly under their cloaks, to walk in silence, not to look around but to keep their eyes firmly fixed on the ground. The result of this is very clear: even in matters of decorum, the male of the species is stronger than the female. [5] You would get a better response from a stone statue than from one of them, or a more admiring glance from a bronze figurine; you might even regard them as more bashful than a newly wed bride in her marriage chamber. And when they sit down to a supper in the mess, you can count yourself lucky to get an answer even to a direct question. That gives you some idea of the care they took over late-teenagers (*paidikoi*) as they grew up.

[Xenophon, *Constitution of the Lakedaimonians* 3 (continued in **D79**)]

Though Xenophon uses the word *paidikoi* only right at the end of the passage, he does so to sum up this stage of their education (compare his closing remarks to section 2 – **D74**), and also at **E50**. At the start of the passage, 'being a youngster' is a single verb, unconnected to *paides/paidikoi*. For the rest of the passage, Xenophon's Greek needs no word for 'boy' or 'teenager' since the adjectives and participles show clearly the gender.

D78   'Secondary' Education of Spartans

[17.1] Once they had got to this age they were allowed to associate with lovers (*erastai*), who were young men (*neoi*) drawn from the higher echelons of society. The older men kept a close eye on them, visiting the gymnasia more frequently and watching them fighting or fooling around with each other. This was no casual activity; in fact the old men all thought of themselves in a way as both parents, teachers, and rulers of all those boys, which ensured that no opportunity was missed nor place neglected for reprimanding or punishing any boy who did wrong. [2] But they went even further:

a *paidonomos* was appointed from among the noblest and most distinguished of the citizens; and he in turn appointed the most responsible and warlike of the so-called *eirens* to be in charge of each *agele* ('herd'). *Eiren* is the name given to those who "graduated" from the class of boys (*paides*) two years previously, while *melleirens*, or would-be-eirens, is what they call the oldest of those still in the class of boys (*paides*). This *eiren*, therefore, is a twenty-year old, and he commands those put under him in practice battles, while in barracks he makes them serve his meals as if they were servants. [3] He gets the bigger ones to gather wood and the smaller ones vegetables. But they have to steal it. So some of them secretly enter gardens, others into the men's messes, slipping inside with the utmost cunning and care. Anyone caught receives a severe beating with a whip for showing himself to be an idle and incompetent thief. They also steal whatever food they can, thus learning to be clever at targeting victims who are asleep or off their guard. [4] The penalty for being caught is a flogging and no dinner. Their rations are deliberately inadequate, so as to force them to use their own resources to stave off hunger, thus encouraging them to take risks and develop low cunning.

This is what the starvation rations are all about: but there is a secondary purpose, which is to encourage physical development. Height is encouraged when excessive intake of food is avoided, because over-eating causes breathlessness and inertia, and compresses the body into grossness and limited stature. Lack of weight, by contrast, is conducive to upward growth, since the body thanks to its inherent lightness is able to grow easily and without encumbrance. [5] The same dietary regime seems also to encourage good looks. A sparse and meagre diet seems to allow a bias towards the physical development of the limbs, whereas the fat and over-fed tend in the opposite direction because of sheer over-weight. And of course the same applies to women in pregnancy: if they take laxatives, they may produce children who are smaller, but they will be lean and beautifully formed, thanks to the lightness of the parent's body-mass, which make it more easily shaped. As for the reasons behind this phenomenon, that I must leave to others to investigate.

[Plutarch, *Life of Lykourgos* 17 (continued in **D80**)]

At the start of this passage, Plutarch seems to be talking about boys from the age of 12 (section 16.6 in **D76**). Their lovers he describes as *neoi* – young men – a usual Greek term, not one specific to the stages of a Spartan education as used by Plutarch, but clearly, from the later context, more than 20. Unlike Xenophon (**D77**), Plutarch does not use the word *paidikoi* ('teenager'): he refers to *eirens* at 20 as having 'graduated' from being *paides* two years before, and with the further designation of *melleirens* which he describes as the oldest *paides,* but more logically means presumably those between 18 and 20.

D79   Young men

[4.1] For young men (*hebontes*) Lykourgos showed by far the greatest concern. He reckoned that if they were properly trained and educated their influence for good on the state as a whole would be the most significant. [2] He realised that where the competitive instinct is given the freest rein, there you find the best choruses to listen to and the most spectacular athletic contests to watch. If, then, he could stimulate a competition for courage among these young men (*hebontes*), he hoped it would spur them to the very heights of manly virtue. Let me now explain how he set about creating these competitions.

[3] The ephors start by selecting the three outstanding members of the year group, who are designated *hippagretai* (guard commanders). Each of these selects a hundred others, openly stating the reasons for choosing this one and rejecting that. [4] As a result, those who fail to win the honour of selection become enemies of those who rejected them and bitter rivals of those who were chosen in their stead. So they all keep an eye on each other to see if any of them offends the established code of honour. [5] This generates the right sort of hostilities, the kind that is dearest to the gods and politically desirable – a rivalry which brings out and makes clear the qualities of excellence in a man, with the separate groups striving constantly for supremacy in such excellence, yet if the need arises striving with all their might as one man to serve the state. [6] This arrangement ensures that everyone takes pains to remain physically fit, because wherever they meet each other fist fights break out. Anyone who happens to be present has the legal right to separate the warring parties; if they refuse to obey him, then the *paidonomos* marches them in front of the ephors, who impose a heavy fine in order to make it clear that one must never allow a fit of hot temper to override the duty of obedience to the laws.

[7] Finally, there were those who had passed through this period of youth and were eligible to take on the highest offices of state. Other Greeks release them from any obligation to maintain their physical fitness, even though they are still required for military service. But for such as these Lykourgos established hunting as the most honourable activity, unless prevented by official obligations. His purpose was to ensure that they could still endure the demands of military service just as well as the young men (*hebontes*).

[Xenophon, *Constitution of the Lakedaimonians* 4 (continued in **D61**)]

The 300 young men chosen each year were the *Hippeis:* although the name means 'knights' they had probably never been actual cavalrymen (Lazenby, *Spartan Army*[2] 15). Instead they were a sort of 'royal guard', and all the *hebontes* would compete for the honour. (For their ceremonial role in escorting and honouring Themistokles in 480 BC, see Hdt. 8.124.3.) Clearly, such competitive behaviour must have been carefully controlled, but we have to assume that under these circumstances the young men were constantly preoccupied with upholding the ideals of Spartan society, in competition with each other as well as in their interaction with the younger boys. This period therefore meant further training in all aspects of an ideal Spartiate's life, and it allowed or even encouraged the young men to jostle for positions within Spartan society before they became full citizens, and served to distinguish the future élite – those who would hold the top military positions. For the *hippeis* see Figuera 'The Spartan *Hippeis*' in *Sparta and War* (2006).

D80   Supervision of Spartan boys by *eirens*
[18.1] The boys (*paides*) take the business of stealing very seriously. There is the legendary account of one who had just stolen a fox cub; he was carrying it hidden under his cloak, and endured the laceration of his stomach by the creature's teeth and nails until it killed him, rather than allowing himself to be found out. This story becomes all the more credible when we think of what happens to present day ephebes, many of whom I have seen being flogged to death at the altar of Artemis Orthia.

[2] When relaxing after supper, the *eiren* might tell one of the boys (*paides*) to sing a song, another to answer some question which required a carefully thought out reply, such as, perhaps, to say who was the best among the citizens or to assess the motives for someone's actions. In this way they learned from the very start to make sound

judgements and to involve themselves in political issues. Anyone who was asked to name a good citizen or a despicable one and could not offer a coherent answer was regard as lazy-minded and showing character deficiencies suggestive of indifference to excellence. [3] Such answers had to be given with reasons and supported with clear and concise arguments in support; anyone offering an inadequate answer was punished by a bite on the thumb from the *eiren*. The *eiren* often inflicted such punishments on the boys (*paides*) in the presence of the elders and magistrates, which allowed him to demonstrate that his punishments were reasonable and fair. They never interfered during the administration of the punishment, but once the boys (*paides*) had gone he was required to give an account of his decision and face an assessment of whether his decision was excessively harsh or alternatively too feeble or lenient. [4] Lovers (*erastai*) were also part and parcel of their boys' (*paides*) reputations, whether good or poor. It is said that a boy (*pais*) once let out a discreditable cry during a fight, so his lover (*erastes*) was fined by the magistrates. This sort of devotion was so heartily approved of among them that even unmarried girls could have lovers among the best and noblest of the women. But such love was not competitive: instead it became the basis for genuine friendship between those who had the same object of their affections, and helped to sustain a long-term shared determination to mould the character of their beloved to the highest level of perfection.

[Plutarch, *Life of Lykourgos* 18]

Though impossible to convey in English, the Greek makes it clear that the last sentence is concerned with male same-sex relations. The two examples we hear about are Lysander & Agesilaos (**E83**) and Archidamos & Kleonymos (**E50**).

D81   Violent team game

Lykourgos set in place laws regarding the constitution but also for the fighting of the ephebes … on the following day, a little before midday, they enter the aforementioned place by bridges. Lots drawn during the night predetermine the route by which each side enters. They fight with fists, kick with their feet, bite, and gouge opponents' eyes. I have just described the way they fight man to man: but they also charge at each other violently in a group and push each other into the water.

[Pausanias, *Description of Greece* 3.14.9–10]

THE ARMY: D82–D97

Warfare was clearly a central concern of the Spartan state and dominated the communal activities of its citizens. Spartiates continued to engage in training for military pursuits, and their preferred leisure activities (exercise, hunting) could be considered as further preparation for war. Consequently, the Spartan army was a well-oiled machine which functioned exceptionally well, especially compared to the infantry of other cities which consisted of men who usually had little time or opportunity for military training (Xen, *Lak. Pol.* 11–12 = **D88–D89**; compare Thuc. 5.66–73 = **E101–E103**). As a result, the Spartans were not only very good at warfare, they also had a fearsome reputation which further enhanced their success. Spartiate hoplites could still make a difference in battle when their numbers had begun to dwindle. It seems clear that the Spartans themselves cultivated their warrior image, not least because it must have been a useful tool of psychological warfare. For example, the Spartans apparently tried to conceal their numbers, those of combatants as well as of the fallen (Thuc, **D83**, Paus. 9.13.11–12, see **E111**). Their comparatively uniform equipment (shields, red cloaks) must have made a strong impression, too, and a Doric *paian* (battle hymn) as sung by the Spartans and their allies could strike irrational fear in Athenians, even when the Dorians in questions were their own allies (Thuc. 7.44.6). The Spartans also liked to boast about the fact that they did not need a city wall: they did not expect to see enemies anywhere close to their own city (Plut. *Lyk.* 19 and **F32**.6).

D82   Spartan leadership

[2] As long as it endured, Sparta enjoyed a way of life more typical of a wise and disciplined individual than of a city bound by a constitution. The poets put it rather better in their tales of Herakles, in which they portray him as ranging the inhabited world dressed in lion skin and carrying his club, clobbering lawless and savage tyrants. Sparta was rather similar: with just her decoding-staff and her threadbare cloaks, she acted as the ruler of a willing and compliant Greece. She put down lawless dynasties and tyrannies in the various states, settled wars by arbitration, and suppressed revolutions, often without even raising a shield, but simply by sending a single envoy, whose commands were instantly obeyed by all, rather as bees gather and unite together in good order when their leader appears. All this is a measure of the state's superiority in good government (*eunomia*) and just dealing.

[3] In the light of all this, and speaking personally, I find it surprising that people say that the Lakedaimonians know how to follow, but they have no idea of leadership, citing with approval King Theopompos' reply to someone's observation that Sparta owed her security to their kings' leadership talents. "On the contrary," he replied, "we owe it to our people's talent for obedience." [4] Where there are no leadership skills, there is no willing obedience; such obedience is a discipline instilled by good leadership. Good leadership creates good followers. And just as the ultimate purpose of horsemanship is to make a horse docile and obedient, so it is the function of the art of political leadership to make a people law-abiding. The achievement of the Lakedaimonians was to instil in the rest of Greece not merely a willingness to follow their leadership, but a positive desire to do so and to be their subjects. [5] Greeks made a habit of asking not for ships or money or even hoplites from them, but a single Spartiate commander. And when they got him, they would treat him with honour and respect, as for example the Sicilians with Gylippos, the Chalkidians with Brasidas, and all the Greeks of Asia with Lysander, Kallikratidas, and Agesilaos. They would call such commanders, wherever they were sent, "harmosts" (governors), or "regulators" of the people and their magistrates, and they looked towards the city of the Spartiates as a whole as a kind of *paidagogos* or teacher of civilised living and well-ordered public life. [6] This was presumably the point of Stratonikos' mocking proposal for a new law putting the Athenians in charge of mysteries and religious processions and the Eleans in charge of the Olympic games, because they ran them so well; but if either of them fell down on the job, the Lakedaimonians should be flogged. Of course he said this for a laugh; but Antisthenes, the Socratic philosopher, was making an entirely serious point when he saw the Thebans arrogantly strutting about after their victory in the battle of Leuktra. "They are just like little boys," he said, "boasting of how they have beaten up their tutor."

[Plutarch, *Life of Lykourgos* 30.2–6]

D83   Spartan secrecy

[5.68.2] The secret nature of their political arrangements makes it impossible to discover the numbers of Lakedaimonians … [5.74.3] as for their own losses, it is difficult to establish the truth …

[Thucydides, *History of the Peloponnesian War* 5.68.2, 5.74.3 (for context see **E101**)]

D84   Emphasis on the military
In respect of the lawgiver's intentions, someone might also criticise (the criticism that Plato makes in his *Laws*), that the whole set up of their institutions is aimed at one aspect of excellence, to do with war, which is valuable as regards exerting power. This indeed was their salvation when they were at war, but their destruction when they were the rulers, because they have no understanding of being at leisure, nor do they go in for any other training as being as important as that for war. And they make a mistake that is just as bad, in believing that good things worth striving for are achieved by virtue not vice (which is true), but they also assume that these objectives are more worthwhile that virtue itself (which is wrong).

[Aristotle, *Politics* 1271a41–1271b10 (continued in **D55**)]

D85   Spartan command structure on the battlefield
[66.3] When the king is in command of the army, all orders emanate from the top. The king gives his relevant orders to the polemarchs, they pass them down to the unit-leaders (*lochagoi*); they pass them to the leaders of 50 men (*pentekonteres*); and they again to the group commanders (*enomotarchai*). [4] As a result any orders that need to be issued are passed along in the same way and speedily implemented, since with a few exceptions nearly all the army comes from their professional Lakedaimonian officer class, and when anything needs to be done it becomes the responsibility of a large number to see to it. ... [70.1] In each unit (*lochos*) there were four companies of fifty men (*pentekostyes*), and in each company four groups (*enomotiai*).

[Thucydides, *History of the Peloponnesian War* 5.66.3–4 and 70.1 (see **E101** and **E103**)]

D86   The *Skiritai*
The *Skiritai* always have this privilege (unique in the Lakedaimonian army) of operating on their own as a unit. ... The *Skiritai* numbered about 600 in all.

[Thucydides, *History of the Peloponnesian War* 5.67.1 and 5.68.3 (see **E101**)]

Skiritai were a lightly-armed unit named after the district of Lakonia, Skiritis, near the Arkadian town of Skiros (Thuc. 5.33), also mentioned in **D7** and in action at the first battle of Mantineia **E101**, **E103**.

D87   The *mora*
Two divisions (*morai*) of Lakedaimonians were there: Ephoros says a *mora* consists of five hundred men; Kallisthenes seven hundred; some others, including Polybius, nine hundred.

[Plutarch, *Pelopidas* 17 = Ephoros, *FGrH* 70 F210 = Kallisthenes, *FGrH* 124 F18]

Plutarch is giving an account of the battle at Tegyra (375 BC, see Diod. 15.37 = **H66**). Ephoros was a fourth-century historian; Kallisthenes (died 327 BC), was a nephew of Aristotle whose *Hellenika* covered 386–356.

D88   Organisation of the army
[11.1] All these advantages were the common property of every citizen, whether in peace or war. But if anyone wishes to understand the system by which he contrived to develop their military superiority over all other states, he can read the following account. [2] First of all the ephors issue a proclamation setting out the age groups required to serve as cavalry, hoplites, and then craftsmen. As a result when they go to

war the Lakedaimonians always have a full complement of all the things men need at home in times of peace. All the standard equipment which an army is likely to require is laid down for delivery, whether on wagons or baggage animals. This ensures that there is little likelihood of anything being forgotten by mistake. [3] Included in his list of compulsory equipment for the battlefield itself, he specified a red cloak and a bronze shield for every man, on the grounds that the cloak was the least effeminate and most warlike kind of uniform and the shield was quick and easy to polish and very slow to rust. Once they had come of age, he allowed men to wear their hair long, believing that it made them look taller, finer champions of freedom, and more terrifying.

[4] Thus equipped, he divided them into six regiments (*morai*) of cavalry and infantry. Each infantry regiment of hoplites had a polemarch, four unit-leaders (*lochagoi*), leaders of 50 men (*pentekonteres*), and sixteen group-commanders (*enomotarchai*). All these companies at the word of command form up into sections, [two], three, or six abreast. [5] Most people think that the Lakonian fighting formations are very complicated; in this they are totally mistaken. In fact the opposite is true. In the Lakonian order of battle, the officers occupy the front rank, and each file is a self-sufficient fighting unit. [6] All this is so easy to understand that anyone who can distinguish one man from another cannot make mistakes: some are required to lead; others commanded to follow. The manoeuvre of changing from column of march into line of battle is given verbally by each section leader at the top of his voice, like a herald, and the consequent battle line, or phalanx formation, can be thinner or deeper as tactics require. The whole system is very easily understood. [7] But in the confusion of an actual battle it quickly becomes much more difficult for a soldier to hold the line with whichever of his comrades he happens to be fighting alongside, unless he has been trained under the Lykourgan system.

[8] Military trainers tend to think these manoeuvres are very difficult; but Lakedaimonians execute them very easily. When their army is marching in column, then of course each section marches behind the one on front. But if an enemy suddenly appears in from of them in battle formation while they are still in marching column, the command is passed from section leader to section leader all down the column to deploy to the left (the shield side), until they stand in phalanx formation facing the enemy. If, by contrast, the enemy suddenly appears behind their marching column, each rank simply does an about turn, so that their strongest line is always facing the enemy. [9] The fact that this leaves the commander on the left is not regarded as a disadvantage, but sometimes even an advantage. For, if the enemy should attempt to outflank them, he would be moving to encircle them on their protected shield side, the left, rather than to the exposed right side. But if for any reason it seems tactically better for the leader to control the right wing, the whole force turns back on itself and the force counter-marches until the leader is on the right and the rearguard on the left. [10] If again the enemy formation appears on the right of their marching column, all they have to do is to order each unit (*lochos*) to deploy to the right, rather like a warship turning its prow to face the enemy, and the effect is to place the rear *lochos* to the right. Suppose the enemy approaches from the left, then they can counter them no less effectively either by immediate counter attack (if in battle formation) or wheeling

their *lochoi* to the left to face their opponents. Once again, the effect is to leave the rear *lochoi* on the left.

[Xenophon, *Constitution of the Lakedaimonians* 11 (continued in **D89**)]

Xenophon was an experienced military commander who had been resident in Sparta. But despite his protestations, it is difficult to believe that Xenophon fully understood what he was talking about and the specifics of this account of Spartan tactics are not entirely clear.

D89   How the Spartans set up camp

[12.1] I shall now explain the principles laid down by Lykourgos for setting up a military encampment. He understood that the corners of a square are defensively useless, so he made camps circular, unless they were set safely on high ground, or had a wall or a river behind them for protection. [2] He had sentries posted looking inwards by day along the lines of the arms stores, to protect them from their friends, not their enemies; the enemy themselves were watched by the cavalry from the highest possible vantages points. [3] In case anyone approached by night, he set the *Skiritai* to patrol a defensive outer ring beyond the central encampment, though nowadays they use foreign mercenaries as well, if there happen to be any serving with them. [4] He insisted that at all times those patrolling the perimeter must carry spears, obviously for the same reason as slaves are forbidden to come near the arms stores. Anyone forced to leave the patrol to relieve himself is required to move away from his comrades and the area of the arms stores for the minimum distance necessary to avoid mutual discomfort and no further. All these rules are fundamentally safety measures. [5] They move camp frequently so as to keep the enemy on edge and to help their allies.

While out of campaign all Lakedaimonians are required by law to exercise regularly. As a result as individuals they all develop a more splendid physique, and at the same time make it clear to others that they are finer embodiments of the citizens of a free nation than other Greeks. Neither the exercise area nor the running track may be larger than the regimental encampment, to ensure that no soldier can ever be far from his weapons. [6] After exercise, the senior polemarch gives the order by herald to sit down, which is their equivalent of roll call and inspection. This is followed by the order to have lunch and very quickly after that the order to change the guard. Then comes rest and recreation until the evening exercise session. [7] After that there is the call to supper, and once they have sung a hymn to the gods who have given them favourable replies, then comes the command to rest by their weapons.

Do not be surprised that I have written at such length. Least of all with the Lakedaimonians would one find any detail of essential military organisation which had escaped their attention.

[Xenophon, *Constitution of the Lakedaimonians* 12 (continued in **D7**)]

D90   Customs when on campaign

[22.1] At such times they also relaxed the strictest application of their *agoge* by suspending the ban on personal grooming, both of hair and the individual decoration of weaponry and clothing. It delighted them to see their young men, like horses at the starting gate, champing at the bit and whinnying with excitement at the coming contest. For this reason they let their hair grow long as soon as they reached the age of twenty and ceased to be ephebes, and especially when danger threatened they took pains to make it look shiny and well combed, remembering a saying of Lykourgos that well groomed hair made a handsome man more elegant and an ugly man even more horrible. [2] Physical exercises were less demanding during campaigns and they gave their young men a regime that was generally less severe and less closely monitored. As a result, for Lakedaimonians alone in all the world, war brought relief from their training for war.

[Plutarch, *Life of Lykourgos* 22.1–2 (continued in **D93**)]

D91   Scarlet cloaks
In wars they use scarlet clothes, since the colour seems to them to be manly and the blood-red hue creates greater fear in inexperienced fighters. In addition it gives the advantage that, if one of them is wounded, this fact is not easily spotted by the enemy, but goes unnoticed because the colour is the same.

[Plutarch, *Spartan Customs* 24 (*Moralia* 238F)]

D92   Marching into battle
The Lakedaimonians advanced with cool deliberation to the sound of flutes from the many musicians in their ranks. This had nothing to do with religion, but was intended to ensure that they advanced at a uniform pace so that their ranks remained in close order, rather than losing cohesion, as tends to happen when a large army advances into battle.

[Thucydides, *History of the Peloponnesian War* 5.70.1 (for context see **E103**)]

D93   Marching into battle II
[2] It was now, when their regiments were all deployed and the enemy coming to close quarters, that the king would simultaneously sacrifice the usual she-goat, command all the army to don their garlands, and order his pipers to play the hymn to Kastor. [3] At the same time he himself set the pace for the marching *paian*, so that the whole effect on their enemies was one of shock and awe, as the army advanced in step with the rhythm of the pipes, in close order with no gaps in the line, with no hint of hesitation, and with their battle hymn ringing in their ears as they marched into deadly danger with courage high and hearts aglow. When soldiers are fired up in this way, they are unlikely to feel fear or uncontrolled aggression, so much as fixity of purpose combined with high hopes and total confidence that God is on their side.

[Plutarch, *Life of Lykourgos* 22.2–3 (continued in **D94**)]

D94   Special place for Spartan Olympic victors
[4] Traditionally the king went into battle with a crowned Olympic champion as his personal bodyguard. The story goes that one such champion, offered a huge bribe at the Olympic games not to compete, refused it and after a prolonged and painful wrestling match with his opponent finally defeated him. Someone asked what profit he had made from his victory compared with the bribe. He answered with a grin: "When we go into battle against our enemies, I'll be the one who guards my king."

[Plutarch, *Life of Lykourgos* 22.4 (continued in **D95**)]

Two pieces of archaeological evidence suggest that Olympic victors may have been given special treatment: the designation on a memorial stone (**B53**) and the tomb of the Spartans in Athens' *Kerameikos* with the subtle marking out of one of the burials (see **B25a**).

D95   Spartan tactic of not pursuing enemies

When they had put their enemies to flight and the day was theirs, the Lakedaimonians would only follow the fugitives far enough to consolidate their victory by such pursuit and then quickly return to base, thinking it shameful and rather un-Greek to hack their enemies to pieces and slaughter them, when they had cried off the contest and made a run for it. This was not only admirable and generous, but also thoroughly sound policy. Their opponents knew very well that those who stood their ground would be killed, while those that surrendered were spared. So they reckoned that flight was a better bet than resistance.

[Plutarch, *Life of Lykourgos* 22.5 (continued in **D15**)]

D96   Spartan treatment of cowards

[9.1] Another admirable feature of Lykourgan policy was to create a culture in the state where a noble death was seen as preferable by far to a disgraceful life. Anyone who researches this will find the result is a lower casualty rate than in cities where soldiers choose to run away from danger. [2] In fact, to tell the truth, survival usually seems to favour the bold far more often than the coward. For courage is the easier way and sweeter, its resources greater and more potent its power. After all, glory follows most readily in the footsteps of the brave and all men desire to fight beside the bravest. [3] But I must of course record as well the method he employed to bring all this about. It is obvious, of course. He simply ensured that brave men won rewards and cowards misery. [4] Elsewhere anyone found guilty of cowardice simply gets a bad reputation – nothing more. He goes to the same markets as the brave man, sits beside him, goes to the same gymnasium, if he so chooses. But in Lakedaimon, everyone would be ashamed to share a meal with a coward in the same mess, or to wrestle with him at the gymnasium. [5] Often when sides are being picked for ball games, it is the coward who gets left out; in the choral competitions, he is pushed off to the most ignominious position in the line; in the street he must stand aside for others; when seated he must stand up even for his juniors; his female relatives may well not marry and so he must support them at home and explain to them why his cowardice is responsible for their unmarried state; he must put up with a hearth and home without a wife beside him, and yet at the same time accept the standard fines for remaining a bachelor; he cannot walk about looking cheerfully well-groomed or try to present himself as a man of impeccable reputation; if he does, he will be beaten up by better men than he. [6] With such a burden of disgrace heaped upon cowards, it is hardly surprising that men there prefer death to a life of such dishonour and disgrace.

[Xenophon, *Constitution of the Lakedaimonians* 9 (continued in **D12**)]

For a comprehensive treatement, see Ducat, 'The Spartan "tremblers"' in *Sparta and War* (2006), based on this and other passages, including **A8** (Tyrtaios), **F21** (Hdt.), **E52** (Thuc.), **D97**.

D97   Spartan songs

The majority were songs of praise, which celebrated those who had died for Sparta as being blessed by the gods, or castigated as cowards those who 'trembled', describing them as living lives of misery and misfortune.

[Plutarch, *Life of Lykourgos* 21.2 = *Moralia* 238a]

NAVAL COMMAND (NAVARCHY): D98–D99

Though the Spartiate Eurybiadas was given command of the combined Greek fleet at Artemision and Salamis in 480 BC (**E116**), the post of *nauarchos* ('navarch' or 'admiral') was not a traditional office or one that the Spartans could plausibly attribute to Lykourgos. Its first occupant was Knemos who held it in summer 430 and 429 (Thuc. 2.66.2 and 2.80), but it seems at this stage to have been an occasional office, with the strict one-year tenure introduced only *c.* 408 BC. It became an enormously important post with special arrangements having to be made for Lysander, whose appointment as deputy navarch (see **E125**) provides the context for **D99** (also Plut. *Lysander* 7.2), and for Aristotle's comment on it being virtually another kingship (i.e. equivalent in power when on campaign) , see below (**D98**) and Cartledge, *Agesilaos* 80–81.

D98   Naval command

Some people have also criticised the law about the navarchs, and they are rightly critical, since it is responsible for unrest. This is because on top of the kings who are permanent generals, the navarchy has been established as virtually another kingship.

[Aristotle, *Politics* 1271a37–41 (continued in **D84**)]

D99   Naval command for one year and one term only

It is not legal with them for the same man to be navarch twice.

[Xenophon, *Hellenika* 2.1.7, (continued in **E125**)]

THE PELOPONNESIAN LEAGUE: D100–D102

From the eighth century onwards Sparta was one of the great powers in the Peloponnese. The conquest of Messenia created one of the largest *polis* territories in the Greek world. More important, however, were Sparta's efforts to bring almost all Peloponnesian states into an alliance under her leadership, which made her the most powerful state in Greece during the late Archaic period (Hdt. 1.68 = **H10**), and one of two 'superpowers' on the Greek mainland during the fifth and early fourth century. Relations within the Peloponnese were never without conflict, but the longevity of the Peloponnesian league and its effective use on many occasions should be considered a success.

In the sixth century the Spartans turned from attempts to subjugate their neighbours to a new strategy: they began to form alliances with Peloponnesian states. Traditionally, Sparta's agreement with Tegea, probably in the 550's BC, is seen as the first of many such agreements of an alliance which became the Peloponnesian League of the classical period. In fact, it seems that even earlier, Sparta was already very active in forging links with many cities. In the Peloponnese, the Spartans could offer support against the other potentially large power, Argos, and they also acquired a reputation for helping cities to remove tyrants. In any case, by the late sixth century many states on the peninsula were allies of Sparta, namely all Arkadians, the Eleans in the west and a number of states in the north-east (in the vicinity of Argos), especially Corinth, which was to play a crucial role in the alliance. Herodotus saw the beginning of Sparta's system of alliances as a turning point which made her the largest power in Greece at the time (Hdt. 1.65–8 = **H8, H10**). Thucydides 2.9.2 (= **D100**) gives a clear description of the size of the league in 431 BC, and the league reached its greatest extent at some stage during the Peloponnesian War, when all of Achaia on the coast of the Corinthian Gulf was added. Argos always remained outside the alliance. After the end of the Peloponnesian War Sparta began to lose allies, most importantly Corinth, which was dissatisfied with the outcome of the war. Diodoros gives a list of allies in 378 BC (**D101**). The league was dissolved in the aftermath of the battle of Leuktra (371 BC), when the Arkadians in particular decided to found their own regional state, and see **E145** for apparent Spartan recognition that they have nothing to offer their allies.

It is not clear when Sparta's set of alliances came to be seen as one entity, the organisation we call the Peloponnesian League, while the official term in ancient texts is 'the Lakedaimonians and their allies', often 'the Peloponnesians' for short. It seems that from the beginning the allies were obliged to contribute troops to Spartan campaigns, initially probably without having a say in decisions about campaigns. The abortive campaign of Kleomenes against Athens, *c*. 506 BC (**E14**) seems to have resulted in Sparta consulting her allies (**E138**). See **E137–E145** for the League in practice, including formalisation of the process at some stage (the exact chronology is not clear), with formal league councils at Sparta and votes by allies by the beginning of the Peloponnesian War, though only Sparta could summon a League congress (see **E139**).

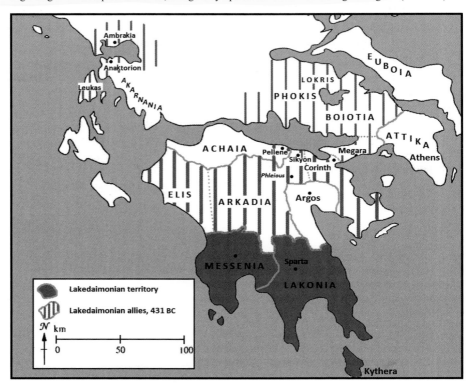

Map 6: Peloponnesian League in 431 BC

D100   The Peloponnesian League in 431 BC

[2] The following states were allies of the Lakedaimonians. All the Peloponnesians states south of the Isthmus, except Argos and the Achaians, who remained on friendly terms with both sides. Only Pellene of the Achaian states supported her from the start, but later all the other Achaian cities followed her. Outside the Peloponnese those allied to her were the Megarians, Boiotians, Lokrians, Phokians, Ambrakiots, Leukadians, and Anaktorians. [3] Those who provided naval resources were Corinth, Megara, Sikyon, Pellene, Elis, Ambrakia, and Leukas, while Boiotia, Phokis, and Lokris supplied cavalry.

[Thucydides, *History of the Peloponnesian War* 2.9.2–3]

D101   Major reorganization of the league, 378 BC

The Lakedaimonians, seeing that they could not hold the allies back from pushing to leave the alliance, stopped being as uncompromising as before and treated the cities sympathetically. By making contacts and granting favours they made all the allies more loyal. Seeing that the war was escalating and requiring great attention, they eagerly made preparations of various sorts, especially for the even better organization and deployment of their soldiers and services. [2] They divided the cities and the soldiers levied for the war into ten parts. The Lakedaimonians comprised the first of these, the Arkadians the second and third, the fourth the Eleans, the fifth the Achaians; the Corinthians and Megarians formed the sixth, the seventh the Sikyonians, and men from Phleious and Akte, the eighth the Akarnanians, the ninth the Phokians and Lokrians, and last the Olynthians and the allies living in Thrace. One hoplite was thought to be worth two lightly-armed men, and one cavalryman the equivalent of four hoplites.

[Diodoros, *Library of History* 15.31.1–2]

D102   League members allowed to provide money rather than troops, 378 BC

Discussion took place about whether cities who wished could provide silver instead of men, at a rate of three Aiginetan obols per man; any city that provided cavalry, could give payment at four times the rate for a man; and if any failed to provide a force, the Lakedaimonians could level a fine at one *stater* per man per day.

[Xenophon, *Hellenika* 5.2.21]

SECTION E
SPARTAN INSTITUTIONS IN PRACTICE

THE SPARTAN EXECUTIVE IN ACTION: (E1–E50)
Section **D** presented sources on the political structure of Sparta from writers attempting to define the powers and roles played of kings (**D1–D11**), *gerousia* (**D12–D15**), ephors (**D16–D21**) and the popular assembly (**D23**). A range of sources in this section show how things might operate in practice. Given that a particular feature of Sparta was its 'mixed constitution' (see note on kings before **D1**) it's not surprising that the sources should reveal considerable interaction and often tension between the different executive bodies (see **E47**). The sources below are therefore presented in a chronological order of the events they describe. Kings are referred to in **E1–E5, E7–E10, E12–E24, E29, E39, E41, E43–E50**; and as being held to account in **E19, E20, E23, E25, E26, E44, E136, H21**; regent **E24–E27, H20**; *gerousia* **E8, E28, E44, E47, E50 E53a**; ephors in **E5–E8, E19, E20, E23, E24, E26, E30–E32, E42–E44, E47, E50, E53, E112, E131, E135, E144, E155**; assembly **E28–E31, E43**.

E1   Ancestry of Leotychidas II and the Eurypontid kings

The general and naval commander was Leotychidas who was from the other house of kings. He was the son of Menares, son of Agesilaos, son of Hippokratidas, son of Leotychidas, son of Anaxilas, son of Archidamos, son of Anaxandridas, son of Theopompos, son of Nikandros, son of Charillos, son of Eunomos, son of Polydektes, son of Prytanis, son of Eurypon, son of Prokles, son of Aristodemos, son of Aristomachos, son of Kleodaios, son of Hyllos, son of Herakles. All of these, except for the two named after Leotychidas were kings of Sparta.

[Herodotus, *Histories* 8.131.2–3]

Herodotus here describes the allied Greek fleet gathering at Aigina in 479. His account of Thermopylai (7.204 = **F10**) had given Leonidas' Agiad ancestry, but here Herodotus clearly says he is giving both Leotychidas' ancestry and a list of (Eurypontid) kings. His lists, however, are not the same as those provided by Pausanias (**E3, E4**). For the complex question of the reliability of the names given by Hdt and Paus, see Appendix 3 in Cartledge *SL* 293–298, and for a summary, the lists given in *OCD³* under 'Sparta' (Cartledge and others).

E2   Leotychidas I

[…] is the son of Leotychidas, the king of Sparta.

[Alkman, fragment 5 = P. Oxy 2390, fr.2, col.2]

This fragment of a commentary on Alkman, found on a papyrus at Oxyrhynchos confirms that Leotychidas (I) was king (as Hdt., **E1**, against Paus., **E4**), since Alkman predates Leotychidas II. Leotychidas' known son and successor was Hippokratidas.

E3   Pausanias on Agiad kings

Eurysthenes, Agis, Echestratos, Labotas, Doryssos, Agesilaos, Archelaos, Teleklos, Alkamenes, Polydoros, Eurykrates, Anaxandros, Eurykrates, Leon, Anaxandridas, Kleomenes, Leonidas (brother), Pleistarchos, Pleistoanax (son of the regent Pausanias and great-grandson of Anaxandridas), Pausanias, Agesipolis, Kleombrotos (brother), Agesipolis (II), Kleomenes (II), (brother).

[Pausanias, *Description of Greece* 3.2.1 – 3.6.2]

E4   Pausanias on Eurypontid kings

Prokles, Soös, Eurypon, Prytanis, Eunomos, Polydektes, Charillos, Nikandros, Theopompos, Zeuxidamos (grandson), Anaxidamos, Archidamos, Agasikles, Ariston, Demaratos, Leotychidas (II) (not son), Archidamos (II) (grandson), Agis, Agesilaos (II) (brother), Archidamos (III).

[Pausanias, *Description of Greece* 3.7.1 – 3.10.3]

Both these 'lists' are extracted from the information given by Pausanias about the kings and their roles in Spartan history which he splits into their separate houses ('I shall go through each of their houses separately and not mix them both together as one and the same.' 3.1.9). Pausanias also gives the relationship between the kings: where not indicated otherwise above, Pausanias says explicitly that son succeeded father.

E5   Chilon puts down tyrannies in Greece

Chilon the Lakonian, who was ephor and general, and Anaxandridas put down tyrannies among the Greeks: in Sikyon, Aeschines; and Hippias, son of Peisist[ratos in Athens].

[Rylands Papyrus 18.2.5–13 = Anonymous, *FGrH* 105 F1]

We know nothing of the context of this papyrus. Plutarch, *On the Malice of Herodotus* 21 gives a list of eight tyrannies ended by Sparta, but his list appears unreliable (Osborne, *Greece in the Making*, 290).

E6   Chilon tries to prevent tyranny in Athens

Chilon the Lakedaimonian happened to be present. On seeing the portent he advised Hippokrates either not to marry and have children, or if he happened to have a wife, to divorce her, or to disown his son if he happened to have one. But Hippokrates was not willing to obey Chilon's advice, and Peisistratos was born after this.

[Herodotus, *Histories* 1.59.2–3]

The chronology is impossible as Peisistratos was already prominent in Athens several years before Chilon's ephorate. In any case Peisistratos was not a *tyrannos* in the later sense of a tyrant (Thuc. 6.54). But the story shows how firmly Chilon and Sparta later came to be associated with opposition to tyranny in Greece.

E7   Chilon as the first significant ephor

Chilon, son of Damagetas, was a Lakedaimonian. … He became ephor in the 55th Olympiad [560 BC] (Pamphile says in the 56th [556 BC]). Sosikrates says that he first became ephor when Euthydemos was archon. He was the first to introduce ephors being yoked alongside the kings, though Satyros says it was Lykourgos.

[Diogenes Laertius, 1.68]

Diogenes Laertius (probably 2nd/3rd century AD) wrote an account of Greek philosophers, starting with short lifes of the 'Seven Sages' of Greece, including Chilon. The account includes several sayings of Chilon, and clearly used a wide range of earlier historians. Chilon is mentioned in Hdt and was heroized at Sparta = **C34–C35**.

KING KLEOMENES: E8–E23

Herodotus appears consistently to underestimate Kleomenes, in everything from his length of reign – 'Kleomenes ruled no great length of time' (Hdt. 5.48) – but actually around 30 years – to his personal qualities and behaviour. In reality, Kleomenes was clearly one of the most important Spartan kings of any period, pursuing an interventionist foreign policy (**E12–E14, E17, E18, E21**). His reign also saw the formation of the Peloponnesian League (**E138**). His policies created considerable opposition (**E19, E20**) and it is possible, even likely, that one of Herodotus' oral sources was one of the descendants of Demaratos, rival king to Kleomenes. For an assessment of Kleomenes, see A. Griffiths, 'Was Kleomenes Mad?' in Powell, *Classical Sparta* (1989).

E8   Kleomenes' birth, *c.* 550 BC

Anaxandridas had married his own niece, to whom he was devoted, but there were no children. [39.2] In view of the situation, the ephors summoned him to appear before them and made the following declaration: "Even if you are indifferent to your own interests," they said, "as far as we are concerned it is unacceptable that the lineage of Eurysthenes should die out. You may have a wife; but she has produced no children. Marry someone else. If you do, you will delight the Spartiates." Anaxandridas replied that he would do no such thing; he had a wife who was utterly blameless; their advice that he should get rid of her and marry someone else was grossly improper. He had no intention of taking their advice.

[40.1] At that the ephors and members of the *gerousia* talked the matter over and brought Anaxandridas a new proposal. "We realise," they said," that you are devoted to your present wife. But it is important that you follow our suggestions and do not obstruct them, so as to avoid some more serious action against you by the Spartiates. [40.2] We are not asking you to divorce your present wife; you may continue to maintain her in the style to which she is accustomed. But you must marry a second woman as well, to produce children and guarantee the succession. Anaxandridas agreed to this suggestion and thereafter kept two wives and two separate households – a thoroughly un-Spartiate procedure.

[41.1] Very soon after this his second wife gave birth to a son, Kleomenes, whom I have mentioned above, and thus presented the Lakedaimonians with a successor to the throne. Whereupon his first wife, who had hitherto proved childless, somehow or other happened to become pregnant. [41.2] So then the relatives of the second wife, hearing the news (which was true) that the first wife was pregnant kicked up a tremendous fuss, alleging that she was telling lies and planned to pass off a substitute child as her own. So great were their protests that when the time came for her child to be delivered, the ephors, who did not know whom to believe, even acted as observers, sitting around the mother as she gave birth. [41.3] Having given birth to Dorieus, she rapidly produced another son, Leonidas, and immediately after that another, Kleombrotos, though there are suggestions that these two last were twins. But the second wife, the mother of Kleomenes, who was the daughter of Prinetadas, son of Demarmenos, never had another child.

[Herodotus, *Histories* 5.39–41 (continued below)]

E9   Herodotus on Kleomenes' accession

[1] Kleomenes, so the rumour goes, if not completely mad was certainly not quite *compos mentis*. Dorieus, by contrast, was the brightest and best of his contemporaries, and fully expected that he would inherit the kingdom by virtue of those outstanding qualities. [2] So when, on the death of Anaxandridas, the Lakedaimonians stuck to tradition and confounded his expectations by electing Kleomenes king, by right of primogeniture, he was exceedingly angry.

[Herodotus, *Histories* 5.42 (continued in **H13**)]

VARIOUS SPARTAN ATTEMPTS TO CONTROL ATHENS: E10–E14
Hdt. 1.59–64 gives an account of how Peisistratos had finally (*c.* 546 BC) established himself in Athens as *tyrannos*, that is to say a sole ruler, without the fully negative implications that 'tyrant' presently came to acquire in the Greek world and to this day. Peisistratos' rule seems to have been distincty enlightened (Thuc. 6.54), and he was succeeded by his son, Hippias, in 527, who is known from the Athenian archon-list (ML 6), to have had important aristocratic families serve as archon (chief magistrate) under his rule, including Kleisthenes, the head of the Alkmeonid family in 525–4. The more oppressive 'tyranny' came later, after the assassination of Hippias' brother in what Thuc. makes clear (6.53–59) was *not* a political act. One modern explanation of Sparta's involvement in Athens is that it wished to pre-empt a pro-Persian Athens. More plausibly, Sparta saw the opportunity to add an Athens, grateful for the removal of an increasingly unpopular ruler, to her network of allies (Osborne, *Greece in the Making,* 294).

E10   Thucydides on the end of Peisistratid rule

[53.3] The people knew from what they had heard that the tyranny of Peisistratos and his children had become hard to tolerate towards its end, and also that it had been overthrown not by the Athenians themselves, nor by Harmodios, but by the Lakedaimonians … [59.4] [*After Harmodios had killed Hipparchos*], Hippias ruled three more years as tyrant of Athens, but then in the fourth year his rule was ended by the Lakedaimonians and the Alkmeonid exiles.

[Thucydides, *History of the Peloponnesian War,* 6.53.3 and 6.59.4]

Thuc. in describing fears in Athens in 415 BC of attempts to re-establish a tyranny offers a lengthy digression intended to correct popular views about the Peisistratid tyranny.

E11   Abortive Spartan attempt to depose Peisistratids from Athens, *c.* 512

[1] The Athenians say that the Alkmeonids while residing at Delphi bribed the Pythian priestess with money so that whenever Spartiates came to consult the oracle either on individual or state business she would tell them to free Athens. [2] The Lakedaimonians, since they kept receiving the same oracle, sent Anchimolios, son of Aster, one of their most distinguished citizens, with an army to drive the Peisistratids out of Athens, although they were very good friends of theirs: nonetheless the wishes of the gods were more important than those of men. The Lakedaimonians sent the force across the sea in boats, [3] and it landed at Phaleron. But the Peisistratids, being forewarned had called on the Thessalians for help, since they had an alliance with them. The Thessalians, accepting their request, sent one thousand cavalry with their king, Kineas of Konda. Backed by these allies, the Peisistratids devised the following plan: [4] they cut down trees on the plain of Phaleron to make it possible for cavalry to operate there and launched a cavalry attack on the camp. In the attack they killed many Lakedaimonians, including Anchimolios himself, and drove the survivors back

to their ships. So the first expedition from Lakedaimon ended, and Anchimolios was buried at Alopeke in Attika, near the Temple of Herakles at Kynosargos.

[Herodotus, *Histories* 5.63]

The Alkmeonids were an aristocratic Athenian family, who initially supported the Peisistratids (Peisistratos and his sons Hippias and Hipparchos). Hdt's explanation that the Spartans were simply obeying the (bribed) Delphic oracle is hard to believe. Certainly Sparta under Kleomenes tried to expand influence over Argos (**E17**) and Athens.

E12   Kleomenes invades Attika and deposes Hippias from Athens, 510 BC

[64.1] Later on the Lakedaimonians despatched a larger force to Athens, accepting King Kleomenes, son of Anaxandridas as leader of the expedition, and not sending it by sea, by but land. [64.2] When they invaded Attic territory, Thessalian cavalry engaged them, but rapidly withdrew, when more than forty had fallen: the survivors went straight back to Thessaly as best they could. Kleomenes, when he reached the city, together with those of the Athenians who wished to be free, besieged the tyrants, walled in on the akropolis. [65.1] The Lakedaimonians would certainly not have taken the Peisistratids (since they had not intended to undertake a siege, and the Peisistratids had provided themselves with ample food and water), but would have besieged them for a few days before returning to Sparta. [65.2] But as it was, something happened which was disastrous for them, but at the same time lucky for their opponents: the children of the Peisistratids were captured as they were being smuggled out of the country. [65.3] When this happened, all their plans had to be abandoned: the terms they accepted to recover their children, as stipulated by the Athenians, were that they should withdraw from Attika within five days.

[Herodotus, *Histories* 5.64–65]

E13   Abortive attempt of Kleomenes to expel Kleisthenes from Athens, 508 BC

According to Hdt, after the expulsion of Hippias, Kleisthenes the head of the Alkmeonid family gained power over his main rival Isagoras by enlisting the support of the people (Hdt. 5.66).

Kleisthenes, with the support of the masses, was much stronger than his rivals. [70.1] As for the defeated Isagoras, he took the following measures: he summoned Kleomenes the Lakedaimonian, who had been his guest (*xenos*) while besieging the Peisistratids. (It was alleged that Kleomenes had slept with Isagoras' wife.) [70.2] Kleomenes first sent a messenger to Athens that Kleisthenes should be thrown out alongside many other Athenians whom he labelled as 'accursed'. … [*Herodotus explains the story involving an ancestor of Kleisthenes*].

[72.1] So Kleomenes sent a message that Kleisthenes and 'the accursed' should be thrown out, and Kleisthenes withdrew of his own accord. Nonetheless Kleomenes came to Athens with a small band of men, and on his arrival banished seven hundred Athenian families suggested by Isagoras. After doing this he made a second attempt to abolish the council and put government in the hands of three hundred supporters of Isagoras. [72.2] The council resisted and refused to obey, and Kleomenes, Isagoras and his supporters occupied the akropolis. The rest of the Athenians, acting in unison, besieged them there for two days: on the third day the Lakedaimonians amongst them left the country under a truce.

[Herodotus, *Histories* 5.70 and 5.72]

E14 Abortive attempt to restore Isagoras, 506 BC

[74.1] Kleomenes, feeling that he had been insulted by the Athenians in words and actions, gathered an army from across the Peloponnese. He did not declare it openly, but wished to punish the Athenian people and set up as a tyrant Isagoras who had escaped with him from the akropolis. [74.2] Kleomenes invaded Eleusis with a large force and the Boiotians by agreement captured Oinoe and Hysiai, the villages furthest from Athens, while the Chalkidians invaded from the other side and ravaged the countryside of Attika. The Athenians, though attacked on two sides, decided to deal with the Boiotians and Chalkidians later, but to take arms against the Peloponnesians at Eleusis.

[75.1] When the armies were about to engage in battle, the Corinthians were the first to reflect that what they were doing was not right, and changed their minds and withdrew; next Demaratos son of Ariston, the king of the Spartiates, and jointly in command of the army from Lakedaimon did the same, though he had not formerly been at odds with Kleomenes.

(for the result of this disagreement, see **D6** *– 75.2)*

[75.3] Meanwhile the other allies at Eleusis, seeing the kings of the Lakedaimonians at loggerheads, and the Corinthians having already left the ranks, also went back home themselves.

[Herodotus, *Histories* 5.74–75]

A little later, perhaps in 504, Sparta consulted her allies in the Peloponnesian League on whether to attack Athens again, but the allies rejected the idea (presumably Kleomenes' – see **E138**).

SPARTAN HELP REQUESTED FOR IONIAN REVOLT, 499 BC: E15–E16

The Ionian Greek cities of the islands and coastline of Asia Minor (western Turkey) had been part of the Persian empire since *c.* 546 BC. But most followed the lead of Aristagoras of Miletos in 499 BC in overthrowing their local rulers. He sought help from mainland Greece in maintaining their newly won independence (**E15**). Athenian assistance ultimately led to the Persian expedition of 490 BC. In Sparta the request was rejected (**E16**), though the story as told by Hdt conforms too much to stereotypes (potential for Spartans to be corrupted by foreigners; laconic words of wisdom from a small child) for us to have confidence in any details.

E15 Aristagoras of Miletos seeks Spartan help for Ionian revolt, 499 BC

Aristagoras of Miletos, having put an end to the tyrants, ordered that generals should be established in each of the cities, and then sailed on a trireme to Lakedaimon, since he needed to find a powerful ally for himself.

[Herodotus, *Histories* 5.38.2]

E16 Kleomenes refuses to involve Sparta in the Ionian Revolt, 499 BC

[49.1] But it was while Kleomenes was still king that Aristagoras, the tyrant of Miletos, came to Sparta. Now the Lakedaimonians say that at the royal audience Aristagoras produced a map of the whole world, which gave a bird's eye view of all its lands, seas, and rivers engraved on bronze. [49.2] Aristagoras opened the discussions in the following way: "King Kleomenes," he said, "don't be surprised at my enthusiasm to make this visit; the current situation gives me no choice. That we, the sons of the Ionians, should be slaves rather than free men is a disgrace and the source of the utmost misery both to ourselves, to the rest of Greece, and to yourselves as the greatest power in Greece. [49.3] Now, therefore, in the name of the gods I beg you to rescue the Ionians from their slavery, for we are your kinsfolk. For you it will be as easy as walking. For the barbarians are a feeble lot, while in matters of warfare and courage you Lakedaimonians have reached the very pinnacle of success. Look at the way the Persians fight: they use bows and short spears. They go into battle wearing trousers and with turbans on their heads. [49.4] Victory will be a walkover. The inhabitants of the country have more wealth than all the rest of the world put together, in gold, silver, bronze, rich clothing, working animals, slaves. If you want it, it's yours for the taking."

[49.5] "Let me explain to you their geographical relationship. The Lydians are neighbours to the Ionians. Theirs is a fertile country, with rich deposits of silver." And here he pointed out the boundaries of those countries, drawn out on the map, which he had brought with him. "Next to the Lydians' eastern borders," he went on, "are the Phrygians, whose herds and crops are, to the best of my knowledge, the richest in the world. [49.6] Then come the Kappadokians, known to us as Syrians, and beside them the Kilikians, whose territory reaches the sea; and lying off their coast here you can see the island of Cyprus. The Kilikians pay the Persians an annual tribute of 500 talents. Next to them come the Armenians, also very rich in cattle, and beyond them here are the Matieni, as you can see. [49.7] Next to them, here you can see the Kissians, and here lying on the banks of the river Choaspes, is Susa, where the Great King lives and keeps his treasure houses. If you capture Susa, you can confidently compete with Zeus for wealth.

[49.8] You seem to feel you must go to war with the Messenians, your rivals, and the Arkadians and the Argives, over some tiny patch of poor quality land with miniscule boundaries, even though they have none of the reserves of gold or silver, which might inspire men to fight and die for. Yet now you are offered the chance of an easy conquest of the whole of Asia; could the choice be any easier?"

[49.9] When Aristagoras had finished, Kleomenes replied that he would give him a decision in three days' time. [50.1] That was as far as the discussion went, but when the day of decision arrived, they met again, and Kleomenes asked Aristagoras how many days' journey it would be to reach the king's capital at Susa from the Ionian coast. [50.2] Hitherto Aristagoras had played his cards very skilfully and successfully misled the king; but now he slipped up badly. He should have concealed the truth, if he wanted the Lakedaimonians to launch an invasion of Asia; instead he admitted that it involved a journey of about three months. [50.3] He was about to describe the route when Kleomenes cut him short. "Milesian stranger," he declared, "get out of Sparta before sunset. What an appalling idea to suggest to the Lakedaimonians that they should launch an expedition to a place that is three months' march from the sea.

[51.1] After that, Kleomenes went back into his house, but Aristagoras got hold of a suppliant's olive branch and followed him. When he had got inside, he begged Kleomenes to send his daughter away and to hear what he had to say, since he was now a suppliant. Kleomenes' daughter, was in the room standing beside her father. She was his only child, eight or nine years old, and her name was Gorgo. Kleomenes told him to say what he had to say and not to be inhibited by the presence of the child. [51.2] So Aristagoras began by offering him a bribe of ten talents if he would do what he had asked. When Kleomenes refused, Aristagoras gradually increased his offer until his bid had reached the sum of fifty talents. At that point the child exclaimed, "Father, this stranger will destroy you if you don't go away at once." [51.3] Kleomenes was so impressed by his daughter's advice that he retired to another room. As for Aristagoras, he left Sparta for good, having failed to get any further opportunity to give Kleomenes details of the route to Susa.

[Herodotus, *Histories* 5.49–51]

E17   Spartans inflict heavy defeat on Argos at Sepeia, *c.* 494 BC
[76.1] What happened was this. Kleomenes had once consulted the Delphic oracle and was told that he would capture Argos. So he led the Spartiates against them and got as far as the river Erasinos …. On arrival there, Kleomenes had offered a sacrifice to the river but proved totally unable to gain a favourable omen for his crossing. [76.2] He declared that he admired the river for refusing to betray its people, but declared that the Argives were not going to get off so lightly. So he turned around and marched his army down to Thyrea, where he sacrificed a bull to the sea, embarked his troops and sailed them to Nauplia, in the territory of Tiryns.

[77.1] When they got news of this, the Argives hurried to the coast in defence of their territory. Once they reached the district known as Sepeia, near Tiryns, they pitched camp not very far from the Lakedaimonians. At this point the Argives had no fear of a pitched battle, but were worried about falling into a trap. [77.2] The reason for this was that there had been an oracle, given by the Delphic priestess jointly to themselves and the Milesians, which went as follows:
> But when the female overcomes the male
> And drives him out, winning great glory among the Argives,
> That shall be the beginning of cheek-mangling grief for Argive women.
> So, some day, shall a man of the future times declare that
> The dread thrice-coiled serpent is destroyed, tamed by the spear.

[77.3] The Argives were alarmed by the coincidence of all these events. Their best solution seemed to be to make use of the enemy trumpeters and match the orders they issued. So whenever the Spartiate trumpeter sounded an order to their troops, the Argives did exactly the same. [78.1] Once Kleomenes realised that the Argives were matching exactly the orders issued by his own trumpeters, his sent out an instruction to his army that when the trumpeters sounded the call for dinner, they should in fact pick up their weapons again and charge the Argives. [78.2] It turned out exactly as he had ordered. They fell upon the Argives while they were preparing their meal as per the trumpeters' instructions, slaughtered many of them, and drove an even greater number of them to flee to the sacred grove of Argos, where they surrounded them and kept them tightly guarded. …

… [83] Argos, however, suffered such a shortage of manpower that their slaves actually took charge of administration, holding the chief offices and managing its affairs until the children of their dead soldiers came of age.

[Herodotus, *Histories* 6.76–78 and 83]

E18   Argive losses at Sepeia
The Argives sent heralds to Delphi to ask the god what was the best thing for them to do. The reason for sending for advice was that sixty thousand of them had recently been killed by Kleomenes, son of Anaxandridas.

[Herodotus, *Histories* 7. 148.2]

Hdt. is discussing how individual Greek states decided whether to fight the Persians in 480 or to submit.

E19   Kleomenes on trial, *c.* 493 BC
On his return, Kleomenes' enemies haled him before the ephors, alleging that he had taken bribes not to capture Argos, even though he could easily have done so.

[Herodotus, *Histories* 6.82.1]

E20   Demaratos and Kleomenes intrigue against each other, 491 BC
[61.1] At this time Kleomenes was in Aigina working in the general interests of all Greece, but Demaratos continued to spread malicious gossip about him, not out of any affection for the people of Aigina, but out of sheer jealousy and spite. So when Kleomenes got home from Aigina he started looking for ways to deprive Demaratos of his right to the kingship. He soon found the following way to weaken his position: When Ariston was king in Sparta he had no children, despite the fact that he had married twice. [61.2] He refused to acknowledge that he might himself be the reason, and therefore married for the third time.
(story of Ariston's third marriage omitted here ...)
[63.1] And that is how Ariston came to dispose of his second wife and married his third; and before the usual nine months were complete she gave birth to Demaratos, as a premature baby. [63.2] One of his servants brought the news to Ariston that the child was born, when he was actually presiding in the state chair in formal session with the ephors. But he was well aware of the date of his marriage and worked out on his fingers the number of months that had elapsed since then. He swore loudly and exclaimed, "It can't be mine." The ephors heard this statement, but for the time being took no action. As the boy grew up Ariston had a change of heart and regretted his original words, because he was convinced that Demaratos was indeed his son. [63.3] The origin of the name Demaratos is worth recording. Sometime previously all the Spartiate citizens prayed publicly that a male heir should be born to Ariston, because he was greatly admired as the best of all the kings of Sparta. Demaratos means, 'The People's Prayer', and that is how he got his name.

[64.1] As time went by, Ariston died and Demaratos became king. Inevitably, however, it seems that the story was bound to come out and put an end to the reign of Demaratos. He had twice given offence to Kleomenes, first of all when he pulled his army out of the battle at Eleusis, and the second time when Kleomenes had led an expedition against the pro-Persian party on Aigina.

[65.1] Kleomenes was determined now to get his own back against Demaratos. So he made an agreement with Agis' grandson, Leotychidas, the son of Menares, to the effect that if he supported him in his bid to replace Demaratos as king, Leotychidas would support him in return in his campaign against the Aiginetans. [65.2] Leotychidas hated Demaratos and the main cause of the feud was as follows: Leotychidas had been engaged to marry Perkalos, the daughter of Chilon, who was himself the son of Demarmenos. But by a bit of sharp practice Demaratos had carried her off and married her himself. [65.3] That was the origin of Demaratos' hatred for Leotychidas, and now on the instigation of Kleomenes he denounced Demaratos on oath, swearing that he was not the legitimate king of the Lakedaimonians, since he was not the child of Ariston. After that he prosecuted him, and in evidence he repeated the story of the words spoken by Ariston when his servant had reported to him that he had had a son. He reminded the court of how he had calculated the months, sworn loudly, and declared that the child was not his. [65.4] On the basis of this account Leotychidas sought to prove that Demaratos could not be the son of Ariston, and consequently could not be the legitimate king of Sparta either. He introduced as witnesses those ephors who had been present on that occasion and had heard the words spoken by Ariston.

[66.1] The upshot of all this was that there was violent disagreement about the rival claims, and the Lakedaimonians decided to consult the Delphic oracle on the question of whether Demaratos was or was not the son of Ariston. [66.2] The decision to refer to the oracle was primarily due to the cunning of Kleomenes, who then suborned one of the most influential citizens of Delphi, Kobon, the son of Aristophantos, into persuading Perialla, the Pythian priestess, to give the reply which Kleomenes wanted. [66.3] So in answer to the question posed by the ambassadors she declared that Demaratos was not the son of Ariston. Later, when all this came to light, Kobon was exiled from Delphi while Perialla, the priestess, was dismissed from her office.

[Herodotus, *Histories* 6.61 and 63–66]

Aigina, the island opposite Athens' harbour was independent, prosperous and strategically vital. It had submitted to Darius in 492 BC, prompting Kleomenes to intervene. Demaratos' secret opposition (Hdt. 6.49–51) causes Hdt. to digress on the origins of the dual kingship and the privileges of the kings (6.52 = **D2** and 6.56–9 = **D5, D8, D10**) before again picking up the events of 492 at the start of this passage.

E21 Kleomenes acts to secure Aigina for the Greek interest, before 491 BC

[1] As for Kleomenes, following the success of his scheme against Demaratos, he immediately led an expedition against the Aiginetans, with Leotychidas in support. He still had a bitter grudge against them for the way they had blackened his reputation [2] With both the kings ranged against them, the Aiginetans decided that there was no point in any further resistance. So the Lakedaimonians seized their ten richest and most aristocratic citizens including Krios, the son of Polykritos, and Kasambos, the son of Aristokrates, their two most powerful of all. These they transported to Attika and left them as hostages in the custody of the Athenians, who were the Aiginetans' bitterest enemies.

[Herodotus, *Histories* 6.73]

E22 Kleomenes' madness and death, *c.* 490 BC

[74.1] After this, when Kleomenes' plots against Demaratos became generally known, through fear of Spartiate retribution he lost his nerve and escaped to Thessaly. From there he moved on to Arkadia and began to foment trouble, trying to incite the Arkadians to attack Sparta by getting them to swear an oath to follow him wherever he might lead them.

[75.1] When they heard what Kleomenes had been up to, the Lakedaimonians became alarmed and recalled him and restored him to the same powers as he had originally enjoyed. He had always had a somewhat unstable personality, but almost as soon as he had returned home, some sort of mental illness overcame him, and he began poking every Spartiate that he came across in the face with his sceptre. [2] Once he started behaving like this and was clearly mad, his relatives put him in the stocks. Finding himself under restraint like this and realising that he had been left alone with just one guard, he asked him for a knife. The guard at first refused, but Kleomenes threatened him with dire consequences once he was released and this terrified the guard, who was only a helot. [3] Once he had got hold of the knife, Kleomenes began to mutilate himself, starting with his shins and then cutting strips of flesh along the length of his body from shins to thighs, and from thighs to hips and flanks, until finally he reached his stomach and cut it into strips, till he died.

[Herodotus, *Histories* 6.74.1 and 75]

Accusations of treachery as well as madness and suicide may have been invented by Kleomenes' opponents to justify his imprisonment or even assassination (Osborne, *Greece in the Making* 336 and Griffiths 'Was Kleomenes Mad?' in Powell, *Classical Sparta* (1989).

E23   Leotychidas on trial, *c.* 490 BC

On learning of the death of Kleomenes, the Aiginetans sent envoys to Sparta to denounce Leotychidas for keeping their hostages detained in Athens. The Lakedaimonians convened a legal enquiry and decided that the Aiginetans had indeed been outrageously treated by Leotychidas. They voted to surrender him to the Aiginetans in return for the hostages still detained in Athens.

[Herodotus, *Histories* 6.85.1]

PAUSANIAS: E24–E27
Pausanias was the grandson of King Anaxandridas. After the deaths in 480 of his uncle Leonidas and his father, Kleombrotos, he became regent to his cousin, along with, it seems, the military privileges of a king. His generalship was successful at Plataia (**E84–E86** and Hdt. 9.46–64 – 'Pausanias won the finest victory of any that we know') and elsewhere (Thuc. 1.94 = **H20**), but his arrogance was disastrous for Sparta and evidenced by all the sources (Hdt. 8.3 = **E27**; Thuc. 1.95 and 1.130–4 = **E25, E26**; Plut. *Kimon* 6, *Aristides* 23) and by his own words (**B6, B7**).

E24   Pausanias as regent

[1] The ephors immediately took his advice to heart, and without telling the messengers who had come from the cities anything, dispatched by night 5,000 Spartiates, each with seven helots in attendance, and with Pausanias, the son of Kleombrotos, entrusted with command. [2] Leadership now belonged to Pleistarchos the son of Leonidas. But he was still a boy and Pausanias was his guardian and cousin. Pausanias' father, Kleombrotos son of Anaxandridas was no longer alive, having died a short time after bringing the army back from building the wall at the Isthmos. ... [3] Pausanias chose Euryanax son of Dorieus a man from his own family as his second-in-command.

[Herodotus, *Histories* 9.10]

The advice, given by Chileus of Tegea 'who had the greatest influence of any *xenos* in Lakedaimon' (Hdt. 9.9.1) was that the Spartans risked having the Athenians go over to the Persians if they were not more proactive in trying to drive the Persian army under Mardonius out of Greece in 479 BC. For Anaxandridas and Kleombrotos, see **E8**.

E25   Pausanias' behaviour leads Sparta to lose naval hegemony, *c.* 478 BC

[1] Already however the other Greeks were aggrieved at his bullying, especially the Ionians and those who had recently been freed from the King. Constantly approaching the Athenians, they asked them to lead them on account of their shared origins and not to leave them at Pausanias' mercy if he should use force. [2] The Athenians accepted these requests and turned their attention to not ignoring them and to making changes as seemed best to them. [3] Meanwhile the Lakedaimonians recalled Pausanias to investigate what they had heard. Many crimes were indeed alleged by the Greeks who came, and his command seemed a close approximation to tyranny. [4] It also happened that he was recalled at the same time that the allies, except for those from the Peloponnese, switched over to the Athenians because of their hatred for him. [5] On his arrival at Lakedaimon, Pausanias was convicted of personal offences against individuals, but absolved of blame on the most serious charges, the most important of which was collaboration with the Persians, which seemed to have been very blatant. [6] The Lakedaimonians did not send him out again in command, but sent Dorkis and a few others in his place with a small force. But the allies would no longer accept their command. [7] When they realised this, they returned home, and the Lakedaimonians no longer sent out anyone else, fearing that those who went out there became corrupted, as they saw had happened to Pausanias; wishing to disengage from war with Persia; and thinking that the Athenians were quite capable of leadership and well-disposed to them at the present time.

[Thucydides, *History of the Peloponnesian War* 1.95]

E26   The regent Pausanias' behaviour offends Sparta, *c.* 478–469

[130.1] Up until this time Pausanias had been held in high regard by the Greeks because of his leadership at the battle of Platatia. But from that point on he gave himself more and more airs and graces and was no longer able to live in the usual style, but wore Persian dress as he went out of Byzantium, had a Persian and Egyptian bodyguard as he marched through Thrace, had his table served in the Persian way, and could not conceal his intentions but showed his great ambitions for the future in little deeds. [130.2] He made himself difficult to approach and displayed so violent a temper to all alike that no one could go near him. That in particular is why the alliance switched to the Athenians.

[131.1] The Lakedaimonians had first recalled him for this very reason, but then he sailed out for a second time on a ship from Hermione without their authority, and seemed to be acting in the same way; and when he had been besieged and forced out of Byzantium by the Athenians, he refused to return to Sparta and instead set himself up at Kolonai in the Troad. There he was reported to them as having dealings with the Persians and spending time there with ulterior motives. The ephors could tolerate this no longer, but sent a messenger and a written command that if he did not stay with the messenger the Lakedaimonians would declare war on him. [131.2] Pausanias wished to behave as unsuspiciously as possible, trusting in his money to escape the accusation, and so returned to Sparta for the second time. At first he was thrown into prison by the ephors (the ephors are allowed to do this to a king), but later he managed to get let out and offered himself for trial to be questioned on these matters by anyone who wished to.

[132.1] The Spartiates had no clear evidence, nor did his enemies, nor the city as a whole which they could rely on sufficiently to punish a man from the king's family, and who was the acting king (for he was first cousin and guardian to Pleistarchos, son of Leonidas, who was king but a minor). [132.2] But, by breaking rules of behaviour and imitating foreign ways, he had given considerable grounds for the suspicion that he did not think his present position was good enough. They also examined other cases of how he had changed from his normal way of life, for example when, on a previous occasion, he had thought it appropriate to have inscribed on the tripod which the Greeks had dedicated at Delphi as a sacred offering from the Persians, the following poem:

> The Greek leader, when he destroyed the Persian army,
> Pausanias, dedicated this memorial to Phoibos.

[132.3] The Lakedaimonians immediately erased this poem from the tripod, re-inscribed the names of all the states which together brought down the Persians and put it back up. Even then this seemed to be very wrong on Pausanias' part, and now when the situation had reached the current point, it seemed to provide an exact parallel for his current behaviour. [132.4] In addition they learnt that he was having dealings with some helots, as was in fact the case: he was promising them freedom and citizenship if they joined in his uprising and helped him carry it out. [132.5] But neither immediately, nor when some helots informed on him, did they believe it or think that they should take any action against him, adopting their usual policy towards their own people of being slow to make any irreversible decision about a Spartiate without incontrovertible proof. Finally, it is said that a man from Argilos, who was about to take Pausanias' most recent letter to Artabazos, and who had been Pausanias' favourite and was most trusted by him, turned informer. He had become fearful after noticing that none of the messengers sent before him had returned; so, having made a copy of the seal so as not to be found out if he was mistaken in his thought or if Pausanias were to ask to change what he had written, he opened the letter and found in it just what he had expected there would be – written instructions that he should be killed.

[133] It was only when he showed the letter that the ephors were more convinced, but still wished to hear in person some admission from Pausanias' lips. The man went to Tainaron as a suppliant as part of a plan and made himself a double hut with a partition behind which he concealed some ephors. When Pausanias came and asked him the reason for his supplication, they got to know the full story: the man asked about what had been written about him and exposed other details one by one, that he had never in his errands to the king put him at risk, yet had been marked out for death just like most of the go-betweens. Pausanias accepted all that he said but asked him not to be angry at the current situation, but pledged that he could safely leave the temple and told him to make the journey as quickly as possible and not to delay the negotiations.

[134.1] The ephors then went away after hearing exactly and now knowing for certain what had happened, and they made to arrest him in the city. The story is that when he was about to be arrested in the street, he realised why they were coming, from seeing the expression of one of the approaching ephors, while another, out of loyalty to him revealed their mission by an imperceptible nod of the head. He ran towards the temple of the goddess of the Bronze House, whose precinct was nearby, and took refuge there. He went into a small building within the sacred area so as not to have to endure being out in the open, and lay low. [134.2] They initially were too late in their pursuit but then removed the roof of the building, kept a watch on him inside the doors, and walled him up, trapped inside; then they besieged him and starved him out. [134.3] When he was on the point of expiring just where he was, inside the building, they noticed and carried him out of the sacred area, still breathing, though he died as soon as he was taken out. [134.4] They intended to throw him into the Kaiadas, but then they decided to dig a grave somewhere nearby. Later the god at Delphi gave an oracle that his tomb should be moved to where he died (and it now lies just at the front of the precinct as writing on the *stelai* shows); that what they had done had brought a curse; and that they should give two bodies to the goddess of the Bronze House in return for the one. So they made and dedicated two bronze statues for Pausanias.

[Thucydides, *History of the Peloponnesian War* 1.130–134]

Kaiadas: a pit for condemned criminals.

E27 Athens takes away Spartan naval hegemony

Once they had driven out the Persians and were then taking the contest to Persia, the Athenians took the hegemony from the Lakedaimonians, using Pausanias' *hubris* as an excuse.

[Herodotus, *Histories* 8.3.2]

Herodotus' point here is that the Athenians had only yielded naval command in the Second Persian War to Eurybiadas (see **E116**) to prevent disunity and in the interests of Greece.

E28 Debate in the *gerousia* and assembly about naval hegemony, 475 BC

[1] When Dromokleides was archon at Athens, the Romans elected Marcus Fabius and Gnaeus Manlius as consuls [475 BC]. In the same year, the Lakedaimonians were angry at having thrown away their hegemony at sea. And so they blamed the Greeks who had switched from their side and threatened appropriate action against them. [2] A meeting of the *gerousia* was held at which they discussed war against the Athenians over the hegemony at sea. [3] Similarly, when a meeting of the general assembly was held, the younger men and most of the others were very keen to recover the hegemony, thinking that if they could do so, they would benefit from great wealth; that Sparta generally would become greater and stronger; and that private households would achieve a significant increase in prosperity. … [5] As almost all the citizens were very much in favour of this proposal, and the *gerousia* was meeting to consider it, no one expected anyone to dare to suggest any alternative. [6] But one of the members of the *gerousia*, named Hetoimaridas, a descendant of Herakles, who was well thought of by his fellow citizens for his character, took it upon himself to suggest that they allow the Athenians to maintain the hegemony, since it would not be in Sparta's interests to fight over the sea. He managed to make good points to support his surprising proposal and unexpectedly won over the *gerousia* and the people.

[Diodoros, *Library of History* 11.50]

DEBATE IN SPARTA ON THE PELOPONNESIAN WAR: E29–E31
The debate in Sparta in 432 BC on whether the Athenians had broken the Thirty Years' Peace (Thuc. 1.67 = **E140**) prompts the first great set-piece debate in Thucydides' history, unique in giving four speeches. He presents a speech by the Corinthians urging their Spartan allies to go to war (1.68–71 = **E141**), a reply by Athenian ambassadors who happened to be present on other business (1.72–78) and then the debate within the Spartan assembly (below, **E29** and **E30**). For excellent introduction and commentary see Hornblower, *Commentary* vol. I, 107–132.

E29 Speech of King Archidamos at the debate in Sparta, 432 BC

[79.1] Once the Lakedaimonians had heard the complaints of their allies against the Athenians and the Athenian response, they ordered all non-Lakedaimonians present to withdraw and proceeded to hold their own debate about the current state of affairs. [79.2] There was broad agreement amongst those present that the Athenians had already acted illegally and that war should be declared as soon as possible. But at this point their own king, Archidamos, who had a great reputation for wisdom and moderation, came forward and made a speech.

[80.1] "My fellow Lakedaimonians," he said, "I personally have had long experience of many wars and I see many of my own contemporaries here among you. I doubt if any of them will share what seems to be the general enthusiasm for an undertaking which has little to commend it and carries high risks. [80.2] Anyone who thinks seriously about it will realise that in a war such as you are now debating the stakes are of the very highest. [80.3] When we go to war with neighbouring cities or our fellow Peloponnesians, our resources are broadly equivalent, and we can choose our opponents and strike quickly. But the Athenians live at a distance; their seamanship is superb and in all other respects their resources are formidable; their private and public finances are enormous; they have ships, cavalry, weaponry, and manpower beyond that of any other single Greek state; and in addition they have many allies whose taxes add to their revenues. There is no way in which we can go to war with them expecting an easy victory. What gives us the confidence to go rushing into war without the most careful preparation? [80.4] Our navy? We are outnumbered, and it will take time to build up its numbers and train the crews. What about financial reserves? Here the situation is much worse still. There is nothing in the state treasury, and individuals will prove reluctant contributors.

[81.1] "Perhaps some of you have great faith in our army and its superiority in weaponry and size. We can simply invade them and devastate their lands. [81.2] But the Athenians control plenty of land beyond the borders of Attika, which will enable them to supply all they need by sea. [81.3] Even if we try to persuade their allies to revolt, we shall require ships to support them with, since the majority are islanders. [81.4] What then will be our strategy for fighting a war like this? If we cannot win at sea nor deprive them of the resources with which they maintain their navy, we shall be the ones that will suffer. [81.5] We will not be able to settle with them on honourable terms, especially if we are the ones that look like the aggressors. [81.6] Let us not deceive ourselves by imagining that the war will quickly come to an end if we ravage their territory. Rather, I fear, we shall leave this war as a legacy to our children. Those Athenians are a proud people; they are not going to be tied to their land, like helots, and they have enough experience of warfare to be willing to face it unafraid.

[82.1] "Nevertheless, I am not suggesting that we should cheerfully allow them to harm our allies or ignore the fact that they are plotting against us. I am proposing that we do not yet take up arms; but that we should send an embassy to them and set out the basis of our grievances, without openly threatening hostilities or suggesting that we are going to roll over and let them walk all over us. Meanwhile, let us strengthen our own resources by winning over allies among both Greeks and foreigners, anywhere in fact where we can add to our naval and financial resources. Given that we are the targets of Athenian plots, we can hardly be criticised for seeking our own survival by winning over Greeks and foreigners alike to our alliance. At the same time, we need to put our own house in order. [82.2] If diplomacy succeeds and they listen to our representations, all well and good. If not, after two or three years we shall be much better equipped to attack them, if that seems the right thing to do. [82.3] And when they see us sending out the same message in our preparations as in our diplomacy, perhaps they will give way, when they count their present blessings – their land as yet un-ravaged and their resources as yet undiminished. [82.4] Look at their land as a kind of hostage – the better it is cared for the more valuable it is. We should spare it for as long as we can and avoid making them less amenable to persuasion by driving them to desperation. [82.5] If we are carried away by the complaints of our allies and ravage their lands with first making proper preparations, there is a real danger that we will inflict much greater shame and misfortune upon the Peloponnese. [82.6] As for such complaints, whether from cities or individuals, settlements can always be arranged by negotiation. But when such individual complaints give rise to a united declaration of war, there is no knowing how things will turn out and an honourable settlement becomes extremely difficult.

[83.1] "Don't let anyone try to tell you that it is cowardice for us to hesitate to attack a single city when there are so many of us. [83.2] Their allies match ours in numbers – and they pay taxes as well. And war is not just a question of weapons, but also of the money which supplies effective weaponry, especially when a land power is challenging a maritime one. [83.3] So let us get the money right first, before we get carried away by the speeches of our allies. After all, whatever the outcome, good or bad, we are the ones that will get the most of the blame or credit. So let as take our time to calmly assess the possible outcomes. [84.1] Most people criticise us for being slow and cautious – well, there is nothing in that to be ashamed of. More haste at the beginning makes for less speed at the end when preparations are inadequate. Ours is a city whose fame and freedom are universally admired. [84.2] This can best be seen as a mark of intelligence and self-control. We are the only ones who manage to avoid arrogance in prosperity or defeatism in the face of misfortune. We are not moved by delight at the flattery of those who urge us to take risks against our better judgement, any more than we will give way through shame at the critical abuse of who seek to spur us into action. [84.3] Thanks to our well-ordered society, we are good warriors and sound policy makers. As warriors, our code of honour depends above all upon our capacity for self-control; our courage upon our sense of shame. As policy makers, our education system (*paideuomenoi*) teaches us not to think ourselves too clever to respect our laws, while severe discipline gives us the self-control to avoid disobeying them. We avoid being too clever by half to the point of uselessness – such as, for example, producing an admirable verbal criticism of our enemy's strategy while proving ourselves incapable of matching action to words. Rather we learn to think that our neighbours' character is pretty well the same as our own and that words are no guide to the operations of blind chance. [84.4] Our preparations are based on the realities and assume that our enemies are not fools; we find grounds for optimism in the quality of our own precautionary preparation, rather than any expectation that our enemy will make mistakes. People are pretty well the same the world over; those who succeed are those whose education (*paideuetai*) has been the most demanding.

[85.1] "That is certainly the sort of training which our ancestors have handed down to us. Having enjoyed such benefits from it, let us preserve it and not casually throw it away. Let us not be pressurised into some sort of hasty debate over the space of a single day, when such vital issues are at stake – our lives, finances, cities, and our glorious past. Let us take our time. We can afford to do so, because far more than others we have the strength. [85.2] Send an embassy to the Athenians to raise the issue of Poteidaia and the complaints of unfair treatment from our allies. This has got to be the right course, since they have agreed to submit to arbitration, and when someone makes such an offer it is wrong to attack him as if he has done you wrong. But at the same time, prepare for war. This is the best decision you can make and the one that is most likely to alarm your enemies."

That was the speech of Archidamos.

[Thucydides, *History of the Peloponnesian War* 1.79–85]

As with all speeches given by ancient historians, this is at best an approximation of Archidamos' real speech – in Thucydides' famous formulation, 'my method has been to make each speaker say roughly what I think was required in the situation, while keeping as closely as possible to the overall sense of what was actually said' (2.22.1). Here he will have had the added difficulty that this speech was given in a 'closed session' of the assembly, with only Spartans present (79.1), and it is hard to imagine him having the chance to ask about the debate before his exile from Athens in 424. Even when he did, he came up against 'the secret nature of their political arrangements' (**D83**). Nonetheless the crucial point as regards Spartan institutions is that the king, a member of the *gerousia* and future commander-in-chief of the campaign comes forward to put his view. Though based on long experience and his reputation, it is a view, not a command nor state policy – and, of course, it is rejected by popular vote.

E30 Speech of the ephor Sthenelaïdas at the debate in Sparta, 432 BC

The final speaker was Sthenelaïdas, one of the ephors for the year. His speech was as follows:

[86.1] "I don't understand all these long-winded speeches by the Athenians. They have plenty to say about their own merits, but have made no attempt to rebut the charge that they have behaved disgracefully towards our allies and the people of the Peloponnese. And yet, if in the past they proved themselves such heroes against the Persians, but are now showing such hostility toward us, then they deserve to be punished twice over for turning from heroism to illegality. [2] We, by contrast, have been models of consistency, both against the Persians and now. If we have got any sense at all, we shall not look away when our allies are victims of aggression, nor play for time instead of going to their aid; they are already now suffering severely. [3] Others may have rich resources in money, ships and cavalry; but we have loyal allies and we must not betray them to the Athenians. This is not something to be settled by law-suits and fine speeches; fine speeches are not what are damaging us; we must seek redress at once and with all the forces at our command. [4] Don't try to tell me that the best thing to do when we are under attack is to form a committee to discuss the matter; that is something which those planning aggression should do, thinking long and hard before acting. [5] So now, cast your votes for war, fellow Lakedaimonians, and be worthy of Sparta. Don't let the Athenians expand their empire. Don't betray your allies. Rather, with the gods' help, let us go out and fight the aggressors."

[Thucydides, *History of the Peloponnesian War* 1.85.3–86]

Nothing else is known about Sthenelaïdas. The start of his speech refers to a speech made by some Athenian ambassadors who happened to be in Sparta, and reported by Thuc. 1.73–78.

E31   Vote in the Spartan assembly on declaring war, 432 BC

[1] After this speech, in his capacity as presiding ephor, he put the question to the vote in the assembly of the Lakedaimonians. [2] Lakedaimonians take decisions by acclamation rather than casting votes, and he pretended that he could not tell from their shouts which side of the debate had won. In reality, he wanted them to make their vote clearly and unequivocally, and thus to inspire them to action. So he made the following announcement: "Lakedaimonians, those of you who think that the treaties have been broken and that the Athenians are at fault, kindly stand over there" – and he pointed to the appropriate area – "and those of you who disagree, stand over there on the other side." [3] The two sides separated and there was a large majority for those who thought the treaties had been broken. [4] They then recalled their allies to the assembly and told them that the decision had been taken that the Athenians were the aggressors, but that they wanted to put the decision to the vote in the presence of their whole alliance, so that the decision for war, if such it proved to be, would be unanimous. [5] After that the allies returned home having achieved their objective, while the Athenian delegation did likewise, once they had cleared up all the business on their agenda.

[Thucydides, *History of the Peloponnesian War* 1.87 (continued in **H37**)]

This passage is valuable for telling us the normal procedure of the Spartan assembly (compare **D13**, **D15** on elections to *gerousia* etc.) and how it was altered for this occasion, as would certainly have been remembered by Thucydides' informants. The division may have been intended to bring moral pressure on the undecided to go along with the majority and be seen supporting the brave and patriotic choice, especially as the single most charismatic and authoritative Spartan (Archidamos) was against the motion.

E32   List of eponymous ephors, 431–404

Lysander gave all these things back to the Lakedaimonians at the end of the summer in which twenty-eight years and six months of war came to an end. During this time the ephors who gave their names to the years were as follows, first Ainesias in whose time of office the war began, then, after him, the following: Brasidas, Isanor, Sostratidas, Exarchos, Agesistratos, Angenidas, Onomakles, Zeuxippos, Pityas, Pleistolas, Kleinomachos, Ilarchos, Leon, Chairilas, Patesiadas, Kleosthenes, Lykarios, Eperatos, Onomantios, Alexippidas, Misgolaidas, Isias, Arakos, Euarchippos, Pantakles, Pityas, Archytas, Eudios.

[Xenophon, *Hellenika* 2.3.9–10]

Although it is thought that this list was added later to the texts of Xenophon, there is no reason to doubt the list, since where names are known from Thuc, they match on all five occasions.

BRASIDAS: E33–E40

Brasidas is one of the most prominent Spartan commanders in Thucydides' account. The historian knew him as a military opponent, failing to defend Amphipolis from his attack in 424. In his resulting exile, it seems very likely that he met Brasidas and thus that Thuc. was well informed about Brasidas' operations. **E34** is Thucydides' first mention of Brasidas and his language suggests some official Spartan award, but no such system is known. What is known (Xen. *Hell.* 2.3.10 = **E32**) is that Brasidas was ephor for 431/0 (entering office in Sept 431) suggesting that his exploits that summer may have prompted his election as ephor. He is mentioned as a naval adviser (in 429 and 427 Thuc. 2.85, 3.69), and as one of the Spartan leaders in 429 (Thuc. 2.93). At Pylos in 425 he commanded a trireme (Thuc. 4.11–12 = **E88**) with conspicuous courage. He led an expeditionary force to northern Greece in 424 (Thuc. 4.78–88, 4.102–116, 4.120–129) winning over a number of Athens' allied city states. These included Skione where he was 'crowned with a golden crown as the liberator of Greece' and treated like a winning athlete; and Amphipolis which he captured from Thucydides. He was clearly a very able and popular general, 'not a bad speaker for a Spartan' (Thuc. 4.84.2: litotes, but from a very Athenian perspective – a very good speaker *for a Spartan*). But the comments on the jealousy of the Spartan leaders (**E37**) suggest that the Spartan system found it difficult to harness his talents, although **E36** suggests that he was carrying out approved Spartan policy. He was killed leading a daring and successful improvised attack on an Athenian force near Amphipolis in 422 (**E38**). For an assessment of Brasidas, see Hornblower, *Commentary* vol. II, 38–61.

E33   Brasidas compared to Achilles

For what Achilles was like, one could compare Brasidas or others.

[Plato, *Symposium* 221c]

Plato is actually making the point that no one can compare with Socrates. But in a dialogue carefully set in the Athens of 416 BC it is suggestive of Brasidas' great reputation six years after his death and in Plato's own day (*c.* 429–347 BC), that he could be compared to the greatest Greek hero.

E34   Introduction of Brasidas

Brasidas the son of Tellis, a Spartiate, happened to be in these parts in charge of a garrison. When he perceived what was happening he went to help those in that area with one hundred hoplites. Charging straight through the Athenian force which was scattered across the countryside or concentrating on the wall, he burst into Methone, and though he lost a few of his men in his attack he saved the town, and for his act of daring became the first to be decorated in Sparta in the war.

[Thucydides, *History of the Peloponnesian War* 2.25.2 (431 BC)]

Methone/Mothone was a perioikic town just on the extreme south-west corner of Messenia (see Map 4).

E35   Praise for Brasidas I

[1] The Lakedaimonians dispatched Brasidas who was very keen to be sent, as were the Chalkidians. He was thought of in Sparta as a man who would always get things done and since being sent out had proved a great asset to the Lakedaimonians. [2] He immediately came across to the cities as fair and moderate and he caused many to switch sides, and gained other places which were betrayed to him. The result was that the Lakedaimonians were able to bargain from a position of strength about the exchange or return of places (as indeed they did) and that the impact of war was reduced on the Peloponnesian side. Even later, after the war in Sicily, the integrity and intelligence Brasidas showed then, seen at first hand by some, by others known from report, created great goodwill towards the Lakedaimonians amongst Athens' allies. [3] For he was the first man sent out, and as he seemed good in all respects, he created a clear expectation that all the others would be like him.

[Thucydides, *History of the Peloponnesian War* 4.81 (424 BC)]

E36   Brasidas makes offers guaranteed by the Spartan authorities

[4.86.1] "I myself have not come here to harm you, but for the liberation of Greece, having bound the Lakedaimonian authorities by the strongest oaths that any people whom I bring over to be allies will be autonomous." ... [4.88.1] (The Akanthians) made him commit to the oaths which the Lakedaimonian authorities had sworn to in sending him out, that any peoples he brought over would be autonomous allies, and with this guarantee, admitted his army.

[Thucydides, *History of the Peloponnesian War* 4.86.1, 4.88.1 (424 BC)]

E37   Praise for Brasidas II

[2] Brasidas was conducting himself with moderation in other actions, and in his speeches everywhere he declared that he had been sent to free Greece. [3] When the cities that were subject to Athens learnt about the capture of Amphipolis, the qualities he had shown and his gentleness, they became most eager to revolt, and they sent messages to him in secret, urging him to visit them and hoping that they would be the first to change sides. [4] They showed no awareness of the danger, deceiving themselves that the extent of Athenian power was not as great as it was later shown to be. They judged things by vague hopes rather than realistic assessment, since all men naturally apply unrealistic hopes to what they desire, but cut through what they do not want to admit with arbitrary reasoning. [5] At the same time the recent defeat of the Athenians by the Boiotians, and Brasidas' statements – attractive though untrue – that the Athenians had been unwilling at Nisaia to fight against the small force under his command, encouraged them and made them believe that no army would ever come against them. [6] But the biggest factor in making them ready to take any risk was the excitement they had at the present moment and the thought that they would experience real Lakedaimonians for the first time. Realising this, the Athenians sent garrisons to the cities as best they could at short notice and in the winter, while Brasidas sent orders to Lakedaimon asking for a force to be sent out and that he be allowed to prepare to build triremes at Strymon. [7] The Lakedaimonians did not agree to this, partly because of the jealousy felt by their leaders, partly because they wished rather to recover the men from the island and to end the war.

[Thucydides, *History of the Peloponnesian War* 4.108 (424/3 BC)]

E38   Brasidas' public funeral and hero worship at Amphipolis, 422 BC

After this they gave Brasidas a public funeral in the city in front of where the *agora* now is, and all the allies marched behind his body in full armour. Since then the Amphipolitans, after setting up a precinct around his tombstone, have performed sacrifices for him as a hero, have given games in his honour and annual offerings, and have dedicated the colony to him as its founder, knocking down the buildings in honour of Hagnon and removing any traces of monuments that might survive of his founding of the colony. They considered Brasidas to have been their saviour and for the moment played up their alliance with the Lakedaimonians in fear of the Athenians. But Hagnon they thought less useful to them and less pleasant to hold in honour, given their hostility to the Athenians.

[Thucydides, *History of the Peloponnesian War* 5.11.1 (422 BC)]

Hagnon, an Athenian, had founded Amphipolis (see Map 1) only 15 years before, in 437 BC.

E39 **Pleistoanax favours peace**

But when the Athenians had also suffered the defeat at Amphipolis and Kleon had died and Brasidas too, who were those on both sides most opposed to peace (the latter because of his good fortune and the honour he got from war, the former becasuse he thought that in a time of quiet his wrongdoing would be more manifest and his slanders would be less believed) then those most eager for leadership on both sides, Pleistoanax, son of Pausanias, king of the Lakedaimonians and Nikias son of Nikeratos, who at the time had the greatest reputation for generalship, grew more keen on peace.

[Thucydides, *History of the Peloponnesian War* 5.16]

E40 **Chance of peace after the deaths of those who ground down Greece, 421**

(In Aristophanes' Peace, War, living on a Mount Olympos vacated by the gods in disgust at the Greeks' behaviour, is making himself a meal by mashing together various Greek states. He has just sent his servant, Uproar, to borrow a pestle from Athens further to grind down the Greeks. They are watched by Trygaios, representing an ordinary Athenian.)

UPROAR:	Hey!
WAR:	What is it? Haven't you got it?
UPROAR:	The bad news is,
	He's dead, the Athenians' grinder,
	The leather-seller who wrecked Greece. 270
TRYGAIOS:	(*aside*) Hooray! Your Majesty, Queen Athena, he did well
	Dying just when the city wanted him.
WAR:	Well go and get another one from Lakedaimon then.
UPROAR:	Yes, sir.
WAR:	And come back quickly. 275
	(*276–9 Trygaios asks the audience to pray that Uproar doesn't make it back*)
UPROAR:	Alack, alas! Woe is me and yet more woe! 280
WAR:	What is it? Have you still not got it?
UPROAR:	No! It's gone –
	The Lakedaimonians' grinder has been lost too.
WAR:	How, you miserable wretch?
UPROAR:	Up over in Thrace,
	They lent it to some other folk and lost it.
TRYGAIOS:	Well done, well done indeed, Dioskouroi! 285
	Perhaps all may be well: courage, men!
WAR:	(*to Uproar*) Get all this stuff and take it back inside.
	I'll go in and make a pestle myself. *(Exit)* 288
TRYGAIOS:	(*289–291: Trygaios rejoices, quoting poetry obscure to us*)
	Now's our great chance, men of Greece, 292
	To get rid of all these troubles and fights,
	And to drag out Peace, whom we all love,
	Before some other pestle stops us! 295

[Aristophanes, *Peace* 267–295 (performed 421 BC)]

This contemporary comedy agrees with Thucydides (**E39**) in seeing Kleon and Brasidas as the chief war-mongers on each side. The Athenian audience would immediately have identified Kleon as the 'leather-seller' (line 270; an allusion frequently made by Aristophanes to his slave-produced family wealth). Brasidas campaigned in Thrace from 424 BC, being killed there in 422 (see **E38**).

E41   Powers of King Agis, 413/2 BC

Agis was persuaded to hold off from Euboia, but to assist the Lesbians in their revolt. He appointed as their harmost Alkamenes, who had been about to sail to Euboia; the Boiotians promised ten ships and Agis another ten. [3] He did all this independently of the Lakedaimonian state. For Agis, as long as he was at Dekeleia with his own army, had full powers to dispatch an expedition wherever he wished, to levy an army, and to raise money. And for that whole time, one could say that the allies were subject to him rather than to the Lakedaimonian state, since he had his own army and was powerful wherever he was.

[Thucydides, *History of the Peloponnesian War* 8.5.2–3]

King Agis II, (confusingly of the Eurypontid, not the Agiad house) reigned *c.* 427–400. His success at Mantineia in 418 BC, (Thuc. 5.65–5.75 = **E100–E104**) restored his reputation after criticism for his handling of an expedition against Argos earlier in the year (Thuc. 5.59–60, 63, 65 = **E97–E98, E100**); for some of his reported sayings, **F32**; for his death see **E45**.

E42   *xenia* between Alkibiades and Endios, ephor 412

The Lakedaimonians were much more in favour of the proposals of Tissaphernes and the Chians, since Alkibiades was working with them. He had strong ties of ancestral guest-friendship (*xenia*) with Endios who was serving as ephor, and it was a result of this *xenia* that his family had a Lakonian name, since Endios' father was called Alkibiades.

[Thucydides, *History of the Peloponnesian War* 8.6.3]

In 412, the Spartans had rival proposals for an alliance with Persian forces against Athens: one came jointly the Chians and from Tissaphernes (satrap of Asia Minor – for his motives see **E150**); the other from Pharnabazos (satrap of Phrygia). This passage is interesting for the workings of *xenia* in Greek politics. The Spartans accept the Chian alliance, after sending a perioikic spy to Chios (**E55**).

E43   King Pausanias sympathises with the democrats at Peiraieus, 403 BC

[28] Both the thirty at Eleusis and those on the list (of the Three Thousand) in Athens sent ambassadors to Lakedaimon to ask for help because the democrats had revolted from the Lakedaimonians. Lysander reckoned that the people at Peiraieus could quickly be forced to surrender by a siege by land and sea if their supplies were cut off, and arranged for the oligarchs to have loan of one hundred talents, for himself to be sent out as harmost by land and for his brother to command the navy. [29] He himself went out to Eleusis and brought together a large group of hoplites from the Peloponnese. The navarch guarded the sea so that no one could sail in with supplies. Therefore those in Peiraieus were once again quickly in trouble, while those in Athens were again confident with Lysander on their side. While this was going on, King Pausanias, being jealous that Lysander in effecting this bloackade would increase his reputation and would make Athens his own, got the support of three of the ephors and held a levy. [30] All the allies followed him, except the Boiotians and Corinthians.

[Some skirmishes take place including those resulting in the death of the Lakedaimonians buried in Athens (B25)]

[35] Pausanias put up a trophy and then retreated. Even as things had turned out he was not angry with them but sent a secret message to give instructions to the party in Peiraieus as to what should be said by the ambassadors sent to him and to the ephors with him: they did so. He also caused a split within the party in Athens and told them that as many people should gather and approach him to say that they had no wish to make war on the party in Peiraieus, but rather to make an agreement with them and that both should be friends with the Lakedaimonians. [36] Naukleidas, one of the ephors, was also happy to hear this. For it is customary for two of the ephors to go on campaign with the king, and he was then present together with one other, and both of them were with Pausanias' strategy rather than Lysander's. Therefore they were very keen to send the messengers from Peiraieus to make a treaty with the Lakedaimonians, along with two men from the party in the city, Kephisphon and Meletos who were acting as individuals. [37] When, however, they were on their way to Lakedaimon, the party in the city also sent a delegation to act on their behalf, and to say that they were making unconditional surrender of the walls they held and of their own persons; and they said that they thought that the Peiraieus party, if they claimed to be friends of the Lakedaimonians, should surrender Peiraieus and Mounychia too. [38] When the ephors and the assembly had heard all these embassies, they despatched fifteen men to Athens and instructed them to negotiate with Pausanias as to what seemed best.

[Xenophon, *Hellenika* 2.4.28–30 and 35–38]

E44   Narrow acquittal of King Pausanias in 403 BC
When Pausanias returned from Athens after fighting a pointless battle, his enemies put him on trial. In the case of the king of the Lakedaimonians, the court that sat consisted of the twenty-eight so-called elders and the ruling ephors, along with the king of the other house. Fourteen of the elders together with Agis (II), the king of the other house, decided that Pausanias was guilty, but the rest of the court voted for acquittal.

[Pausanias, *Description of Greece* 3.5.2]

The context of the trial was the rival views on how to treat the defeated Athens and the influence of Lysander. See **E43** and **E144**, and, for the trial itself, Cartledge, *Agesilaos* 134–5.

AGESILAOS: E45– E50
The case of Agesilaos (reigned 400–360 BC) above all shows how a king could use extra-constitutional means to break the theoretical limits to royal power. He did this by creating over his long reign a network of friendship and patronage at home, and ties of *xenia* abroad. For more details on the methods of patronage practised by Agesilaos see Cartledge, *Agesilaos and the Crisis of Sparta,* London 1987, 143–159, followed by Hodkinson, *PWCS* 348–50 and 361–5. We are dependent for our information on Agesilaos on Xenophon who campaigned with him in Asia and in Greece, and was exiled from Athens for fighting on Agesilaos' side against fellow Greeks at Koroneia in 394 BC. Agesilaos is prominent in Xenophon's *Hellenika*, and was also the subject of a separate, posthumous, encomium, *Agesilaos.* Plutarch's *Life* is derived from these (see e.g. **E46, E47**). For a full-length modern study see Cartledge, *Agesilaos.*

E45   The succession of Agesilaos, 400 BC
[1] After this Agis went to Delphi and offered to the appointed spoils to the god. On his way back, he fell sick at Heraia, being now an old man, and although he was still alive when they brought him home to Lakedaimon, he died shortly after. He received

a burial more splendid than belongs to man. When the required days of mourning had been observed and it was necessary to appoint a king, Leotychidas, who claimed to be a son of Agis, and Agesilaos, a brother of Agis, competed for the kingship.

[Xenophon, *Hellenika* 3.3.1]

E46   Xenophon on the paradox of Agesilaos' great power
He behaved towards his country in such a way that by obeying it in every respect [he gained the greatest power], and being eager to help his companions he created friends who would do anything for him.

[Xenophon, *Agesilaos* 6.4]

E47   Plutarch explains the paradox of Agesilaos' power
What Xenophon says – that by obeying his country in every respect he gained the greatest power, so that he could do whatever he liked – can be explained as follows: The ephors and the elders had the greatest power at that time under the constitution. The former rule for just a one-off year, the elders hold their office for life, both groups being appointed so that the kings should not be absolute rulers, as I have written regarding Lysander. By tradition, right from very start, the kings have continued to adopt a quarrelsome and contrary attitude to them. [3] But Agesilaos went the other route, stopping fighting and clashing with them; he courted them, beginning everything he did with them. If he was summoned, he rushed there at a pace quicker than a march; whenever he happened to be seated on the throne, doing official business, he would stand up when the ephors came in; whenever someone was appointed to the *gerousia*, he would send him a cloak and an ox as a mark of respect. [4] As a result while appearing to respect and increase the status of their office, no one noticed that he was increasing his own power and adding to the king's position a greatness which was given out of goodwill towards him personally.

[Plutarch, *Agesilaos* 6.4]

E48   Agesilaos' various 'networks'
His relations described him as "a devoted family man"; his close associates as "someone who would do anything for you"; by those who served him as "not someone who would forget people"; by the oppressed as "a champion"; by companions on the battlefield "their saviour, second only to the gods".

[Xenophon, *Agesilaos* 11.13]

We can discern some of the reality beyond Xenophon's admiration for the man he had fought for, and who almost certainly granted him his Spartan estate. Agesilaos appointed his brother-in-law Peisander as navarch in 394 (Xen. *Hell.* 3.4.29) and was exceptionally generous to his mother's relations in giving them half the property he inherited from King Agis, 'because he saw that they were in poverty' (Xen. *Agesilaos* 4.5). His close associates will have included important men from Agesilaos' own social class of political and military importance (see **E50** for the assumption that a group in the *gerousia* would vote with him). Those who served him probably were ordinary citizens: there seems to have been considerable scope by this time for wealthy Spartans to exert patronage by providing their mess contributions – in return their 'clients' would have served him by voting for his policies and candidates in the assembly. Such may be the basis for his generosity (**E49** below and Xen. *Ages.* 4.1 'many acknowledged receiving many benefits from him').

E49   Agesilaos' generosity

In spending his money he was not merely fair but generous, thinking that all that being just requires is not taking money from others whereas being generous means providing benefits to others from one's own wealth.

[Xenophon, *Agesilaos* 11.8]

E50   The Sphodrias affair, 378 BC

[Sphodrias, harmost of Thespiai was bribed by Thebans to invade Attika and provoke a war. Through incompetence he managed merely to provoke a diplomatic incident (5.4.20–23)].

[24] The ephors summoned Sphodrias to face capital charges. He, however, refused, fearing the result, but despite this refusal to face trial, he was acquitted – a verdict which many regard as the most unjust ever reached in Lakedaimon. The reason was as follows: [25] Sphodrias' son, Kleonymos, was of an age just past being a boy (*pais*), and was the best-looking and most highly regarded of his peers. Archidamos, the son of Agesilaos, happened to be in love with him. … [26] Therefore Sphodrias said to Kleonymos, "You, my son, could save your father, by begging Archidamos to get Agesilaos on my side at my trial." Kleonymos, when he heard this, plucked up the courage to approach Archidamos to beg him, for his sake, to save his father.

[(5.4.27–31) Archidamos in turn eventually approaches his father, the first time unsuccessfully and then a second time …]

[31] "I know it is the case, father, that if Sphodrias had done nothing wrong, you would have had him acquitted: as it is, if he has done something wrong, let him receive your pardon, for our sakes." Agesilaos replied, "Well then, if we can do it honourably, it shall be done." Archidamos went away without much hope when he heard this answer. [32] One of Sphodrias' friends, when talking to Etymokles, said, "I imagine that all you friends of Agesilaos are going to put Sphrodrias to death." Etymokles replied, "By Zeus, that would mean our acting differently from Agesilaos who tells everyone he talks to that it's impossible that Sphrodrias is not guilty, but that when someone has done absolutely everything right as boy (*pais*), late-teenager (*paidikos*) and young man (*hebon*), it is hard to put him to death. For Sparta has need of such men in her army." [33] He told Kleonymos what he had heard, and Kleonymos was delighted and went to say to Achidamos, "We know that you are looking after us: you can rest assured that we shall try to ensure that you are never ashamed of our friendship."

[Xenophon, *Hellenika* 5.4.24–26 and 31–33]

Trials on capital charges were heard before the *gerousia* – see **D12–D15**. In 382 Agesilaos had defended the unofficial actions of Phoibidas (**H59, H60**), probably saving him from being condemned to death and paying his fine. In this case, Sphodrias expected Agesilaos to be against him. The influence of Agesilaos was clearly very considerable – the story constantly takes it for granted that there is a grouping 'friends of Agesilaos' who will vote with him. By this date any members elected to the *gerousia* before Agesilaos' accession (400 BC) were either dead or at least 82. The reasoning 'Sparta has need of such soldiers' is suggestive of *oliganthropia* (**D28–D29**). **Boy, teenager and young man**: Agesilaos/Xenophon uses the terms used of pupils at the three stages of a Spartan education – *pais, paidikos, hebon*, as Xen. *Constitution* 2–4 = **D74, D77, D79**). He here admits (compare **D74**) that Archidamos was the pederastic lover (*erastes*) of the young Kleonymos. For the episode see Cartledge, *Agesilaos* 136–8 and 156–8.

SPARTAN SOCIETY IN PRACTICE: E51–E69

Texts providing generalisations about Spartan Society, as well as introductory material are in Section **D** (**D24–D45**). This section gives texts which show particular historical episodes casting light on how Spartan society worked in practice. For ructions in early Spartan society resulting in the foundation of Tarentum, see **H5–H6**. The arrangement here follows the pattern of section **D** in working down the social hierarchy, though naturally some texts deal with several groups within society.

E51   Separate Spartan burials of the dead at Plataia

[1] When the Greeks had assigned the plunder at Plataia, they each buried their dead separately. The Lakedaimonians made three tombs: in one they buried the priests, including Poseidonios, Amompharetos, Philokyon and Kallikrates. [2] So the priests were in one of the tombs, the other Spartiates were in another, and the helots in the third.

[Herodotus, *Histories* 9.85.1–2]

Some Herodotus manuscripts have the word *ireas* (priests), but others have *(e)irenas* which would mean that the *eirens* ('young men') received a separate burial. 'Priests' is probably the right reading, and given above. Confirmation of subtly different demarcations of status within burial seems to be confirmed by the tomb of the Spartans in Athens' *Kerameikos,* see **B25**.

E52   Sphakteria: Helots freed, but Spartiates deprived of citizenship

[1] That same summer, the soldiers who had gone out with Brasidas had already returned home from Thrace, having been brought back by Klearidas under the terms of the treaty. The Lakedaimonians passed a decree declaring that the helots who had fought with Brasidas should be set free and allowed to live wherever they liked. Soon afterwards they settled them with other *neodamodeis* in Lepreon, which lies on the borders of Lakonia and Elis, with which they were already at loggerheads. [2] As for their soldiers from the island <of Sphakteria> who had surrendered their weapons and been taken prisoner, they feared that they might be plotting a revolution because they expected to be punished in some way for the disaster and lose their citizenship. So they deprived them of their citizenship, even though some of them already held high positions, a penalty which meant that they were unable to hold any office or pursue any commercial activity such as buying and selling. In due course, however, they were reinstated.

[Thucydides, *History of the Peloponnesian War* 5.34 (421 BC)]

E53a   The Kinadon Conspiracy I (*c.* 399 BC): how to topple Spartan society

Within five days of the end of the sacrifice, someone reported a conspiracy to the ephors and that the leader of it was Kinadon. [5] He was young in appearance and strong in spirit, but not one of the equals (*homoioi*). When the ephors asked how he said the plan would be carried out, the informant said that Kinadon had taken him to the edge of the agora and told him to count how many Spartiates were in the *agora*. "And I," he said, "counted the king, the ephors, the members of the *gerousia*, and about forty others, and asked 'Why did you tell me to count them, Kinadon?' He said, 'Imagine that these are your enemies, and all the others are your allies – more than four thousand of them in the *agora*.'" And he said that as they met people in the streets he had pointed out one man here and two there as their enemies and all the rest as their allies; and out of all those who happened to be on the estates of the Spartiates, one enemy – the owner, but many allies on each estate.

[6] The ephors asked how many Kinadon said knew about the matter, he said that Kinadon said that amongst his group and amongst the leaders, those in the know were reliable but not very many; but what they said was that they knew on behalf of all, helots and *neodamodeis*, and the *hypomeiones* ('men of lesser status'), and the *periokoi*. For amongst them, whenever a word was said about Spartiates, no one could hide the fact that they would gladly eat them even raw.

[7] When the ephors asked, "Where did they say they would get the weapons from?", the informer claimed that Kinadon said, "Those of us in the army obviously have our own weapons," and that as for the masses, he led him to iron-works and showed him many knives, many swords, many skewers, many axes and hatchets, many sickles. And he said that Kinadon said that all those things that men use to work on the land, on timber, and in quarries, were similarly weapons, and that most other trades had tools that would serve as weapons, especially against unarmed opponents. When he was further asked at what time this would happen he said that he had been told not to go away.

[Xenophon, *Hellenika* 3.3.4–7]

E53b   The Kinadon Conspiracy II (*c.* 399 BC): how the authorities reacted
[8] When they heard this, the ephors thought that the plots he described had been carefully laid and were very worried; they did not summon the so-called 'little assembly' but instead, summoning one of the elders here and another one there, they decided to dispatch Kinadon to Aulon with some other revolutionaries and to bring back some of the inhabitants of Aulon and some helots whose names were written on the coded message. They also ordered him to bring back a woman, said to be the most beautiful there who seemed to be corrupting the Lakedaimonians who went there whether young or old.

[9] Kinadon had previously done other such jobs for the ephors. And on this occasion they gave the coded message to him on which were written the names of the people to be arrested. He asked which young men he should take with him. They replied, "Go and tell the most senior of the kings' bodyguards (*hippagretai*) to send with you six or seven of those who happen to be around." But they had taken care that the *hippagretai* knew whom to send, and that those being sent knew that Kinadon should be arrested. They also told Kinadon that they would send three carts so that they would not need to bring back the prisoners on foot, concealing, as far as they could that they were sending for one man – Kinadon.

[10] They did not arrest him in the city because they did not know how widespread the conspiracy was and they wished to hear first from Kinadon who his accomplices were before they were aware that information had been laid against them, so that they did not run away. Those arresting him intended to detain Kinadon, learn from him the names of the conspirators, and send them in writing to the ephors as soon as possible. The ephors took the matter so seriously that they even sent a whole division (*mora*) of cavalry with them to Aulon.

[11] When Kinadon had been taken, a cavalryman brought the names of those he had denounced, and the ephors immediately arrested Tisamenos the seer and the most prominent of the others. Kinadon was brought back and questioned. He admitted everything and named the conspirators. Finally they asked him what his aim had been in doing this. He answered "To be no one's inferior in Lakedaimon." After this his hands were bound, his neck put in a halter and he and those with him were led round the city being flogged and tortured. And so they met their punishment.

[Xenophon, *Hellenika* 3.3.8–11]

Xenophon mentions *hypomeiones* (people of 'lesser status') at 3.3.6, and strongly implies that this was the status of Kinadon himself (3.3.11 – 'to be no one's inferior'), but this is the only use of the term. They were presumably descendants of *homoioi* who had lost their status: this might be through poverty (and being unable to contribute to the *syssitia*); through failure to complete their training or be elected to a mess; or for being convicted of misconduct. At the same time some helots were given freedom and certain rights as *neodamodeis*, although they did not attain full citizen status. This measure may have been introduced to slow the decline of Spartiate numbers, especially in the army. We should remember that within the account Kinadon has every reason to exaggerate the discrepancy in numbers on each side (*gerousia* (30) + 5 ephors + 40 against 4,000), the extent to which the various 'intermediate' classes of *hypomeiones*, *neodamodeis, perioikoi* would identify with helots rather than Spartiates and even the extent of helot hatred for the Spartiates. After all the Spartan state managed to remain stable until 370/69 BC, and in the end it was a major invasion by Thebans and Peloponnesians, rather than a revolution, which brought about change. But it is crucial to understand that even in the city of Sparta the Spartiates were probably a small minority, although we rarely, if ever, hear of the lives and activities of all those other inhabitants. Cartledge, *SL* 267–270 gives a fuller analysis of Xenophon's account and the wider questions it raises.

E54   'Inferiors' form the cavalry

… But as regards the Lakedaimonians, at that time their cavalry were an absolute disgrace. [11] This was because it was the very richest who bred the horses, but it was only when the call-up was announced that the man enlisted arrived to collect his horse and whatever weapons were given him and take the field at once. In addition the troops on horses were the most incapable physically and the least ambitious.

[Xenophon, *Hellenika* 6.4.10–11 (371 BC)]

Cartledge, *SL* 268–9 interprets this description of the mounted troops as being those who had failed the *agoge*. Christesen's new interpretation of the Damonon inscription (see **C83**) shows that the Spartans tried consciously to improve their cavalry – albeit without long-term success.

PERIOIKOI: E55–E59

For introduction to the *perioikoi*, including discussion of some of the texts below, see pages 105–6. *Perioikoi* also helped at Sphakteria – **E87**.

E55   A *perioikos* used as a spy, 421 BC

Nevertheless the Lakedaimonians first sent a man called Phrynis, a *perioikos,* to Chios as a spy to see if they had as many ships as they said and if the city had sufficient other resources for what had been planned.

[Thucydides, *History of the Peloponnesian War* 8.6.4]

The use of a *perioikos* may have been for better secrecy, though the eventual alliance also results in another *perioikos* being put in charge of Spartan ships (and men) – **E56**. They are the only two *perioikoi* named in Thucydides.

E56   A *perioikos* in command of ships, 412 BC

Eualas, a Spartiate, commanded the army; Deiniadas, a *perioikos*, the ships.

[Thucydides, *History of the Peloponnesian War* 8.22.1]

Deiniadas (perhaps from Gytheion) commanded 13 ships, part of the force sent to help Chios foment revolts against Athens (**E42** and **E55**).

E57   Agesipolis' expedition to Olynthos, 381 BC

Having decided on this course of action, they sent out King Agesipolis as leader and with him went thirty Spartiates just as with Agesilaos in Asia. [9] Many of the better sort of *perioikoi* volunteered to go with him, as did foreigners known as 'the trained' and illegitimate children of Spartiates – a fine-looking group well acquainted with the ideals of the city.

[Xenophon, *Hellenika* 5.3.8–9]

E58   Agesilaos returns from expedition to Arkadia, 370 BC

Once in Lakonia, he sent the Spartiates home and released the *perioikoi* to their own towns (*poleis*).

[Xenophon, *Hellenika* 6.5.21]

E59   *Periokoi* revolt, 370 BC

Some of the *perioikoi* were there, appealing to the Thebans and insisting that they would revolt if they would only make an appearance in the countryside. They said that the *perioikoi* had just been summoned by the Spartiates but were unwilling to help them.

[Xenophon, *Hellenika* 6.5.25]

HELOTS: E60–E69

For introduction to the helots, see pages 106–8 and 111, and on the helot system and general treatment of helots, see **D32–D44**. In addition to the texts below, showing how they were treated on specific occasions, see **E92** (Pylos & Sphakteria); **E52, E99, E101, E131, F21** when they are used in battle; **E22** for use as a guard. For potential helot revolts, see **E26, E53**.

E60   A Messenian Revolt in 491/0?

When the Athenians sent ambassadors everywhere to seek help, no one was willing, except the Lakedaimonians. But they were hindered by the war that was then taking place against the Messenians and maybe by something else – we cannot say – and they arrived just one day after the battle of Marathon.

[Plato, *Laws* 1.698DE]

Besides this statement of Plato, which is clear, but written 100 years later, there are various other scraps of evidence (set out by Cartledge, *SL* 132–3) supporting a revolt or war around this time, which though Herodotus does not mention it, could make better sense of their refusal to help the Athenians immediately.

E61   Helots collect plunder after battle of Plataia, 479 BC

[9.80.1] Pausanias made an order that none of the plunder should be touched, but ordered the helots to collect the valuable items. They dispersed throughout the camp and found tents furnished with gold and silver, couches plated with gold and silver, golden mixing-bowls, plates and other drinking vessels … [9.80.3] The helots stole many items which they sold to the Aiginetans, but produced many treasures which they could not hide. This was the start of the great wealth of the Aiginetans who bought the gold from the helots as if it was really the bronze the helots thought. [9.81.1] When the valuables had been collected, a tenth part was removed for the god at Delphi, from which the golden tripod was set up which stands on the three-headed snake next to the altar …

[Herodotus, *Histories* 9.80.1 and 9.80.3 – 9.81.1]

For the three-headed snake (the Serpent Column), see **B5**.

EARTHQUAKE AND HELOT REVOLT, 465/4 – ?455 BC: E62–E67

This episode, vital for Sparta's internal and external relations is tied by Thucydides (**E62**) to the revolt of Thasos, which can be placed in 465/4 BC (for the nexus of dates, see Hornblower, *Commentary* vol I 154). Diodoros' dating (**E63**) is actually 469 BC, while Plutarch's text (**E64**) says 'in the fourteenth year of Archidamos' 456/5 BC, so is to be emended to 'fourth' = 466/5. Both Thuc. 1.103.1 (**E62**) and Diod. 11.64.4 say the revolt lasted 10 years. Modern scholars doubt whether Sparta could have fought a major battle at Tanagra in 458 BC if the helot revolt was still going on, and suggest that the figures in the text are wrong. For discussion of the revolt, see Cartledge, *SL* 186–191.

E62   Thucydides' account of earthquake and helot revolt

[101.1] The people of Thasos were now under siege, having been defeated in battle by the Athenians. So they appealed to the Lakedaimonians to help them by launching an invasion of Attika. [101.2] Unknown to the Athenians, they secretly made a promise to do so. Preparations were well in hand, but they were interrupted by an earthquake, which occurred at about the same time and led to a revolt by the helots. (The majority of the helots were descendants of the original indigenous population of Messenia, who had been enslaved by the Lakedaimonians. Thus they were all known as Messenians). Together with the neighbouring *perioikoi* of Thouria and Aithaia, they seceded to Mount Ithome. *[101.3 – the people of Thasos, with no prospect of Spartan help, surrender to Athens.]*

[102.1] The Lakedaimonians soon found that their war against the helots on Ithome was becoming protracted and appealed for help to their allies, including the Athenians. The Athenians went to their aid with a substantial force, led by Kimon. [102.2] The Lakedaimonians had asked for their assistance because the Athenians had particular expertise in siege warfare, at which the long duration of their own siege operations had shown the Lakedaimonians to be clearly deficient. Otherwise they would have succeeded in taking the place by storm. [102.3] It was as a result of this campaign that a breach between the Athenians and Lakedaimonians first became apparent. Finding that they could not take the place by storm, the Lakedaimonians became alarmed by the daring originality of Athenian tactics; once they also came to recognise that the Athenians' political outlook was very different from their own, they began to fear that they might develop sympathies with the helots on Ithome and even change sides.

So they sent them home – the only allies treated in this way. They gave no hint of their suspicions, but simply stated that they had no further need of them. [102.4] The Athenians realised that they had not been dismissed for any such respectable reason and that somehow they had become suspect. They were deeply offended and felt that they should not have been treated in this way by the Lakedaimonians. Once they returned home, they immediately abrogated their existing anti-Persian alliance with them and made a treaty of alliance with their enemies, the Argives; both of them then jointly established an alliance with the Thessalians on identical terms.

[103.1] The helots, now in the tenth year of the siege of Mount Ithome, found themselves unable to hold out any longer. So they made peace with the Lakedaimonians on the following terms: they were to leave the Peloponnese under safe conduct and never again set foot in it. Anyone caught so doing would become the slave of anyone that captured him. [103.2] There had also been an earlier oracle from the Pythia at Delphi to the Lakedaimonians instructing them "to release the suppliant of Zeus of Ithome." [103.3] So the helots, along with their wives and children, left Ithome for exile, but were given a warm welcome by the Athenians because of the ill-feeling there that now existed towards the Lakedaimonians. They settled them in the town of Naupaktos, which they now held, having recently captured it from the Ozolian Lokrians.

[Thucydides, *History of the Peloponnesian War* 1.101–3]

This passage comes from Thucydides' *'pentekontaetia'* ('fifty-year period') in which he describes how Sparta and Athens went from being allies against the Persians to fight the Peloponnesian War. Thuc. gives more attention to this event than to many in the period, but naturally concentrates on Sparta and Athens. That many or most other Greek states seem to have sent help is suggested by other passages in Thuc. – Aigina 2.28.2, Plataia 3.54.5 (**E65**).

E62b   Previous Spartan impiety as cause of the earthquake

For once when some helots had sought refuge at Poseidon's temple [at Tainaron], the Lakedaimonians had granted them safe conduct, only to lead them away to be killed. They think that this was what brought the great earthquake at Sparta upon them.

[Thucydides, *History of the Peloponnesian War* 1.128.1]

At the start of the Peloponnesian War both sides tried to make political and diplomatic capital by bringing up previous acts of impiety. The particular episode can only be dated by the assumption that memories of it were strong in 465/4 BC.

E63   Diodoros' account of earthquake and helot revolt

[1] When Phaion was archon in Athens, at Rome Lucius Furius Mediolanus and Marcus Manilius Vaso received the consulship. This year a great and incredible disaster befell the Lakedaimonians. There were great earthquakes in Sparta resulting in houses falling down completely and more than twenty thousand Lakedaimonians died. [2] Since the city was being brought down and houses were falling continually for a long period, many people were caught and killed by the collapse of walls, and the earthquake caused no little destruction of household property. [3] They suffered this disaster because of some god as it were wreaking vengeance on them, but other dangers befell them by human agency for the following reasons. [4] The helots and Messenians who were hostile to the Lakedaimonians had kept quiet up until then, in

fear of the superior power of Sparta: but when they saw that the majority of them had been killed in the earthquake, they felt contempt for the survivors who were few in number. Therefore they made an agreement with one another and joined a common war against the Lakedaimonians. [5] The king of the Lakedaimonians, Archidamos, by his own foresight saved the citizens both in the earthquake and in the war in which he bravely resisted the attackers. [6] For when the city was in the grip of the terrible earthquake, he was the first Spartiate to seize all his armour and rush from the city to the countryside, calling on the other citizens to do the same.

[Diodoros, *Library of History* 11.63.1–6]

E64   Plutarch's account of earthquake and helot revolt
[4] In the fourth year in which Archidamos son of Zeuxidamos was king in Sparta, the land of the Lakedaimonians was split by many chasms by the largest earthquake ever known. Mount Taygetos was shaken so that many peaks broke away, and the entire city was devastated, except for five houses – the earthquake threw down all the rest. [5] It is said that just before the earthquake, the ephebes and the young men (*neaniskoi*) were exercising under the colonnade when a hare appeared. The young men ran out to chase it for fun, while the ephebes stayed behind in the gymnasium which collapsed, killing them all together. Their tomb is still called 'The Earthquake Tomb'. [6] Archidamos quickly understood from the immediate danger the one that would follow, and when he saw the citizens attempting to save their most valued possessions from their houses, ordered the trumpet signal for the attack of an enemy to be given, so that they would gather round him under arms. At that critical time, this alone saved Sparta, since the helots rushed together from all over the countryside to despatch those Spartiates who had survived. [7] But when they found them in arms, they withdrew to their towns and waged open war, persuading quite a few *perioikoi* to do so, and being joined in their attack on the Spartiates by the Messenians.

[Plutarch, *Life of Kimon* 16.4–7 (continued in **G1**)]

E65   Plataian help in the helot revolt
"For you in particular, Lakedaimonians, at the time when the greatest anxiety befell Sparta, after the earthquake, when the helots revolted at Ithome, we sent one third of our men to your assistance. This should not be forgotten."

[Thucydides, *History of the Peloponnesian War* 3.54.5 (427 BC)]

Part of the speech of the Plataians (very longstanding allies of Athens) given them by Thuc. when they are effectively put on trial for their lives by the Spartans after the capture of their city in 427 BC.

E66   Veteran of Plataia killed at Stenykleros in Messenian revolt, after 464 BC
Mardonius was killed by Arimnestos, a man of great reputation in Sparta, who after the Persian Wars, fought a battle with three hundred men at Stenykleros in the war against all the Messenians, leading to his own death and those of his three hundred men.

[Herodotus, *Histories* 9.64]

E67   Lysistrata on Athenian help for Sparta in the Helot Revolt, *c.* 462 BC

LYSISTRATA: Men of Lakonia, I turn to you next;
                You know, of course, when once Lakonian Perikleidas
                Came here and sat at our altars as a suppliant of
                The Athenians, deathly pale in his scarlet cloak,   1140
                Begging for an army? You were hard pressed then
                By the Messenians and the god's earthquake at the same time.
                And Kimon went with four thousand hoplites
                And saved the whole of Lakedaimon.
                That was the treatment you received then from Athens,   1145
                And do you now devastate a land that treated you well?

[Aristophanes, *Lysistrata* 1137–1146 (performed 411 BC)]

Aristophanes adds some details to Thucydides' account, and is in turn supplememented by Plut. (**G1**). Perikleidas was clearly chosen by Sparta as being pro-Athenian, or even an official *proxenos*: his own name suggests a link with the Athenian statesman, Perikles; and he named his son (a signatory to a treaty of 423 – Thuc. 4.119.1) 'Athenaios', just as Kimon's son was 'Lakedaimonios' (Thuc. 1.45.2). Aristophanes' figure of 4,000 hoplites, would be half the Athenian force which fought at Plataia.

For Messenian dedication of spears from Spartan and Athenian spoils, see B9

E68   Helot massacre

[1] With the Athenians putting a lot of pressure on the area, in particular on their own territory, the Lakedaimonians hoped that by sending an army north in support of Athens' allies they would cause the same sort of difficulties for her as they themselves were suffering, and that this would divert their war effort away from the Peloponnese. A key factor in their calculation was the willingness of those allies to provide supplies for their army and the fact that they were seeking support for a planned revolt. [2] They also welcomed an opportunity to send some of their helot population out of the country, in case the current situation and the capture of Pylos might encourage them to plot revolution. [3] They were also motivated by the helots' youthful vigour and their large population, since as far as the Lakedaimonians were concerned, considerations of security *were always paramount in matters regarding the helots* [or] *against the helots were always paramount.* They issued a proclamation commanding them to choose from their own number those who claimed to have the most outstanding military records. It sounded as if they were going to give them their freedom; in fact it was a test which they thought would enable them to identify those whose strong personalities would encourage them to be the first to claim their freedom. These, they thought, would also be the first to turn against them. [4] They selected about 2,000 of them, put garlands on their heads, and marched them around the shrines as if it was part of their freedom ceremonial. After that they were never seen again and no one knows how each of them was done away with. On this occasion too they were willing enough to send out about 700 of them as hoplites with Brasidas, though the rest of his army were mercenaries recruited from the Peloponnese.

[Thucydides, *History of the Peloponnesian War* 4.80]

Note that Thucydides leaves the helot massacre undated: though presented within the context of Pylos, the massacre of 2,000 is a different occasion from enlisting 700 as hoplites, and is introduced by Thucydides as another example of defence against the helots being paramount, but there is no indication of its date (see Hornblower, *Commentary* vol II page 266). It is also hard to imagine how one could kill so many helots without a trace. For the difficulty of determining exactly what Thucydides meant in the passage asterisked, see **D39**.

E69 Helots help the Spartans in 370 BC

[28] As for the citizens, the women, who had never seen an enemy, could not even endure the sight of the smoke. The Spartiates, living in a city without walls, were posted at intervals, one here, another there, and so kept guard – although they were what they appeared to be, very few in number. The authorities also passed a decree announcing to the helots that whoever wished to take up arms and join the ranks, they should be given a solemn pledge of freedom in return for their assistance in the war. [29] More than six thousand helots, it is said, enrolled themselves. This aroused a new fear, as when they were marshalled together, their number was considered excessive. However when it was learnt that the mercenaries from Orchomenos remained loyal and that the Lakedaimonians received reinforcements from Phleious, Corinth, Epidauros, Pellene and some other states, the Spartiates were less afraid of those who had been enlisted.

[Xenophon, *Hellenika* 6.5.28–9]

For Sparta's disastrous defeat at Leuktra in 371 BC, see **E106–E112**. Despite the Spartan rally and the fact that many helots and periokic communities probably remained loyal, Epaminondas could surely have captured Sparta. Instead he inflicted terminal damage on Sparta by turning instead to Messenia, where he was able to give lasting force to the helot revolt which followed Leuktra by supervising the refounding of their city. No direct mention of this major event is recorded by Xenophon who presumably could not bear to narrate this disaster for Spartans, just as the Spartans themselves stubbornly refused to recognise Messene as independent (see **H74**).

E70 Xenophon's criticism of contemporary Sparta (*c.* 380 BC)

[1] If someone were to ask me whether I think that Lykourgos' laws remain unchanged to this day, I have to confess in all honesty that I could not say so with any confidence. [2] I do know that in earlier times the Lakedaimonians chose to stay at home, living together as a community of modest means rather than ruling as governors in other Greek cities and being corrupted by the flattery of their subjects. [3] I know, too, that in former days they were frightened to be caught in possession of gold; whereas nowadays some of them are even happy to make a display of their wealth. [4] I know that for this very reason in the olden days they used to expel immigrants and made it illegal for their own citizens to live abroad, so as to discourage idleness through excessive exposure to foreign influences. Yet I am all too well aware that nowadays their so-called "leading citizens" desire nothing more than to live out their days as the governors of foreign communities. [5] There was a time when the summit of ambition was to be a worthy leader. Now they will do anything to become a leader, rather than strive to be worthy of the office. [6] This is why in the good old days the Greek cities used to come to Lakedaimon and beg them to take the lead against those they saw as having wronged them. But now many of them beg one another instead to take the lead in preventing Lakedaimonians ever becoming their leaders again. [8] But none of these criticisms is at all surprising, since it is all too clear that modern Lakedaimonians obey the laws of neither the gods nor Lykourgos.

[Xenophon, *Constitution of the Lakedaimonians* 14 (continued in **D9**)]

Xenophon provides a major source of our information on the institutions of classical Sparta. His *Constitution of the Lakedaimonians* gives a consistently admiring standpoint, with the solitary exception of this 'notoriously problematic chapter' (Cartledge *SL* 258). It must surely represent Xenophon's disillusionment with Sparta after the catastrophic defeat at Leuktra in 371 BC, but it is not clear whether it was added after the rest of the *Constitution* and the question is complicated by its position in the manuscript as the penultimate chapter, rather than final chapter it should have been.

SPARTAN PROPERTY AND WEALTH: E71–E76

For all the strictures on Spartan property and wealth seen in **D52–D59**, it is clear that great wealth existed in Sparta in all periods. In addition to the sources below, see the evidence for Spartan success in equestrian events (**C50–C58**) and the Damonon inscription (**C83**). Some sources below argue Sparta's failure was a result of the influx of wealth after her victory in the Peloponnesian War, but a far more likely explanation is Sparta's diminishing manpower (**D28–D29**).

For more on this topic, see work by Stephen Hodkinson, culminating in *Property and Wealth in Classical Sparta* (Classical Press of Wales, 2000). He has concluded "that Sparta's public institutions and austere lifestyle in operation during the classical period were—on the long view—a temporary imposition upon a more enduring privately-oriented, wealth-based society. Already by the later fifth century Sparta was being transformed back into a plutocratic society, as she had previously been before the 'sixth-century revolution'". (Hodkinson, NSW notes 2000, ch. 13).

E71   Bronze figure of a reclining banqueter

[BM 1954,1018.1]

Bronze figure of a reclining banqueter from the tripod-support of a bronze bowl. The smiling banqueter is shown reclining on a couch, his left hand holding a shallow dish, his right resting on his raised right knee. 10.16 cm in length. Probably made in Lakonia, *c.* 530–500 BC, and thought to have been found at the Sanctuary of Zeus at Dodona. It need not, of course, show any individual diner, let alone a Spartiate one, since it could equally well have been made for external consumption.

E72   Sparta's wealth

For if you wish to look at the riches of the Lakedaimonians, you would realise that they leave those here far behind. For they have all their own land and also that of Messenia; nor would there be any comparison with theirs in terms of size or quality; nor even in ownership of slaves of other sorts but especially helots; nor of horses or other farm animals which have pasture throughout Messenia. But even if put all this to one side, there is not in all Greece as much gold and silver as in private hands in Lakedaimon: this is because for many generations now it has been coming in there from all the

Greeks, and frequently from foreigners too, but it does not go out anywhere. Instead, just as in Aesop's fable, when the vixen told the lion that the footprints clearly pointed in one direction, so it is with coinage going into Lakedaimon, but no one is able to see it coming out to anywhere else. Therefore one must know that in gold and silver, the people there are the richest of the Greeks, and the king the richest of them, since the greatest and highest amounts received are for the kings, and additionally, the tax paid by the Lakedaimonians as tribute to the king is not small.

[Plato, *Alcibiades* 1.122d–123b]

The dramatic date of this dialogue is *c.* 433 BC.

E73   Xouthias inscription

To Xouthias, son of Philachaios, two hundred *mnai*. If he comes in person, let him take them. If he is dead, they are his sons', once they have been young men (*hebontes*) for five years. If he has no family left, they belong to those judged to own them: the Tegeans are to judge according to the law.

To Xouthias, son of Philachaios, four hundred *mnai* of silver. If he is alive, let him take them. If he is not alive, let his legitimate sons take them, once they have been young men (*hebontes*) for five years. If they are not alive, let his legitimate daughters take them. If they are not alive, let his illegitimate children take them. If his illegitimate children are not alive, let his relations take them. If there is a dispute, let the Tegeans decide according to the law.

[*IG* 5.2.159]

This bronze plaque was found at Tegea in Arkadia, and dates to the mid-fifth century BC. It is often assumed to relate to a Spartiate, unable to deposit money at home, see C.H.de Carvalho Gomes, *ZPE* 108 (1995) 103–106, though this is doubted by Hodkinson, *PWCS* 167.

E74   Lykourgan rules on money incompatible with empire

As long as they aimed to rule over their neighbouring towns, or even over the Peloponnesians, they could manage this with the resources Lakonia itself could supply: they had at hand provisions for their campaigns, and could rapidly return home or send supplies across. [8] But when they began to send out expeditions across the seas, or to campaign with infantry outside the Peloponnese, it became clear that neither currency made of iron nor the exchange of annual crops, as laid down by the laws of Lykourgos would make up for the shortfall in what they needed, [9] since the situation required a common currency and materials from abroad. [10] Therefore they were forced to make approaches to the Persians, to impose tribute on the islanders and to make all the Greeks pay, since they realised that under the laws laid down by Lykourgos, hegemony over Greece was not possible, or even having any influence in affairs at all.

[Polybius, *Histories* 6.49]

E75   Money brought for public use corrupts Spartan society, c. 400 BC

But the most sensible of the Spartiates, not least because of this, feared the power of money and that it was affecting the citizens; so they rebuked Lysander and begged the ephors remove all the silver and gold from the city as if an imported pollution. The ephors considered the proposal. And Theopompos says that the ephor Skiraphidas [2] or Phlogidas declared that they ought not to receive gold and silver coin into the city but use that of their own country. ... [4] When the friends of Lysander opposed the proposal, and were eager that the money remained in the city, it was decided that money of this sort be put to public use; also if anyone was caught possessing this money for private use, they determined the punishment should be death, as if Lykourgus feared the coin, not the love of money which came with the coin. Rather than solving this problem, by preventing an individual holding the money privately, in fact it increased because of the city's possession of the money, making its use a means of gaining reputation and honour. [5] For it was not possible for those who saw it honoured for public use to despise it as worthless for private use and to consider what was so prized and approved in public to be of no value for anyone's personal use.

[Plutarch, *Life of Lysander* 17.1–2 and 4–5 = Theopompos, *FGrH* 115 F332]

Though Lysander apparently sent all the money he gained to the Spartan authorities (compare **E136** – dying poor), his associate Gylippos was caught embezzling and went into exile (Plut. *Lys.* 16.1 – 17.1).

E76   Sparta corrupted

But in the reign of Agis coinage first began to pour into Sparta and, with the coming of money, greed and a desire for wealth developed under the influence of Lysander. He himself was totally incorruptible, but he filled his country with a love of riches and luxury by bringing back gold and silver from the war, thus undermining the legislation of Lykourgos.

[Plutarch, *Life of Lykourgos* 30.1]

E77   'Extras' at the mess-meal (as quoted by Athenaios)

a)   [141b] Concerning the meal of the *phidition*, Dikaiarchos writes as follows in his book entitled *Tripolitikos* (Three types of government) "the first dinner is set out separately for each person and no dish is shared with anyone else; then each person has as much barley-bread as he wants, and a cup is placed by each person to drink whenever he wants. The cooked dish is always the same for everyone – boiled pork, but sometimes none of this at all, except a small portion weighing about 16 grams and besides this nothing at all except the broth from it which is sufficient to last the whole dinner for everyone; then perhaps some olives, or cheese, or a fig; or they might have a bonus – fish or hare or pigeon or [141c] something of that sort; then after eating quickly, there is brought round what are called 'extras'. Each man contributes to the *phidition* (mess) about 1½ Attic *medimnoi* (75 litres) of barley, eleven or twelve *choes* of wine (35 litres), and in addition a certain weight of cheese and figs; finally, for the meat, 10 Aiginetan obols.

b)   Sphairos in the third book of his *Lakedaimonian Constitution* writes, "Those at the *phidition* also bring 'extras' – sometimes what many of them have caught while hunting, [141d] but the rich bring bread and what is in season from their fields, in the right quantity for that meeting, thinking that providing more than sufficient would be excessive, and that it would not be eaten.

c)   And Molpis says, "After the meal it is always the done thing for something to be brought by someone, or sometimes by more than one person, a course, prepared by them at home, which they call the 'extra'. It would not be the done thing for anyone providing it to bring anything they had bought, for they do not provide it for pleasure or because of an uncontrolled appetite, but to make a show of their skill [141e] in hunting; and many who breed animals give generously of their produce. This course would be pigeons, geese, turtle-doves, thrushes, blackbirds, hares, lambs, kids. And the cooks always announce who has provided something, so that everyone might know his love of hunting and his eagerness on their behalf.

[Athenaios, *Scholars at Dinner* 4.19 = Sphairos, *FGrH* 581 F1 = Molpis, *FGrH* 590 F2c]

Dikaiarchos of Messana was a polymath student of Aristotle who wrote *c.* 320–300 BC: the start of his account is clearly intended to form a contrast with Athenians meals where dishes would be shared and *symposia* where cups would be passed round (compare Kritias **D60**). Sphairos, another philosopher, advised Kleomenes III who reigned 235–222 BC. Molpis was a Lakonian writer, probably of the Hellenistic period. Since none of these accounts is from the classical period, we cannot be sure whether they describe practices continued from classical times or later changes, in particular the introduction of farmed animals. For discussion see Hodkinson, *PWCS* 356–8.

SPARTAN WOMEN: E78–E81
Our (non-Spartan) sources are very male orientated (contrast Alkman's poetry), and give us only occasional information about Spartan women. Some are concerned with the strategic use of women in marriages: these were inevitably conducted within the narrow constraints of Spartan society, often in the case of royal marriages within the family itself – so Leonidas married Gorgo, daughter of his half-brother (and former king) **E78**, and Archidamos a step-aunt **E79**. For other royal marriages see **E8** (Hdt on Anaxandridas) and Pomeroy, *Spartan Women* 73–4. Several stories and sayings of Gorgo are preserved (besides that at **E78**), attesting to her spirit and intelligence. Plutarch made a collection of *Famous Sayings of Spartan Women* (translated in Talbert, *Plutarch on Sparta*). Most are very stereotypical and unattributed (30 of the 40), including the most famous (**F35**). For epitaphs to women, see **B35, B54, B55**.

E78   Gorgo solves a secret message
When the message reached Lakedaimon, the Lakedaimonians could not understand it, until, so I have learnt, the daughter of Kleomenes and wife of Leonidas herself came up with the idea and told them to scrape off the wax and find the message written on the wood.

[Herodotus, *Histories* 7.239.4]

Kleomenes and Leonidas were step-brothers (Hdt. 5.41) so Leonidas married his step-niece. For the context of the message, hidden on a seemingly blank wax-tablet, see **F26**.

E79   Archidamos' marriage to Lampito
[1] Leotychidas had a son Zeuxidamos who did not rule in Sparta as he died before his father, leaving a son, Archidamos. [2] After losing Zeuxidamos, Leotychidas married again, to a woman called Eurydame, sister of Menios and daughter of Diaktoridas, who gave him no male heir, but a daughter, Lampito whom he gave in marriage to Archidamos.

[Herodotus, *Histories* 6.71.1–2]

E80   Agesilaos pleases his wife by appointing her brother

But in then putting Peisander in command of the fleet Agesilaos was thought to have
made a mistake, since there were older and more intelligent men available, but he did
not pay attention to the good of his country, but honoured a relative to please his wife,
the sister of Peisander, in giving him naval command.

[Plutarch, *Life of Agesilaos* 10.6]

Agesilaos' wife's influence is not mentioned by Xenophon, describing the appointment at *Hell.* 3.4.27 (395 BC).

E81   Killings of a mother and aunt

Theopompos in his 56th book of *Histories* says that Xenopeitheia the mother of
Lysandridas was the most beautiful woman in the Peloponnese. The Lakedaimonians
killed her and her sister Chryse, when King Agesilaos, after a power struggle, caused
Lysandridas his enemy to be banished by the Lakedaimonians.

[Athenaios, *Scholars at Dinner* 13.89 = Theopompos, *FGrH* 115 F240]

We don't know anything else about this episode: Hodkinson, *PWCS* 439.

EDUCATION: E82–E83

Except for the unusual case of Agesilaos, we have no information on the education of any individual
Spartan. This, of course, was the point: the system was the same for absolutely everybody, except likely
future kings.

E82   Agesilaos goes through the '*agoge*'

Archidamos, son of Zeuxidamas, after a distinguished reign over the Lakedaimonians,
left a son, Agis, by Lampido, a woman of noble birth; and a much younger son,
Agesilaos, by Eupolia, daughter of Melesippidas. Since Agis was the rightful king by
law, Agesilaos seemed likely to pass his life as a private citizen, and was put through
the so-called '*agoge*' at Lakedaimon. This was a harsh and painful way of life but
one which taught the young men to be obedient. It was this, they say, that led to
Sparta being dubbed 'man-breaking' by Simonides as having customs which made
her citizens especially obedient to her laws and submissive, just like horses which
are broken in from the very start. The law exempts boys being raised as future kings
from this compulsory practice. But Agesilaos was unique in this that he came to rule
after being educated to obey. As a result he was, of all kings, the one much the most
in sympathy with his subjects, in that to his natural leadership and regal qualities were
added consideration for others and a popular touch, from his education (*agoge*).

[Plutarch, *Life of Agesilaos* 1]

E83   Lysander as lover of Agesilaos

While in the so-called 'herds' (*agelai*) of the boys being raised, he had Lysander as his
lover (*erastes*) who was particularly struck with his natural decency.

[Plutarch, *Life of Agesilaos* 2.1]

One of the two known historical examples of the pederastic relationships institutionalised into the
Spartan education (cf. **E50**). Plutarch continues by extolling the goodness of his character and behaviour.
Xenophon's *Agesilaos* omits any mention of Agesilaos' childhood, or indeed of Lysander.

THE ARMY: E84–E104

This section contains accounts of those campaigns which usefully reveal aspects of the Spartan military machine. For Thermopylai, see **F9–F26**. Campaigns are presented in chronological order. Plataia (479 BC: **E84–E86**), Pylos/Sphakteria (424 BC: **E87–E96**), Mantineia (418 BC: **E99–E104**), Leuktra (371 BC: **E106–E112**).

PLATAIA, 479 BC: E84–E86

After the defeat of the Persian fleet at Salamis in 480 BC, King Xerxes himself withdrew together with the remainder of his fleet, leaving Mardonius, his nephew, in charge of the Persian forces. The following year, Mardonius while withdrawing from Attika was forced to battle near the town of Plataia. For the despatch of Spartan troops under the regent Pausanias, see **E24**. Herodotus' full account of the build-up, battle, and aftermath is at 9.1–86. In addition to the passages below, see **E51, E61, H22, E66** for further extracts from Herodotus' account, and also **A21** and **A22** (Simonides' epic poem and epigram) and **B5** and **B6** (Greek victory monument). Thucydides naturally makes the Plataians of 429–7 BC recall the battle when facing Spartan aggression in the Peloponnesian War (2.71, 2.74; 3.54 = **E65**, 3.58). For a modern analysis of the battle, see Lazenby, *Spartan Army²* 120–139 and Rees, *Great Battles of the Classical World*, (Pen & Sword 2016).

E84   Seven helots for every Spartiate at Plataia

[28.2] After this, those who had recently arrived and those who had come at the start were drawn up as follows. Ten thousand Lakedaimonians held the right wing: of them, five thousand were Spartiates who were guarded by thirty-five thousand light-armed helots – seven serving each man. [28.3] The Lakedaimonians chose the Tegeans to stand next to them, to honour them and because they were courageous: there were fifteen hundred of them. After them stood five thousand Corinthians, and they obtained permission from Pausanias for the three hundred Poteidaians from Pallene to stand next to them. [28.4] Then there were six hundred men from Orchomenos in Arkadia, and three thousand men from Sikyon. Then eight hundred from Epidauros. Beside them were stationed one thousand men from Troizen, and next to them two hundred from Lepreon, four hundred from Mykenai and Tiryns, one thousand from Phleious. [28.5] Next to them stood three hundred from Hermione, six hundred from Eretria and Styra, four hundred from Chalkis, five hundred from Ambrakia. Next were eight hundred men from Leukas and Anaktorion, and two hundred from Pale in Kephallenia. Next to them were stationed five hundred men from Aigina, three thousand from Megara, six hundred from Plataia. Last of all were the Athenians, holding the left wing and numbering eight thousand. Aristeides son of Lysimachos was in command. [29.1] All these troops, except the seven men accompanying each Spartiate, were hoplites, and their total number was 38,700. This was the total of hoplites who came together against the Persians. There was also a large number of lightly-armed troops, the 35,000 with the force of Spartiates, seven for each man, each trained for war. [29.2] Other lightly-armed troops of the other Lakedaimonians and Greeks, being one for each man, made 34,500.

[Herodotus, *Histories* 9.28–9]

Hdt. had also mentioned each of the 5,000 Spartiates taking 7 helots at 9.10 = **E24**.

E85   Amompharetos disobeys orders at Plataia, 479 BC

[53.1] The forces were encamped around the Temple of Hera, and Pausanias, seeing them moving away from the camp, instructed the Lakedaimonians to take up their weapons and go in the same direction as those heading off, thinking that they were going to the rendez-vous agreed. [53.2] The other officers were ready to obey Pausanias, but Amompharetos, son of Polyadas, the unit-leader (*lochagos*) of the Pitanate unit said that he would not run away from foreigners nor deliberately bring shame on Sparta, and was amazed to see what was being done, since he had not been present at the previous discussion. [53.3] Pausanias and Euryanax took his refusal to obey them very badly, but thought it still worse to abandon the Pitanate unit just because he had taken this attitude, since if they left to carry out the plan agreed with the Greeks, Amompharetos himself and his men would perish through being left behind. [53.4] Reasoning thus they held the Lakonian camp in position and tried to persuade him that he should not act in this way. [54.1] While they were speaking to Amompharetos, the only man of the Lakedaimonians and Tegeans left behind, the Athenians were acting as follows: they had also kept themselves stationary where they had been drawn up, understanding that the plans of the Lakedaimonians were the opposite of what they said they were.

[Herodotus, *Histories* 9.53–54]

Herodotus' narrative shows an allied council agreeing to move the Greek army to a new position, but with most in fact simply retreating to another location. Amompharetos, refuses to obey his commanders (it's not clear whether he objected to any repositioning or saw the reality of the allied retreat), but avoids repercussions. On the contrary, Hdt. describes him (9.71.2–4) as one of the three to have fought most bravely, and that he was given special honours after his death in the battle (see also 9.85 = **E51**). This episode suggests that the downside to the rigid education system and strict adherence to a very simple set of strong values was a certain inflexibility when straightforward solutions were not an option. It also suggests that courage was so crucial it could be regarded as more important than obedience.

E86   Spartans, Tegeans and Athenians fight at Plataia, 479 BC

[61.2] Thus the Lakedaimonians and Tegeans were left alone, the former numbering fifty thousand including their lightly-armed troops, the Tegeans, who refused to part from the Lakedaimonians, three thousand. They made a sacrifice on the point of engaging with Mardonius and his army, [61.3] but the sacrifices were not propitious for them, and at the same time many of them fell and many more were wounded, since the Persians made a wicker-work and shot a vast number of arrows so that the Spartiates were hard pressed. With the sacrifices also not turning out well, Pausanias looked to the temple of Hera at Plataia and called upon the goddess, asking that they should not be cheated of their hopes. [62.1] Even while he was still calling on her, the Tegeans rose up at the front and went at the Persians, and immediately after Pausanias' prayer, the Lakedaimonians who were conducting the sacrifices found the omens favourable. So, finally, the Lakedaimonians too went at the Persians, and the Persians facing them stopped shooting arrows. [62.2] The first fight took place at the wicker shield. When this had fallen, there was a great fight at the temple of Demeter, lasting a long time, which came to a mêlée, since the Persians kept seizing and breaking the Greek spears. [62.3] The Persians were not inferior in resolve and strength, but were poorly armed, untrained and not equal in skill to those they were facing. Darting out singly, or massed in groups of ten or more or less, they fell on the Spartiates and were killed. [63.1] Where Mardonius happened to be, fighting from a white horse, and with a contingent of the thousand best Persians around him, there they pressed especially hard on their opponents. As long as he remained alive, they held out and resisted and took down many Lakedaimonians: [63.2] but when Mardonius died and the strongest part of the army, drawn up around him fell, then the others turned to flight and yielded to the Lakedaimonians. What most damaged them was their lack of body armour, since they were fighting a battle, unprotected, against heavily-armed men.

[Herodotus, *Histories* 9.61–63]

PYLOS AND SPHAKTERIA: E87–E96

In the spring of 425, the start of the seventh year of the Peloponnesian War, the Athenians sent a force of forty ships to Sicily, via Kerkyra (= Corcyra = Corfu). While sailing round the Peloponnese, a storm forced the fleet to put into Pylos in Messenia. Once there, one of the commanders, Demosthenes, saw the potential to fortify the place and cause trouble for the Spartans. The troops did so, while waiting for good weather to continue their voyage to Kerkyra, and left Demosthenes with just a garrison of five ships and their crews (Thuc. 4.2–5). The Spartans had invaded Attika to ravage the territory at the start of the spring. Thucydides' clear account (4.1–41) is further elucidated by Hornblower, *Commentary* vol. II, 149–197, Lazenby, *Spartan Army²* 140–150, and Shepherd, *Pylos and Sphacteria 425* BC (Osprey 2013), with excellent illustrations. For dedications by Athenians and Messenians celebrating Pylos, see **B13** and **B14**.

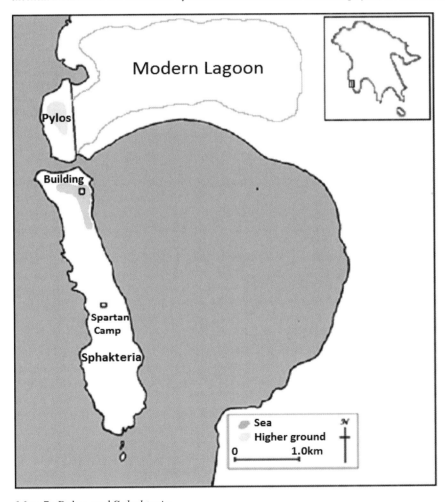

Map 7: Pylos and Sphakteria

E87   Pylos & Sphakteria I: Spartans hurry to expel the Athenians

[1] After the Peloponnesians pulled back from Attika, the Spartiates themselves and the *perioikoi* who lived closest went immediately to help at Pylos. The other Lakedaimonians approached more slowly since they had just come from another expedition. [2] In addition the message went all round the Peloponnese to come to help at Pylos as quickly as possible, and they sent for their sixty ships at Kerkyra which were carried across the isthmus at Leukas, and reached Pylos unnoticed by the Athenian ships at Zakynthos. The land force was already there. [3] Demosthenes, while the Peloponnesian ships were still on their way, managed in time to send off two ships to tell Eurymedon and the Athenians in the fleet at Zakynthos that they should come as Pylos was in danger. [4] The ships sailed quickly as Demosthenes had asked. The Lakedaimonians prepared to attack the fort by land and sea, expecting that they would easily take a building constructed in haste and manned by only a few people. [5] Anticipating that the Attic ships from Zakynthos would come to help, they intended, if they had not already captured the fort, to block the approaches to the harbour, so that the Athenians could not anchor there. [6] For the island called Sphakteria stretches out at the side of the harbour and lies close to it, making the harbour safe and the approaches narrow. There is space for two ships to sail through the side by Pylos, where the Athenian fort was, and on the other side for eight or nine. The whole island is wooded and trackless, since no one lives there, and is around 2 miles in length. [7] They intended to block the approaches with ships put close together with their prows facing outwards. And fearing that the Athenians would use the island as a base to fight them, they sent hoplites across to it and stationed others on the mainland. [8] Thus both island and mainland would be hostile to the Athenians, with nowhere to land (the area of Pylos, outside the harbour-entrance, faced the open sea and had no harbours from which they could set out to relieve their men). They could probably therefore avoid a sea battle and danger in besieging a place without much food because it had been seized at short notice. [9] With this in mind they began to send across to the island hoplites chosen by lot from all their units. These crossed over and others took their places in turn until the final ones were trapped there, numbering four hundred and twenty and the helots who served them. Epitadas son of Molobros commanded them.

[Thucydides, *History of the Peloponnesian War* 4.8]

E88   Pylos & Sphakteria II: Spartan navy fails to force a landing

[11.1] This is what Demosthenes said to encourage them, and the Athenians gained confidence and went down to take up positions right by the sea. [2] The Lakedaimonians began their attack on the fort by land with their army and with their forty-three ships led by the Spartiate Thrasymelidas, son of Kratesikles, who sailed with them. His attack came where Demosthenes was ready for it, [3] and the Athenians made their defence on both landward and seaward sides. The Lakedaimonians divided their ships into small groups because there was not space to use more, and they took turns to make their attacks and recover, with the greatest eagerness and shouts of encouragement to break through somehow and take the fort. [4] In the very forefront of everything was Brasidas. He was captain of a trireme and saw that the coastline was rough and that the other captains and helmsmen, even where it seemed possible to land, were hanging back and taking care not to wreck their ships. He shouted out that it was stupid to grudge some wood and look on when the enemy had made fortifications in their country, and ordered the Lakedaimonians to break up their ships but force a landing, and the allies not to hang back in return for all the benefits the Lakedaimonians had given them, but to sacrifice their ships in their hour of need and run them aground and get their men off, however they could, to take control of the land.

[12.1] He urged the others to do this, forced his own helmsman to run his ship aground and made for the gangway. As he tried to disembark he was cut off by the Athenians, received many wounds and fell down unconscious into the outrigger. His shield slipped off his arm into the sea and later, when it came to land, the Athenians recovered it and used it in the trophy which they set up for repelling this attack. [2] The others made every effort, but were unable to disembark, owing to the difficulty of the terrain and the fact that the Athenians stayed in place and gave no ground. [3] So it turned out that the Athenians were on land in Lakonia, warding off the Lakedaimonians who were attacking by sea, while the Lakedaimonians attempted a landing from ships on their own territory held by their Athenians enemies. Opinion generally was at that time that the Lakedaimonians were mostly landsmen and strongest in their infantry, while the Athenians were the seafarers and completely dominant with their ships.

[Thucydides, *History of the Peloponnesian War* 4.11–12]

E89   Pylos & Sphakteria III: Athenian navy cuts off Spartiates on Sphakteria
[13.1] So after making attacks throughout this day and for part of the next, the Lakedaimonians called a halt. On the third day they sent some of their ship to Asine for wood to make siege-engines, intending to use them to take the area facing the harbour which had a high wall but was the best place to land. [2] Meanwhile the Athenian ships from Zakynthos arrived, fifty in number since they had been reinforced by some from the garrison at Naupaktos and four from Chios. [3] When they saw both mainland and island full of hoplites, and the ships in the harbour making no move to come out to meet them, with nowhere else to anchor, they went first to the island of Prote, not far away and uninhabited, and built a camp there. On the next day they put out to sea, prepared to fight a battle if the Lakedaimonians wished to sail out into open waters, or else to sail into the harbour. [4] The Lakedaimonians did not put out to sea to meet them, nor had they managed to close off the approaches as they had intended: instead they were idling about on land, manning their ships and getting ready to fight a battle in the huge harbour if any ship sailed in.

[14.1] The Athenians, realising this, attacked them through both entrances. They fell on and put to flight most of the ships which were in open waters and facing them; pursuing them over the short distances they disabled many and captured five, one of these with all its crew. Then they attacked the remaining ones which had escaped onto the shore. Others were still being manned and were attacked before they could put to sea: some of them, left empty by their crews rushing to flee, were pulled off the beach and towed away. [2] When they saw this, the Lakedaimonians were devastated at this disaster, since their men were cut off on the island, and rushed to the rescue, even going into the sea fully armed to grab hold of the ships and pull them back. In this crisis, everyone thought that if he was not there and personally involved everything would come to a stop. [3] There was enormous confusion and, regarding the ships, a reversal of what both sides were used to: the Lakedaimonians in their haste and panic, were, so to speak, doing nothing other than fighting a naval battle from land, while the Athenians, with the upper hand but wishing to make the most of their current advantage, were fighting a land battle from the ships. [4] Much effort was spent on both sides and after many casualties they disengaged. By this time the Lakedaimonians had rescued their empty ships except those captured at the start. [5] Both sides returned to their camps and the Athenians erected a trophy, returned the bodies and took possession of the wrecked ships. They also immediately began to sail around the island to keep watch over the men cut off there. The Peloponnesians on the mainland and all those who had come as reinforcements from everywhere remained in position on the land opposite Pylos.

[Thucydides, *History of the Peloponnesian War* 4.13–14]

E90   Pylos & Sphakteria IV: temporary truce
When news of events at Pylos reached Sparta, they decided, in the wake of so great a disaster, to send the magistrates down to the camp to see for themselves and decide immediately what they thought. When they saw that it was impossible to rescue the men, they did not want to put them at risk of suffering starvation or being overpowered by force of numbers. So they decided to make a truce about the situation at Pylos with the Athenian generals, if they were willing, and to send ambassadors to Athens about a treaty, and to try to get their men brought out as soon as possible.

[Thucydides, *History of the Peloponnesian War* 4.15]

The treaty proposed by the Spartans was rejected since the ambassadors were not empowered to offer the territorial concessions demanded by the Athenians at the instigation of Kleon (Thuc. 4.16–22).

E91   Pylos & Sphakteria V: end of truce, resumption of hostilities
[1] When they arrived back, the truce about Pylos was immediately at an end and the Lakedaimonians asked for their ships as had been agreed. But the Athenians, alleging that an attack on the walls had taken place in breach of the truce, as well as other things not worth mentioning, did not return them, sticking staunchly to what had been said, that the treaty would be void in the event of any breach. The Lakedaimonians denied this and called on the gods to witness Athenian injustice regarding their ships. Then they returned to camp and resumed hostilities. [2] Both sides were now fighting at Pylos to the full extent of their powers: the Athenians were sailing around the island with two ships going in opposite directions all day long, while at night they all rode at anchor, except on the side facing the open sea when there was a wind; in addition twenty ships had arrived from Athens to join their blockade, making seventy in all. The Peloponnesians camped on the mainland and made attacks on the wall, looking out for some opportunity to arise to save their men.

[Thucydides, *History of the Peloponnesian War* 4.23]

E92   Pylos & Sphakteria VI: measures and counter-measures to get food to the Spartans
[1] At Pylos the Athenians were still surrounding the Lakedaimonians on the island, while the camp of the Peloponnesians still remained in position on the mainland. [2] Lack of food and water made it very difficult for the Athenians to maintain their watch, since there was only the one spring on the akropolis of Pylos, and this was not large,

but the majority of the men struggled through the shingle to get what water they could from the sea. [3] Conditions were cramped for those encamped in a small area, and the ships had no harbour, so they took it in turns to forage for food on land and to anchor in open seas. [4] But the time it was taking was the greatest source of demoralisation, since they had thought that they would finish the siege within in few days against men on a desert island with only salt-water to drink. [5] The reason was that the Lakedaimonians had made it known that anyone wishing to take across to the island flour, wine, cheese or any other food that would help those besieged, would be given a large amount of money, and any helots doing so were promised their freedom. [6] And people took the risk to take food across, especially helots who set out from wherever they were in the Peloponnese and sailed across by night to the parts of the island facing the sea. [7] They kept a close eye out for a breeze to carry them in, since it was easier for them to slip past the watching triremes when the breeze was from the sea, as this made it impossible to stay at anchor all round the island, while for the helots the voyage across became free of risk. They took boats across for a fee that had been agreed, and the hoplites kept watch over the island's landing places. Any who took a chance in calm seas were caught. [8] Divers also swam under water to the island from the harbour pulling behind them on a string bags with honeyed poppy-cakes and crushed linseed. At first those on guard, did not notice them but later they did. [9] So each side used every means possible to send food across or to spot this being done.

[Thucydides, *History of the Peloponnesian War* 4.26]

The Athenians now feared that they had failed to take full advantage of the situation. Kleon responded by criticising the general Nikias for not taking decisive action. Nikias called Kleon's bluff by offering to stand aside for him; Kleon tried to back out, but found himself trumped by popular opinion; he eventually boasted that he would bring back the Spartans, dead or alive, within twenty days – prompting ridicule (Thuc. 4.27–28). Meanwhile a fire on the island had removed much of the tree-cover, making the landing, already being planned by the Athenian general, Demosthenes, much easier. On Kleon's arrival he called on the Spartans to surrender (4.29–30). Thucydides portrays Kleon as an absolute demagogue, willing to promise anything for his political advantage. We must sympathise with Thucydides' view of a man who twice proposed mass executions of citizens of captured city states, while bearing in mind that Kleon also instigated Thucydides' exile.

E93   Pylos & Sphakteria VII: Athenian attack on Sphakteria
[31.1] These terms were rejected. The Athenians held back for one day, and on the next set out by night, putting all their hoplites onto a few ships. Before dawn a few set foot on either side of the island, that facing the sea and that facing the harbour, roughly eight hundred hoplites. They advanced at a run against the first lookout post on the island. [31.2] These had been set out as follows: in the first one were around thirty hoplites; most of them, including Epitadas their commander occupied the middle and flattest part of the island, near the water-supply; a small group guarded the furthest part of the island, over towards Pylos, which rose up sheer from the sea and was the part of the island least prone to attack. There was also a guard post there, built long before of rough stones which they thought could be useful if they were caught needing to retreat. This is how the troops were stationed.

[32.1] The Athenians immediately killed the first guards whom they overran. They were still in their beds or taking up their weapons since they had been unaware of the landing and thought they the ships were sailing to their usual night-time anchorage.

[32.2] At first dawn, the other force came ashore from just over seventy ships, the whole crews except for the bottom tier of rowers. The men had different types of equipment, with eight hundred archers and an equal number of spearmen; there were those of the Messenians who had come to help and all the others holding the area of Pylos except for those guarding the walls. [32.3] Under Demosthenes' instructions, they separated into groups of more or less two hundred, took hold of the highest points on the island so as to make things as difficult as possible for an enemy who would be surrounded on all sides and have no means of forming their troops in response: they would be exposed on both flanks to superior numbers, and if they advanced on those in front, they would be shot at by those in the rear, if on those on their flanks, by those already in position on either side. [32.4] And in whatever direction they went, there would always be lightly-armed enemy forces who would pose the greatest difficulty in being strong from long range with their arrows, javelins, stones and sling-shots, and impossible to get close to, since they were still powerful even in flight but would press hard on retreating opponents. These were the tactics which Demosthenes had initially planned for the landing, and which he actually employed.

[33.1] The men under Epitadas, the majority of the force on the island, when they saw the first garrison destroyed and the army advancing against them, drew themselves up and advanced against the Athenian hoplites, wishing to engage. They were positioned immediately opposite them, while the lightly-armed troops were on the flanks and to the rear. [33.2] However they were not able to engage with these hoplites nor use their own experience, since the lightly-armed troops kept them back by shooting at them from both sides, while the Athenian hoplites did not advance to meet them but stayed still. They could force back the lightly-armed fighters whenever they ran up to press closely on them, but they would turn round again and defend themselves, and since they were lightly equipped and could easily get a head start when running away, the Lakedaimonians in their armour could not pursue them through terrain which was naturally difficult and rough because previously uninhabited.

[34.1] So they skirmished with one another for a short while, but when the Lakedaimonians were no longer able to dart out quickly where someone attacked them, the lightly-armed troops realised that they were already slower to defend themselves and took the greatest of confidence in seeing this. They seemed to outnumber them greatly and had become used to their no longer appearing quite as terrible to them, in that they had not suffered anything to justify their expectations, whereas when they had first landed they had been enslaved by the thought that they would face Lakedaimonians. Now despising them, they shouted in unison and rushed on them, casting stones, javelins and arrows – whatever each one had to hand. [34.2] At the shout and simultaneous charge, terror descended on people who were unused to such fighting; in addition a great cloud of ash was arising from the newly-burnt wood, and it was impossible to see in front of one because of the arrows and stones being thrown from so many men together with the cloud of ash. [34.3] The situation now became critical for the Lakedaimonians, since their felt caps did not keep off the arrows and the points of the javelins broke off where they were struck, and they had no way to help themselves, hindered by not being able to see in front of them, unable to hear instructions to each other because of the greater shouting of their enemies, with danger on all sides, and no hope of any means to defend themselves and be saved.

[35.1] In the end, with many already wounded through always being kept on the same spot, they closed together and made for the building at the end of the island, which was not far off, and those guarding it. When they gave ground, the lightly-armed men, further encouraged, gave an even louder shout and pressed hard on them. [35.2] Any Lakedaimonians who were overtaken as they retreated were killed, but most escaped to the building. Together with the guards there, they positioned themselves around the whole building to defend it wherever it was attacked. [35.3] The Athenians followed behind, but were not able, because of the strength of the location, to encircle or surround it, but tried to force their way with a direct frontal assault. [35.4] For a long time – the greatest part of the day – both sides endured great suffering from the battle, from thirst, and from the heat of the sun, as the Athenians tried to drive the Lakedaimonians from the high ground, while they tried not to give way. It was easier for the Lakedaimonians to defend themselves than before since they were not encircled on all sides.

[36.1] With no end to the fighting in sight, the Messenian leader came up to Kleon and Demosthenes and said that they were wasting their efforts: if they were willing to give him some of the archers and lightly-armed troops, he would go round the back of the Lakedaimonians by whatever route he could find, and thought he could force a way in. [36.2] Taking the troops he had asked for, he set off from an area out of view so that they could not see him and climbed the steep cliffs of the island by whatever route was possible, where the Lakedaimonians kept no guard, trusting the strength of the location. With great difficulty he just about made it round without being noticed, and suddenly appeared on high ground behind them and terrified them by his unexpected appearance, while greatly encouraging those who saw what they had been looking out for. [36.3] The Lakedaimonians were now being assailed from both sides and were in the same trouble, to compare small with large, as at Thermopylai; there they were destroyed by the path which led the Persians around them; here they were now attacked from both sides and could hold out no longer. Fighting a few against many, and weak in body through lack of food, they began to fall back and the Athenians now took control of the approaches.

[Thucydides, *History of the Peloponnesian War* 4.31–36]

E94   Pylos & Sphakteria VIII: Surrender of the Spartiates

[37.1] Kleon and Demosthenes wanted to take the Lakedaimonians alive and bring them back to Athens. They rather hoped that they were so demoralised that when they heard the proclamation they would recognise that their situation was hopeless and give up their weapons. [37.2] So through a herald they invited them, if they were willing, to hand over their weapons and surrender themselves to the Athenians unconditionally. [38.1] When they heard this, most of the Lakedaimonians dropped their shields and waved their hands, signalling that they accepted the terms of the proclamation. After that a truce was declared and the two sides met to discuss terms, Kleon and Demosthenes for the Athenians, and Styphon the son of Pharax for the Lakedaimonians: their original general, Epitadas, was already dead, while his appointed successor, Hippagretas, was still alive but as good as dead and lying among the corpses. Styphon was third in command, officially appointed to take over if anything happened to the first two. [38.2] Styphon and his associates stated that they wished to send a messenger to the Lakedaimonians on the mainland to ask them what action to take. [38.3] The Athenians refused, but themselves invited

Lakedaimonian representatives. After two or three sets of exploratory discussions, the final representative of the Lakedaimonians from the mainland reported to the prisoners that "The Lakedaimonians have decided that you must make your own decision, but it must not bring disgrace." And so, after debating the matter among themselves, they handed over their weapons and surrendered. [38.4] For the rest of that day and that night the Athenians kept their prisoners under guard. The following morning they set up a trophy on the island and made their preparations for setting sail. They distributed the prisoners for safe custody among the various trireme commanders, while the Lakedaimonians sent over a herald and transported the dead back to the mainland.

[38.5] The following are the numbers of those killed and taken alive: 420 hoplites in all crossed over to the island. Of these 292 were taken alive and transported to Athens, of whom about 120 were Spartiates; the rest lost their lives. Athenians casualties were minimal, since there had not been any hand-to-hand fighting.

[Thucydides, *History of the Peloponnesian War* 4.37–38]

E95   Pylos & Sphakteria IX: Summary and reaction in Greece
[39.1] The whole length of time which the men spent trapped on the island after the sea battle was seventy-two days. [39.2] Of this period, they were properly fed for around the twenty days when the ambassadors went away to negotiate; for the remaining time they were kept going by supplies brought in secret. And there was even food and other provisions found when the island was captured, since the leader Epitadas had been providing the men with less than was available. [39.3] Now the Athenians and Peloponnesians both withdrew their armies from Pylos and went back home, and Kleon's promise, crazy though it had been, was fulfilled, since he led his men back home within twenty days, as he promised.

[40.1] This was for the Greeks the most extraordinary thing to have happened in the war. For they thought the Lakedaimonians would not surrender their weapons through starvation or any other force, but would keep them, fight as long as they were able and die fighting. [40.2] Nor did they believe that the men who surrendered were the equals of those who died. Sometime later an Athenian taunted one of the men taken prisoner on the island by asking whether the great and good Lakedaimonians were the dead ones; he replied that the women's weapons (meaning arrows) were worth a lot if they could pick out the brave, making it clear that anyone who happened to be in the way of the stones and arrows was killed.

[Thucydides, *History of the Peloponnesian War* 4.39–40]

E96   Kleon steals Demosthenes' 'Spartan Cake' at Pylos
DEMOSTHENES: A little while back
                    I'd made a Lakonian cake at Pylos, all by myself   55
                    And he had the nerve to run up, grab it himself
                    And serve it, though it was made by me!

[Aristophanes, *Knights* 54–57 (performed 424 BC)]

Aristophanes makes Demosthenes (as himself) complain that Paphlagon (a very transparent disguise for Kleon) took all the credit from him for the victory at Pylos/Sphakteria.

AGIS AND THE MANTINEIA CAMPAIGN, 418 BC: E97–E104
Argos and Sparta had been long-standing rivals and enemies, see **H11** for the 'Battle of the Champions' *c.* 546 BC and **E17**, **E18** for Kleomenes' crushing defeat of Argos, *c.* 494 BC. In 451 BC Argos and Sparta had agreed on a peace for 30 years. Argos did indeed remain neutral for this period and therefore avoided involvement in the first part of the Peloponnesian War. As it happened, the treaty expired around the time when Sparta concluded peace with Athens (421 BC), so the Argives found themselves in a position where they could form an alliance with Athens, Mantineia and Elis: 420–418 BC; Thuc. 5.47–56). In the mid-summer of 418, Sparta sent a large expedition against Argos and her allies. Sparta's force under King Agis included helots and forces from the Peloponnesian league. Agis manages to outmanoeuvre and surround the Argive forces near Argos, before Athenian cavalry could arrive (Thuc. 5.57–59.3) …

E97   Agis unilaterally decides not to fight the Argives, 418 BC
[59.4] Most of the Argive army and their allies had no idea of the danger they were in. Indeed they reckoned that they would have the advantage of fighting an army of Lakedaimonians which was on Argive territory and close to their own city. [59.5] But two members of the Argive forces, Thrasylos, one of their five generals, and Alkiphron, the Lakedaimonians' *proxenos*, went forward to hold a parley with King Agis just before the armies clashed, and persuaded him to avoid joining battle. They said that the Argives were willing to exchange guarantees provided they were fair and equivalent, if the Lakedaimonians had any grievances against them, and that they would make a treaty to keep the peace for the future. [60.1] These proposals were made entirely on their own initiative and without the authority of their army as a whole. Agis, too, accepted their proposals on his own and without the consent of anyone else; indeed he sought advice from no one except one of the senior commanders of his army whom he let into the secret. A four-month truce was agreed during which the Argives were required to make good their promises. Agis immediately led his army away without a word of explanation to his allies.

[60.2] The Lakedaimonians and their allies followed his lead, as their law required, but among themselves they were furious with Agis. They believed that they had been lucky enough to join battle under highly favourable circumstances with the enemy surrounded on all sides by infantry and cavalry, and yet they had simply marched away without any achievement to match their formidable resources. [60.3] After all this was the finest Greek army that had ever been brought together, and it had been seen publicly en masse while still at its fullest strength at Nemea: the whole army of the Lakedaimonians had been there, together with men from Arkadia, Boiotia, Corinth, Sikyon, Pellene, Phleious, and Megara, all of them with the cream of their troops, and the whole force was clearly capable of taking on not just the Argive alliance but any other alliance as well which happened to come to their aid. [60.4] And so the army contingents went home and dispersed to their various cities in a mood of bitter discontent with Agis.

[Thucydides, *History of the Peloponnesian War* 5.59–60]

E98   Sanctions placed on Agis as a result
[1] When the Lakedaimonians returned from Argos having agreed the four month truce, they were bitterly angry with Agis for his failure to defeat the Argives when, as they thought, they had had such an unprecedented opportunity for doing so, since it was never easy to gather together such a large allied army of such high quality. [2] But when they heard the news that Orchomenos had been captured, their sense

of outrage was intensified, and in a frenzy of anger which was unlike their usual behaviour they voted to tear down his house and to fine him 10,000 drachmas. [3] He begged them not to do so, promising to redeem his disgrace by heroic action when he next took the field, and after that they could do whatever they wished. [4] So they suspended the fine and the destruction of his house, but passed a temporary measure, of a kind hitherto unheard of in Sparta, by which ten senior Spartiate officials would be appointed as his advisers, and that he would not be allowed to lead an army out of the city without their official sanction.

[Thucydides, *History of the Peloponnesian War* 5.63]

BATTLE OF MANTINEIA, 418 BC
'Thucydides uses the battle of Mantineia to feed in paradigmatic material about ancient hoplite battles' (Hornblower, *Commentary* vol III, pages 163–4). For a military analysis of the battle, see Lazenby, *Spartan Army2* 151–160, Rees, *Great Battles of the Classical World,* (Pen & Sword 2016), or for a very brief summary of this battle and later battles at Mantineia in 362 and 207 BC as encapsulating the main stages of Greek warfare, see Lazenby on 'Mantinea, battles of' in *OCD³*.

E99   Mantineia I: Spartans gather a large army to prevent loss of Tegea
[1] Meanwhile news reached the Lakedaimonians from their supporters in Tegea that, unless they came very quickly, the city would secede from them and go over to the Argives and their allies; indeed it had all but done so already. [2] This finally spurred them into action, and they mustered all their forces, Lakedaimonians and helots alike, to go to their aid with the largest army they had ever raised. [3] They made a forced march to Mainalian Orestheion, and sent messages ahead to their allies, the Arkadians, to call up their forces and then to follow in their footsteps to Tegea. They themselves marched their whole army as far as Orestheion, but then sent back a sixth part consisting of the oldest and youngest to act as a home defence force; the rest of the army then advanced to Tegea, to be joined soon afterwards by their Arkadian allies. [4] They also sent messages to the Corinthians, Boiotians, Phokians and Lokrians to come to Mantineia as a matter of urgency. But for some of them this gave very little warning, and it was no easy matter for them to cross hostile territory which blocked their way unless they waited for one another and moved as a united force. But they pressed forward as best they could. Meanwhile the Lakedaimonians, taking with them those of their Arkadian allies who had already arrived, moved forward into Mantineian territory, established their camp, and proceeded to lay waste the countryside.

[Thucydides, *History of the Peloponnesian War* 5.64]

E100   Mantineia II: Argives take up strong position; Agis does not engage them
[1] When the Argives and their allies saw this they took up a strong position protected by difficult terrain and drew up their battle lines. [2] The Lakedaimonians immediately moved against them, advancing to within a stone's throw or javelin range. But then one of the old soldiers in the army who had seen what a strong position they were advancing against shouted to Agis that that he was trying to cure one disease with another, by which he meant that he was too eager to try and make their present unfavourable situation a form of reparation for the retreat from Argos which had earned him such discredit. [3] Either because of what the soldier shouted or because

he had himself suddenly had a change of mind, Agis quickly led his army back again before battle was actually joined. [4] He then moved into Tegean territory and began to divert its river into Mantineian territory. The Mantineians and Tegeans are always at loggerheads about this, because of the damage which its waters do to whichever part of the countryside they flows into. His plan was that when the pro-Mantineian forces (that is the Argives and their allies) realised that the river was being diverted in their direction, they would come down off their high ground to prevent it, and so the battle would then be fought on level ground.

[5] Agis remained where he was for the whole of that day, organising the diversion of river. But the Argives and their allies were initially non-plussed by the Lakedaimonians' sudden retreat and had no idea what to make of it all. So, when the enemy backed off and disappeared from sight, they simply held their ground and made no attempt to pursue them. But then they started to blame their own generals once again, because just as on the previous occasion, when they had been successfully trapped in front of Argos, the Lakedaimonians had managed to slip away. Now they were once more running away with no one following them in hot pursuit. So the Lakedaimonians were quietly getting away to safety, while the Argives themselves were being betrayed. [6] At first the generals were thoroughly confused by it all, but then they led their forces down from the high ground, advanced onto the plain, and set up camp fully intending to launch an attack on the enemy.

[Thucydides, *History of the Peloponnesian War* 5.65]

E101   Mantineia III: both sides deploy for battle

[66.1] Next day the Argives and their allies formed up in order of battle, intending to fight if the opportunity arose. As for the Lakedaimonians, they were on their way back to their camp at the temple of Herakles after their operations to divert the water supply, when suddenly at no great distance they came upon their opponents, who had now come forward down off their hill top, lined up in full battle order. [66.2] In this moment of potential crisis the Lakedaimonians were more startled than anyone could ever remember. They had to organise themselves with a minimum of warning and every man immediately took up his own position as fast as he could, while King Agis issued the necessary specific orders, as the law required. ...

[Thucydides now explains the general command structure of the Lakedaimonians in battle – see **D85***]*

[67.1] On this occasion the left wing was held by the *Skiritai*, who always have this privilege (unique in the Lakedaimonian army) of operating on their own as a unit. Next to them were the soldiers of Brasidas' Thracian contingents, which included helots who had been freed for their services in the field; then came the Lakedaimonians, ranged by companies, next to them the Arkadians, then the Mainalians, and on the right wing the Tegeans, together with a few Lakedaimonians stationed on the outer edges of their formation. Their cavalry was stationed on both wings. [67.2] So much for the line-up of the Lakedaimonians. On their opponents' side, the Mantineians held the right wing, since the whole operation was taking place on their territory; next to them their own allies from Arkadia; then the thousand élite troops from Argos, to whom at public expense their city had given long-term professional military training; next to them the rest of the Argive army, and then their allies, the Kleonaians and

Orneans; finally on the left wing were the Athenians together with their own cavalry who had accompanied them.

[68.1] These were the dispositions of each side and certainly the army of the Lakedaimonians looked the larger. [68.2] But it would be impossible for me to give the exact numbers of the forces on either side, whether of the individual units or the whole armies. The secret nature of their political arrangements makes it impossible to discover the numbers of Lakedaimonians, and as for the others, the natural human tendency to exaggerate one's own resources makes all estimates unreliable. Nevertheless, it is possible to make an estimate of the Lakedaimonian contingent on this occasion by the following method: [68.3] Excluding the *Skiritai*, who numbered about 600 in all, seven units *(lochoi)* fought in this battle. In each unit there were four companies *(pentekostyes)*, and in each company four groups *(enomotiai)*. The front rank of each group had four men, but the depth behind them varied according to the judgement of the different unit leaders *(lochagoi)*; but on average they stood usually about eight deep. The front line, excluding the *Skiritai*, was therefore 448 men.

[Thucydides, *History of the Peloponnesian War* 5.66–68]

Thucydides' numbers are very problematic. If 4 men from each group (*enomotia*) stood in the front and they were usually 8 deep, that makes 32 men in each *enomotia*; 4 *enomotiai* in each *pentekostys* and 4 *pentekostyes* in each *lochos* gives a total for each *lochos* of 32 x 4 x 4 = 512 men. With 7 *lochoi* that would make a force of 3,584 which is close enough to 448 spread out usually 8 deep (448 x 8 = 3,576). Even adding 600 *Skiritai*, however, this is nowhere near enough to make the Spartan army (without some allies (5.64.4)) not only 'look larger' (68.1) but 'be larger' (71.2), since the combined Argive forces can be estimated at something like 11,000 (calculated by Lazenby, *The Peloponnesian War: A Military Study,* 2004 and supported by Hornblower, *Comm.* vol. III.181) with 1,000 élite and purely Argive troops alone). So it is widely assumed that Thuc.'s totals should be doubled because he missed out the *mora* (Xen. *Lak.Pol.* 11.4 = **D88**). But even then, there are further complications and it may simply be right to conclude (as at 5.68.2) that the secretive Spartans did not want Thucydides to understand the structure of their army (Hornblower, *Comm.* vol. III.182).

E102   Mantineia IV: encouragement for the troops

[1] As they were just about to join battle, morale-boosting speeches were made by their respective commanders to each side along the following lines: the Mantineians were reminded that the battle was for their country; at stake was their independence or slavery, the loss of that independence or the re-imposition of slavery once again. The Argives were told that they were battling to recover their traditional leadership role in the Peloponnese, their rightful share of the lands there, and the prevention of its total loss for ever, and revenge for the wrongs done to them by a people who were their enemies as well as neighbours. As for the Athenians, they were exhorted to realise that it was a glorious thing not to be defeated while fighting on behalf of their many loyal allies, and that if they could defeat the Lakedaimonians within the Peloponnese, their control of their own empire would be the greater and stronger, and never again would anyone launch an attack on their country. [2] Such were the exhortations addressed to the Argives and their allies. But the Lakedaimonians preferred mutual encouragement among themselves addressed man to man, accompanied by their battle hymns, as their own way of reminding each other that they were brave men, since they were well aware of the fact that their lengthy training for action was a far better source of safety than a few hasty speeches however eloquently spoken.

[Thucydides, *History of the Peloponnesian War* 5.69]

E103   Mantineia V: the battle itself

[70.1] After that the battle was joined. The Argives and their allies charged into action with violence and passion; the Lakedaimonians with cool deliberation to the sound of flutes from the many musicians in their ranks. This had nothing to do with religion, but was intended to ensure that they advanced at a uniform pace so that their ranks remained in close order, rather than losing cohesion, as tends to happen when a large army advances into battle. [71.1] As the lines approached, King Agis decided on the following tactics. In the advance to action there is a universal tendency in all armies to drift towards the right and for each side's right wing to overlap its enemy's left, because fear causes each soldier to try to guard his unprotected side as far as he can behind the cover of the shield of the man on his immediate right, imagining that the more closely packed together they are, the safer he will be. The fundamental reason for this lies with the men on the extreme right wing, who are always eager to protect their own unguarded side from their enemy and thus they communicate their own anxiety to the others all along the line. [71.2] So too on this occasion: the Mantineians extended well beyond the *Skiritai*; the Lakedaimonians and Tegeans on their own right wing stretched even further beyond the opposing Athenians, because their army was the larger. [71.3] Agis feared that his own left wing would be encircled, because it seemed to him that the Mantineians had achieved an excessive overlap. So he signalled to the *Skiritai* and Brasidas' Thracian units to move outwards and away from the main force so as to match the Mantineian line. This created a space into which he ordered his generals Hipponoidas and Aristokles commanding two units on the right wing to detach them and bring them round and insert them into the gap. He assumed that his own right would still extend beyond the enemy left while the line facing the Mantineians would be significantly reinforced.

[72.1] As it turned out, because the armies were already manoeuvring for the attack and the message to Aristokles and Hipponoidas came at such short notice, they refused to obey orders, and as a result later faced a charge of cowardice and were exiled from Sparta. Meanwhile the enemy managed to launch their attack before the *Skiritai* could bring their line together and close up their ranks again, despite Agis' instructions to do so when the two right wing units failed to arrive. [72.2] In this the Lakedaimonians were clearly outmanoeuvred, but when it came to sheer courage in battle they now proved themselves a match for any. [72.3] Once the battle came to close quarters, the Mantineian right wing routed the *Skiritai* and Brasidas' Thracian units; then they and their allies, together with the thousand élite Argive troops, charged into the gap which had still not been closed up, surrounded and killed many of the Lakedaimonians and forced them to retreat, driving them back as far as their wagon train and killing some of the older soldiers who were stationed there. [72.4] So in this area the Lakedaimonians certainly had the worst of it. But in other parts of the battlefield, especially in the centre where King Agis himself was stationed with his bodyguard of 300 so-called knights, the Lakedaimonians launched an assault upon the older soldiers of the Argive army (usually referred to as the Five Companies) together with the Kleonaians and Orneans and the Athenians who were positioned alongside them. They routed them so comprehensively that many of them failed even to hold up against the initial assault but simply fled when the Lakedaimonians charged, some of them being trampled underfoot in their efforts to escape before the Lakedaimonians reached them.

[73.1] Once the army of the Argives and their allies had yielded the initiative in this way, there were several simultaneous developments. The Argive centre lost contact with its two wings while the Lakedaimonians and Tegeans with their overlapping right wing began to encircle the Athenians, who were as a result facing danger on two fronts, becoming encircled from behind and already defeated in front. They would certainly have sustained the most severe losses of all the army if they had not had their own cavalry in close support. [73.2] In addition, as it happened, Agis had seen that his own left wing, facing the Mantineians and the Argive élite troops, was in serious difficulty, so he ordered all the rest of his army to race to support the part of his army that was facing imminent defeat. [73.3] This manoeuvre allowed the Athenians and the Argive troops with them who had already been defeated to slip away to safety, while the Lakedaimonian army was moving past them and away from their position. The Mantineians and their allies together with the Argive élite detachments lost all thought of continuing to press home their attacks on the enemy; instead, realising that their own side had been defeated and that the Lakedaimonians were moving in on them, they turned tail and fled. [73.4] Of the Mantineians a large number were killed, though the Argive élite largely escaped. But the pursuit and the retreat did not last very long. The Lakedaimonians will fight long and hard to hold their ground until their enemy's flight has tipped the scales of battle; once that has been achieved, their pursuit is short lived and over no great distance.

[Thucydides, *History of the Peloponnesian War* 5.70–73]

For the 300 'knights' (actually infantry) forming the king's bodyguard, see Hdt. 8.124.3 and Xen. *Lak. Pol.* 4.3 = **D79**. Thuc.'s comments about Spartan non-pursuit of fleeing enemies is echoed by Plutarch's comment **D95**.

E104   Mantineia VI: summary of the battle and its aftermath

[74.1] That represents as accurate an account of the battle as I can achieve; it was certainly the greatest battle among the Greeks for a very long time and brought into confrontation their most prestigious cities. [74.2] The Lakedaimonians lined up in front of the enemy dead and immediately put up a trophy, stripped the corpses of their weaponry, collected their own casualties and took them back to Tegea, where they buried them. They gave back the enemy dead under a truce. [74.3] The Argives, Orneans, and Kleonaians lost about 700 men, the Mantineians about 200, and the Athenians and Aiginetans together another 200, including both their generals. On the Lakedaimonian side, allied casualties were negligible; as for their own losses, it is difficult to establish the truth, but anecdotal evidence suggests they were about 300 dead.

[75.1] When this battle was still in the future, Pleistonoanax, the other king, brought an army of reinforcements, consisting of older and younger soldiers, to support his army. He got as far as Tegea when he learned of the victory and so he went home again. [75.2] Meanwhile the Lakedaimonians also sent messengers to turn back their allied reinforcements coming from Corinth and beyond the Isthmus, while they themselves returned home and allowed their allies to stand down. As it happened to be the period of the festival of Karneian Apollo, they held the appropriate celebrations. [75.3] By this single victorious action the Lakedaimonians expunged all the unfavourable comments about them in the Greek world, whether the charge of cowardice arising from the Sphakteria disaster or the more general criticism of their incompetence or dilatory responses elsewhere. The general perception was that they had suffered from a run of bad luck, but that their essential quality as Lakedaimonians remained untarnished.

[Thucydides, *History of the Peloponnesian War* 5.74–75 (continued in **H42**)]

E105   The composition of the Spartan army in 394

*Although Sparta had a traditional dislike of archers (see Thuc. 4.40.2 = **E95**), following Pylos their army was often accompanied by squadrons of allied archers.*
[16] And now I will state the numbers on either side. The Lakedaimonian hoplites totalled six thousand men; there must have been almost three thousand of the Eleans, Triphylians, Akrorians, and Lasionians, with one thousand five hundred of the Sikyonians, and not less than three thousand from Epidauros, Troizen, Hermione and Halieis. Also the Lakedaimonians had around seven hundred cavalry, about three hundred Cretan bowmen who accompanied the army, and in addition no fewer than four hundred slingers of the Marganians, Letrinians, and Amphidolians. However the men of Phleious would not join them as they said that they were keeping a holy truce. This was the force on the side of the Lakedaimonians.

[Xenophon, *Hellenika* 4.2.16]

Six thousand. This figure is not, of course, the number of Spartiates. Though we cannot be certain, this may have been as low as 2,500 or 2,000 (Cartledge *SL* 239–40).

THE BATTLE OF LEUKTRA, 371 BC: E106–E112
On several occasions Sparta had taken military action against what she seems to have seen as the Theban threat to her hegemony. In 371 she attempted to capitalise on Thebes not having agreed to the Common Peace sworn earlier that year (see **H67**). Cleombrotos led a Spartan allied force into Boiotia. The Thebans eventually decided to give battle, and the battle was fought with roughly equal forces. The main military innovation was the Thebans positioning their best forces on their left (usually in phalanx warfare, commanders placed their best troops on their right.)

Accounts of Leuktra survive from Xenophon (*Hell.* 6.4.1–20), Diodoros (15.51–56), Pausanias (9.13) and Plutarch (*Pelopidas* 20–23). Xenophon, though contemporary, gives his account entirely from the Spartan side: he does not once in his whole account mention Epaminondas, architect of the Theban victory, or Pelopidas or the 'Sacred Band'. Diodoros' account, derived largely from the lost Ephoros, is largely a rhetorical set-piece. Plutarch gives the best account from the Theban perspective in writing the Life of the Theban general, Pelopidas. For a modern, military analysis of the battle, see Lazenby, *Spartan Army²* 176–188.

E106   Spartan victory expected
[In 371/0 BC] The Thebans, not being included in the treaty were forced to face the Lakedaimonians in war on their own, since no city could fight with them as they had all agreed to the common peace. [2] Since the Thebans were on their own, the Lakedaimonians decided to wage war against them and enslave them completely. The preparations of the Lakedaimonians were made quite openly and the Thebans were without allies, so everyone assumed that they would be defeated by the Spartiates.

[Diodoros, *Library of History* 15.51]

E107   Spartan and Theban cavalry contrasted
[10] And then, since there was a plain in the space between the two armies, the Lakedaimonians stationed their cavalry in front of their phalanx, and the Thebans in like manner stationed theirs opposite them. As a result of the war with the

Orchomenians and the Thespians, the cavalry of the Thebans was in good order; but as regards the Lakedaimonians, at that time their cavalry were an absolute disgrace. [11] This was because it was the very richest who bred the horses, but it was only when the call-up was announced that the man enlisted arrived to collect his horse and whatever weapons were given him and take the field at once. In addition the troops on horses were the most incapable physically and the least ambitious.

[Xenophon, *Hellenika* 6.4.10–11]

E108   The disposition of the forces

On the Lakedaimonian side, the descendants of Herakles, King Kleombrotos and Archidamos son of King Agesilaos, were stationed in command of the wings. On the Boiotian side, Epaminondas employed an unprecedented formation of his own and brought about, through his own generalship, the celebrated victory. [2] He picked the best men from his entire force and stationed them in one part, intending the see the contest through amongst them. The weakest he drew up on the other wing, with orders to avoid battle by gradually withdrawing as the enemy advanced. By putting his phalanx at a slant, he thought to decide the battle on the wing which had his chosen fighters. [3] When on both sides the trumpets gave the signal for war and the forces yelled at the first charge, the Lakedaimonians made their phalanx into a crescent shape and attacked on both wings, while the Boiotians gave ground on one wing, but on the other engaged with their enemy at the double.

[Diodoros, *Library of History* 15.55–56]

E109   Theban infantry defeat Spartan infantry

[12] This, then, was the cavalry on each side. As for the infantry, it was said that the Lakedaimonians led each half-company into battle three files abreast and that, as a result, the phalanx was not more than twelve men deep. On the other hand, the Thebans were drawn up in a formation of at least fifty shields deep, reckoning that if they could conquer the area around the king, then the rest would be easy to overcome. [13] Then Kleombrotos began to advance against the enemy. However, first of all, even before his troops so much as realised that he was advancing, the cavalry had already engaged and the Lakedaimonian forces were quickly diminished. Then in their flight, they fell upon their own hoplites, and at the same moment, the Theban forces now charged at them. Nevertheless, Kleombrotos and his men at first gained the upper hand in the battle. This is clearly shown by the fact that they would not have been able to take him up and carry him off while still alive unless those who were fighting in front of him had been winning at that time.

[14] But when Deinon, the polemarch, had been killed, along with Sphodrias, one of the king's tent-companions, and his son Kleonymos, and then the royal bodyguard and the troops known as 'the polemarch's own', then the others fell back under the pressure of the Theban masses. And the left wing of the Lakedaimonians, when they saw that the right wing was being pushed back, gave way too. Although many had fallen and they had been defeated, once they had crossed the ditch which was in front of their camp, they halted and grounded their arms at the place where they had set out from. In fact, the camp was not on ground which was entirely flat but rather on a hill-slope. After this disaster, there were some of the Lakedaimonians who thought

that what had happened was unbearable and said that they should prevent the enemy from setting up a trophy and recover the bodies of the dead by fighting, rather than by means of a truce.

[15] However, when the polemarchs saw that the whole number of the Lakedaimonians (of nearly a thousand in total) had been killed and that also four hundred of the seven hundred Spartiates present had fallen, they realised that none of their allies had any spirit left for fighting and, indeed, that some of them were not upset with the way the battle had gone. They therefore called a meeting of the most important persons and discussed what they should do. All agreed that it was best to recover the bodies of the dead by a truce and they sent a herald to request this. And so, after this, the Thebans set up a trophy and handed back the bodies under a truce.

[Xenophon, *Hellenika* 6.4.12–15]

E110   Plutarch's account of Leuktra, 371 BC
[1] In the battle, Epaminondas was drawing his phalanx to the left so that he could separate the right wing of the Spartans as far as possible from the other Greeks and supplant Kleombrotos with a fierce charge of his column on that wing. However, the enemy understood what he was doing and began to change their battle-formation. [2] They opened up and extended their right wing and began to surround Epaminondas, enclosing him with their superior numbers. But Pelopidas came swiftly forward with his band of three hundred before Kleombrotos could fully extend his wing, close his line and return the men again to their formations and fell upon the Spartans while they were in disarray. Now the Spartans were the best drilled soldiers and most skilled in the arts of warfare, and were trained and accustomed to any change of formation without confusion and to follow any fellow fighter, and to come together in formation and fight as well as ever whenever danger threatened. [4] However in this battle Epaminondas and his phalanx bore down on them alone, neglecting the other Greeks, and Pelopidas fell upon them with such incredible speed and boldness that their spirit and skill were so broken that there began such a flight and slaughter of the Spartans that had never been seen before. And so, although Epaminondas was the Boiotarch, Pelopidas, who had no high office but was only the captain of a small contingent, won as much glory as Epaminondas did for the victory.

[Plutarch, *Pelopidas* 23]

E111   The Spartan Dead at Leuktra, 371 BC
The most famous victory of all those won by Greek over Greeks was achieved by the Thebans. On the following day the Lakedaimonians gave thought to burying their dead and despatched a messenger to the Thebans. Epaminondas, being aware that the Lakedaimonians were always inclined to conceal their misfortunes, said that he would allow their allies to recover their dead first, and that after they had taken them away he thought it right for the Lakedaimonians to bury their dead. [12] Some of the allies did not do this at all because none of the dead were theirs, while it was obvious that others had a small number of dead. So when the Lakedaimonians buried their dead, it was proven clearly that the dead were Spartiates. Of the Thebans and those Boiotians who stood with them, forty-seven men died, of actual Lakedaimonians, more than one thousand.

[Pausanias, *Description of Greece* 9.13.11–12]

E112   News of the Spartan defeat reaches Sparta
The man bringing news of the disaster arrived at Lakedaimon on the last day of the Gymnopaidiai while the men's chorus was inside. The ephors when they heard of the disaster were naturally grief-stricken, but they did not take them off stage, but allowed them to complete the competition. Furthermore, although they gave the names of the dead to their relatives, they gave orders that the women bear their suffering in silence and avoid cries of mourning. And so, on the following day, those whose relatives had been killed could be seen in public with bright and cheerful faces, while those whose relatives had been reported as living (of whom there were few to be seen), these few were walking around gloomy and despondent.

[Xenophon, *Hellenika* 6.4.16]

Xenophon probably witnessed the events he describes here, which formed the basis for the slightly elaborated version in Plutarch, *Agesilaos* 29. The wider results of this stunning defeat were great disturbance in 370 BC throughout the Peloponnese, within Lakonia (**E59, E69**) and in cities previously allied to Sparta (Diodoros 15.40.1). Sparta responded with a show of force in Arkadia, led by Agesilaos, but he was driven back by a Greek alliance, supported by Thebes (Xen. *Hell.* 6.5.10–12, Diodoros 15.63.4). In response the Thebans were persuaded, especially by some of the *perioikoi,* to invade Lakonia, led by Epaminondas (Xen. *Hell.* 6.5.25–32; Diodoros 15.63.3–65.5) and resulting in the foundation of Messene and other cities (**H70–H72**).

E113   The 'Tearless' battle, 368 BC
Agesilaos, due to his old age, declined military service but his son, Archidamos, defeated the Arkadians with the help of a force sent by Dionysos of Sicily in what has become known as the 'Tearless Battle'. In this battle, he slaughtered many of the enemy without the loss of a single Spartan. However, this victory clearly revealed the present weakness of Sparta. For in the past, victory was considered such a natural occurrence that the only sacrifice to the gods for their successes was a cockerel. The soldiers never boasted and the citizens never displayed any joy at the news of victory. Even after the battle of Mantineia, as described by Thucydides, the messenger who first reported the news of the victory received no other reward than a piece of meat, which the magistrates sent from their mess. But now at the news of this victory, the Spartans were unable to restrain themselves. Agesilaos went out to meet and embrace Archidamos on his return with tears of joy in his eyes and the magistrates followed him. Then old men and women marched down to the river Eurotas, lifting their hands and thanking the gods that Sparta was now free of the disgrace and indignity which had befallen her and once again saw the bright light of day. Before this battle, it is said that Spartan men were so ashamed of their defeats that they would not dare even to look their wives in the face.

[Plutarch, *Life of Agesilaos* 33]

Xen. *Hell.* 7.1 also gives an account of the battle. It was only a temporary respite for Sparta. The success may even have prompted the foundation of Megalopolis (Diodoros 15.72.3–4) as a check on Spartan ambitions (see **H72**). The 360s were 'a period of kaleidoscopically shifting alliances, intermittent warfare and periodic revolutions rounded off by major but indecisive pitched battle.' (Cartledge *SL* 257). With Sparta continuing to lose some allies and regain others, the end of the Peloponnesian League came in *c.* 365 BC (**E145**). A few years later, the (second) Battle of Mantineia ended Epaminondas' life and the Theban hegemony.

E114   Second Battle of Mantineia, 362 BC

Helping the Mantineians were the Eleans, Lakedaimonians, Athenians, and some others: altogether they numbered more than 20,000 infantry, and about 2,000 cavalrymen. Fighting with the Tegeans were most of the bravest Arkadians, also Achaians, Boiotians, Argives, some other Peloponnesians and allies from outside: all in all over 30,000 infantry were assembled and no fewer than 3,000 cavalrymen.

[85.1] Both sides moved eagerly down together for a contest to decide everything, with their armies in formation, while the soothsayers on both sides made sacrifices and proclaimed that victory was pre-ordained by the gods. ... [3] Initially a cavalry battle was joined on the wings in which they outdid each other in eagerness to win glory. [4] The Athenians cavalry attacked the Thebans, but were defeated not so much in quality of horses, nor their own skills, nor their experience of horsemanship – for in none of these areas was the Athenian cavalry lacking; but in numbers and equipment of light-armed troops, and in strategic deployment they fell far short of their enemy. The Athenians only had a few javelin-throwers, while the Thebans had three times the number of slingers and javelin-throwers sent from the areas around Thessaly. [5] These peoples from childhood put all their efforts into this sort of warfare, and usually had a great impact in battles through their experience with these weapons. So the Athenians, being badly wounded by the lightly-armed troops, and exhausted by those facing them, all turned and fled. [6] But by fleeing beyond the wings, they made good their defeat, since their retreat did not take out their own phalanx but coincided with them falling in with the Euboians and some mercenaries who had been sent to seize the neighbouring high ground, engaging with them and killing them all. [7] The Theban cavalry did not pursue those fleeing but by charging at the lines of men drawn up opposite did all they could to outflank the infantry. A stiff battle took place: just as the exhausted Athenians were turning to flee, the cavalry commander of the Eleans, stationed in the rear came to support those fleeing, threw down many Boiotians and turned the course of the battle. [8] So the Elean cavalry appeared on the left wing and made good the defeat of their allies. On the other wing, the cavalry forces clashed with each other for a short time while the battle remained in the balance, but then those fighting for Mantineia were forced back by the bravery and greater number of the Boiotian and Thessalian cavalry, and with considerable loss retreated into their own phalanx.

[86.1] This, then, was the result of the cavalry battle for each side. But when the infantry forces came hand-to-hand with their opponents, they created a mighty and amazing struggle. For never in a contest of Greeks against Greeks was so great a force of soldiers drawn up; nor leaders of such reputations; nor did soldiers display their bravery in battle more effectively. [2] For the most effective infantry fighters of that period, the Boiotians and the Lakedaimonians were drawn up facing each other and were the first to engage in battle, with no thought of sparing their lives.

[Diodoros, *Library of History* 15.84.4–86.1]

Despite the eagerness for **contest to decide everything** (85.1), the infantry battle was indecisive. Epaminondas, attempting to break the deadlock by leading a charge was mortally wounded and both sides claimed victory (15.86.2–88.1). Xenophon's account of the battle (7.5.15–26) is less detailed than Diodoros', but must have been incredibly hard for him to write (see **E115** and note). Overall this battle featuring significant use of cavalry also marks an important shift in warfare from the traditional hoplite battle, (e.g. the *First* Battle of Mantineia – and see entry in *OCD³* 'Mantineia, battles of' for the *Third* battle in 207 BC.).

E115   A dignified and moving tribute

Good men among the Athenian cavalry were killed, and very evidently, those whom they killed themselves were good men too.

[Xenophon, *Hellenika* 7.5.17]

Amongst the 'good men' killed, in a cavalry engagement before the main battle was Xenophon's own son, Gryllos (Paus. 8.11.6; Diog. Laert 2.54).

THE NAVY: E116–E136

Sparta traditionally had no need for a navy to control her land empire within the Peloponnese, nor to protect trade interests. But Sparta could clearly muster enough naval expertise to launch an expedition against the island of Samos (just off the coast of Asia Minor) *c.*525 BC (**H12**); for Dorieus to attempt to found overseas colonies *c.* 520 and 510 BC (**H13, H14**); for the first attempt to depose the Peisistratids to be sent by sea (**E11**); and for Kleomenes' refusal to involve Sparta in the Ionian revolt to be based on the 3–month journey from the Ionian coast to Sardis, not on the voyage across the Aegean (Hdt. 5.49.9 = **E16**). Eurybiadas is given naval command of the allied forces at Artemision and Salamsi (**E116**) and Pausanias is in charge of the allied successes in Cyprus and Byzantium in 478 BC (Thuc. 1.94). Nonetheless Perikles was clearly right in his assessment in 431 BC (Thuc. 1.142–3 = **G3**) that naval superiority made Athens almost impregnable (compare Thuc. 2.83–92 on operations in the Gulf of Corinth in 429 BC).

E116   Spartan naval command at Artemision and Salamis, 480 BC

[2.1] The total number of ships brought together at Artemision, excepting the fifty-oared galleys, was 271. The Spartiates provided the general in supreme command, Eurybiadas, son of Eurykleidas. This was because the allies had said that if a Lakonian was not in command they would not follow Athenian leaders but would break up the intended expedition.

[42.1] Far more ships, from more states had been brought together (at Salamis) than had fought at Artemision. The naval commander then was the same man as at Artemision, Eurybiadas, son of Eurykleidas, a Spartiate, but not of the royal family. It was, however, the Athenians who provided by far the most ships and the best sailors.

[Herodotus, *Histories* 8.2.1–2 and 8.42.1–2]

Herodotus gives exact numbers of the ships involved in each battle (8.2.2 and 8.43–47). In summary, the numbers for Artemision and Salamis respectively were: Sparta 10 and 16; Corinth 40 and 40; Athens 127 and 180. Overall totals were 271 and 378, so on each occasion, Athens provided just under half the fleet and the combined Peloponnesian contribution was around one quarter. Eurybiadas is prominent in Hdt's account of the tactical discussions (8.57–64, 74, 79, 108) and was awarded the prize for valour (8.124.2), but it was clearly the Athenian Themistokles who was the driving force, signally honoured by the Spartans (8.124.2–3).

E117   Spartan allies to build ships at start of Peloponnesian War, 431 BC

The Lakedaimonians instructed those in Italy and Sicily who had chosen their side to build a number of ships proportionate to their size of city, to make their total number five hundred.

[Thucydides, *History of the Peloponnesian War* 2.7.2]

E118   Spartan naval tactics 413/2 BC

Therefore Agis their king immediately set out that winter with an expeditionary force from Dekeleia and levied money from the allies for a fleet. Turning then to Oita on the Malian Gulf, because of the long-standing hatred between them he seized a lot of their property and obtained ransom payment for it. The Achaians of Phthia and other cities subject to Thessaly in the area he forced to surrender hostages and money despite criticism and opposition from the Thessalians. He sent the hostages to Corinth and tried to bring them into the alliance. The Lakedaimonians made an assessment that the cities should contribute by building one hundred ships, and that they and the Boiotians should each contribute twenty-five. Phokis and Lokris would contribute fifteen; Corinth fifteen; Arkadia, Pellene and Sikyon ten; Megara, Troizen, Epidauros and Hermione ten.

[Thucydides, *History of the Peloponnesian War* 8.3]

LYSANDER AND THE NAVARCHY: E119–E136

Plutarch's biography describes Lysander as descended from an impoverished branch of the Heraklid family (i.e. distantly related to the kings). Other late sources make him a *mothax* (see **D30, D31**): in other words a client of a wealthy family. He was the older lover of Agesilaos (reigned 400–360 BC). He came swiftly to prominence as navarch in 408/7, where he crucially made friends with Cyrus, the younger son of Darius II, at the time in command of Asia Minor. He thereby (see **E120** and **E126**) gained the very significant financial support necessary to get good sailors and defeat the Athenians at sea, firstly in a small battle at Notion in 407 BC (see **E121–E124**) which importantly resulted in the disgrace of Alkibiades and then (with Lysander technically vice-navarch, since Spartan law did not permit second terms of appointment – **E125**) in the decisive battle of Aigospotamoi which ended the Peloponnesian War (**E127–E128**). This resulted in fame (**B23**) and hero-worship for Lysander (literally, see **C37–C38**) and enormous wealth flooding into Sparta (**E75, E76**). Lysander's policy of installing small oligarchic councils (*dekarchies*) in former democracies was opposed by King Pausanias and eventually the ephors (**E43**), and he also fell out with King Agesilaos (**E132**), but he remained a very important politician and commander until his death while invading Boiotia in 395 BC (Xen. *Hell.* 3.5.17–20). For Lysander and the navarchy, see Cartledge, *Agesilaos* 79–82.

E119   Lysander appointed navarch, 408/7 BC

Not long before this the Lakedaimonians had sent out Lysander as navarch to replace Kratesippidas who had finished his term.

[Xenophon, *Hellenika* 1.5.1]

E120   Lysander gets money from Cyrus of Persia for the Spartan navy, 408/7 BC

When he learnt that Cyrus, the Great King's son, had arrived in Sardis, he went up there to talk with him, and accuse Tissaphernes. Tissaphernes had orders to help the Lakedaimonians and drive the Athenians from the sea, but he appeared to be unprepared, even giving up because of Alkibiades and destroying the fleet with poor resources. [2] Indeed it was what Cyrus wanted to have Tissaphernes blamed, since he was a worthless character and was privately opposed to Cyrus. So as a result of this, and because of other behaviour, Lysander pleased Cyrus; especially because he was inclined towards being agreeable in conversation, he shifted the youth in favour of the war. [3] Cyrus once gave a feast for Lysander when he wished to leave, and he asked him not to reject the fellow-feelings and friendship between them, but told him to ask whatever he would like and said that there was absolutely nothing he could not have. Lysander replied "Since therefore, Cyrus, you are so kind, I beg and entreat you to add one obol to the pay of the sailors so that they take four obols instead of three". [4] So Cyrus was pleased with the honour of the man and gave him 10,000 *darics*. From this amount he paid out an obol to the sailors and, making a name for himself, in a short time he made the ships of his enemies empty.

[Plutarch, *Lysander* 4.1–4]

For this episode, see Xen. *Hell.* 1.5.6–7. For Cyrus, see introduction to **E151**. For *darics* – the gold coin of the Persian Achaemenid empire, see **E155b**.

FOUR ACCOUNTS OF THE BATTLE OF NOTION, 407 BC: E121–E124
These different accounts are of interest for us in showing how the historical tradition operates (see table below). Plutarch clearly followed the details provided by Xenophon. Diodoros clearly used a different source, probably Ephoros (whose work is lost). With the discovery at Oxyrhynchos of large fragments of an historical narrative, it can now be seen that Diodoros and Ephoros followed this historian. He cannot be identified for certain, and hence is referred to as 'The Oxyrhynchos Historian', but seems to have been a near contemporary of the events he describes and a reliable historian. For 'The Oxyrhynchos Historian', see McKechnie & Kern, *Hellenica Oxyrhynchia* (Warminster 1998), and for the accounts of Notion, see A. Andrewes, 'Notion and Kyzikos: the sources compared' in *JHS* 102 (1982), 15–25.

	Oxyrhynchos Hist.	Xenophon, *Hell.*	Diodoros	Plutarch, *Lysander*
Athenian ships launched	10	2	10	2
Lysander's initial force	All	Small force	All	A few
Athenian losses	22	15	22	15

E121   Battle of Notion I: The Oxyrhynchos Historian

[1] As was usual [...] to send ships [...] them, he manned the [ten] fastest triremes and [ordered] the others to lie in wait until [the enemy ships] should be a long way from land, while [he himself] sailed ahead towards Ephesos [...] to bring the ships over to himself. [2] [But Lysander] on sighting them [launched] thirteen ships which previously [...]. These sank Antiochos [...] and destroyed [...]; the ships of the Athenians [which were sailing together] immediately [took fright and turned] back, [not] intending to fight a proper battle. Lysander, however, pursued the enemy with [all] his triremes. [3] [The rest] of the Athenians seeing the Lakedaimonians had put out to sea in pursuit of the ten Athenian ships embarked [immediately] to rush to the aid of [their ships]. But the quick onset of the enemy meant that they could not man the triremes in time; but they put out a little way from the harbour of the [Kolophonians] with most of them, but the ones sailing at the front [...]. The sailors in their confusion, without fighting [...] and retreated from the enemy in disorder. The Lakedaimonians, seeing the Athenians fleeing, pressed on, destroying or capturing twenty-two ships, and trapped the rest [in Notion]. [4] So the Lakedaimonians, having achieved this victory, set up a trophy by the harbour of the city and went back.

[Oxyrhynchos Historian, 4]

E122 Battle of Notion II: Xenophon

Alkibiades, on hearing that Thrasyboulos had advanced beyond the Peloponnese to fortify Phokaia sailed to meet him, leaving his helmsman Antiochos in charge of the ships, with orders not to sail against Lysander's ships. [12] But Antiochos with his own ship and one other sailed from Notion to the harbour of Ephesos right past the prows of Lysander's ships. [13] Lysander at first launched a small number of his ships in pursuit, but when the Athenians went to help Antiochos with more ships, Lysander sailed out with all his ships in formation. Then the Athenians also launched the rest of their ships from Notion, putting out one by one. [14] Therefore the battle took place with one side in formation, but the Athenians with their ships scattered until they fled, having lost fifteen triremes. Most of the men escaped, but some were taken prisoner. Lysander took his ships back with him, set up a trophy at Notion and sailed on to Ephesos, while the Athenians went to Samos.

[Xenophon, *Hellenika* 1.5.11–14]

E123 Battle of Notion III: Diodoros

[1] When Alkibiades learnt that Lysander was fitting out a fleet at Ephesos, he put to sea for Ephesos with all his ships. He sailed up to the harbours, since no one came out to fight him, and harboured most of his ships at Notion, putting Antiochos, his own helmsman, in command of them, with orders not to fight a battle until he was there himself. Meanwhile he took his troops-ships and sailed quickly to Klazomenai since this city, an ally of the Athenians, was suffering badly from having its land ravaged by some of its exiles. [2] But Antiochos, being naturally impetuous and wanting to achieve something spectacular by himself, ignored Alkibiades' orders. He manned the ten best ships, ordered the other captains to have the others ready in case they had to fight a battle, and sailed up to the enemy, provoking them to fight. [3] Lysander had learnt about Alkibiades' departure from some deserters and thought this was a chance to do something worthy of Sparta. So he put to sea with all his ships and sank the leading ship of the ten which Antiochos had taken as his flagship. He then put the others to flight and went in pursuit until the Athenian captains manned the other ships and rushed to help, but not in formation. [4] A battle took place between all the ships not far from land, and the Athenians were defeated because of their disorder and lost twenty-two ships; a few men were taken prisoner while the rest swam to shore.

[Diodoros, *Library of History* 13.71.1–4]

E124 Battle of Notion IV: Plutarch

When Alkibiades sailed from Samos to Phokaia, leaving Antiochos, his pilot, in command of the fleet, Antiochos, as though to insult Lysander and display his confidence, sailed into the harbour of Ephesos with two triremes. He rowed past their anchorage with laughter and a lot of noise in a swaggering manner; Lysander was angered by this and at first launching a few of his triremes, he pursued him; then he saw that the other Athenians were coming to his aid, so he launched the full fleet, and finally the engagement resulted in a battle. [2] Lysander was victorious, capturing fifteen triremes, and he set up a trophy. At this, the people in the city of Athens deposed Alkibiades from his command;

[Plutarch, *Lysander* 5]

E125   Lysander appointed as vice-navarch, 405 BC

[6] After this the Chians and the rest of the allies gathered at Ephesos and decided, in light of the situation, to send ambassadors to Lakedaimon to report the facts and to ask for Lysander as commander of the fleet, as Lysander was popular among the allies as a result of his former command, when he won the battle of Notion.

[7] And so ambassadors were sent, accompanied by envoys from Cyrus with the same request. And the Lakedaimonians granted them Arakos as navarch and Lysander as second-in-command, for it was contrary to their laws for a man to hold the office of navarch twice. Nevertheless, they handed over the ships to the command of Lysander, with the war now having lasted for twenty-five years.

[Xenophon, *Hellenika* 2.1.6–7]

E126   Cyrus entrusts to Lysander his revenues as hyper-satrap of Asia

[13] Cyrus then sent for Lysander, for a messenger had arrived from his father with word that he was ill and had summoned him. He was at Thamneria in Persia, near the land of the Cadusians against whom he had made an expedition, for they were in revolt.

[14] When Lysander arrived, Cyrus warned him not to battle the Athenians unless he far outnumbered them in ships. For, Cyrus said, both the King and he had abundant amounts of money and as a result, it would be possible to man many ships. He then gave to Lysander all the tribute which came in from his cities and belonged to him personally, and also handed over the balance he had to hand. After he had reminded Lysander how good a friend he was both to the Lakedaimonian state and to him personally, Cyrus began his journey to his father.

[Xenophon, *Hellenika 2.1.13–14]*

See Plut. *Lysander* 9.2. For Cyrus and his 'hyper-satrapy' see introduction to **E151**.

E127   Build up to battle of Aigospotamoi, 405 BC

[17] Meanwhile Lysander sailed from Rhodes along the coast of Ionia to the Hellespont, in order to prevent the grain ships from passing out and to take revenge on the cities which had revolted from the Lakedaimonians. The Athenians likewise set out from Chios, keeping to the open sea; [18] for Asia was hostile to them. But Lysander sailed along the coast from Abydos to Lampsakos, which was an ally of the Athenians. The people of Abydos and the other cities were on the shore to support him, as they were commanded by Thorax, a Lakedaimonian.

[19] Then they attacked Lampsakos and captured it by storm. The soldiers plundered it. Lampsakos was a wealthy city, full of wine and grain and all kinds of other supplies. However Lysander released all of the free people who were captured. [20] The Athenians, who had been sailing closely behind Lysander's fleet, anchored at Elaious in the Chersonese with one hundred and eighty ships. While they were preparing their breakfast there, the news about Lampsakos was reported to them, and they set out immediately for Sestos. [21] From there, as soon as they had replenished their supplies, they sailed to Aigospotamoi, which is opposite Lampsakos (the Hellespont at this point is about two miles wide). There they dined.

[22] During the following night, at dawn, Lysander gave the signal for his men to take breakfast and board their ships. After everything was prepared for battle and the side screens were stretched out, he gave orders that no one should move from his position or set out. [23] At daybreak, the Athenians drew up their ships in line for battle at the mouth of the harbour. However, since Lysander did not set out against them, they sailed back again later in the day to Aigospotamoi. [24] Then Lysander ordered his swiftest ships to follow the Athenians and, when they had disembarked, to observe what they did, and then to sail back and report to him. He did not disembark his men from their ships until these scout-ships had returned. This he did for four days; and the Athenians continued to draw themselves up for battle.

[Xenophon, *Hellenika* 2.1.17–24]

In *Hellenika* 2.1.25–26, Alkibiades, the controversial Athenian politician, warns the Athenian generals of the weakness of the position of their navy but is brusquely told that he is not in charge.

E128 Battle of Aigospotamoi, 405 BC

[27] Lysander, on the fifth day that the Athenians sailed out against him, ordered his men who followed them back to sail back to him and to hoist a shield at the midway point. Lysander's men did just as he had ordered as soon as they saw that the enemy had disembarked and had scattered up and down the Chersonese. The Athenians had been doing this far more freely every day, not only because they had bought their provisions at a distance, but also because they treated Lysander with contempt for not putting out to meet them. [28] But now Lysander signalled immediately to his fleet to sail with all speed, and Thorax with his troops went with the fleet. When Konon saw the oncoming attack, he signalled the Athenians to hasten to their ships with all their strength. But since his men were scattered here and there, some of the ships had only two banks of oars manned, some only had one, and others were entirely empty. Konon's own ship and the seven others accompanying him, which were fully manned, set out to sea in close formation with the *Paralos*. However Lysander captured all the rest on the beach. He also rounded up most of the crew-men on the shore, although some had fled to neighbouring strongholds.

[29] When Konon, fleeing with his nine ships, realised that the Athenian cause was utterly lost, he put in at Abarnis, the promontory of Lampsakos, and there he seized the sails that belonged to Lysander's ships. He then sailed away to seek refuge with Euagoras in Cyprus with eight ships, while the *Paralos* went to Athens with the news of what had happened.

[Xenophon, *Hellenika* 2.1.27–28]

The *Paralos* was the state trireme, used more for public missions than as a warship.

E129 Lysander's treachery at Thasos, 405 BC

Lysander took control of Thasos. Many of the population were on the side of Athens and were in hiding in fear of the Spartan, but he assembled the people of Thasos in the sanctuary of Herakles and came out with a generous speech, that it was vital to pardon those in hiding because of the change in government, and that they should be assured that nothing would happen to them, and should have confidence in what he said as being spoken in a sanctuary and especially that of Herakles their ancestor. The

Thasians who had been in hiding put their trust in his generous speech and came out; but Lysander after waiting a few days to make them even less fearful, ordered that they should be rounded up and killed.

[Polyaenus, *Stratagems* 1.45.4]

Polyaenus was a Macedonian writer of the 2nd century AD. In his *Stratagems*, he compiled episodes from Greek and Roman military history. This episode is not mentioned by Xenophon or Plutarch's *Life of Lysander*, but Nepos (*Life of Lysander* 2) mentions his behaviour in Thasos in 405 as an example of his cruelty and treachery. The Oxyrhynchos Historian may be the original source.

E130   Lysander sets up a dekarchy in Samos, 404 BC

Lysander handed over the city and everything in it to its former citizens, appointing ten rulers as its guardians, and then released the allied naval forces back to their cities. [8] He sailed to Lakedaimon with the Lakonian ships, taking the prows of the captured ships, all but twelve of the triremes from Peiraieus, the crowns which he had received as personal presents from the cities, the 470 talents of silver which still remained from the tribute which Cyrus had provided him to pay for the war, and everything else he had obtained in the war. [9] All of this he handed over to the Lakedaimonians at the end of the summer.

[Xenophon, *Hellenika* 2.3.7–9 (404 BC)]

Other dekarchies (councils of ten extreme oligarchs) were also established in Thasos (Nepos, *Lysander* 3.1), in Peiraieus 404–3 BC, and elsewhere (Diod. Sic. 14.3.4; 14.10.1; Nepos, *Lys.* 2.1) to run affairs in cities formerly part of the Athenian empire. As unelected tyrants answerable only to Lysander, they quickly became extremely unpopular. Their model, the 'Thirty Tyrants' of Athens, was overthrown in 403 BC, and those in the cities of Asia Minor followed quickly. King Pausanias had a majority of ephors supporting him against Lysander in 403/2 BC, see **E43**, though some other dekarchies may have lasted until Sparta's defeat at Knidos (394) or the King's Peace (386).

E131   Lysander hopes to restablish the dekarchies, 396 BC

[2] The Lakedaimonians were in a state of great expectation and anxiety. They gathered together their allies and deliberated what they should do. Lysander, believing that the Greeks were far superior on the sea and aware that the land force which had gone to the country with Cyrus had returned safely, persuaded Agesilaos to make an expedition to Asia if the Lakedaimonians would give him thirty Spartiates, two thousand freed helots, and a contingent of six thousand of the allies. Apart from these motives, Lysander in addition wished to accompany Agesilaos himself, so that with the aid of Agesilaos he might re-establish the dekarchies which had been set up in the cities by him but had been overthrown by the ephors, who had issued a decree restoring to the cities their ancient form of government.

[Xenophon, *Hellenika* 3.4.2 (396 BC)]

E132   Lysander annoys Agesilaos by his regal behaviour

[7] Since Lysander was so famous, people were courting him thinking that he could obtain from Agesilaos whatever they wanted. Therefore there was always such a great crowd following him around, asking for favours, that he appeared to be the king and Agesilaos a private citizen. [8] It became apparent later that this infuriated Agesilaos too, while the other thirty Spartiates were not able to keep silent in their

jealousy, but spoke to Agesilaos about Lysander acting improperly by conducting himself with greater pomp than in a monarchy. Lysander then began to introduce people to Agesilaos, but he began to send away with rejections all those people he knew Lysander was working with.

[Xenophon, *Hellenika* 3.4.7–8 (397 BC)]

E133   Lysander hopes to be elected king

[2] Consequently Lysander arrogantly thought to abolish the kingship of the Heraklids and to make all Spartiates eligible to choose their kings. For he hoped that rule would very quickly come to him because of the very great and glorious deed he had achieved. [3] Realising that the Lakedaimonians took great notice of oracles, he tried to corrupt the priestess at Delphi with money.

[Diodoros, *Library of History* 14.13.2–3]

E134   Lysander aims at an elective kingship

[24.4] He had achieved great fame for his actions and acquired many friends and much power. So he was angry because he saw the city, whose power had been increased by his efforts, being ruled by others who had no better claim by birth than his. He planned to take the rule of the state from the control of these two families and hand it over to all the Heraklids [24.5] although some say, not just to the Heraklids, but to the Spartiates in general. His intention was that the privilege of monarchy should not only be for those descended from Herakles, but for all, like Herakles, chosen for his excellence, which had raised him to the honours of the gods. He hoped that, once the kingship was decided in this way, no other Spartiate would be chosen before himself. [25.1] Therefore at first he made preparations to persuade his citizens himself, and he learnt carefully a speech written for this proposal by Kleon, the Halikarnassian. Then he realised that the extraordinary nature and importance of his revolutionary change needed more vigorous support; so he raised machinery, like in tragedy, to pressure his citizens, [25.2] putting together and supplying oracles and prophecies declared by Apollo.

[Plutarch, *Life of Lysander* 24.4–25.2]

E135   Lysander's speech proposing elected kings

[3] At a later time, so Ephoros says, there was an argument in Sparta between her allies and it was necessary to examine the writings by him which Lysander kept. Agesilaos went to his house to do this. There he is said to have found a book, in which was written the speech concerning the constitution that they needed to remove the monarchy from the Eurypontids and Agiads, giving everyone the opportunity, and making it a choice from the best Lakedaimonians. [4] Agesilaos was in a hurry to publish the speech to the citizens and show them what sort of citizen Lysander had truly been. But Lakratidas, a sensible man, and the leading ephor at that time, stopped Agesilaos, and said that he should not dig up Lysander, but bury such a cleverly written and plausible speech with him.

[Plutarch, *Life of Lysander* 30.3–4 = Ephoros, *FGrH* 70 F207]

Xenophon makes no mention of this when commenting about Lysander's regal behaviour (**E132** above)

E136   Lysander dies a poor man

Because Lysander had died in such a manner, the Lakedaimonians were at the time so angry that they put King Pausanias on trial for his life; he did not defend this charge but fled to Tegea; there he lived out his life as a suppliant in the sanctuary of Athena. [2] For the poverty of Lysander, which was revealed on his death, made his excellence more obvious to all, since despite all the wealth and power, and such support and favour from cities and the Persian King, he had not, even in some small way, added to his own family's wealth and status. This is what Theopompos records, who is more trustworthy when he praises than when he criticises, for he finds it more pleasing to criticise than to praise.

[Plutarch, *Life of Lysander* 30.1–2 = Theopompos, *FGrH* 115 F333]

THE PELOPONNESIAN LEAGUE: E137–E145

For the Peloponnesian League, see **D100–D102**. The only epigraphic Spartan treaty from before the third century BC is with the Aitoloi Erxadieis (**B15**) – an undated treaty with a previously unknown people. It contains what is generally thought to be the basic clause 'to follow the Lakedaimonians wherever they may lead and to have the same friends and enemies as the Lakedaimonians.' The initial actions of the Peloponnesians in following Kleomenes to Attika *c.* 506 BC (Hdt. 5.74 = **E14**) suggest they were following such a pledge and similar language is used by Hdt. in describing Kleomenes' attempt to use the Arkadians for his own ends (6.74.1 = **E22**). But Bolmarcich, 'The Date of the "Oath of the Peloponnesian League"' in *Historia* 57 (2008), 65–79 argues that it was deliberately and pointedly created to be used by Athens in surrendering to Sparta in 404/3 BC (**E144**). For criticisms of the structure of the Peloponnesian league attributed by Thucydides to Perikles, see **G3**.

E137   Treaty with Tegea

a)   The Lakedaimonians, after being reconciled with the Tegeans made a treaty and set up a joint *stele* on the River Alpheios, in which, amongst other terms, it was written to expel the Messenians from the land and that it was not allowed to make people 'good'. Aristotle in explaining this says that it means not to kill for help towards the pro-Spartan Tegeans.

b)   Aristotle says that in the treaty of the Arkadians with the Lakedaimonians it is written to make no one 'good' for help towards the pro-Spartan Tegeans, i.e. to kill no one.

[Plutarch, *Moralia* 292b and 277bc = *Greek Questions* 5 and
Roman Questions 52]

Plutarch's source was almost certainly one of the many *Greek Constitutions* produced by Aristotle's students. The explanation of making people 'good', as a euphemism for killing them was challenged by Jacoby who thought that it meant that they (i.e. the Messenians) should not be made citizens. Braun, 'Khrestous poiein' in *CQ* 44, 1994 40–45 defends the original reading that pro-Spartans in Tegea must not be killed. The treaty itself is undatable, with suggestions including after the second Messenian War (mid-7th C); the mid-6th C (coinciding with Spartan conquest of Tegea, see **H10**); or various 5th C dates.

E138   Spartans consult allies before trying to restore Hippias, *c.*504 BC

[1] Then, when the Lakedaimonians found the oracles and saw that the Athenians' power was increasing and that they were not at all ready to obey them, they realised that the people of Attika, now free, would become as powerful as them, whereas they would be weak and ready to submit to their rule if held down under an absolute ruler. When they learnt this, they sent for Hippias, son of Peisistratos from Sigeion in the Hellespont. [2] When Hippias answered their summons, they sent messengers to their other allies to say that they Spartiates had this to say, "Our allies, we admit that we have been mistaken: misled by fraudulent oracles, we have driven out from their fatherland men who were very friendly to us and who had undertaken to keep Athens subservient. And in doing so, we have surrendered the city to the thankless mob, which, once freed by us, emerged to insult and expel us and our king. They have increased in reputation and strength as their neighbours, the Boiotians and Chalkidians are only too well aware, and others might soon learn if they don't watch out. [3] These are the mistakes we made then: now we shall try to repair them, together with you. It was for this reason that we called this man, Hippias, and you from your cities, so that with joint resolve and joint expedition we should take him back to Athens and restore what we took away.

[Herodotus, *Histories* 5.91]

Hdt tells us (5.92α) that allied opposition was expressed by the Corinthian delegate likening Sparta's proposal to restore tyranny to the recommendation that men should live in the sea and fish on land, emphasising the reputation of Sparta as ending tyrannies throughout Greece, see **E5** and note, **E6**, **F4**.

E139   Peloponnesian League vote on Samian revolt from Athens, 440 BC

[40.5] For when the Samians revolted from you [the Athenians], we [the Corinthians] did not vote against you when the other Peloponnesians were divided in voting on whether to help Samos. We clearly opposed the motion and maintained that a state should have the right to punish its own allies. … [41.2] The help we gave you regarding the Samians when it was due to us that the Peloponnesians did not send help, allowed you to punish the Samians.

[Thucydides, *History of the Peloponnesian War* 1.40.5]

In 440, Athens installed a democracy in Samos, a member of the Delian League. This prompted an armed revolt which Athens suppressed in 439. Thucydides gives an account in 1.115–7 in his '*pentekontaetia*' but the account there makes no mention of Spartan thoughts of intervention. Instead these had been referred to in the speech Thuc. gives to the Corinthians above, urging Athens not to form an alliance with Corinth's colony-turned-opponents, Corcyra. The brief passage above provides important evidence for the way the Peloponnesian League operated: Sparta had the choice whether or not to call a meeting in the first place. Only if it did, could action be taken. The Athenian decree of 440/39 making settlement with Samos (ML56 = OR 139) contains fragmentary mention of the [Pelo]ponnes[ians]. See Hornblower, *Commentary* vol I, 83–4; Cartledge, *Sparta and Samos* 262–3.

THE LEAGUE AND THE PELOPONNESIAN WAR 432–404 BC: E140–E144
For remarks on debate in 432, see the introductory note to E29–E31.

E140   Peloponnesian League meets to discuss war with Athens, 432 BC

[66.1] Athens and the Peloponnesians had similar pretexts for war against each other: on the Corinthian side, that their own colony of Poteidaia, with Corinthian and Peloponnesian citizens resident there, was being besieged by the Athenians; on the Athenian side that one of their own tribute-paying cities had been induced to revolt and that the Corinthians had openly gone and joined the Poteidaians in their fight with Athens.

[67.1] Nevertheless, war had not yet broken out and the truce was still in force. The Corinthians had been operating covertly. But now, with Poteidaia under siege, they brought things into the open, since some of their citizens were still inside the city and they feared they might lose it. They sent urgent messages to the allies to send delegations to Lakedaimon and when they themselves got there they vigorously denounced the Athenians for breaking the truce and committing aggression against the Peloponnese. [67.2] The people of Aigina did not send a formal delegation, because they feared Athenian retaliation, but they gave strong tacit support to the Corinthians in encouraging a declaration of war, claiming that they had not been given the independence promised to them under the terms of the truce. [67.3] The Lakedaimonians summoned to one of their regular assemblies both their own allies and anyone else who claimed to have suffered aggression at the hands of the Athenians. There they offered them opportunity to report their grievances. [67.4] Many of them came forward with their individual complaints, but it was the Megarians in particular who listed a number of other issues, but in particular the fact that, in breach of the terms of the truce, they were excluded from all the ports of the Athenian empire and from markets in Attika. The final speech came from the Corinthians, who had allowed previous speakers to work up the feelings of the Lakedaimonians against Athens. They spoke as follows:

[Thucydides, *History of the Peloponnesian War* 1.66–67]

E141   Corinthian speech urging war with Athens

[68.1] "Lakedaimonians, your trust in your own constitution and society makes you less ready to trust others, when we have something to say. You take from it a sense of caution, but in dealing with external matters what you use is more like ignorance. [68.2] We have often warned in advance that we would be harmed by the Athenians, but each time you did not take the lesson that we were teaching you, but instead suspected that the speakers had motives of their own which differed from yours. And this is why you have called your allies here too late – not before they suffered but only now we are in the thick of it. Therefore we have the most right to speak, since we have the greatest complaint in being wronged by the Athenians and ignored by you.

[68.3] "Now if they were somehow wronging Greece surreptitiously, it would be necessary to teach people who did not know. But as it is, why make a long speech, when you see some people being enslaved, and see them plotting against others, not least our own allies, and that they have been preparing for a long while in advance to go to war some day. [68.4] They would not otherwise have stolen Kerkyra and held it despite our efforts, or besieged Poteidaia, since the latter is the most useful place from which to conduct operations towards Thrace, while the former provided the largest navy for the Peloponnesians.

[69.1] "And for these mistakes you are to blame, firstly for having allowed them to fortify their city after the Persian Wars and later build the Long Walls, and even now for depriving of their freedom not only those enslaved by them but now even your allies. It is not the enslaver, but the man who could stop it, but just looks on who is more truly responsible for the action, if indeed he bears a reputation for virtue in setting Greece free. [69.2] Now we have, with difficulty, obtained a meeting, but still with no clear purpose. For we should not be considering whether we are being wronged, but how to defend ourselves, since men of action make their plans in advance and do not wait to move against those who have still not made up their minds. [69.3] And we know the way in which the Athenians little by little move against their neighbours. At present they are rather cautious because they think they can get away with it because you have not noticed; once they realise that you are aware, but ignore it, they will press on strongly. [69.4] For you Lakedaimonians are the only Greeks who take no action and defend yourselves not by a show of strength but by the promise of it, and the only ones who break the power of your enemies not at the start but when it has doubled. [69.5] Yet you were said to be 'reliable', though more in words than deeds. For we ourselves know that the Persians came from the ends of the earth to the Peloponnese before meeting any resistance worthy of the name from you. And now you ignore the Athenians, who are not far off like them, but close at hand, and instead of moving against them, you would rather defend yourselves when they attack, and leave to chance the result of your contest against people who have become much stronger. In addition you know that the Persian king failed largely through his own mistakes, and that so far against the Athenians too we have survived more by their mistakes than by your assistance, since placing their hopes and trust in you, rather than in preparing themselves has already ruined several states. [69.6] And let no one think that this is said out of enmity, rather than as a matter of taking responsibility. For when friends make mistakes it is a matter taking responsibility: accusations are for wrongs done by enemies.

[70.1] "And while we are on the subject, there is another point, which we believe can be legitimately made in criticism of our neighbours, such as yourselves, especially given the very great differences that exist between you and the Athenians, of which you seem to be completely unaware. Indeed, you have never really analysed the qualities of these Athenians against whom you are proposing to make war, and their national characteristics which are so utterly different from your own. [70.2] These Athenians are imaginative, quick witted in conception, and swift in the execution of any enterprise. By contrast you are a conservative people, preferring to preserve the status quo, hostile to new ideas, and reluctant to take even the most essential steps to remedy a situation. [70.3] Then again, Athenians are courageous to the point of absurdity, willing to take risks beyond the bounds of common sense, and optimistic even in the most dire circumstances. But you Lakedaimonians are slaves to mediocrity, always doing less than your capacities or analysis suggest is possible; you are deeply suspicious of even rock-solid arguments, because you cannot believe that the good times will ever come again. [70.4] They activate; you procrastinate. They get out and about; you stay at home. For them such activity is seen as a source of potential profit; for you it represents the possibility of loss. [70.5] For them any success is the basis for further advance, a setback a matter of minimal retreat. [70.6] Furthermore, for Athenians their lives are not their own, but expendable in the service of their city;

their talents though their own are there to be used for their city's advantage. [70.7] Unsuccessful projects they regard as personal losses; successful projects as minor gains on the way to greater future success. Any genuine failure is immediately remedied by the development of some new enterprise. Uniquely, for them to conceive an idea is to achieve it, almost immediately, thanks to the speed with which they think of it and then put it into action. [70.8] All the story of their lives is one of toil and danger; least of all mankind do they enjoy what they have got, because they are always striving for more; for them a holiday is an opportunity for necessary action, untroubled peace a misfortune, leisure a wearisome bore. [70.9] In fact the most accurate assessment of them that anyone can offer is to say that Nature has designed them to get no pleasure from peace for themselves, nor to allow anyone else to do so either.

[71.1] "That is the sort of city you are up against, Lakedaimonians. And yet you continue to procrastinate; you seem unable to realise that peace usually comes to those who by their preparations show themselves champions of justice, and by their resolution make it clear that they will not tolerate injustice. But yours seems to be a two-pronged policy: to avoid provoking anyone else, while taking steps to protect only yourselves from harm. [71.2] This would hardly be a recipe for success even if the next door city were like yourselves. But now, as we have just explained, by contrast with the Athenians your whole outlook is totally out of date. [71.3] As with all technical processes, new skills constantly need to be mastered. For any city existing in a state of peace, of course the established systems are the best. But for those confronted by frequent emergencies, frequent fresh strategies are no less essential. That is why the Athenians, thanks to their wide-ranging initiatives, have developed a state that is far better adapted than yours to changing circumstances.

[71.4] "The time has come to put an end to your present policy of inertia. Now is the time to help your allies, especially the people of Poteidaia, as you promised. You must launch an immediate invasion of Attika, before you simply deliver your own friends and kinsfolk into the hands of your bitterest enemies and send the rest of us off in despair to seek an alternative alliance. [71.5] We would not be doing anything unlawful in the eyes of the gods by whom we swore our oaths nor in the eyes of those who are now watching our actions closely. Treaties are broken, not by those who change their allegiance because they have been abandoned by their so-called allies, but by those very allies who fail to supply the help which they promised under oath to give. [71.6] Provided you show yourselves willing to respond, we shall remain your enthusiastic allies. It would be sacrilegious to do otherwise by changing sides and we could never find anyone else whose values are so closely allied to our own. [71.7] Think about all this very carefully. As leaders of the Peloponnese, prove your mettle by showing yourselves worthy of your ancestors who bequeathed it to you."

[Thucydides, *History of the Peloponnesian War* 1.68–71]

For general remarks about speeches in Thucydides, see note on **E29**. The Corinthian speech is followed immediately in Thucydides' narrative by one from an Athenian delegation which was at the meeting on other business (Thuc. 1.72–78), and who must surely have reported back at Athens that they made a reply to the Corinthians. On the other hand, we must wonder whether the speech as presented by Thuc., is not unduly aggressive and provocative; whether its considerable praise of Athens and criticism of Sparta, especially section 70, could really have been delivered; or whether Thuc. is not taking the opportunity, early in his history to set up the national characteristics of the two sides.

E142   Spartans call a final meeting of the Peloponnesian League to ratify war, 432 BC

Even so, the Lakedaimonians summoned their allies to yet another assembly, wishing to take a vote on whether war was an unavoidable necessity. The allied delegates arrived and at the assembly made their opinions clear, most of them denouncing the Athenians and recommending a declaration of war.

[Thucydides, *History of the Peloponnesian War* 1.119.1]

E143   The League votes for the fifty years peace, 421 BC

Throughout this winter people met for talks; as spring approached, preparations for a first move by the Lakedaimonians involving setting up forts in enemy territory were announced in the cities, with the aim of getting the Athenians to take notice. After meetings had carried on with many demands, it was mutually agreed that after giving back what each side had taken by war, peace would be made; the Athenians would keep Nisaia, since when they asked for the return of Plataia the Thebans said that they had taken that place not by force, but by agreement with inhabitants who did not betray the city but came onto their side: and the Athenians said that it was the same case with Nisaia. Then the Lakedaimonians summoned their allies and all except for Boiotia, Corinth, Elis, and Megara, who did not like the terms, voted to end hostilities. So they made the agreement, performed the rites, and made an oath with the Athenians, and the Athenians with the Lakedaimonians in the following words. *[see **B17** for the treaty]*

[Thucydides, *History of the Peloponnesian War* 5.17.2]

E144   League vote on accepting Athenian surrender, 404 BC

[19] When Theramenes and the other ambassadors were at Sellasia and were asked with what proposals they had come, they replied that they had full power to negotiate a peace. The ephors then gave orders to summon them to Lakedaimon. When they arrived, the ephors called an assembly. Many Greeks, the Corinthians and Thebans in particular, opposed making a treaty with the Athenians and favoured destroying their city. [20] The Lakedaimonians, however, said that they would not enslave a Greek city which had done such great service amid the greatest dangers that had befallen Greece. Instead, they offered to make peace on the condition that the Athenians should destroy the long walls and the walls of Peiraieus, hand over all of their ships except twelve, allow their exiles to return, count the same people friends and enemies as the Lakedaimonians did, and follow the Lakedaimonians both by land and by sea wherever they should lead.

[23] After [the Athenian assembly agreed to these terms] Lysander sailed into the Peiraieus, the exiles were returned, and the Lacedaemonians and their allies began to tear down the walls to the music of flute-girls with great enthusiasm, thinking that this was the day that heralded freedom for Greece.

[Xenophon, *Hellenika* 2.2.19–20 and 23]

For the terms dictated by the Spartan ephors see **B24**. For the idea that the terms of the Spartan alliance were deliberately coined for Athens' surrender, see introductory note to **E137–E145**. For the question of why Sparta vetoed Athens' destruction, see Powell in *Sparta and War* (2006).

E145   The effective end of the Peloponnesian League, 366 BC

[8] "Lakedaimonians, we have come to you as your friends, thinking it right that you should tell us if you can see any safety for us if we continue fighting: but if you consider that our position is hopeless, that you join us in making peace if it would benefit you too, since we would more gladly be saved with you than with anyone else. But if you reckon that your advantage lies in continuing to fight, we ask you to allow us to make peace. For if we are saved we may perhaps at some future point have the opportunity of helping you; but if we are destroyed now, we could clearly never do so." [9] When they heard this, the Lakedaimonians advised the Corinthians to make peace and backed those allies who did not wish to fight alongside them in ceasing to do so. For their own part, they said that they would fight and do whatever god pleased – but never would they submit to being deprived of Messene which they had received from their fathers. [10] So when the Corinthians heard this, they went to Thebes to make peace.

[Xenophon, *Hellenika* 7.4.8–10]

SPARTA AND PERSIA: E146–E156
Sparta and Persia seem to have remained technically at war until 412 BC (Hornblower, *Greek World*[3] 74, citing Lewis, *Sparta and Persia* 62) so it is no surprise that we hear very little of any Spartan dealings with Persia for much of the fifth century. Within the Peloponnesian War, Persian assistance for Sparta would be hard to square with Sparta's claim to be liberating Greece (Thuc. 2.8). But many critics feel that Thucydides failed to make enough of Persian involvements up to 411 BC: though perhaps (see, for example Hornblower, *Commentary* vol. III 770–1) he intended to include previous Persian involvement when introducing Cyrus whose importance he clearly recognised (**E146**). There are almost no Persian sources to help us: Kuhrt's comprehensive *The Persian Empire: a Corpus of Sources from the Achaemenid period* (550–330 BC) contains about 70 sources mentioning Sparta(ns) in the index, but all bar one (a Lycian inscription, **E149**) are by Greek writers!

E146   Cyrus' importance foreshadowed

The Athenians still held out for eight (?) years against their initial enemies, and the Sicilians who joined them, even when most of their allies had revolted, and later when Cyrus, the son of the Persian king joined in and provided money for the Peloponnesians for their fleet. Even then, they did not surrender before they had brought about their own downfall and defeat through internal dissent. Such great advantages at the time were more than enough for Perikles to predict that Athens would easily come through a war against the Peloponnesians.

[Thucydides, *History of the Peloponnesian War* 2.65.12–13]

Thucydides here looks ahead to the reasons for Athens' eventual defeat, while seeking to justify Perikles for having led Athens into the war. The passage comes shortly after Thuc. presents Perikles' final speech (2.60–64) and his 'obituary' (2.65). Towards the start of the passage the manuscripts give the figure of 3 years, which is clearly a mistake: the restoration of 10 or 8 depends on whether the starting point is taken as the disaster in Sicily (413 BC) or the oligarchic revolution (411).

E147   Spartan contacts with Persia, 430 BC

At the end of the summer, Aristeus of Corinth, the Lakedaimonian ambassadors, Aneristos, Nikolaos, and Pratodamos, together with Timagoras from Tegea and an Argive acting as a private individual, named Pollis, journeyed to Asia to see the Persian king, to see if they could persuade him to provide money and to join the war.

[Thucydides, *History of the Peloponnesian War* 2.67.1]

The ambassadors did not make it to Persia, but only to Thrace, where they were handed over to the Athenians who executed them without trial, as Thuc. goes on to tell us (2.67.3–4) – a notorious incident also mentioned by Hdt 7.137 = **E148**, below.

E148   Betrayal of Spartan ambassadors sent to negotiate with Persia in 430

These messengers were sent to Asia by the Lakedaimonians, but betrayed by Sitalkes, son of Teres, the king of Thrace, and by Nymphodoros, son of Pythas, a man from Abdera. They were taken prisoner at Bisanthe in the Hellespont, transported to Attika and put to death by the Athenians.

[Herodotus, *Histories* 7.137.3]

E149   Lycian inscribed monument at Xanthus

The Spartans (?) … began (?) to … Tissaphernes … son of Hydarnes and the Persians in Caunus, and in alliance with Spartalia against Athens, the Persians fought the army. I became judge for them. They issued a double guarantee (?). Both in Hytenna a *stele* shall be set down for Maliya, in place/on the spot … the fighters (?) … And in Caunus likewise (?) a *stele* shall be put down for the local precinct and for Maliya and for Artemis and for the King of Caunus.

[Xanthus pillar = Kuhrt, *The Persian Empire* 8.29 (trans. Kuhrt)]

4m high pillar, topped by grave chamber, thought to have been erected around 400 BC by a Lycian dynast in honour of his father. The 412/1 Persia-Sparta treaty (**B22**) was agreed at Caunus (Thuc. 8.57) and this text in Lycian seems to record that meeting.

E150   Persian satrap promises maintenance to League forces, 411 BC

Tissaphernes called in the Peloponnesians and promised that he would provide maintenance. He had recently been appointed by the King and owed the tributes from his province which because of the Athenians he had been unable to extract from the Greek cities. He thought that if he did the Athenians harm, he would be more likely to get in the tribute, secure an alliance between the Lakedaimonians and the King, and bring in, alive or dead, Amorges, bastard son of Pissouthnes, who had revolted in Karia, as the King has ordered him.

[Thucydides, *History of the Peloponnesian War* 8.5.5]

CYRUS, SON OF DARIUS II

Cyrus was the second son of the Persian king Darius II. In 408 BC, when maybe as young as 16, he was sent to Asia with special control over several satrapies (provinces) in the area. He gave the Peloponnesians the financial support crucial for their naval success against Athens (see Xen. *Hell.* 1.5.6–7, **E120**, **E146** and **E126**). After the death of his father (405 BC), he revolted against his elder brother, Artaxerxes, enlisting help from Greeks (**E151**), including a large force of mercenaries. He was killed in battle at Cunaxa in 401: the return journey of the 'Ten Thousand' remaining mercenaries was told by Xenophon (*Anabasis*) who took charge after other Greek leaders, including the Spartiate exile Klearchos, had been rounded up and killed by the Persians under Tissaphernes. The capabilities shown by Greek mercenaries as well as the new political situation in Greece encouraged further Greek military involvement in Asia Minor in the following years, until the settlement of the King's Peace in 387/6.

E151   Spartan involvement in Cyrus' rebellion in Persia, 401 BC

Cyrus also sent ambassadors to the Lakedaimonians to remind them of how he had helped them in the war against the Athenians and to urge them to ally themselves with him. The Lakedaimonians, thinking that the war would be of benefit to them, decided to help Cyrus and dispatched ambassadors to their navarch, called Samios, to instruct him to do whatever Cyrus ordered. [5] Samios had 25 triremes and sailed with them to Ephesos ready to act fully in support of Cyrus' naval commander. The Lakedaimonians also sent 800 foot soldiers under the command of Cheirisophos.

[Diodoros, *Library of History* 14.19.4–5]

E152   Continued Spartan involvement in Asia, 400–397

Tissaphernes had clearly been of great service to the King in his war with his brother. Therefore he was sent as satrap of the areas he had previously ruled, and those of Cyrus too. He immediately demanded that all the cities of Ionia should submit to him. They wished to be free, and also feared Tissaphernes because they had chosen to support Cyrus while he was alive, not him. So they refused to let him into their cities, but instead sent envoys to the Lakedaimonians asking them, as the champions of the whole of Greece, to protect the Greeks of Asia too, to stop their land being ravaged and to preserve their freedom. [4] So the Lakedaimonians sent out Thibron as their harmost, giving him an army of almost 1,000 *neodamodeis* and about 4,000 Peloponnesians.

[Xenophon, *Hellenika* 3.1.3–4]

Sparta continued to fight the Persians in Asia under Thibron and then Derkylidas (Xen. *Hell.* 3.1.5 – 3.2.20 over the next few years, before Agesilaos launched a far larger expedition in 396 BC (below).

E153   Agesilaos' mission to liberate Ionian Greeks, 396 BC

[3] Agesilaos wanted to go to sacrifice at Aulis, where Agamemnon had sacrificed when he sailed to Troy. … [5] When he first arrived, Tissaphernes sent to ask him what he wanted. Agesilaos replied that he had come so that the cities in Asia would be as independent as those back home in Greece.

[Xenophon, *Hellenika* 3.4.3 and 5]

Xenophon gives accounts of Agesilaos' campaigns in Asia, 396–4 BC in *Agesilaos* 1.9–38 and *Hellenika* 3.4 and 4.1. His wish to imitate Agamamenon shows his desire to lead a panhellenic force of conquest (compare Xen. *Agesilaos* 1.8).

E154   Spartan successes in Asia – the Battle of Sardis in 395 BC

[He made] Xenokles, a Spartiate, [the commander] of [..x..] hoplites and [x-]hundred lightly-armed troops, and [ordered that when the Persians] were marching to fight his men […] should be arranged for battle. […] He got his army up at daybreak and [again] led them forward. The Persians, as usual, kept up with them; some of them made an attack on the Greeks; others rode around them on horseback; others pursued them across the plain in disorder. [5] Xenokles, when he thought it the right moment to engage the enemy, sent the Peloponnesians from their ambush at the double. When the Persians all saw the Greek charging them, they fled right across the plain. Agesilaos seeing their panic sent the lightly-armed troops from his army as well as the cavalry to pursue them, and they fell on the Persians together with those from the ambush. [6] They went in pursuit of the enemy, but not for very long as they could not catch them, being mostly cavalry or troops without armour. But they killed around six hundred and broke off their pursuit and went to the Persian camp. They took the garrison by surprise before it was properly prepared and captured it, taking a large amount of food, many men, much equipment and money belonging to various people including Tissaphernes himself.

[Oxyrhynchos Historian, 11.4–6]

The fragmentary account is followed by Diodoros (14.80), though he multiplies the Persian deaths by 10! Xenophon, who was part of Agesilaos' forces, gives a significantly different account of the battle (*Hell.* 3.4.23–24 – no ambush) and of the whole campaign. It is not clear who is more reliable (see, e.g. *Appendix* p.405–6 in the 'Penguin' translation of Xenophon).

E155 Persian bribery prompts Corinthian War and Agesilaos' recall, 395 BC

[1] Many parts of Asia were now revolting from the Persians; Agesilaos restored order in the cities and re-established the proper form of governments, without resorting to bloodshed or banishment. Next he resolved to carry the war away from the coast and to march further up into the country, and to attack the King of Persia himself and the wealth of Susa and Ecbatana. Above all, he wanted to deprive the King of sitting at leisure on his throne, arbitrating between the conflicts of the Greeks, and bribing their demagogues. [2] But just at this moment came unhappy news from Sparta. Epikydidas arrived to inform Agesilaos that Sparta was involved in a great war in Greece and that the ephors were summoning him to give assistance at home.

[6] Persian coinage was stamped with the figure of an archer. Agesilaos said that the Great King was driving him out of Asia with 10,000 'Archers'. For this was the sum of money which had been sent to Athens and Thebes and distributed among the popular leaders there, thus inciting these states to hostility against Sparta.

[Plutarch, *Agesilaos 15.1–2, 6]*

Plutarch follows Xenophon, *Hellenika* 3.5.1–2 in the Persians creating an anti-Sparta alliance in Greece to divert Agesilaos from Persia. But the Oxyrhynchos Historian (**E156**) is 'wiser or less biased' (Cartledge, *SL* 237) in suggesting the main cause was mounting hostility to Sparta.

E155b A gold Persian *daric*

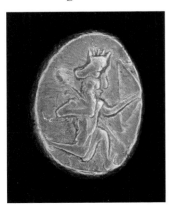

Contemporary gold *daric* coin, from the Oxus treasure, (5th or 4th centuries BC) now in the British Museum. The coin measures 16.5mm x 13 mm and weighs 8.5 g.

The design of a king, crowned, as a warrior (archer) is on one side only and remained, with minor variants, the only *daric* design from inception, *c.* 500 BC to the end of the Achaemenid empire in 330 BC. See A. Kuhrt, *The Persian Empire* (2007) fig.11.35 and 8.28 note 5.

[British Museum no. 124080 = BM 1897,1231.177]

E156   Persian bribery *not* a factor in Corinthian War

[2] The opposition [sc. of the Athenian populace] towards Sparta was sharpened by the supporters of Epikrates and Kephalos, since they were very eager for the city to go to war, and had been, not since talking to Timokrates and [taking] the gold [but long] before that. Some, however, say that it was the money from him that was [responsible for their actions] along with people in Boiotia, and in [other cities] previously mentioned, ignoring the fact that [all of them] had long been hostile to the Lakedaimonians and on the lookout for a way to get [their cities] to go to war. For the Argives and the Boiotians hated the Lakedaimonians because they had made friends with the opposition groups within the city; those in Athens were eager to change the Athenians from peaceful non-interference and lead them to war and interventionist policies, as a means for them to get money from the public finances. [3] Most of the Corinthians who sought a change of policy were, like the Argives and Boiotians, hostile to the Lakedaimonians. … [5] So it was for these reasons, much more than for Pharnabazus' gold, that people in the cities just mentioned were inclined to hate the Lakedaimonians.

[Oxyrhynchos Historian 7.2–3 and 7.5]

SPARTAN COLONY AT HERAKLEIA TRACHINIA: E157–158

Thucydides provides quite a lot of detail about this settlement, clear evidence of Sparta's ability to take innovative strategic decisions. Despite what Thuc. implies in **E158**, Spartan involvement continued (Xen. *Hell.* 1.2.18, Diod. 14.38.4–5) until 395 BC. Diodoros 12.59 provides further details about the colony and see Hornblower, *Commentary* vol I, 501–8. The episode may be indicative of problems Sparta found with appointments of governors over non-Spartan populations (compare *OCD³* for the idea that Herakleia may have had the first 'harmosts', (military governors) widely used after 404 BC).

E157   Colony of Herakleia established but badly administered, 426 to 420/419

[92.1] At this time the Lakedaimonians established a colony at Herakleia in Trachis for the following reasons: … [92.4] they wished to help the people of Trachis and Doris, and they thought that establishment of a city for them would be of advantage in the war with Athens, since a fleet could be prepared there to operate against Euboia, which was only a short sea-crossing away, and it would also be useful on the route to Thrace. All in all they were keen to found a city there. [92.5] So first they asked the god at Delphi who told them to do so. They sent out colonists from their own people and the *perioikoi*, and they told anyone who wished to from the rest of Greece to join, except Ionians and Achaians and some other groups. Three Lakedaimonian colonists were in charge, Leon, Alkidas and Damagon. They founded the city and built walls for it from scratch. It is now called Herakleia, about five miles from Thermopylai and two and a half from the sea. [92.6] They built dockyards and built a wall at the narrow pass at Thermopylai to strengthen its defences. …

[93.2] The reason [sc. why Herakleia did not succeed in damaging Athenian interests] was that the Thessalians who were the major power in that area, and also the people in whose territory the colony was founded feared having to live right next to a very strong power used spoiling tactics to fight against the new arrivals until they wore them down. This was despite the fact that there had been a large number of them at first (each and every one of the Lakedaimonian colonists went full of confidence, imagining that the city would be sure to last). However the Lakedaimonian rulers who arrived were themselves largely responsible for ruining the situation, and decreasing the population, since they frightened away many colonists by governing harshly and often unfairly, thus making it easy for the neighbouring people to win out.

[Thucydides, *History of the Peloponnesian War* 3.92–93]

E158   Defeat of Herakleia and reasons for its failure, 420/419

[51.1] The following winter, a battle took place between the people of Herakleia in Trachis, and the Ainianians, Dolopians, Malians, and some of the Thessalians. [51.2] They are all close neighbours of Herakleia and hostile to it, because it had been set up on their territory specifically as a fortified outpost against them. From the moment the city was established these tribes had opposed it and done everything they could to make it untenable. On this occasion they defeated the Herakleians, and the Lakedaimonian commander, Xenares son of Knidis, was killed, along with a significant number of Herakleians. [52] At the very beginning of the following summer the Boiotians seized control of Herakleia. It had been devastated by the battle described above, but also by the incompetent administration of the Lakedaimonian governor, Agesippidas, for which they expelled him.

[Thucydides, *History of the Peloponnesian War* 5.51–52]

E159   Alcibiades' advice to Sparta on tactics in the war with Athens, 415/4 BC

You should build a fort at Dekeleia in Attika, something the Athenians have always feared most, and which they think is the only thing they have not had to experience in the war. … I shall sum up the main points (omitting many others) about how building this fort in enemy territory will benefit you and hinder your opponents. Regarding what the land produces, most will be captured by you, the rest will come of its own accord: they will immediately be deprived of the revenues from the silver mine at Laureion, and from the land and law-courts; in particular income from tribute from their allies will reduce when they respect them less, knowing that you are now fighting them with all your strength.

[Thucydides, *History of the Peloponnesian War* 6.91]

SECTION F
THE SPARTAN MIRAGE

THE SPARTAN MIRAGE

The concept of a Spartan 'mirage' was first suggested by François Ollier (*Le Mirage spartiate*, Lyon & Paris 1933). He highlighted the ongoing idealisation and distortion of traditions about Spartan society recorded in ancient literature. As Rawson (*Spartan Tradition*) has shown, the interpretation and re-invention of Sparta did not end in late antiquity, and the process of re-inventing Sparta for new times and contexts is still continuing: see recent interpretations of Sparta and its history in the popular media, e.g. the new interpretation of the battle of Thermopylai in Frank Miller's graphic novel *300* and the recent film version; various historical novels, e.g. S. Pressfield, *Gates of Fire*.

In spite of Ollier's work, scholars who studied Sparta were slow in taking his warning on board, and a real change in the general outlook of Spartan studies did not arrive before the 1990's. An extreme position would suggest that all evidence for Sparta is so distorted that it is impossible to study Sparta herself, and we are reduced to tracing outsiders' perceptions and late 'reconstructions' of Spartan customs which never actually existed in the classical period. This is an over pessimistic stance, but caution is advisable and can actually bring new insights. Kennell (*Gymnasium of Virtue*) shows that a careful assessment of the sources will sometimes force us to change ideas about Spartan life which have themselves become part of a cherished tradition. But such an approach does not only discard details, it also adds new perspectives. For example, Sparta no longer appears as a static society, and it has become possible to distinguish many layers of tradition and change throughout antiquity. Today, interest in Sparta reaches well beyond the Archaic and Classical period, and it has become clear that in order to interpret later authors' reports of Sparta, we also have to understand the life of the Hellenistic and Roman city (note Cartledge & Spawforth, *Hellenistic and Roman Sparta*).

The 'Spartan Mirage' is a sum of stereotypes that came to dominate the Spartan image. Cartledge (*Spartan Reflections* 170) lists three crucial components of the myth as we find it in our ancient texts: firstly, the idea that Sparta had been free of civil strife since time (almost) immemorial; second, this was due to the fact that all Spartans dutifully followed the laws of Lykourgos; and third, these laws affected every aspect of Spartan life, and were in some respect very different from those of other Greek states. We are therefore presented with a single-minded community of proud warriors who submit to self-imposed discipline, austerity and obedience. The tradition describes a society where individuals gave up private interests and collectively agreed on a set of values and goals; as a consequence they achieved power and glory, and, individually as well as collectively, demonstrated that they were capable of great heroism. Outsiders' views of Sparta cannot avoid these stereotypes: favourable comments as well as criticism (e.g. modern comparisons with totalitarian states) are based on the same familiar elements of the legend. Because of the prevalence of these ideas about Sparta it is probably impossible for us to find out 'what life was really like' in classical Sparta. Were the rules really ever as rigid as the sources suggest? How far was conformity enforced, and was there room for a range of talents and personalities? Many of our sources, especially Xenophon (*Lak. Pol.*) describe an ancient system, but also suggest that the ideal Spartan lifestyle was a thing of the past. If this could be said as early as in the early fourth century, perhaps the Spartans never really fully complied with the strict standards we hear about, but nevertheless maintained a set of ideals and considered them as an 'original' system as it had been in 'the good old days' (that never were).

Why was the 'myth of Sparta' such an attractive image? Sparta dominated interstate politics in mainland Greece throughout the Archaic and Classical period, and she continued to be influential long afterwards. As Herodotus (1.65–6, 7.104) shows, the question about Sparta's secret of success was already a matter of discussion in the fifth century, and her laws and society were seen as a crucial factor. Moreover, the Spartan way of life seemed impervious to change and conspicuously old-fashioned: all those who hankered for the good old times and feared decadence could look to Sparta for a different model which seemed to avoid many political and social problems that troubled so many Greek *poleis*. Spartan austerity and simplicity, and her stubborn emphasis on simple traditional values looked like a perfect (though elsewhere unattainable) recipe for avoiding political turmoil, corruption and civil strife. The relative difficulty of visiting Sparta and getting to know the Spartans themselves at first hand would have contributed to their mystique. Many traditions about Spartans were simply good stories to pass on, for example the many examples of exceptional heroism, especially during the Persian Wars: the battle of Thermopylai in particular had a lasting impact on the Spartan image (**F9–F26**, also **F29**). We are told that stories of heroism are exactly what the Spartans talked about over dinner (**D61**). In addition, there were many examples of poignant (and sometimes humorous) Spartan comments: Laconic brevity made for attractive quotations, and by the Roman period, Plutarch could assemble a whole collection of the best examples (**F30–F35**), and he also inserts quotations into his Spartan biographies. We cannot know whether any of these are authentic, but together they can serve as a perfect illustration of the main themes of the Spartan 'mirage'.

LYKOURGOS: F1–F7

The whole first chapter of Plutarch's *Life of Lykourgos*, (**F2** below) should be required reading for anyone who approaches the question of Lykourgos or uses Plutarch's *Lykourgos* as a source. Plutarch, whose main interest was moral philosophy rather than historiography, expressed his doubts, but nevertheless proceeded to write a whole detailed biography. Scholars today, however, have to aspire to higher standards of historicity. Lykourgos is at the centre of the 'Spartan mirage', and it is best to consider him a mythical figure: as the Spartan legend developed, most aspects of Spartan culture which made their society so unique were attached to one person: the legendary lawgiver Lykourgos. If there ever was a historical figure Lykourgos who had some hand in the development of early Spartan laws, we have no means of disentangling the legends that grew around him to get an idea of one man's achievements. However, the figure might be entirely mythical: as Cartledge (*The Spartans. An Epic History*, 57–9) has pointed out, the name Lykourgos, 'Wolf-worker', comes close to some epithets of Apollo, and according to the legend this god and his oracle at Delphi are also closely connected with the origin story of the Spartan state. Earlier scholarly works on Sparta attempted to 'reconstruct' a historical Lykourgos by establishing a date and by creating a more or less plausible narrative of his achievements. This approach is outdated: the development of the Spartan constitution should be seen as a lengthy process, and in more recent studies the interest in Lykourgos as a 'historical' figure has shifted to the formation of the legend in parallel with perceptions of Spartan society, both in Sparta and beyond.

In fact, we can detect significant changes of the story in our literary sources: it seems that ideas about Lykourgos were still developing in the late archaic and classical period. Tyrtaios, at any rate, does not mention Lykourgos at all. Since we only have a few short fragments of his poetry, an argument from silence may seem of little value, but firstly, we have a fragment of his take on the early Spartan laws, and secondly, later authors, particularly Plutarch, were aware of the value of Tyrtaios as an early authentic source, and therefore the passages they selected for quotation or paraphrase probably favour the historically most informative passages of his poetry. Be this as it may, Tyrtaios (**A4**) seems to suggest that the Spartans received their constitution from Delphi. Even this early version looks like an attempt to legitimise the outcomes of a political process by presenting the constitution as divinely inspired. We do not know when Lykourgos entered the scene. Herodotus' account (1.65 = **F3**) is the earliest ancient reference to the Spartan lawgiver. This version also shows the involvement of Delphi; the oracle's doubts about Lykourgos' identity (a hero? a god?) probably reflect contradictions in the tradition about him. Moreover, Herodotus knew that some credited the oracle with the whole Spartan constitution, but he also offers a Spartan version of the origin story which centres on Lykourgos' initiative and efforts to create the laws. The legend was to become much more detailed later on, but Herodotus' version includes the essentials, namely that the Spartan political system and way of life was the result of one man's legislative efforts at some point in the past.

Xenophon's *Constitution of the Spartans* represents a further step in the creation of the myth: the tradition becomes more detailed, and we also hear more about the motivation behind specific regulations. Lykourgos has now become a wise and prescient figure who had an ingenious solution for almost any problem that might arise in Greek *polis* society. These ideas no doubt were influenced by the interests of political philosophy (see Plato's *Laws* or *Republic*), which experimented with the idea of law codes that would create an ideal society. Lykourgos would have seemed an ideal 'historical' example, but such discussions would also invite the instructive and explanatory embellishment of the story that we see in Xenophon's work. By the time Plutarch compiled his biography, there was a whole body of scholarly writings on the subject: Plutarch cites over fifty works, and his attention to earlier traditions illustrates the range of ideas and interpretations that had become attached to the fabled figure of Lykourgos.

While there is little mileage in any discussion of a 'historical Lykourgos', the ancient tradition offers us a good opportunity to discuss the development of the legend, and its reception in different contexts in antiquity. It seems clear that the core tradition about Lykourgos originated in Sparta, presumably at some stage between the mid-seventh and the mid-fifth century BC. Lykourgos came to be a symbol for all things Spartan, both in Sparta and abroad. The legend of the lawgiver particularly emphasised the idea of a traditional Sparta, which had, after one moment of innovation in the distant past, strictly stood by its laws without any further changes **F4, F6**. As we have seen, the Spartan system did evolve, and still underwent some changes in the classical period. The legend of Lykourgos, however, emphasised a notion of traditional, unchangeable values and stability in Spartan society, allowing the Spartans to think of their own way of life as constant and ancestral, while discouraging any calls for radical reform or change. This notion of a stable ancestral law code also inspired awe among other Greeks, for whom constitutional reform or upheaval was a fairly common occurrence.

Such a process of myth-making should not be dismissed as cynical 'spin', even if the legend was no doubt of some use in political contexts (see Flower in Powell & Hodkinson, *Sparta Beyond the Mirage,* ch. 7, on the 'invention of tradition' in Sparta). The legend of Lykourgos developed over centuries, responding to the needs of Spartans and their outside observers at different times: we are dealing with a dynamic set of stories that developed and grew in the telling, for example in response to questions about the origins of particular customs. Individual features of the Spartan constitution would also inspire stories about the lawgiver's motivation for particular measures, and more tales would be added to the legend. This process continued when, after the upheavals of the late classical and Hellenistic period, the Spartans tried to restore (or re-invent) their ancestral constitution. As Kennell (*Gymnasium of Virtue*) and Cartledge & Spawforth (*Hellenistic and Roman Sparta,* 197–211) have shown, such efforts meant that many new ideas were presented as ancient, and Lykourgos would yet again be called upon to help integrating them with the ancestral constitution. In this way many details that defined the changing Spartan way of life over the centuries were 'traced back' to Lykourgos, until he could indeed be seen as the originator of most features of Spartan culture, or, more accurately, a universal unifying symbol of the 'Spartan cultures' of different periods.

F1   Xenophon on when Lykourgos lived

It is clear that these laws are of great antiquity, since Lykourgos is said to have lived in the days of the Heraklids, the sons of Herakles. But though they are so very old, even today they still seem very odd to the rest of Greece. What makes it even more extraordinary is that everyone admires these arrangements, but no state wants to imitate them.

[Xenophon, *Constitution of the Lakedaimonians* 10.8 (continued in **D88**)]

F2   The impossibility of writing about Lykourgos

[1] There is a general lack of agreement about the life of Lykourgos, the lawgiver, both in its broad perspective and its particulars, since accounts vary about his origins, travels, and death. Above all, the record of his legal and constitutional reforms is inconsistent, the history of the times in which he lived being, perhaps, the most widely disputed subject of all. Some say that he reached the pinnacle of his career at the same time as Iphitos, with whom he was instrumental in establishing the Olympic truce. The philosopher Aristotle is one of these and he offers as evidence the discus at Olympia, on which an inscription with the name of Lykourgos is preserved. [2] Others such as Eratosthenes and Apollodoros base their chronological calculations on the hereditary kings of Sparta to demonstrate that Lykourgos pre-dates the first Olympiad [776 BC] by a significant period. Timaios suggests that there were two Lykourgoses in Sparta at very different periods, and that their joint achievements were credited to one of them because of his legendary status; he suggests that the elder one was in fact a near contemporary of Homer – indeed some sources even suggest that he met Homer face to face. [3] One might suspect Xenophon of a certain over-simplification,

when he suggests that Lykourgos lived in the time of the Heraklids, because of course even the most recent kings at Sparta were Heraklid by lineage. But his reference was presumably to those early famous Heraklids most closely related to Herakles himself.

[Plutarch, *Life of Lykourgos* 1]

F3 Lykourgos – Herodotus provides the earliest historical mention

[65.2] In still earlier times they had probably been the worst governed of almost all the Greek states, both in domestic policy and in their relations with other cities, since they refused to have anything to do with foreigners. But they now enjoyed excellent government and I shall explain how this came about. A very distinguished Spartiate called Lykourgos went to Delphi to consult the oracle. As he entered the shrine, the Pythia immediately greeted him with the following words:

[65.3]   *You have come, Lykourgos, to this my prosperous temple,*
         Dear as you are to Zeus and all the gods that dwell in Olympos.
         I know not whether to worship you as hero or god.
         Yet more and yet more I believe that you will be a god, Lykourgos.

[65.4] Some sources state, in addition, that the Pythia outlined for him the current system of government for the Spartiates; but the Lakedaimonians themselves say that Lykourgos brought these ideas back from Crete when he became the guardian of his nephew Leobotas, who was king of the Spartiates. [65.5] In fact, as soon as he became his guardian and regent, he changed the whole constitution and firmly enforced the new laws. He then reorganised the army, establishing the system of sworn comrades, operating in thirty-man units, and eating together in their own messes. Lykourgos was also responsible for the institution of the ephorate and the *gerousia*. [66.1] These changes were responsible for the excellent system of government, and when Lykourgos died they put up a temple to him and greatly honoured his memory.

[Herodotus, *Histories* 1.65.2–66.1 (see **H8** and **H9** for context)]

The third line of the oracle quoted by Herodotus and Diodoros (**F5**) uses a verb from the Greek word 'oracle' (*manteion*), here translated 'to worship'; the choice then is whether to worship him as *theos* (god) or *anthropos* – normally 'man', but here, in the context of worship, meaning 'hero', as for example Menelaos or Agamemnon (**C29–C33**) were 'hero-worshipped'. The response, though presented as being given spontaneously to the visiting Lykourgos may well have been a response to a Spartan question on how they should worship him.

F4 400 years of the same constitution?

Eventually the Athenian tyrants and also those from the rest of Greece which had mostly come under tyranny even earlier had been mostly – except for the final ones in Sicily – been deposed by the Lakedaimonians. Lakedaimon itself, after being founded by the Dorians who now live there, had suffered internal strife for the greatest period we know about, but nevertheless had also had a system of law and order since very ancient times and had never been ruled by tyrants. For four hundred years and more, until the end of the Peloponnesian War, the Lakedaimonians have had the same constitution, through which they have been able to bring about change in other states.

[Thucydides, *History of the Peloponnesian War* 1.18.1]

Even the highly intelligent and sceptical Thuc. agrees with the tradition in Hdt (above) that Sparta had changed suddenly and entirely from lawlessness (*anomia*) to good order (*eunomia*), though he omits mention of Lykourgos. Thucydides' figure of over 400 years may be based on a calculation of the generations of kings from Lykourgos to the Peloponnesian War, but for a variety of good reasons, modern scholars think that this would place a new system of stable government for Sparta too early (Hornblower, *Commentary* vol. I pp.51–54).

F5   Lykourgos visits Delphi

[1] Such was the magnitude of Lykourgos' virtue that when he came to Delphi, the Pythian priestess uttered the following oracle:

> *You have come, Lykourgos, to this my prosperous temple,*
> *Dear as you are to Zeus and all the gods that dwell in Olympos.*
> *I know not whether to worship you as hero or god.*
> *Yet more and yet more I believe that you will be a god, Lykourgos.*
> *You have come to inquire after good government: and I shall*
> *Grant you such as no other city on the earth will possess.*

[2] He also asked the Pythian what sort of institutions he should establish as would most benefit the Spartiates. She replied that he should make laws that one group should govern fairly and the other should obey their rulers. When he asked again what the people governing fairly and those obeying their rulers should do, she gave this oracle.

> *There are two roads as far apart from each other as is possible,*
> *One leading to the honoured abode of freedom.*
> *The other to the house of slavery which men wish to escape.*
> *The one is travelled by courage and lovely concord,*
> *And this is the path you should lead your people.*
> *The other is where people go because of strife*
> *And weak folly: guard against it most carefully.*

[3] The main point was that the greatest care was to be taken for concord and bravery, since only through these can freedom be safeguarded, while without it there is no benefit for a man, subject to others, to have those things which most people wrongly assume are good. For all such things belong to the leader not those who follow orders. So someone who wishes to obtain good things for himself rather than for others must first establish freedom. [4] The oracle instructed that care was to be taken of both things, since either thing without the other could be of no benefit to the possessor, since there was no benefit for brave men if they quarrelled or for complete agreement among cowards.

[5] Lykourgos also received an oracle from Delphi about love of money which is remembered in the form of a proverb, "Love of money will destroy Sparta – nothing else." [6] The Pythian priestess gave Lykourgos an oracle about the constitution of the state as follows,

[Diodoros here gives 10 lines of verse equivalent to Tyrtaios 4 = A4]

[7] Those who do not maintain reverence towards the divine observe far less what is right as regards men. [8] The Lakedaimonians, adhering to the laws of Lykourgos grew from humble beginnings into the greatest power in Greece, and maintained their leadership for more than 400 years. But after this by gradually letting each of their institutions slip, by declining into luxury and idleness, and being so corrupted that they used money and piled up wealth, they lost their foremost place.

[Diodoros, *Library of History* 7.12.1–8]

F6   Unchanging nature of Spartan constitution

His city remained preeminent in Greece for its good government and high reputation by following the laws of Lykourgos for some five hundred years; not one of the fourteen kings who succeeded him, down to the time of Agis, son of Archidamos, made any changes to his settlement. Far from weakening the constitution, the creation of the ephorate strengthened it, since it appeared to be a democratic measure, but in fact it made the aristocracy more secure.

[Plutarch, *Life of Lykourgos* 29.6]

Even putting aside the question of whether Lykourgos really existed, there is an obvious contradiction in this passage that the constitution 1) did not change at all, and 2) the creation of the ephorate strengthened it. Agis II reigned 427–400.

F7   Lykourgos' reputation and legacy

[1] Yet it was never Lykourgos' intention originally to leave his city as the ruler of so many others. He saw the happiness of each individual and of the city in the same light, each being derived from virtuous living and at unity with itself. The primary purpose of all his legislation and regulations was to ensure that for as long as possible they should live as free men, responsible for their own destinies, and moderate in the conduct of their lives. [2] This was the basic principle adopted by Plato for his *Republic*, by Diogenes, and Zeno, and by all those who have been praised for their attempts to write about such matters, though their only legacy has been books and words. But it was not just books and words that Lykourgos left behind; he brought into the light of day a real constitution, one which is beyond imitation. For those who imagine that such an arrangement is the stuff of philosophical fantasy, he has produced in actual reality a model for a whole state devoted to philosophical ideals. For that reason he is rightly praised as the greatest of all the Greek statesmen that have ever lived. [3] For the same reason Aristotle states that he received less honour from the Lakedaimonians than he deserved, even though they were the highest ever accorded. In fact he has a temple there, and annual sacrifices to him as if he was a god. There is a legend, too, that when they brought his remains back home, his tomb was struck by lightning. They say that this has very rarely happened to any other famous man since, except Euripides, who died and was buried near Arethusa in Macedonia. For lovers of Euripides, therefore, this is a powerful testimony to his greatness, that he alone experienced after his death something that had previously only happened to one who was a profoundly holy man and beloved of the gods.

[Plutarch, *Life of Lykourgos* 31.1–3]

F8   Spartan myth of never losing a battle

Before Leuktra, no setback had ever befallen the Lakedaimonians, with the result that they did not admit that they had ever been beaten in an infantry contest: for they say that Leonidas won but had insufficient followers for a wholesale slaughter of the Persians, and that what the Athenians and Demosthenes managed on the island of Sphakteria was a ruse of war and not a victory.

[Pausanias, *Description of Greece* 1.13.5]

THERMOPYLAI: F9–F26
The Spartans themselves clearly understood that their reputation abroad was an asset, and as far as we can tell, they were keen to cultivate their image and to be on best 'Spartan behaviour' when they interacted with outsiders. In fact, they played a crucial role in creating and maintaining the Spartan mirage (on Spartan propaganda see Hooker in Powell, *Classical Sparta*, ch. 5). For example, the battle of Thermopylai had a significant impact on their reputation with other Greeks: a crushing defeat soon became the most famous example of Spartan valour (rather like Britain's 'Dunkirk spirit' in WWII). By the time Herodotus composed his report, a few decades after the event, the battle had already become a celebrated example of Greek (especially Spartan) heroism which became one of the most memorable passages in his work and, arguably, all of Greek historiography. Herodotus' account comes with striking Laconic statements ('come and get them'; 'we shall fight in the shade') and impressive details about the Spartans' behaviour in the face of adversity. At the same time, other Greek forces get very little attention: few ever remember that 700 men from Thespiai and 400 Thebans also stayed to the bitter end (Hdt. 7.202, 7.222 = **F18**), or that the Spartans were probably accompanied by *periokoi* and helots who also lost their lives. Nevertheless, the event is generally known as the struggle of the 300 Spartans. We have good evidence that the Spartans actively invested in the memory of this battle: the leading poet of the day, Simonides of Keos, wrote epigrams for memorials on the battlefield (Paus. 9.2.4, see **A22**), and also a more substantial work about the Persian wars, which, as far as we can tell from the fragments (see **A21**), focused on the Spartans and echoed the Homeric epics to cast the events in a heroic light. If this work was commissioned by the Spartans, perhaps for a commemorative ceremony at Thermopylai very soon after the Persian Wars ended, then the myth-making began almost immediately after the event. For modern accounts see Lazenby, *The Defence of Greece* 1993.

F9   Thermopylai I: The Greek alliance
[202.1] The contingents of the Greek army waiting for the Persians at Thermopylai were as follows: hoplites from the Peloponnese: Spartiates – 300; Tegea and Mantineia – 1,000 (500 each); Orchomenos (in Arkadia) – 120; rest of Arkadia – 1,000; Corinth – 400; Phleious – 200; Mycenae – 80.[1] Hoplites from Boiotia: Thespiai – 700; Thebes – 400.

[203.1] From elsewhere, in answer to the general call to arms, the Opuntian Lokrians had sent their whole army, and the Phokians 1,000 men. They had been persuaded to do so by an appeal from their fellow Greeks, who had sent them despatches to explain that they were themselves only the vanguard of the army, and that the rest of the allied forces were expected any day now. Meanwhile the sea would be defended by the Athenians and the Aiginetans, and the rest of the naval contingents. So there was no need for alarm. [203.2] It was not a god who was marching against Greece but a mortal man, and there was not, nor ever would be, a man who was not from the day he was born liable to misfortune – and the greater the man, the bigger the misfortune that was likely to befall him. Their invader was himself a mere mortal and must inevitably fall from his present exalted position. With this reassurance the Lokrians and Phokians had marched to Trachis in support of the alliance.

F10   Thermopylai II: Leonidas
[204.1] These allied states were each commanded by their own leaders, but the supreme commander of the whole army was Leonidas the Lakedaimonian, the most respected of all the generals. His father and grandfather were Anaxandridas and Leon,

---

[1]   This gives a total from the Peloponnese of 3,100, which can be matched with the 4,000 of the epigram at 7.228.1 if one assumes a total of 900 helots, three for each Spartiate. Helots are not mentioned in the figures here, but died in significant numbers (Hdt 8.25.1 = **F28**). *Perioikoi* are not mentioned in Hdt's account, so another possibility is that they should make up the total. Isocrates, an Athenian orator, 436–338 BC says that 1,000 Lakedaimonians fought at Thermopylai (*Panegyricus* 90, cf. *Archidamos* 99).

and through them he traced his pedigree back to Hyllos, the son of Herakles through their forebears Eurykratidas, Anaxandros, Eurykrates, Polydoros, Alkamenes, Teleklos, Archelaos, Agesilaos, Doryssos, Labotas, Echestratos, Agis, Eurysthenes, Aristodamos, Aristomachos, and Kleodaios.[2] But his accession to the throne at Sparta was entirely unexpected. [205.1] He had two older brothers, Kleomenes and Dorieus, and thoughts of kingship had never crossed his mind. But Kleomenes died without a male heir, and since Dorieus was already dead, having been killed in Sicily, Leonidas naturally came to the throne, because he was older than Kleombrotos, the youngest of Anaxandridas' sons.[3] He had the added advantage of being married to Kleomenes' daughter.[4]

F11   Thermopylai III: Leonidas' contingent

[205.2] So Leonidas arrived at Thermopylai accompanied by his hand-picked bodyguard of three hundred men which the law assigned to him, all of them fathers of living sons. En route he had also picked up the 400 Thebans listed above, commanded by Leontiades the son of Eurymachos. [205.3] The reason why Leonidas was so careful to include the Thebans among his troops, alone of the Greek contingents, was because their loyalty to the Greek cause was highly suspect. So he summoned them to support the war effort in order to discover whether they would send troops as requested, or refuse and thus openly deny their allegiance to the allied cause. They did comply, though their loyalties lay elsewhere.[5]

[206.1] The body of 300 hoplites accompanying Leonidas had been sent by the Spartiates ahead of the main contingent so that the sight of them would inspire the other allied states to join the war, instead of going over to the Persian side as they would have done had they seen the Lakedaimonians hanging back. Once they had finished celebrating the Karneia,[6] they planned to leave a garrison force in Sparta and to join the army with all their forces as quickly as possible. [206.2] The remaining allies had similar plans, for it also happened to coincide with the time of the Olympic festival and none of them expected the battle of Thermopylai to be decided so quickly. So they had all sent token forces as an advance guard. [207.1] These Greek troops at Thermopylai were now faced with a dilemma. As the Persian army approached, they were sufficiently alarmed and contemplated a strategic withdrawal. The Peloponnesian contingents generally were all for retiring to the Peloponnese and mounting a defence of the Isthmus, but confronted by the protests of the Phokians and Lokrians at the proposal Leonidas ruled in favour of staying where they were and sending urgent appeals for reinforcements to the allied cities, explaining that they were hopelessly outnumbered.

---

[2]   Hdt. similarly gives the ancestry of Leotychidas, the other (Eurypontid) king at 8.131.2 (= **E1**) when describing his command of the fleet. Pausanias gives an almost identical list (**E3**).

[3]   For Anaxandridas' children from two wives, see **E8, E9**.

[4]   His step-niece, Gorgo, see **E78, F26, F30, F31** (for Leonidas' final words to her).

[5]   This explanation obviously makes no sense. Instead Diodoros, 11.4.7 gives the right explanation, that Thebes was bitterly divided, with the majority in favour of medizing. The four hundred Thebans to fight with Leonidas obviously did so out of great conviction, and in awareness that their views probably meant they had no place in Thebes whatever the outcome.

[6]   See **C60–C67**.

F12   Thermopylai IV: Xerxes' reconnaissance

[208.1] While all this was being debated, Xerxes sent out a cavalry soldier to make a reconnaissance, assess the Greek numbers, and to observe their preparations. While still up in Thessaly, he had heard that a small force was quartered there led by the Lakedaimonians under Leonidas, of the house of Herakles. [208.2] The rider approached the camp and surveyed the area, but in fact failed to observe the whole encampment, because the wall had now been repaired and was well guarded, but the troops stationed behind it were out of sight. All he could observe were the troops out in front of the wall, whose weapons had been grounded in front of it. [208.3] As it happened, the Lakedaimonians were on forward defence duty at this moment, and the rider watched in amazement as some stripped for exercise, others combed their hair; but he did make a note of their numbers. Once he had made careful assessment of the whole site, he slipped quietly back to his own camp. For no one had pursued him, nor indeed had they paid the slightest attention to him. On his return he reported all that he had seen to Xerxes.

F13   Thermopylai V: Demaratos' praise of Sparta

[209.1] This report left Xerxes bewildered; he could not understand the reality of the situation, which was that the Lakedaimonians were preparing to slay or be slain, as bravely as possible. As far as he was concerned, it was simply ludicrous. [209.2] So he sent for Demaratos,[7] the son of Ariston, who happened to have accompanied the army, and when he appeared he gave him all the details of the spy's report and asked him to explain the meaning of the Lakedaimonians' behaviour. "I told you once before about these men," he replied, "when we were setting out for Greece. But you simply laughed at me when I explained how I foresaw the way things would turn out for this expedition. My highest priority, your Majesty, is to strive to tell you the truth. [209.3] So please pay close attention to me this time. These men have come here to fight us for control of this pass, and they are getting ready in their traditional manner. When they expect to be fighting for their lives, they pay particular attention to the grooming of their hair. [209.4] But if you can defeat these men and the rest still at home in Sparta, there is no other nation in the world, Great King, that will be able to raise a finger to resist you. For now your battle is against the finest kingdom and the bravest soldiers in the whole of Greece." [209.5] Xerxes found this statement totally incredible and asked him for the second time how on earth such a small army could resist his own forces. "Call me a liar, Great King," replied Demaratos, "if things do not turn out exactly as I have predicted." But despite his protestation, the King refused to be persuaded.

F14   Thermopylai VI: First Persian attack

[210.1] So for four days he maintained his position, hoping that the Greeks would make a run for it. But on the fifth day, when they had still not disappeared but were continuing to hold their ground in a way that seemed to him a combination of lunacy and impertinence, he lost his temper and ordered the Medes and Kissians into battle to take them alive and bring them back to him for inspection. [210.2] The Medes charged into the Greeks and suffered enormous losses; fresh troops took their place, but despite such casualties they could not dislodge the Greeks from their position.

---

[7]   Former king of Sparta, removed through Kleomenes' plotting (**E20**).

They made it clear to everyone there, not least the Great King himself, that despite his overwhelming numbers, he lacked good soldiers. And so it went on all day long.

[211.1] In the end after savage losses the Medes were recalled. Their place was taken by the élite troops of the Persian army led by Hydarnes and known by the King as 'The Immortals'. They went into battle with an arrogance born of the certainty of an easy victory. [211.2] But once the battle was joined, they did no better than the Median forces. They suffered the same level of casualties, simply because they were fighting in a confined space with shorter spears than those of the Greeks and had no opportunity to take advantage of their superior numbers. [211.3] For the Lakedaimonians it proved a battle of legendary proportions. They showed clearly that it was a case of professionals against mere amateurs in the art of war. One of their tactics was to turn their backs as if in a disorderly retreat; at this the barbarians seeing them fleeing went after them with noisy and confused shouts; but then when the enemy were almost on them, the Lakedaimonians would wheel round and confront their attackers and by this manoeuvre slaughtered innumerable Persians. Though they did also suffer casualties, for the Lakedaimonians these were very limited. When all their efforts to capture the pass proved fruitless despite a variety of different tactics, whether in full force or otherwise, the Persians withdrew to their own camp. [212.1] In the course of these various assaults, the story goes that Xerxes who was watching the battle leapt three times from his throne in sheer terror for his troops.

F15   Thermopylai VII: Second Persian attack

That was the outcome of the day's fighting, and the next proved no more successful for the barbarians. They launched their attack in the expectation that Greek numbers were so small that they would have been traumatised by the fighting of the previous day and would no longer be able to offer serious resistance. [212.2] But the Greeks remained in good order, deployed according to their individual states, and thus able to join the battle in turn. The only exception were the Phokians, who had been stationed on the mountain to guard the pathway. Finding that things had gone no better than on the previous day the Persians again withdrew to their camp.

F16   Thermopylai VIII: Epialtes offers to help Xerxes

[213.1] Faced with this state of affairs, Xerxes was at a loss. But at this point a native of Malis called Epialtes, the son of Eurydemos, sought an audience with him, clearly expecting that he would get some great reward. He told the King of a pathway that led across the mountain to Thermopylai – and by this act of treachery he undermined the Greeks' defences and caused the deaths of their soldiers. [213.2] Later Epialtes fled to Thessaly in fear for his life at the hands of the Lakedaimonians, and during his exile a price was put on his head by the people of Pylai, when the Amphiktyonic Council met there.[8] But when he ultimately returned to Antikyra he was killed by the Trachian, Athenades, [213.3] for an entirely different reason which I shall relate at some later point in this history,[9] though the Lakedaimonians honoured Athenades for what he had done. That, finally, was the end of Epialtes.

---

[8]   Made up of members from across Greece to deal mainly with the sanctuary at Delphi.
[9]   Hdt. does not do so.

[214.1] There is, however, an entirely different story, which alleges that Phanagoras' son, Onetes of Karystos, and Korydallos of Antikyra, were the men who spoke to the King and led the Persians across the mountain. I don't believe it, [214.2] for reasons which can be readily substantiated by the following facts: the members of the Amphiktyonic Council, presumably on the basis of the most reliable evidence, put up the reward for the death of Epialtes of Trachis,[10] and not for that of Onetes and Korydallos. Secondly, it is common knowledge, that this charge of treachery was Epialtes' motive for seeking to escape. [214.3] Of course, since he was a native of Malis, Onetes might have known of the existence of the mountain track, if he had been familiar with the area. But the traitor who led the Persians along that mountain track was Epialtes and I am naming him as the guilty party.

[215.1] When he heard Epialtes' proposal, Xerxes was delighted and his whole mood changed. He despatched Hydarnes and his troops and they left camp at dusk, at about the time when the lamps are lit. Local Malians had originally discovered this track and used it to guide the Thessalians in their attack on Phokis at a time when the Phokians had sealed the pass with a wall and as a result had little fear of military attacks upon them. Ever since then, nothing good has ever come of it for the Malians.

F17   Thermopylai IX: The Persians take the mountain pass
[216.1] The route of the track is as follows: it starts at the river Asopos, which pours through a narrow mountain gorge, and then it runs along the ridge of Mount Anopaia, after which the track is named. It comes to an end at the city of Alpenos, the first Lokrian settlement one reaches *en route* from Malis, near the Black Buttock Rock and the Kerkopians' Seats, where the track is also at its narrowest. [217.1] That is a description of the route which the Persians followed. And so, having crossed the Asopos, they marched through the night with the peaks of Mount Oita to their right and the Trachinian mountains to their left, till dawn found them near the summit of Mount Anopaia. [217.2] As I have already explained, there was a guard post on the mountain, consisting of a thousand Phokian hoplites, whose task it was to protect their own country and defend the mountain track, while the pass below was defended by the forces I have already described. The Phokians had volunteered to defend the mountain track and Leonidas had been happy to accept their offer.

[218.1] The Persian approach had been concealed from the Phokians by the thick oak forests which grew on the mountain. There was no wind and the Phokians only became aware of their approach as they reached the top from the inevitable sound of rustling leaves under the Persians' feet, which made a considerable amount of noise. The Phokians ran to their positions, strapped on their armour, and almost immediately the Persians were upon them. [218.2] They were startled to see men arming themselves, since they had not expected to encounter hostile forces in this position. At this point Hydarnes feared that the Phokians might be Lakedaimonians, and asked Epialtes what nationality they were. Once Epialtes had given him the facts, he deployed his Persians for battle. [218.3.] The Phokians found themselves under heavy fire from a hail of arrows and retreated rapidly to the summit of the mountain

---

[10] Trachis was the major settlement in the area, Malis, around the Malian Gulf. Hence Epialtes can be described as either 'of Malis' or 'of Trachis'.

under the mistaken assumption that they were the primary targets of the Persian attack. There they prepared to sell their lives dearly. They were mistaken, of course – the Persians following Epialtes and Hydarnes simply ignored them and instead hurried on down the track at the double.

F18   Thermopylai X: Leonidas decides the Spartiates should remain
[219.1] For the Greek defenders of Thermopylai the first warning that death was on its way to them with the dawn came when Megistias, the soothsayer, read it in the entrails of his sacrifices; this was followed by reports from deserters who brought the news while it was still dark about the Persians' move to outflank them; but finally, as day broke, the look-outs on the hills came running down from the mountain tops. [219.2] The Greeks called a council of war and opinions proved sharply divided, some refusing to desert their posts; others arguing for the opposite. Given this sharp division of opinion, some beat a hasty retreat and scattered to their respective cities while others prepared to stand their ground with Leonidas. But there is a different account as well. [220.1] This states that it was Leonidas himself who took the decision to send them home, in an effort to save lives. But for himself and the Spartiate troops who accompanied him, it seemed the height of dishonour to desert the post which they had originally come to defend. [220.2] For myself, I think that the most likely explanation is that Leonidas realised that the allies' morale had collapsed and that they were not prepared to risk their lives any further; so he dismissed them, but recognised that it would be dishonourable to run away himself. The result was that by deciding to stand his ground he won a glory that will never die and Sparta's own prosperity was preserved. [220.3] For when the Spartiates originally sought the advice of the Pythia about the forthcoming war, she had declared that either Lakedaimon would be devastated by the barbarians or else one of her kings must die. This prophecy was pronounced in hexameter verse, as follows:

[220.4]   *Dwellers in Sparta, the land of the wide open spaces, I tell you*
            The fate of your city of glorious renown – by the sons of the Persians
            It shall be sacked; or if not, Lakedaimon's frontiers must be wasted
            In grief for the death of a king who is born of the Heraklid line.
            He cannot be stayed by the courage of bulls or the strength of great lions;
            For mighty as Zeus is his power and nothing shall hold him in check
            Till one of these twain is consumed in his utter destruction.

I believe that it was the recollection of this oracle as well as a desire to win for Spartiates alone a glory that was unique which persuaded Leonidas to dismiss the allied forces, rather than some difference of opinion which led to such a disorderly retreat from the field of battle by those who departed. [221.1] There is powerful evidence for this in the conduct of Megistias, the Akarnanian soothsayer said to be a descendant of Melampos, who had accompanied the army and had warned them of the outcome of events from his inspection of the sacrificial entrails. He had clearly been instructed by Leonidas to flee, so as to avoid being killed. But despite this he had refused to go and instead sent away his only son who was also serving with the army. [222.1] So now the allied forces obeyed Leonidas' orders, abandoned their positions, and escaped. Only the Thespians and Thebans stayed behind together with the Lakedaimonians. Of these, the Thebans stayed reluctantly and much against their will, because Leonidas had kept them there rather as if they were hostages;[11] but the Thespians were notably willing allies, and steadfastly refused to abandon Leonidas and his troops, preferring to stand and die beside them.[12] Their commander was Demophilos, the son of Diadromes.

F19   Thermopylai XI: Third Persian attack

[223.1] As the sun lifted over the hills, Xerxes poured libations and then waited until about the hour when the markets begin to fill before launching his attack. He was following the advice of Epialtes, who had explained that, compared with the lengthy climb and march involved in Hydarnes' flanking movement, the downhill approach from his own position on high ground was direct and involved a much shorter distance. [223.2] And so Xerxes' troops advanced, while the Greek forces with Leonidas fully aware that they were going out to die, made far more aggressive charges than before right up to the mouth of the gorge, where it began to widen out. Previously they had remained within the defences of the wall or else made sallies only as far as the narrowest part. [223.3] But now they joined battle out beyond the narrows and inflicted enormous casualties on the barbarians, whose company commanders armed with whips kept lashing their troops and driving them forward from behind. Many of them fell into the sea and drowned; a far greater number were trampled to death by their own soldiers; casualties were a matter of indifference to them. [223.4] As for the Greeks, they knew that death was a certainty now that the enemy had found a way round the mountain, so they set out to give their finest possible display of force with a reckless disregard for their own safety.

[224.1] By now, for most of them, their spears were shattered, so they went for the Persians with their swords and it was at this point in the heat of the battle that Leonidas fell, fighting like a hero, and alongside him many other famous Lakedaimonians, whose names I have recorded in recognition of their great achievement. Indeed, I have discovered the names of all three hundred Lakedaimonians who fell that day.[13] [224.2] Amongst their many casualties a great number of Persians from famous families also fell, including two sons of Darius, Abrocomes and Hyperanthes, his children by Phratagune, the daughter of Artanes, Darius' brother, the son of Hystaspes and grandson of Arsames. His gift of Phratagune to Darius was the same as handing over to him his whole estate, since she was his only child. [225.1] So Xerxes lost two brothers in the course of that battle. Meanwhile a ferocious battle ensued between Greeks and Persians over the body of Leonidas until at last by sheer courage the Greeks carried it away, having driven back the Persians no fewer than four times. And that was how matters stood until the force with Epialtes arrived.

F20   Thermopylai XII: Final Greek defence

[225.2] This was the point at which the Greeks realised that they were now fighting a very different sort of battle. So they now altered their position and pulled back into the narrow section of the pass behind the wall and (apart from the Thebans) concentrated their forces in a single body on a small hillock at the entrance to the pass, where to

---

11   See note 1
12   Note that there were 700 of them. Perhaps they realised their city would be destroyed (Hdt 8.50).
13   Perhaps from the memorial in Sparta mentioned by Pausanias, **F27**. One or two of the 300 did not fall
     (**F21**).

this day there stands a stone statue of a lion in memory of Leonidas. [225.3] On this spot they resisted to the last, with swords, if they still had them, and then with their hands and teeth until the barbarian attacks from all sides overwhelmed them, those attacking from the front having torn down the defensive wall, while the flanking force came in from behind.

[226.1] Of the Lakedaimonians and Thespians who fought there so heroically, tradition has it that the bravest of all was a Spartiate, Dienekes. His most famous comment came shortly before the battle with the Persians was joined. A man from Trachis told him that when the Persians fired their arrows, there were so many that they shut out the sun. [226.2] He was unperturbed by this description of the sheer size of Persian forces. "This is excellent news," he said," which the stranger from Trachis brings us. If the Persians shut out the sun, we'll be fighting in the shade instead." There are other such witticisms by which Dienekes, the Lakedaimonian, will always be remembered.[14] [227.1] Second only to Dienekes for courage were two Lakedaimonian brothers, Alpheios and Maron, the sons of Orsiphantos,[15] while for the Thespians, Dithyrambos, the son of Harmatides, wins the accolade for courage.

[228.1] They buried the dead where they had fallen, including those who had died before the rest were sent away by Leonidas. In honour of all the slain they set up the following inscription:
> *Once in this place, against three million men allied,*
> *Four thousand Peloponnesians fought and died.*[16]

[228.2] That was the inscription dedicated to the whole allied force together; but a second inscription was set up to honour especially the Spartiate contingent:
> *Tell the Lakedaemonians, passer-by,*
> *We followed orders, and here now we lie.*

[228.3] That was for the Lakedaimonians; but this was for their soothsayer, Megistias:
> *Here stands the tomb of famed Megistias, whom Persians slew*
> *When Spercheios' streams they crossed. A prophet, he knew*
> *The Fates, and clearly saw Death on his way,*
> *But with his Spartan leaders chose to stay.*

[228.4] It was the Amphiktyons who had these epitaphs inscribed on stone pillars in honour of the dead, apart from the one for the prophet Megistias, which was the work of Simonides, son of Leoprepes, who inscribed it in honour of their lifelong friendship.[17]

---

[14]   In fact Plutarch, *Sayings of Spartans,* attributes the comment about arrows creating shade to Leonidas (Saying 6), along with others, see **F31**.

[15]   They received a memorial in Sparta, metioned by Pausanias 3.12.9.

[16]   There is considerable confusion here. The three million figure is a rounding of the 2,641,610 calculated by Hdt's source (7.185) and is obviously impossible in terms of logistics. *CAH* IV[2] 534 suggests 220,000 for the army. More problematic are the Greek figures: 4,000 could fit with the numbers who fought given by Hdt (see note 1), but most of those did not die at Thermopylai. Those who made a final stand were those of the **one** thousand, (700 from Thespiai in Boiotia and only 300 Spartiates from the Peloponnese) who had survived until day 3 of the battle.

[17]   Simonides was the great contemporary Greek poet commissioned to write various poems, including **A22** (probably for Spartan dead at Thermopylai) and **A21** (for victory at Plataia).

F21   Thermopylai XIII: Eurytos and Aristodamos

[229.1] Of the three hundred, it is said that just two, Eurytos and Aristodamos, shared the same excuse, which might have allowed them to get back safely to Sparta together. They had been released from military duty by Leonidas and were resting at Alpenoi suffering from an acute eye infection. If they had preferred not to go home, they could have chosen instead to die together along with their comrades. But faced with these two options, they could not agree but chose different courses. When Eurytos learned of the Persians' flanking movement, he demanded his weapons and donned his armour, and ordered his helot servant to lead him to the scene of battle. This the helot did and then ran away, while Eurytos plunged into the thick of the fighting and there lost his life. But Aristodamos lost his nerve and stayed behind at Alpenoi. [229.2] Now if Aristodamos alone had been sick and returned to Sparta, or if the two of them together had made the journey home, I suspect the Spartiates would not have been particularly angry about it. But now that one of them had lost his life while the other one had used the same excuse to avoid death in battle, inevitably there was a feeling of anger towards Aristodamos.

[230.1] But the sources vary in their account of how it was that Aristodamos got back safely to Sparta, and some offer a rather different explanation. They suggest that he was in fact sent out of the camp with a message; and though he could have returned to join in the fighting, he chose not to, and managed to survive by dilly-dallying on the way. But a fellow despatch carrier, who had been sent out with him, returned to fight and lost his life. [231.1] When he got home to Lakedaimon, Aristodamos was greeted with shame and disgrace of the following kind: no Spartiate would give him a light for his fire or even speak to him and he was nicknamed "Lily-livered Aristodamos." But afterwards, at the battle of Plataia, he redeemed himself and his disgrace was forgotten.[18] [232.1] There is said to have been one other survivor of the Three Hundred. His name was Pantites and he had been sent to Thessaly with despatches. But when he got back to Sparta he was in such disgrace that he hanged himself.

F22   Thermopylai XIV: The Thebans surrender

[233.1] The Thebans commanded by Leontiades fought against the Persians under compulsion while they were still part of the Greek contingents. But once the retreat under pressure of Leonidas and his Greeks to the Mound showed them that the Persians were gaining the upper hand, they detached themselves from the defenders and with arms raised in surrender they approached the barbarians shouting out (with absolute truth) that they were Persian supporters, that they had been among the first to offer earth and water to the Great King, and that they had come to Thermopylai under compulsion and bore no responsibility for the losses inflicted on the King's forces. [233.2] Their claim, backed as it was by the Thessalians, saved their lives. But there was a price to pay, none the less. Some of them were in fact killed when the Persians first became aware of their approach; and all of them, on Xerxes' orders, were branded with the royal stamp, starting with Leontiades, their commander, whose son Eurymachos was later killed by the Plataians, when in command of four hundred Thebans at the capture of their city.[19]

---

[18]   Hdt. 9.71
[19]   Thuc. 2.5.7 – that battle was in summer 431 BC.

F23   Thermopylai XV: Demaratos' analysis of the battle

[234.1] So much for the tale of the Greek defence of Thermopylai. Afterwards Xerxes sent of Demaratos and asked him a series of questions. "Demaratos," he began, "you are a loyal friend; you tell the truth and everything has turned out as you predicted. So now, tell me how many more Lakedaimonians there are, and how many of them are warriors like these, some of them or all of them?" [234.2] "Great King," replied Demaratos, "the population of the Lakedaimonians as a whole is enormous and their cities numerous. But I shall tell you what you really need to know. In Lakedaimon there is one city, called Sparta, with a population of about eight thousand men. Every one of them is a match for those who fought here. The other Lakedaemonians are not their equals, but good soldiers all the same." To which the King replied, "Demaratos, please tell me how on earth we are to defeat these people with a minimum of casualties? You must understand how their minds work, since you were once their king."

[235.1] "Great King," Demaratos replied, "if you seriously want my advice, then it is my duty to explain what I think is the best plan. Suppose you were to send three hundred warships into Lakonian territory. [235.2] There is an island lying off the coast called Kythera.[20] Chilon, the wisest man that ever lived amomg us, said that the best possible thing for the Spartiates would be if Kythera were abolished and sunk to the bottom of the sea. He always feared that one day it would become the base for the project I am about to suggest. Of course he did not foresee this particular expedition of yours; but he always feared for something like it from somewhere. [235.3] Using Kythera as a base, launch a terror campaign against the Lakedaimonians from there. While they are preoccupied with a domestic campaign, they will be far less of a problem for you by helping the rest of Greece while your army is conquering it. Once the rest of Greece has been subjugated, Lakonia will be helpless when she is left standing alone. [235.4] If, however, you reject this plan, this is what you must expect. The Peloponnesian Isthmus is narrow. There the united forces of the Peloponnesians will combine against you and you will face more ferocious battles than any you have faced so far. If, however, you do as I say, the Isthmus and these cities will be yours without a fight."

F24   Thermopylai XVI: Achaemenes' analysis

[236.1] Xerxes' brother, Achaemenes, butted in at this point. He was the commander of the fleet and had been listening to the conversation, and was afraid that Xerxes was coming round to Demaratos' proposal. "Your Majesty," he said, "I can see that you like the sound of this man's suggestions. But he clearly envies you your good fortune and may even be a traitor into the bargain. It is typical of the way all Greeks like to behave. They begrudge a man's success and hate their superiors. [236.2] Look at the facts as they now are: we have lost four hundred ships by shipwreck.[21] If you send another three hundred from our fleet to go sailing round the Peloponnese, the enemy will match us for numbers. Keep the whole fleet together and they will be a formidable force to be reckoned with, and the enemy will not think it worthwhile to challenge us. The total naval force will be there in support of the army; and the army will advance in tandem with the navy. If you separate them, you will be no use to them, nor they to

---

20   Kythera was seized by the Athenians in 456/5 (**H26**) and 424 (Thuc. 4.53–56 and cf. **B16**).
21   At Artemision, at the same time as the first few days fighting at Thermopylai, Hdt. 7.188–190.

you. [236.3] Think this through clearly and you can discount anything the enemy may do; you need not worry about their strategy, where they will make a stand, or what their numbers are. They are perfectly capable of working out their own salvation, just as we are. If the Lakedaimonians choose to fight again, they have no way of making up for the losses they have already sustained."

F25   Thermopylai XVII: Xerxes' treatment of Demaratos and Leonidas
[237.1] "Achaemenes," Xerxes replied, "I think you are talking good sense and I shall do exactly what you suggest. But Demaratos gave me what he hoped was the best possible advice, though his judgement is not as good as yours. [237.2] When I weigh up the quality of his previous advice, I cannot accept your proposition that he is unsympathetic to our cause. There is another consideration also: citizens of the same state often become jealous of the success of one of their fellow citizens, though they may well conceal their hostility. It takes a man of quite exceptional integrity to give what he thinks is the very best advice to a fellow citizen in those circumstances. Such people are extraordinarily rare. [237.3] But when it is the case of a friend from another country doing well, then feelings are entirely different and a citizen will feel the utmost goodwill towards him. And when asked for advice he will offer the very best he can. Demaratos is my guest-friend (*xenos*) and I must command you to refrain in future from all forms of malicious comment against him."

[238.1] After this declaration, Xerxes toured the battlefield to inspect the bodies of the dead. When he came upon the corpse of Leonidas and learned that he was the king and general of the Lakedaimonians, he ordered him to be decapitated and his head stuck on a pole. [238.2] It is clear to me on the basis of this action above all, as well as a mass of other evidence, that the King hated Leonidas in his lifetime more fiercely than any other man. Nothing else would ever have persuaded him to mutilate the corpse in this way, since no other nation I know of honours heroism in warfare as the Persians do. But his men carried out his instructions according to orders.

**F26   Thermopylai XVIII: earlier story of Demaratos' secret warning
            to Sparta**
[239.1] As a postscript to my record of these events, let me return to an earlier point in my story. The Lakedaimonians had been the first to get wind of the King's expedition to Greece. They immediately consulted the Delphic oracle and received the answer (to which I alluded a little while back)[22] in circumstances that were really rather remarkable. [239.2] Demaratos, the son of Ariston, was living in Persia as an exile at the time. I assume, and probability is on my side in this, that he felt no particular goodwill towards the Lakedaimonians at the time. One can only speculate about whether what he did was the result of latent affection or malicious pleasure. Once Xerxes had decided to launch his campaign, Demaratos (who was living in Susa) discovered the plan and wanted to get a warning to the Lakedaimonians. [239.3] Given the serious risk of discovery, he could not work out how best to send the message. In the end he thought of the following device: he took a pair of writing tablets and scraped the wax off them and then wrote on the wood the details of the King's intentions. After that he covered over the writing with a fresh application of

---
[22]   Hdt. 7.220.4 = **F18.**

wax, so that the tablets would cause no problems to the checkpoint guards along the route. [239.4] When the message reached Lakedaimon, they could not make head or tail of it until (so I am told) Gorgo, Kleomenes' daughter and the wife of Leonidas, had a brain-wave and told them to scrape off the wax and they would find the message underneath. Her suggestion was accepted and so they discovered the message. Once they had read it, they passed on the news to the rest of Greece. That is the story of what is supposed to have happened.

[Herodotus, *Histories* 7. 202–239]

F27 Leonidas and the 300

Opposite the theatre is a memorial to Pausanias, the general at Plataia, and one to Leonidas. Every year speeches are made there and there is a contest in which only Spartiates may compete. The bones of Leonidas were taken from Thermopylai by [Kleomenes, son of] Pausanias forty years later. There is a *stele* with the names and patronymics of those who stayed to fight the Persians at Thermopylai.

[Pausanias, *Description of Greece* 3.14.1]

The text says that Pausanias moved Leonidas' bones. But the *regent* Pausanias died before 460 BC, while his grandson, *King* Pausanias was not born until *c.* 440 BC. The number forty may be wrong, but since the *writer* Pausanias is normally careful to distinguish between people of the same name, a neater solution is that a son of the *regent* brought back the bones of his great-uncle (W.R. Connor, "Pausanias 3.14.1: A Sidelight on Spartan History *c.* 440 BC?" in *TAPA* 109, 21–27). The timing, which must have been political, might have been related to Athens and Samos (see **E139**): the bones of a king who fought to preserve the freedom of Greece being brought back at a time when there was debate in the Peloponnese over whether to help Samos throw off Athenian rule.

F28 Significant numbers of helots included among Spartan dead

The Persians crossed over, disembarked and viewed the bodies: they all believed that those lying dead were all Lakedaimonians or Thespians, when they were actually seeing dead helots too.

[Herodotus, *Histories* 8.25.1]

Xerxes allegedly invited his navy across from Euboia to view the dead of Thermopylai but only after falsifying the casualty figures by secretly burying all but 1,000 of the Persian dead, and by including helots' corpses among the élite Greek dead (see also note on **F9**).

F29 A parallel for Thermopylai?

They say that Othryades, the only man left alive of the three hundred was ashamed to return to Sparta after his companions had been killed [at the 'Battle of the Champions', *c.* 546 BC] and made away with himself at Thyreai.

[Herodotus, *Histories* 1.82.8 (see **H11** for the battle)]

SPARTAN SAYINGS: F30–F35

The battle of Thermopylai became the source for some of the many famous Spartan sayings. Herdotus' account attributes one of the most famous to Dienekes, and implies that there were others, but later tradition attributes this and others to Leonidas. The ancient world in general was very fond of 'sayings' (for example, Valerius Maximus' *Memorable Deeds and Sayings* in ten books, published *c.* AD 32). The Spartan reputation for bravery, brevity and braininess formed a prime subject for famous sayings: Aristotle's *Rhetoric* mentions 'Laconic sayings' and Plutarch collected *Sayings of Lakedaimonians* and *Sayings of Spartan Women* in his *Moralia* (moral essays 208A–236E and 240C–242D). This includes around 350 'sayings' by 68 men and 4 women, and a further 100 anonymous 'sayings' (some 'sayings' are really anecdotes). Some are attributed to figures who are almost certainly mythological (such as King Soös (= 'Safety')), while many very similar sayings are attributed to different people. The stories then are very little use as genuine historical record, but certainly create an excellent impression of the Spartan mirage. They are translated by Talbert, *Plutarch on Sparta* (Penguin Classics, 2nd ed. 2005).

F30   Sayings of Gorgo

[2] Once when her father told her to give someone corn as a payment, explaining, "He has shown me how to make good wine," she said, "In that case, father, more wine will be drunk and the drinkers will become less manly and less good."

[3] When watching Aristagoras having his shoes put on by one of his servants, she said, "Father, the foreigner has no hands."

[5] When asked by a woman from Attika, "Why are Lakonian wives the only ones who rule their men?" she replied, "Because we alone bear men."

[Plutarch, *Moralia* 240E = *Sayings of Spartan Women,* Gorgo 2, 3, 5]

F31   Sayings of Leonidas, son of Anaxandridas

[2] When asked by his wife Gorgo, as he was setting out to fight the Persians at Thermopylai, if he had any orders for her, he said, "Marry good men and produce good children."

[3] When the ephors said that he was taking too few men to Thermopylai, he replied, "No, too many for the task we're going for." [4] They then said, "Have you any plan of action but to block the Persians' way?" "Not officially, but in reality to die for the Greeks."

[7] Someone else said, "They are near us," "Well then," he said, "We are near them too."

[10] When Xerxes wrote to him, "Hand over your weapons," he wrote back, "Come and get them."

[13] He told his soldiers to eat breakfast as men who would have dinner in Hades.

[15] Wishing to save the lives of some unmarried young men, and knowing that they would not accept this openly, he gave each of them a secret message to send to the ephors. He also wished to save three of the adult men: but they knew what he was thinking and would not accept taking the messages: one of them said, "I followed you to fight, not to be a herald." The second said, "I would be a better man if I stay here." The third said, "I shall not be behind them, but shall fight in the front line."

[Plutarch, *Moralia* 225A–E = *Sayings of Lakedaimonians: Leonidas*]

F32   Sayings of Agis, son of Archidamos

[2] On being asked what sort of learning was most practised in Sparta, he replied, "Knowing how to rule and be ruled."

[3] He said that the Lakedaimonians do not ask how many men the enemy has but where they are.

[4] At Mantineia, when he was prevented from engaging a more numerous enemy, he said, "Someone who wishes to rule many must fight many."

[5] Someone enquired how many Lakedaimonians there were. He replied, "Enough to keep wrong-doers away."

[6] As he walked by the walls of Corinth and saw how tall, strong and extensive they were, he said, "Who are the women who live here?"

[Plutarch, *Moralia* 215D–E = *Sayings of Lakedaimonians: Agis*]

Walls: Lakedaimonians made much of their city not having walls but men to defend it. Similar comments are attributed to Agesilaos (*Saying* 29 and 55, Antalcidas *Saying* 7, Lykourgos *Saying* 28; also Plato *Laws* 778D and Demosthenes *De Corona* 299; Valerius Maximus 3.7 ext. 8).

F33   Argileonis, Brasidas' mother

When his death came about while liberating the Greeks in Thrace, the delegation sent to Lakedaimon came to speak to his mother, Argileonis. The first thing she asked was whether Brasidas had died well. The Thracians sang his praises and said that there was no one else like him. "Being foreigners," she said, "you do not know that. Brasidas was a good man, but Sparta has many better men than he."

[Plutarch, *Moralia* 219D (Brasidas 4) = 190B (Brasidas 3) = 240C (Argileonis 1)]

F34   Sayings of Paidaretos

[2] When not chosen for the three hundred, the highest honour in the state, he left cheerful and smiling. He was called back by the ephors to discover why he was laughing: he replied, "Because I rejoice for a state which has three hundred citizens better than me."

[Plutarch, *Moralia* 231B = *Sayings of Lakedaimonians: Paidaretos*]

Paidaretos or Pedaritos governed Chios and was killed in action there in 411 – Thuc. 8.28, 32–3, 38, 40, 55; Oxy. Hist. 2.1.

F35   With your shield or on it

Another woman, handing her son his shield, encouraged him with the words, "Son, with it or on it."

[Plutarch, *Moralia* 241F = *Sayings of Spartan Women,* 'Unknown women' 16]

This saying, though very famous, is actually quite problematic as dead Spartans were not carried back home at all, but buried where they fell (see e.g. **B43**). Nonetheless this saying was widely quoted (Aristotle, attributing it to Gorgo, as quoted by Stobaeus, *Anthology* 7.31; scholiast on Thuc. 2.39; Valerius Maximus, *Memorable Deeds and Sayings,* 2.7 'foreign' 2).

F36   No cause for tears

To Pitane came Thrasyboulos, on his shield, dead
With seven wounds from Argive hands
All shown on his front. His old father, Tynnichos
Placed his bloodied body on the pyre and said,
"Let tears be shed for cowards. You, my son,
I bury without tears; a son of mine; a son of Sparta."

[*Greek Anthology* 7.229 = Dioskorides 30, and Plutarch, *Moralia* 235A]

Dioskorides seems to have written in the late third century BC. This poem is reproduced in the Greek Anthology and quoted by Plutarch. Ausonius (fourth century AD poet and politician) translated this poem, attesting Rome's continued fascination with the Spartan mirage.

F37   A Spartan mother kills her son

She herself sent death on you, when you turned coward,
Abandoning your duty. Staining the sword in your hollow side
The mother who bore you, Damatrios, spoke thus, holding
The dripping sword covered with her son's blood;
Foaming at the mouth, gnashing her teeth;
Looking with angry eyes, the image of a Lakonian woman.
"Leave the Eurotas and go to Hades. Since you have practised
Cowardly flight you are not my son, nor Lakedaimon's."

[Antipater of Thessalonika 23 (Gow & Page, *GP*)
in *Greek Anthology* 7.531]

Antipater from Thessalonika wrote epigrams at Rome around the time of the birth of Christ. But the idea of a Spartan mother killing her son for cowardice in battle was a common theme for epigram which can be traced from Asklepiades (born *c.* 320 BC, poem 47 (Gow & Page, *HE*)) and Tymnes (*Greek Anthology* 7.433 = Tymnes 6 (Gow & Page, *HE*)), and quoted by Plutarch, *Moralia* 240F–241A) all the way to Palladas in the fourth century AD (9.397).

SECTION G
SOME FIFTH-CENTURY ATHENIAN VIEWS OF SPARTA

G1 Sparta as Athens' partner, *c.* 462 BC

[7] Therefore the Lakedaimonians sent Perikleidas to Athens to ask for help. In his comedy, Aristophanes showed him 'sitting at the altars, deathly pale in his scarlet cloak, begging for an army'. [8] Ephialtes objected and called on the Athenians not to help put back on its feet a city that was a rival to Athens, but to let Spartan arrogance lie trodden underfoot. Kimon, according to Kritias, put his own country's increase in power second to the interests of the Lakedaimonians and persuaded the people to go to their aid with many hoplites. Ion records a quotation of his which particularly moved the Athenians, when he urged them 'not to stand by and watch Greece being hamstrung or Athens losing its partner.'

[Plutarch, *Kimon* 16.7–8 = Ion of Chios, *FGrH* 392 F14 = Kritias 52 (Diels-Kranz)]

This passage is very interesting for Athenian views on Sparta, since Plutarch seems to preserve several contemporary 'soundbites' of the sort that might well have been accurately preserved in writers of the time. His quotation of Aristophanes is exact (see **E67**). Ephialtes' phrase, though not said to be a quotation is certainly memorable. Snippets of the pro-Spartan writings of Kritias (*c.* 460–403 BC) survive in other authors, (see **D40** note): Ion of Chios was author of various works of literature including reminiscences of meeting with various Athenians, including Kimon (Plut. *Kimon* 9.1). The context is the debate in Athens *c.* 462 about whether to send forces to help the Spartans put down the Messenian revolt.

G2 The relative sizes of Sparta and Athens

[10.1] Mykenai was a small city, and indeed any one of the cities of that period [sc. of the Trojan War] would seem unimpressive to us today. But to use that as grounds for believing that the expedition was not as great as the poets and later tradition have suggested would certainly be a mistake. [10.2] For example, if the city of the Lakedaimonians were to be destroyed and abandoned, and all that was left were its temples and the foundations of its buildings, I suspect that future generations would find it impossible to believe historians' accounts of its present power. Yet today they occupy two fifths of the Peloponnese, control the whole of it, and are the leaders of an extensive alliance outside its boundaries as well. Yet to the uninformed observer its physical remains would seem to fall far short of the reality, because it lacks the conventional layout of a modern city, has no temples or extravagant public buildings, and is simply a collection of villages typical of ancient Greek society. But if Athens, by contrast, were to suffer the same fate, the same observer would overestimate its power twice over on the basis of the visible remains of that city.

[Thucydides, *History of the Peloponnesian War* 1.10]

G3 Perikles outlines the weakness of Sparta at the outbreak of war, 431 BC

[141.2] Listen to the resources for war which are available to each side, and be aware that we are not weaker. [3] The Peloponnesians are self-sufficient but have no communal or private wealth; in addition they are inexperienced in warfare that lasts a long time or takes place across the seas, since the wars they wage are short and against one another, because of their poverty. [4] And as such, they are able neither to man ships nor to send out land armies very often, as this involves being away from their properties and paying their own expenses – and anyway the sea is closed to them. [5] Surpluses of resources sustain wars better than emergency taxes. People who are self-sufficient are more ready to fight with their bodies than with their resources: they have confidence that their bodies will survive the dangers; but they are not sure that they will not run out of money, especially if the war drags out longer than they think, as is likely. [6] For in a single battle the Peloponnesians and their allies would be able to withstand all of Greece, but they will not be able to wage a war against a differently prepared opponent: not while they do not employ a single council to achieve quick decisions, nor while they all have equal votes though they come from different groups, each concerned with its own interests. No concerted action is likely to arise from this system. [7] For some of them wish to get the greatest vengeance on some enemy, others to do the least damage to their own interests. Getting together at long intervals, they have a short length of time to consider anything of common concern, but mostly see to their own interests. Each thinks that no damage will be done by their own indifference, but that someone else should be looking out for the general interest. The result is that with all of them thinking about their private interests, they do not notice the destruction of the interest they have in common.

[142.1] The biggest point is that they will be hindered by lack of money, and in the delay when they raise it they will not be active: but opportunities in war do not wait. [2] Nor do I think we have anything to fear from forts being built in our territory, nor from their navy. [3] For it is hard enough for a city to build rival forts in peacetime, and certainly no less so in war for them, when we can build counter-forts. [4] If they can establish a garrison, they could damage some parts of our land with raids and by encouraging slaves to desert, but not sufficiently to prevent our sailing to their land, building forts there and defending them with our navy which is where our strength lies. [5] For we have more experience of operating on land from our navy than they have of naval operations from land. [6] Gaining an understanding of the sea will not come easily to them. [7] For you have not yet fully worked it out, despite training at it since immediately after the Persian Wars. So how can farming men and not seafarers, who will also be denied any practice through always being blockaded by our many ships, do anything of note? [8] Against a small blockade they might bolster their ignorance by numbers and take a risk, but as they will be shut in by large numbers of ships, they will keep inactive and by lack of training will be even less skilful and therefore even more reluctant. [9] Seafaring is a skill, just like any other, and it is not possible to train part-time, whenever one can; it is more the case that nothing else can be done part-time alongside it.

[143.1] If they lay hold of the resources at Olympia or Delphi and try to win over our foreign sailors with higher pay, it would be a threat if we could not match them by putting our own people and metics into the boats. But in fact we can, and most important, we have citizens as helmsmen, and other crewmen better and more numerous than all the rest of Greece. [2] And given the danger, no foreigner would choose to fight with them for a few days' greater pay at the cost of being exiled from their homes and less hope of survival.

[3] This seems to be approximately the state of affairs for the Peloponnesians. Ours is far removed from the weaknesses of theirs which I mentioned, and has other unmatched strengths. [4] If they come against our land on foot, we shall sail against theirs, and ravaging even a part of the Peloponnese will have a far greater effect than ravaging the whole of Attika, since they cannot get other land without a fight, but we have plenty of land in the islands and on the mainland. [5] Power over the sea is a huge advantage. Think about it: if we were islanders, who could be safer from harm? Now we should put ourselves in the frame of mind closest to this, give up our land and houses but keep guard on the sea and our city. We must not fight with the far more numerous Peloponnesians in anger at what we have lost: if we win, we would have to fight again against equal numbers, but if we fail we should also lose our allies who make us strong, since they would not keep quiet if there were not enough of us to control them. We should not mourn for houses or land, but only for the dead. Possessions do not make men, but men gain possessions. And if I thought I could persuade you, I would tell you to go out and destroy them, to show the Peloponnesians that you will not yield for this. [144] I have many other reasons for hoping that you will win through if you can agree not to enlarge your empire in wartime and to run needless risks. I am more afraid of your own mistakes than of the enemy's plans.

[Thucydides, *History of the Peloponnesian War* 1.141–144]

G4   Athens' Constitutional Assets (from Perikles' Funeral Oration)

[37.1] Ours is a constitution which makes no attempt to imitate those of our neighbours. In fact, rather than imitating them, we are more of a model for them. We call it "democracy," because political activity is a matter for the many, not the few. In private disputes all enjoy equality in the eyes of the law; when it comes to public office, what will gain a man preferment is his reputation and how he stands in the eyes of his fellow citizens, not sectional interests, but his own particular merits and potential contribution to the public good. Poverty and consequent obscurity are no impediment, if a man has it in him to benefit the state in any way. [37.2] In public affairs we are a free and open society; in our private everyday relationships with our fellow citizens, we do not conduct our lives on the basis of mutual suspicion and ill feeling if they choose a way of life different from ours, nor do we look askance at their behaviour in a way which may be harmless but certainly gives offence. [37.3] Tolerance is the hallmark of our private lives; our public lives are bound by respect for the law. We pay heed to those who from time to time hold high office; and we obey the laws, both those that exist for the protection of victims of oppression and the unwritten social conventions, which it is an acknowledged disgrace to flout.

[40.1] Ours is an unostentatious love of beauty; an unaffected admiration and love of intellect. Wealth we regard as a source of useful activity, not empty ostentation. Poverty is not something to be ashamed of admitting; the real disgrace is a failure to escape from it. [40.2] We place equal value upon private interests and public engagement, and even those of us whose primary interest is in their own business are nevertheless well briefed on issues of public importance. But what makes us unique is the fact that we regard the politically uninvolved not merely as privately engaged, but publicly useless. At the least, we make our own decisions or reflect carefully and properly on their consequences. We do not regard debate as an impediment to action.

The real impediment is a failure to think through those consequences in open debate before proceeding to the necessary action. [40.3] There is another way in which we are very different from our fellow Greeks: those of us who take the risks are the very ones whose debates have made them all too aware of what those risks are; for others confidence is the product of ignorance; debate breeds timidity. True courage can best be seen in those who have a full appreciation of life's blessings and horrors, but nevertheless brave its dangers undeterred.

[40.4] We differ also from the generality in our broader sense of values. We win friends by our own good deeds to them, not theirs to us. Doing favours creates the greater incentive to retain goodwill already earned; the friendship of a debtor has a blunter edge, since he is all too aware that in returning a favour his motive is born of obligation rather than goodwill. [40.5] But we freely offer our help to others, not out of some cold calculation of future profit, but with the confidence of those who are truly free.

[Thucydides, *History of the Peloponnesian War* 2.37 and 2.40]

G5   Spartan Treachery

CHORUS LEADER: I'm not going to listen to you making long speeches,
                When you've made peace with the Lakonians – I'm going
                    to punish you.
DIKAIOPOLIS: Good citizens, leave the Lakonians out of it,   305
                And hear about my treaty, and whether I was right to make it.
LEADER: How can you possibly mention 'right' if you've ever made peace
                With men who stick to no agreement, oath, or pledge?

[Aristophanes, *Acharnians* 303–308 (performed 425 BC)]

Spartan treachery seems to have been almost proverbial in Athens. Characters in Aristophanes' plays refer to it at *Peace* 623 and 1063–8; and *Lysistrata* 628–9, while Euripides in *Andromache* 445–453 and *Suppliants* 187 makes Andromache (with excellent reasons to hate Sparta), and Adrastos (with no such reason), express similar feelings. For Dikaiopolis' defence of his (and Sparta's) actions, see **H36**.

G6   Lysistrata on Sparta liberating Athens from tyranny, 510 BC

LYSISTRATA: You think I am going to let you Athenians off?
                You know, of course, when you were wearing
                    slavish smocks   1150
                And the Lakedaimonians on the other hand came in arms
                And killed many men of Thessaly
                And many friends and allies of Hippias:
                They alone marched out with you on that day,
                And set you free and instead of slavish smocks   1155
                They clothed your citizen body in a warm cloak again.

[Aristophanes, *Lysistrata* 1149–1156 (performed 411 BC)]

G7   Aristophanes' take on a Spartan song

LAKONIAN: Here, kind sir, you take the bagpipes,
                    So that I can dance the two-step and sing a fine song
                    In honour of the Athenians and also ourselves.

ATHENIAN 2: I beg you by the gods do take the blowers,   1245
                    For I enjoy seeing you all dance.

CHORUS OF LAKEDAIMONIANS:

                    Inspire this youngster, Memory,
                            With the Muse, your daughter, who
                            Knows about us and the Athenians,   1250
                            When, godlike, they attacked
                            The ships at Artemision
                            And defeated the Persians,
                    While we, led by Leonidas,
                            Were like wild boars, I guess,   1255
                            Sharpening their tusks;
                    Foam flowered freely round our cheeks,
                    And foam ran freely down our legs too.
                    For their men were as many as   1260
                    The grains of sand, those Persians.
                            Beast-killing huntress,
                            Come hither, virgin goddess,
                            To grace our treaty,
                            That you may keep us united for a long time.   1265
                    Now let prosperous friendship ever
                    Attend our pact,
                            And let us give up our foxy wiles.   1270
                    O come hither, come,
                            O virgin huntress.

LYSISTRATA: Well now, since the rest of the business is satisfactorily completed,
                    Lakedaimonians, you can take your ladies away, and you
                    Can take yours; let husband stand by wife and wife   1275
                    By husband, and then in view of the happy outcome
                    Let us dance for the gods and take care
                    For the future never to make the same mistake again.

CHORUS OF ATHENIANS:

                    Bring on the dance, and call in the Graces,
                            And invoke Artemis,   1280
                    Invoke her twin who leads the dance,
                            The kindly Healer
                    Invoke the god of Nysa, with his Maenads
                            Eyes ablaze in frenzy
                    And Zeus, flaming with lightning fire;   1285
                            Invoke his blessed Lady consort;

> Then those divinities, whom we shall make
> Unforgetful witnesses
> Concerning the gentle-hearted Peace
> Which the Cyprian goddess made.   1290
>
> Alalai! Hail Paian!
> Raise it high! Iai!
> For victory! Iai!
> Evoi! Evoi! Evai! Evai!

LYSISTRATA: Now give us a new song to add to our new song.   1295

CHORUS OF LAKEDAIMONIANS:

> Leave lovely Taygetos again,
> Lakonian Muse, to come and celebrate
> Fittingly for us the god of Amyklai,
>   And brazen-housed Athena,
> And the noble sons of Tyndareos   1300
>   Who sport beside the Eurotas.
> Step out the dance, hey!
> Prancing lightly, hey!
>   So we may sing of Sparta,
> Which cares about dancing for the gods   1305
>   And stamping feet,
> And like ponies the young girls
>   Beside the Eurotas
> Busily prance, their feet raising
>   Clouds of dust.   1310
> And their hair swings,
>   Like Bacchantes at play who shake the thyrsus.
> They are led by Leda's daughter,
> A chorus-leader pure and pretty.   1315

> But come now, bind up your hair with your hand; stamp with both feet
> Like a deer; and clap your hands too, to help the dance.
> And hymn the goddess, ready for every battle,   1320
>   The Lady of the Brazen House.

[Aristophanes, *Lysistrata* 1241–1321]

The **virgin huntress** (1262–1272) is Artemis; **god of Nysa** (1283) is Dionysos; **Cyprian goddess** (1290) is Aphrodite; **god of Amyklai** (1299) is Apollo; **Bacchantes** (1312) were the female followers of Dionysos; **Leda's daughter** (1314) was Helen of Sparta (= Helen of Troy). The hymn and the whole play ends, appropriately, with Athena, patron goddess of both Athens and Sparta.

SECTION H
AN HISTORICAL OVERVIEW

This chapter attempts to provide an historical overview of Sparta by giving a range of literary sources not covered previously. Given that our earliest historians were writing in the second half of the fifth century, material relating to earlier periods may well tell us more about what was thought later, than what actually happened, especially as none of our authors was a Spartan. So we begin with Thucydides' note of caution. Thereafter the sources are arranged chronologically.

H1   Thucydides on the difficulties of history
In many other instances of things that happen currently and not in the forgotten past, people in the rest of Greece are also mistaken; for example in thinking that the kings of the Lakedaimonians have not one vote each but two; and that they have a 'Pitanate' company, which has never been the case. This is how little effort people make in seeking the truth, rather than accepting readily-available opinions.

[Thucydides, *History of the Peloponnesian War* 1.20.3]

Thuc. here contradicts Hdt (6.57 = **D8** and 9.53.2 = **E85**), though it is not actually clear who is right (Hornblower, *Commentary* vol. I.57–8).

EIGHTH AND SEVENTH-CENTURY SPARTA: H2–H7
Throughout much of Greece, this period was one that saw many colonies being sent out all round the Mediterranean. Sparta indeed colonized Tarentum/Taras in this period (**H5, H6**), but also expanded her territory by conquest, perhaps as an alternative to the varied reasons that led to colonization elsewhere in Greece.

H2   Dorian foundation and civil strife
Lakedaimon itself, after being founded by the Dorians who now live there, had suffered internal strife for the greatest period we know about.

[Thucydides, *History of the Peloponnesian War* 1.18.1: see **F4**]

H3   Settlement of Lakonia
Ephoros says that the people who possessed Lakonia were the Heraklids, Eurysthenes and Prokles. They divided the land into six parts and founded cities. One of the parts, Amyklai, they set apart to give to the man who had betrayed Lakonia* and had persuaded the man who ruled it to accept their terms and go in exile with the Achaians to Ionia. They claimed Sparta as a royal residence for themselves. They sent kings to the other areas, allowing them to take in as fellow citizens any foreigners who wished to, because of the shortage of men. They used Las as an anchorage because of its good harbour; Aigys as a military base against their enemies, since it bordered on those around; Pharis as a treasury because it gave safety from outsiders [... *(short gap in text)* ...]. All the surrounding people (*perioikoi*) were subject to the Spartiates but nevertheless had equal rights, sharing citizenship and offices of state. They were called helots. Agis, the son of Eurysthenes, took away their equality and ordered them to pay tax to Sparta: the rest submitted, but the Heleians who held Helos, revolted,

were taken by force in a war, and condemned to be slaves with the stipulation that their owner was not allowed to free them, nor sell them abroad.

[Ephoros, *FGrH* 70 F 117 = Strabo, *Geography* 8.5.4]

* Strabo's next chapter names him as Philonomos (a name which means 'Lover of law/order').

H4   Spartan conquest of Messenia, *c.* 735–715 BC

Messene was captured after a war lasting nineteen years, as Tyrtaios says [*Strabo here quotes Tyrtaios 5 = A5*] and so the Lakedaimonians divided up Messenia among themselves.

[Strabo, *Geography* 6.3.3]

For the Messenian War, see Tyrtaios, **A5–A6**. The most likely explanation for Sparta's conquest was the wish for more land because of relative overpopulation of the Eurotas Valley (Cartledge *SL* 98–103).

H5   Foundation of Tarentum I (Strabo quoting Antiochos) *c.* 706 BC

Antiochos, in speaking of the founding (of Tarentum), says that once the Messenian War took place, those who had not taken part in the Lakedaimonian forces were judged slaves and called helots, while those children who were had during the campaign were called 'Partheniai' (children of unmarried mothers) and were judged not to have full rights. The Partheniai (there were many of them) did not accept this and conspired against the citizens. ...
   (*When the conspiracy was discovered...*)
Phalanthos was sent to the oracle of the god who gave the response:
      Satyrion I give you, to inhabit the rich land of Taras,
      And to become a bane to the Iapygians.
And so the Partheniai arrived there with Phalanthos, and both the non-Greeks and the Cretans who had previously taken possession of the place, welcomed them.

[Antiochos, *FGrH* 555 F13 = Strabo, *Geography* 6.3.2]

Satyrion is on the 'instep' of S. Italy. Archaeological evidence shows that the distinctive Iapygian pottery design was completely replaced by Greek design from *c.* 700 BC, leading Coldstream, *Geometric Greece* 239, to conclude that 'the place had become an outpost in the territory of the Spartan colony of Taras'.

H6   Foundation of Tarentum II (Strabo quoting Ephoros) *c.* 706 BC

The Partheniai, perceiving that their enterprise had been betrayed, held back, while the Lakedaimonians got the fathers of the Partheniai to persuade them to leave for a colony. And if the place they took possession of was good enough, they should stay there, but if not they could return and divide up among themselves one fifth of Messenia. The men sent out found Greeks fighting foreigners, shared the dangers and founded Taras.

[Ephoros, *FGrH* 70 F216 = Strabo, *Geography* 6.3.3]

Taras/Tarentum is on the 'instep' of S. Italy, about 8 miles NW of Satyrion, but on a far superior natural site of an almost completely enclosed double bay. Literary tradition dates its foundation to 706 BC (*OCD*[3] 'Tarentum'), and this is well within the period of Greek colonisation and 'not contradicted by archaeological finds' (Cartledge *SL* 106).

H7   Battle of Hysiai, 669 BC

There is here a memorial to the Argives who fought in their victory over the Lakedaimonians at Hysiai. This contest I find took place when Peisistratos was archon at Athens, in the fourth year of the twenty-seventh Olympics, when Eurybos of Athens won the stade race. As one goes down to lower-lying ground are the ruins of Hysiai, a town formerly part of the Argolid, where the setback for the Lakedaimonians is said to have taken place.

[Pausanias, *Description of Greece* 2.24.7]

Though this is the only source to mention the battle, Tyrtaios 8 and 23a (**A12** and **A11** respectively) confirm Spartan conflict with Argos. From the archaic period onwards, Argos was Sparta's rival in the Peloponnese, and relations between the two states ranged between open hostilities and uneasy co-existence. Both states had interests in the region along the east coast of the peninsula (Kynouria), and the site of the battle clearly shows that the Spartans were the aggressors (Cartledge *SL* 109).

SPARTA IN THE SIXTH CENTURY: H8–H14

By the middle of this century, Sparta had established herself as the leading power within the Peloponnese (**H8**), and by the end of it, a Peloponnesian League had been formed, see **D100–102**.

H8   Spartan struggles with Tegea, *c.* 600 – 550 BC?

Such was the information Croesus gained about the state of affairs in Athens at the time [when Peisistratos seized power in Athens]. As for the Lakedaimonians, he discovered that they had come through a period of enormous difficulty, but had now defeated the Tegeans in their recent war. In fact, the Lakedaimonians had triumphed in all their other wars during the reign of Leon and Agasikles, and had only come to grief in their struggle with the Tegeans.

[Herodotus, *Histories* 1.65.1 (continued in F3)]

Croesus' reign as king of Lydia ended in 546 BC, in his disastrous attack on the Persian empire. Hdt. presents him here as searching for Greek allies for this attack (1.56.1–2), and thus reporting on how Athens (1.59–64) and Sparta (**H9**, **H10** below) had come to be the most powerful states in Greece. Tegea's location as Sparta's northern neighbour automatically made it a prime target for Spartan aggression, with a series of conflicts between the two communities during the sixth century (Hdt. 1.66–8 = **F3**, **H9**, **H10**). These ended in a treaty (perhaps = **E137**) and Tegea eventually proved to be one of her most faithful allies. With a force of at least 1,500 hoplites (Hdt. 9.28 = **E84**) the city was among the most significant members of the Peloponnesian League, and one of the two leading cities of Arkadia, the other being its northern neighbour Mantineia.

H9   Sparta invades Tegea but is defeated, early sixth century?

[1] Being blessed with fertile land and a large population, the country rapidly grew prosperous and strong. As a result they soon became restless, and contemptuous of the neighbouring Arkadians, whom they regarded as an inferior people. So they consulted the Delphic oracle about the possibility of conquering the whole country. [2] This was the Pythia's reply:

> *You ask me about Arkadia? That is no small matter. Nor shall I consent to it.*
> *Many are the dwellers in Arkadia; acorns are their food.*
> *They will ward you off. Yet I do not begrudge you.*
> *Tegea is my gift to you, wherein to dance and stamp your feet,*
> *And to parcel out her lovely plain with the measuring line.*

[3] When the Lakedaimonians received the news of this oracle, they misunderstood the double meaning of the oracle. So they left the rest of Arkadia alone and launched a campaign against Tegea, confidently carrying with them the shackles for their prospective prisoners. They were in fact defeated in the battle, and those of them that were taken prisoner had to wear the very shackles they had brought along, and to work the "lovely plain" of the Tegeans "with the measuring line." The shackles with which they were bound were preserved in Tegea down to my own time, hanging up around the temple of Athena Alea.

[Herodotus, *Histories* 1.66.1–3: see **F3** and **H10**]

Pausanias 8.47.2 also reports seeing the fetters in the (rebuilt) temple of Athena Alea.

H10   Spartans achieve dominance over Tegea, *c.* 550 BC
[67.1] In this earlier war against the Tegeans the Lakedaimonians always and repeatedly got the worst of it. But by the time of Croesus, in the reign of kings Anaxandridas and Ariston at Lakedaimon, the Spartiates had proved victorious. This is how it came about. [67.2] Having suffered constant defeat in this war at the hands of the Tegeans, they sent envoys to Delphi to ask which god they should seek to propitiate in order to defeat the Tegeans. [67.3] The Pythia declared to them that they must bring home the bones of Orestes, the son of Agamemnon. But they could not find the tomb of Orestes anywhere, so they sent a second embassy to the god to ask where Orestes lay buried. The Pythia gave the following reply to the members of the embassy.
[67.4]   *There is in Arkadia a city, Tegea, standing in a level plain,*
           Where two winds blow by strong necessity;
           Blow counters blow; woe upon woe is piled;
           There the earth, source of all life, holds Agamemnon's son;
           If you bring him home, you shall become the lord of Tegea.
[67.5] Even after they heard this, the Lakedaimonians were still as far as ever from discovering the body. They hunted everywhere, until a Spartiate called Lichas, one of their so-called *agathoergoi* cracked the problem. These *agathoergoi* are the five oldest citizens to graduate from the *Hippeis* each year. Their duty for the year following their graduation is to remain busily engaged on state missions wherever required.

[68.1] Lichas was one of these and by a mixture of luck and intelligence he found the body in Tegea. It was a period when there was a degree of intercourse with Tegea, and Lichas on a visit to Tegea went into a forge, where he saw a smith hammering out iron and was astonished at the spectacle. The smith noted his astonishment and took a moment's rest from his work. [68.2] "Lakonian stranger," he said, "you seem to be surprised to see what I am doing with this piece of iron. Well, you would have been absolutely flabbergasted, if you had seen what I saw recently. [68.3] I wanted to make a well in this workshop here, and as I was digging I came across a coffin, more than ten feet (three metres) long. I could not believe that men ever existed who were taller than they are nowadays, so I opened it and found a corpse as big as the coffin. I measured it and then filled in the hole again." [68.4] That was the smith's account of what he had seen. Lichas thought about what the man had said and decided that this must be the Orestes of the prophecy. He deduced that the smith's pair of bellows was the explanation of the oracle's "two winds"; that the "blow countering blow" referred to the smith's hammer and anvil; and that the "woe piled upon woe" meant the hammering out of the iron, because the discovery of iron represented a succession of woes for humankind. [68.5] On the strength of his deductions he went straight back to Sparta and told them the whole story.

They concocted a scheme, prosecuted him on a false accusation, and exiled him. He went back to Tegea and told the smith the story of his misfortunes and tried unsuccessfully to lease the workshop from him. [68.6] But in time he got his way, and having taken up residence he opened the grave, gathered up the bones, and carried them off back to Sparta. And ever afterwards, whenever the two states came to hostilities, the Lakedaimonians proved by far the stronger. Indeed, by then they had already conquered most of the Peloponnese.

[Herodotus, *Histories* 1.67–68]

This unusual story is not entirely unique: the appropriation of an important hero's relics had a strong symbolic value, and in this case it seems that the Spartans were trying to bridge the gap between themselves as Dorians and non-Doric peoples such as the Arkadians and Achaians by emphasising a connection with one of the mythical rulers of the whole peninsula before the Dorians arrived. We do not know whether this measure did indeed have any direct success: the tomb of Orestes in Sparta survived into Roman times (Paus. 3.11.10), but we have no evidence that this particular mythical connection was of much use later on. Rather than subjugating the Tegeans, the Spartans finally decided to conclude a treaty which may be that of **E137**. The reasons for this momentous step are not clear, but the long Tegean resistance and the position of the city on the main route to Argos and the Isthmus beyond may have played a role, as well as the recognition that controlling a subject territory in the same way as Messenia meant a considerable strain on material resources as well as manpower.

Sparta ends tyranny in Sikyon, *c.* 550 BC – see E5

H11   Sparta and Argos – Battle of the Champions, *c.* 546 BC
[1] At this same time a quarrel had arisen between the Lakedaimonians and the Argives about an area called Thyreai. [2] This was part of the Argolid which the Lakedaimonians had seized and occupied. In addition the land to the west, as far as Malea used to belong to the Argives, both on the mainland and the island of Kythera and the rest of the islands. [3] The Argives marched to the aid of their land which had been seized and agreed after negotiation that three hundred from each side should fight, and whoever won should possess the area. The mass of each army should go back to their own city and not stay for the contest, to avoid the danger of the armies being present and joining the fight if they saw their own side losing. [4] They went away on these terms, and those remaining behind as the chosen champions of each side engaged. Their fight was so closely balanced that out of the six hundred men, three were left alive, on the Argive side, Alkenor and Chromios, and of the Lakedaimonians, Othryades. These men were still alive when night fell. [5] The two Argives ran back to Argos to claim the victory, but the Lakedaimonian Othryades stripped the bodies of the Argives and carried their weapons back to his camp and remained at his post. On the next day both sides were there to learn the result. [6] For a time both said that they had won, the Argives because more of their men had survived, the Lakedaimonians declaring that they had run away while

their man had stayed and stripped the corpses of the Argives. [7] In the end the argument turned into a battle: many men on both sides were killed but the Lakedaimonians won.

[Herodotus, *Histories* 1.82]

Thucydides 5.41.2 refers to this battle as still in the minds of the Argives in 420 BC, and assumes that his readers will be entirely familiar with the 'battle when both sides claimed victory'. Pausanias notes that the graves could still be seen in his day at the site of the battle (2.38.5). For Othryades, see **F29**.

H12   Spartan expedition against Polykrates of Samos, 525 BC
[39.1] While Cambyses was making an expedition against Egypt, the Lakedaimonians made an expedition to Samos against Polykrates, son of Aiakes who had seized control of Samos.

[46.1] When the Samians who had been driven out by Polykrates arrived at Sparta, they came before the magistrates and spoke at great length about their urgent need for help. At this first meeting, the Lakedaimonians replied that they had forgotten the start of the speech and failed to understand what came after. [46.2] After this, at the second meeting, they said nothing, but bringing a sack, said that the sack needed grain. They replied that the word 'sack' was unnecessary, but decided to help them. [47] And so the Lakedaimonians prepared to campaign against Samos. The Samians say that they were returning a favour in that previously they had helped with ships against the Messenians, but the Lakedaimonians say that their expedition was not to help the Samians at their request, but to punish the theft of a bowl and a breastplate.

[54.1] When the Lakedaimonians arrived with a large force, they besieged Samos. Attacking the walls, they advanced to a tower which stood beside the sea over towards the outskirts of the town, but Polykrates himself came to the rescue with a large band of men and drove them back. [54.2] At the upper level of the tower which butts onto a ridge of the hillside, the mercenaries and several of the Samians made a sortie to stop the Lakedaimonians and drove them back for a short while, before being pursued and slain. [55.1] If the Lakedaimonians present that day had been the match for Archias and Lykopes, Samos would have been captured, for they alone followed the fleeing Samians into the walls, but were cut off from getting back and died in the city of Samos. [55.2] I met the grandson of this Archias in Pitana (that was his village), another Archias, son of Samios, who held the Samians in greater honour than any other foreigners, who told me that his father had been given the name Samios because *his* father, Archias, had died fighting heroically in Samos. He said that he honoured the Samians because they had given his grandfather a public funeral. [56.1] The Lakedaimonians besieged Samos for forty days without success and returned to the Peloponnese.

[Herodotus, *Histories* 3.39.1; 3.46–47; 3.54–6]

Sparta was aided by Corinth (Hdt) which may have provided much of the fleet, though clearly *perioikoi* must have helped with this aspect of the expedition. Cartledge (*SL* 123) suggests that in addition to wishing to restore pro-Spartan aristocrats to Samos, there may have been a longer-term anti-Persian motive for the expedition. In any case, the expedition was clearly a failure. See also Cartledge, 'Sparta and Samos: A Special Relationship?' *CQ* 1982.

H13   Dorieus tries to found a colony in Libya, *c.* 520 BC?

[2] Since Dorieus could not bear the thought of living under the rule of Kleomenes, he demanded and received a mandate from the people to lead a body of Lakedaimonians off to found a colony. But, without asking the Delphic oracle in what land he should establish his settlement or following any of the normal procedures for such a venture, in his fit of pique he simply sailed away to Libya with some men from Thera to act as guides. [3] On arrival at Kinyps, he established his settlement beside the river on a stretch of some of the finest land in Libya. After a couple of years he was driven out by the united forces of Makai, Libyans, and Carthaginians and returned to the Peloponnese.

[Herodotus, *Histories* 5.42.2–3 (see also **E8**)]

H14   Dorieus attempts to found a colony in Sicily, *c.* 510 BC

[43] There he was advised by Antichares of Eleon, on the basis of some oracles given to Laios, to go out and found the city of Herakleia in Sicily, allegedly because the whole area of Eryx belonged by right to the descendants of Herakles, the original conqueror of the country. On hearing this, Dorieus went off to Delphi to ask the oracle whether he would be able to capture the area he was being directed to. The Pythia assured him that he would. So Dorieus collected the same body of settlers that he had taken to Libya and coasted along the shores of Italy.

(On the way they may or may not have participated in the sack of Sybaris, datable to 510 BC)

[46] A number of other Lakedaimonians had sailed with Dorieus to help set up the new colony, including Thessalos and Paraibates, Keleas and Euryleon. But when they reached Sicily, they and the whole expeditionary force were defeated and killed by the Phoenicians and Egestans.

[Herodotus, *Histories* 5.43 and 5.46]

Dorieus was the younger son of Anaxandridas, but by his first wife (Hdt. 5.41 – **E8**). The accession of his elder brother Kleomenes (*c.* 520 BC) and the sack of Sybaris, datable to 510 BC give us the approximate dates for these two attempts at colonization, the latter also mentioned by Pausanias (**C35**).

Sparta intervenes in Athens, *c.* 512 – 506 BC see E11–E14
Sparta refuses to help in Ionian revolt, 499 BC see E15, E16
Sparta defeats Argives at Sepeia, *c.* 494 BC see E17, E18
Sparta intervenes in Aigina, *c.* 492 BC see E21

SPARTA AND THE PERSIAN WARS: H15–H19
Unlike Athens, Sparta had refused to help the Ionian Revolt (see **E15–E16**) which was Persia's major cause for war against Athens in 490 BC, and arrived too late to help the Athenians at Marathon (**H16–H17**). Nonetheless Spartan involvement in Aigina (**E21**) seems to have been a pre-emptive move against Aiginetan medizing; and Sparta decisively rejected any medizing herself (**H15**). Sparta was therefore at the forefront of the Greek alliance, providing the supreme commanders for Thermopylai (see **F9–F26**), Artemision & Salamis (**E116**), and Plataia (**E84–E86**).

H15   Spartan treatment of Persian heralds, 491 BC

Xerxes did not dispatch heralds to Athens or Sparta to ask for earth because when
Darius had previously sent them to do this, the Athenians had thrown them into a pit,
and the Lakedaimonians had thrown them into a well and told them to take earth and
water from there to the King.

[Herodotus, *Histories* 7.133.1]

H16   Philippides runs from Athens to Sparta, 490 BC

[105.1] Before this, while they were still in the city, the generals sent a messenger off to
Sparta. This was an Athenian called Philippides who was a specialist all-day runner. ...
[106.1] Philippides reached Sparta from the town of Athens within two days, and spoke
to the leaders, [106.2] "Lakedaimonians, the Athenians have need of you to help them
and not to watch the oldest city in Greece falling into slavery at the hands of foreigners.
For even now Eretria has been enslaved and Greece is weaker by the loss of a fine
city." [106.3] He spoke as he had been told, and the Lakedaimonians wished to help the
Athenians but were not able to do so immediately because they did not want to break
their law: it was the ninth day of the month and they said they could not march until the
full moon.

[Herodotus, *Histories* 6.105–6]

Philippides is the name given by both Herodotus and Plutarch, as opposed to 'Pheidipiddes'. This represents
the authentic story ultimately behind the modern marathon (race), preferable to Plutarch's melodramatic
version. An annual 'Spartathlon' race (246 km from Athens to Sparta) was started in 1983 by a British
classicist and RAF wing commander, John Foden (http://www.spartathlon.gr/en/). Despite Herodotus'
'respectful telling of how the Spartans wanted to help but could not' (Osborne *GM*, 329) scholarly opinion
is divided on Sparta's behaviour: 'The Spartans had promised help; but on being summoned, they typically
claimed that religious scruples prevented them from setting out until the moon was full.' (Murray, *Early
Greece* 1980). 'a runner obtained a promise that the Spartans would come after holding a festival – not
unreasonably: such matters were taken seriously' (Rhodes, *A Short History of Ancient Greece,* 2014). 'Even
if the religious obstruction which they pleaded was genuine, it was an excuse rather than a reason' (Forrest,
History of Sparta 1980). *After* the full moon, the Spartans made considerable haste, with a forced march of
150 miles to Athens and a further 26 to Marathon (**H17**).

H17   Spartans arrive at Marathon too late, 490 BC

Two thousand Lakedaimonians went to Athens after the full moon, in such great haste
to get there that they reached Attika two days after leaving Sparta. Arriving too late
for the battle, they nonetheless wished to see the Persians. After complimenting the
Athenians on their good work, they went back home.

[Herodotus, *Histories* 6.120]

Thermopylai, 480 BC – see F9–F26

H18   Athenian view of Thermopylai and Salamis

[3] That is why we insist that your debt to us is far greater than anything we might owe
to you. When you marched out to war, your own cities were still inhabited and your
interest lay in preserving them for the future; you were far more fearful for your own
people than for us – indeed as long as our city was still secure you never showed up
at all to offer help. But we set out for war from a city that no longer existed, risking
all for what seemed a hopeless cause. Yet in doing so we helped to save both you and

also ourselves. [4] If through fear for our own lands we had changed sides and joined the Persians, as others did; or if through lack of courage we had failed to embark on our ships, because our cause seemed to be irretrievably lost, it would have been futile for you to fight a naval battle, since you would have lacked the ships to do it. For the barbarian his whole campaign would have been a walkover, just as he had hoped…..”

[Thucydides, *History of the Peloponnesian War* 1.74.3–4]

This viewpoint comes from the speech attributed by Thucydides to the Athenians who 'happened to be' at the meeting of the Peloponnesian League in 432 BC, and is supported by Hdt's authorial comment below (**H19**).

H19 Sparta's debt to Athens in 480 BC

[3] Even if many walls had been driven across the Isthmus by the Peloponnesians, the Lakedaimonians would have been let down and deserted by their allies, not because they wanted to, but through compulsion as one by one their cities were captured by the Persian naval force. Having been deserted they would have displayed great deeds and died heroically. Or, before that, having seen the other Greeks medizing, they might have come to an agreement with Xerxes. In either case, Greece would have come under the Persians. For I cannot see what good driving walls across the Isthmus would have been, if the Persian King controlled the seas. … [5] And so it would be quite right to say that the Athenians were the saviours of Greece.

[Herodotus, *Histories* 7.139.3]

Battle of Plataia, 479 BC: See E84–E86 and B5a–b

THE '*PENTEKONTAETIA*' 480–431 BC: H20–H37
The '*Pentekontaetia*' or 'Fifty-year period' is the name generally given to Thucydides' excursus in 1.97–118 for the events which 'happened in the roughly fifty years between Xerxes' retreat and the beginning of this [i.e. the Peloponnesian] war' (Thuc. 1.118.2).

H20 Allied capture of Cyprus and Byzantium from the Persians, 478 BC

Pausanias the son of Kleombrotos was sent out from Lakedaimon as commander of the Greeks, with twenty ships from the Peloponnese. The Athenians sailed with him with thirty ships and a large number of other allies. Under Pausanias' leadership they campaigned against Cyprus and conquered most of it, and then against Byzantium which was held by the Persians, which they captured after a siege.

[Thucydides, *History of the Peloponnesian War* 1.94]

H21 Leotychidas' expedition to Thessaly, *c* 477 BC

[1] Leotychidas did not live to old age in Sparta, but suffered what amounted to a wholesale retribution for what had been done to Demaratos. The circumstances were as follows: He led the Lakedaimonians on an invasion of Thessaly. Total victory was within his grasp, [2] when he was caught red-handed accepting a huge bribe. He was discovered sitting in his tent on a Persian-style glove stuffed with silver coins. He was put on trial and exiled from Sparta, his house was demolished, and he himself died in exile in Tegea. All this took place much later than the events I am currently describing.

[Herodotus, *Histories* 6.72]

H22   Spartans win five contests with the help of Teisamenos (479–457 BC)
The five contests were as follows: first the one at Plataia; then the one that took place
at Tegea against the Tegeans and Argives; after that at Dipaia against all the Arkadians
except those from Mantineia; next in the Messenian war at Ithome; finally at Tanagra,
against the Athenians and Argives.

[Herodotus, *Histories* 9.35]

The Delphic oracle had predicted that Teisamenos of Elis would win five great contests. After he narrowly
failed to win the pentathlon at the Olympics, the Spartans realised that the 'contests' must be battles, so
desperately wanted him on their side: he was thus able to gain Spartan citizenship for himself and his
brother (**D25**). The battles were Plataia 479, Tegea *c.* 473–470, Dipaia *c.* 470–465, the Helot revolt, after
465, Tanagra 458/7. The story is also told by Pausanias 3.12.8.

THE FIRST PELOPONNESIAN WAR, *c.* 461–446 BC: H23–H35
This is the modern term used for a war *c.* 461 to 446 BC, mainly between Athens and Corinth, but also
invoving Sparta. Thucydides mentions several of the episodes, alongside other events in Greece in his
'pentekontaetia' (see intro to **H20–H37**). It was ended by the 'Thirty Years' Peace' (see **H34**, **H35**) between
Athens and Sparta and it was the decision by the Peloponnesian League that Athens had broken its terms
that led to '*The* Peloponnesian War' (see **E140, E142, H37**).

H23   Sparta defeats Athens at battle of Tanagra, 458/7 BC
[107.2] The Phokians launched a campaign against Doris, the mother-city of the
Lakedaimonians, comprising Boion, Kytinion and Erineon, and captured one of these
settlements. The Lakedaimonians, led by Nikomedes son of Kleombrotos, acting
for King Pleistoanax, son of Leonidas, who was still young, went to the aid of their
Dorian kindred with fifteen hundred of their own hoplites and ten thousand allied
hoplites, forced the Phokians to agree to return the city and were ready to return
home. [3] However if they wished to make the sea crossing by the Bay of Krisa,
the Athenians had sailed round with their ships, ready to prevent them. On the other
hand, marching across Geraneia did not seem safe for them, since the Athenians were
in control of Megara and Pegai, and Geraneia is a difficult route and was regularly
guarded by the Athenians, especially at that time when the Lakedaimonians realised
the Athenians intended to block that route. [4] They decided therefore to remain in
Boiotia and consider how they could travel across in greatest safety. In addition there
were Athenian citizens having secret dealings with them in the hope of abolishing the
democracy and the building of the long walls. [5] The Athenians set out against them
in full force, together with a thousand Argives and various other allied troops: in all a
total of fourteen thousand men. [6] They marched thinking that the Lakedaimonians
were trapped there, and suspecting that there was some attempt to overthrow the
democracy. [7] Some Thessalian cavalry forces came with the Athenians, in line with
their treaty, but in the event they went over to the Lakedaimonians.

[108] The battle took place at Tanagra and the Lakedaimonians and their allies were
victorious, but with great slaughter on both sides. The Lakedaimonians went into
Megara, cut down some trees and went back home, through Geraneia and the Isthmus.

[Thucydides, *History of the Peloponnesian War* 1.107–8]

The Spartans commemorated their victory with a golden shield at Olympia, see **B10**. On the other side, up to 400 Argives were commemorated on a stone (ML 35 = OR 111) from Athens' burial quarter, the Kerameikos.

H24 Battle of Oinoe? *c.* 458?

a) The Stoa Poikile first has the Athenians drawn up at Oinoe in Argive territory against the Lakedaimonians. The painting is not of the height of the struggle nor when it has come to a display of valour, but at the beginning of the battle when the men are about to engage.

[Pausanias, *Description of Greece* 1.15.1]

b) These statues are the works of Hypatodoros and Aristogeiton, who made them, as the Argives themselves say, from spoils of the victory which they won at Oinoe in Argive territory with their Athenian allies against the Lakedaimonians.

[Pausanias, *Description of Greece* 10.10.4]

These explanations of works of art by Pausanias are the only references to the battle of Oinoe. The first one describes a painting in the 'Painted Stoa' in Athens' agora; the second, statues dedicated at Delphi depicting the mythological story of the 'Seven against Thebes'. Hornblower, *Commentary* vol 1, page 165, describes the tradition of the battle as 'very obscure'. If it took place, it was most likely during the Athenian-Argive alliance against Sparta (see **E62**).

H25 Tolmides' naval expedition I, 456/5

[108.5] The Athenians, led by Tolmides, son of Tolmaios, sailed around the Peloponnese and burnt the Lakedaimonians' dockyard.

[Thucydides, *History of the Peloponnesian War* 1.108.5]

H26 Tolmides' naval expedition II, 456/5

Tolmides: this man sailed around the Peloponnese with the Athenians and winning great glory, and he captured Boia and Kythera, when Kallias was *archon* in Athens. Tolmides also set fire to the shipyards of the Lakedaimonians.

[Scholiast to Aeschines 2.75 (ed. Dindorf, no.78)]

Aeschines in his speech praised the boldness of Tolmides, so the ancient commentator explains the reference. The dockyard/shipyards were at Gytheion.

H27 Kimon recalled to Athens to make peace, c. 456?

Theopompos in the tenth book of his *Wars against Philip* says, "Before five years had passed, war broke out against the Lakedaimonians and the people sent for Kimon, thinking that because of his *proxenia* he could very quickly bring about peace. On arriving in the city he put an end to the war."

[Theopompos, *FGrH* 115 F88 = Scholiast to Aristeides 46.158.13]

The reference to five years is to his (10 year) ostracism from Athens – but the chronology is very hard to reconcile with other known dates (Hornblower, *Commentary* vol. I.168).

H28   5 year treaty, 451 BC?

Three years later a five-year treaty came into effect between the Peloponnesians and the Athenians.

[Thucydides, *History of the Peloponnesian War* 1.112.1]

H29   Sacred war over Delphi, 449 BC

After this the Lakedaimonians fought the so-called 'Sacred War', in which they took control of the temple at Delphi and handed it back to the people of Delphi. But after the Lakedaimonians had withdrawn, an Athenian force retook control and handed it back to the Phokians.

[Thucydides, *History of the Peloponnesian War* 1.112.3]

H30   Kleandridas' trick at Tegea, before 446 BC

Kleandridas made Tegean aristocrats who were suspected of Lakonizing even more strongly suspected by leaving only their estates unravaged, while destroying those of other people. The Tegeans very angrily brought these men to trial for betrayal. The men feared they would be condemned, and pre-empted the vote by actually betraying the city, being forced by fear to do in reality what they had been wrongly suspected of.

[Polyaenus, *Stratagems* 2.10.3]

For Polyaenus, see **E129**. As ephor in 446 BC Kleandridas advised the young king Pleistoanax on campaign to Athens (Plut. *Perikles* 22 and **H31**), but was convicted for accepting bribes (see **H32**).

H31   Euboia and Megara revolt from Athens, Sparta invades Attika, 446 BC

[1] Not long after this, Euboia revolted from the Athenians and when Perikles had already crossed over with a force of Athenians, he received reports that Megara had revolted, that the Lakedaimonians were about to invade Attika, and that the Athenian guards had been killed by the Megarians, barring those who had escaped to Nisaia. The Megarians had brought in men from Corinth, Sikyon, and Epidauros to help them revolt. Perikles brought his army back from Euboia in haste. [2] And after this the Peloponnesians invaded Attika under the command of Pleistoanax, son of Leonidas, king of the Lakedaimonians: they ravaged the land as far as Eleusis and Thria, but went no further before returning home. [3] The Athenians went back across to Euboia, under Perikles' leadership, subdued the whole island and reached terms with all of the island except for Hestiaia where they drove out the inhabitants and took control of the land themselves.

[Thucydides, *History of the Peloponnesian War* 1.114]

H32   Perikles bribed Pleistoanax to withdraw? 446 BC

There was a very large amount of money in the akropolis: Perikles spent most of it on the war. They say that when accounting for twenty talents, he simply said that it was necessary expenditure. Ephoros says that later, when the Lakedaimonians found this out, they confiscated the property of Kleandridas and fined Pleistoanax 15 talents because they supposed that they had taken bribes from the agents of Perikles to spare the rest of Athenian territory, but that Perikles had not wanted openly to say 'I gave what is unaccounted for to the kings of the Lakedaimonians.'

[Scholiast on Aristophanes, *Clouds* 859 = Ephoros, *FGrH* 70 F193]

Aristophanes' *Clouds,* (first produced in 423, but the existing text represents a revision of 418–6) has a character explaining that he lost his shoes because 'like Perikles, it was necessary'. The scholiast (ancient commentator) explains that topical reference by quoting the historian Ephoros.

H33 Pleistoanax returns 19 years later

Eventually the Lakedaimonians were persuaded to bring Pleistoanax back in the nineteenth year… He had been in exile on Mount Lykaion because he had been suspected of having once being bribed to withdraw from Attika, and in his fear of the Lakedaimonians had lived in a house half within the sanctuary of Zeus.

[Thucydides, *History of the Peloponnesian War* 5.16.3]

H34 The Thirty Years' Peace, 446 BC

Not long after their return, they made a treaty with the Lakedaimonians and their allies for thirty years, in which they gave back Nisaia, Pegai, Troizen and Achaia, places which the Athenians had taken from the Peloponnesians.

[Thucydides, *History of the Peloponnesian War* 1.115]

H35 Terms of the Thirty Years' Peace inscribed at Olympia

In front of this statue of Zeus (by the Council Chamber at Olympia) is a bronze *stele* with the terms of the Thirty Years' Peace between the Lakedaimonians and the Athenians, The Athenians made this after subduing Euboia for the second time, in the third year after the eighty-third Olympics when Krison of Himera won the stade race. It is stated in the terms that the city of Argos has no part in the peace between the Athenians and the Lakedaimonians, but that the Argives and the Athenians may, if they wish, be on friendly terms with each other, outside the treaty.

[Pausanias, *Description of Greece* 5.23.4]

H36 Aristophanes' view of the causes of the Peloponnesian War

Aristophanes' Acharnians was performed in 425 BC. The chorus and main character, Dikaiopolis (his name means Just-city) are from the Attic village of Acharnai, in an area repeatedly ravaged by Peloponnesian invasions. Not surprisingly, they are thoroughly fed up with the war, and Dikaiopolis has even made his own private peace-treaty with Sparta (see G5) which he justifies here.

DIKAIOPOLIS:

Do not be angry, members of the audience,
If, though a beggar, I intend to speak to the Athenians,
About politics, even though it's a comedy,
Since even comedy knows about justice.   500

[501–508: *Dikaiopolis explain that he does not feel he is being treacherous as he is speaking at the Lenaia festival in winter, with few if any foreigners present, rather than the more important, springtime, Dionysia.*]

As for me, I hate the Lakedaimonians a great deal,
And wish that the god of Tainaron once again   510
Shakes all their houses down,
Since I too have had my vines cut down.
And yet, since I'm speaking only amongst friends,
Why do we blame the Lakedaimonians for this?
It was our men, I don't say our city,   515

Remember that I don't say our city,
But useless humanoids, mis-struck,
Worthless, counterfeit and foreign,
Who sneakily reported cloaks from Megara,
And if they saw a melon or a hare anywhere   520
Or a piglet, garlic, or rock-salt, would
Label them as Megarian and have them sold the same day.
This was a minor local dispute.
But then some drunken young gamblers
Went to Megara and stole a whore, Simaitha.   525
So then the garlic-guzzling Megarians took offence,
And retaliated by stealing two whores of Aspasia.
And that was the beginning of war breaking out
Throughout Greece – from three prostitutes.
And then in his anger the Olympian Perikles   530
Thundered and lightened and caused havoc in Greece,
And made laws written like drinking songs,
That the Megarians must not stay on land,
In the agora, on the sea or on the mainland.
And then the Megarians when they were gradually starving   535
Asked the Lakedaimonians to get the decree caused
By the prostitutes overturned.
We refused although they asked repeatedly.
And then there was a clashing of shields.
Someone says, "It's not right." But you tell me what *was* right.   540
Come now, if some Lakedaimonian had sailed his craft out
To report and sell up a Seriphian puppy,
Would you have taken in sitting down? No way.
Of course you would immediately have launched
Three hundred ships …   545

[Aristophanes, *Acharnians* 510–545 (performed 425 BC)]

Poseidon, god of earthquakes, had a temple at **Tainaron** where helots might claim sanctuary. A breach of this was thought to have caused Poseidon to send the earthquake of 464 BC (see **E62**). In the 430s, Athens decreed punitive trade sanctions (the 'Megarian decrees') on **Megara**, a close neighbour of Athens but allied to Sparta. For Thuc. (1.42.2, 1.67.4, and most modern writers) they were not a major cause of the war: Aristophanes represents a different, perhaps more popular view. **Perikles** was the main supporter of the decrees (e.g. Plut. *Perikles* 29–30 (quoting Aristophanes)); **Aspasia** was his mistress, prosecuted around 432 BC by another comic poet (Plut. *Perikles* 32), and Aristophanes' link may just reflect general criticism of Perikles; also literary satire alluding to Helen's abduction starting the Trojan War and to Herodotus' version (*Histories* 1.1 – 1.4). **Seriphos** is a small and remote island in the Aegean, part of the Athenian empire: Spartan interference there would be unthinkable and most unlikely to have provoked Athens to war.

THE PELOPONNESIAN WAR, 431–404 BC: H37–H43
'Fought between Athens and its allies on the one hand and Sparta and its allies on the other; most of it (down to 411) was recorded by the great historian Thucydides and that is the most interesting thing about it.' (Hornblower, *OCD³* under 'Peloponnesian War').

H37   Spartans decide on war with Athens, 432 BC

[87.6] This decision of the assembly that the treaty had been broken was made in the fourteenth year of the existing Thirty Years' Peace, signed in the aftermath of the so-called Euboian episode. [88.1] The Lakedaimonians decided that the treaty had been broken and that war should be declared not so much because of the force of their allies' complaints as their own fear of yet further growth of Athenian power and their realisation that they already controlled the greater part of Greece.

[Thucydides, *History of the Peloponnesian War* 1.87.6 – 1.88.1]

For the meeting and speeches recounted by Thuc. which led to this decision, see **E140–E141** and **E29–E31**.

Pylos and Sphakteria, 425 BC, see E87–E96

H38   Offers of peace thrice rejected by Athenian Assembly after Pylos, 425 BC

HERMES: Peace says that after Pylos she came spontaneously
         Bringing a chest full of treaties for the city
         But three times lost a show of hands in the Assembly.

[Aristophanes, *Peace* 665–667 (performed 421 BC)]

In the comedy the god Hermes is lamenting the fact that the goddess Peace is angry and refusing to talk to the Athenians. Performed within four years of the events to an audience most of whom would have been at the assembly, the detail about three votes must be correct in some way.

H39   Philochoros on the rejection of Spartan peace offer after Pylos, 425 BC

The Lakedaimonians sent envoys to Athens about a peace agreement, after making a truce with regard to their men at Pylos and handing over their ships, 60 in number. Kleon spoke against the peace agreement and it is said that the assembly was sharply divided. When the presiding official came to put the question, those in favour of war won the vote.

[Philochoros, *Attic History, FGrH* 328 F128]

This extract from Philochoros' fourth-century *Attic History* is preserved in a quotation by an ancient commentator on the passage of Aristophanes quoted above. His account suggests a much closer vote than Thuc implies (4.21.2). For the Spartan fleet, handed over to guarantee their good intentions, see Thuc. 4.16.3.

H40   Armistice in the Peloponnesian War, 423 BC

[1] In the spring, and just before the arrival of the following summer, the Lakedaimonians and Athenians agreed an armistice for a single year. The Athenian calculation was that this would prevent Brasidas from winning over any more allies until they themselves had had time during the cessation of hostilities to organise counter-measures. If things then went to plan, they could extend the truce for a further period. The Lakedaimonians guessed that these were the very things that the Athenians had been worried about, but that once they experienced an end to their suffering and general hardships they would

be all the more eager to put an end to them by giving back the prisoners from Pylos and making a more enduring peace settlement. [2] For the Lakedaimonians, recovery of those prisoners was the paramount consideration, while Brasidas' campaign was going so well. And if Brasidas' successes continued and he made up still further for their lost ground, they might indeed be deprived of their prisoners, but the risks of sustained hostilities could be sustained on more level terms, with every likelihood of ultimate victory. [3] So they and their allies agreed to the armistice.

[Thucydides, *History of the Peloponnesian War* 4.117]

H41   Sparta's quarrel with Elis and banishment from the Olympics of 420 BC
[49.1] The Olympic games took place that summer, in which Androsthenes of Arkadia won the *pankration* for the first time. The Lakedaimonians were banned from the temple by the Eleans, and therefore could not sacrifice or participate in the games. They had failed to pay a fine imposed on them under Olympic law by the Eleans, who alleged that they had launched an attack against a fort, Phrykos, and sent their hoplites into Lepreon during the period of the Olympic truce. The fine amounted to two thousand *minai*, two *minai* per hoplite as the law required. [49.2] The Lakedaimonians sent a delegation challenging the judgement on the grounds that it was unjust because the Olympic truce had not yet been announced in Lakedaimon at the time when they despatched the hoplites. [49.3] The Eleans insisted that the armistice was already in force in their country (the declaration is always made amongst them first); that they were at peace with all and not expecting any attack, as laid down by the terms of the truce; and that the Lakedaimonians had broken the law by taking them by surprise. [49.4] The Lakedaimonians replied that there was no longer any need for such a declaration at Lakedaimon if, as the Eleans thought, they had already broken the truce; but in fact they had made the announcement precisely because they did not think they had done wrong and had then immediately ceased hostilities. [49.5] The Eleans remained obdurate and refused to accept their claim to innocence. But they said that if the Lakedaimonians would hand back Lepreon to them, they would forgo their own share of the fine and would themselves pay the share which was owed to the god.

[50.1] When the Lakedaimonians refused to budge, the Eleans made another suggestion. They need not give back Lepreon, if they were unwilling, but since they were so eager to visit the temple, they must go up to the altar of Olympian Zeus and swear before all the Greeks that they genuinely intended to settle the fine at some later date. [50.2] When the Lakedaimonians refused this offer also, they were banned from the temple <and the sacrifices and contests> and sacrificed at home instead. But all the other Greeks apart from Lepreon took part in the festival. [50.3] But the Eleans were still frightened that the Lakedaimonians might try to make their sacrifices by force, so they kept their younger men under arms as a precautionary measure. So the Argives and the Mantineians supplied them with 1000 hoplites each, while the Athenians provided some cavalry, who were waiting in Arpina for the festival.

[Thucydides, *History of the Peloponnesian War* 5.49–50]

Battle of Mantineia, 418: See E99–E104.

H42   Sparta makes peace with Argos, 418 BC
[1] At the very beginning of the following winter, when the celebration of the Karneia was complete, the Lakedaimonians launched another expedition, and when they reached Tegea they sent conciliatory messages ahead of them to Argos. [2] There already existed in Argos a political grouping which was well disposed towards the Lakedaimonians and eager to bring about a dissolution of the democracy there. And now, after the result of the battle of Mantineia, they were in a much better position to persuade the people to reach a settlement. Their primary objective was to make peace with the Lakedaimonians, to follow this up with an alliance, and then to use this as the basis for an assault upon the democracy. [3] At this point Lichas the son of Arkesilaos, who acted as the Argives' *proxenos* to the Lakedamonians, arrived with the offer of two alternatives for the Argives, one if they wanted to continue their hostilities; the other if they preferred to make peace. By coincidence Alkibiades was in Argos at the time, but those who favoured the Lakedaimonians were now much more confident and open about their intentions, and persuaded the Argives to accept the peace proposals.

[Thucydides, *History of the Peloponnesian War* 5.76]

For the exact terms, recorded by Thucydides, see **B20**.

H43   Ransom of prisoners in the Peloponnesian War, 408/7 BC, and other times
Ransom for one *mna:* the Athenians and Lakedaimonians made this agreement in the war between them, to ransom prisoners for one *mna*. Androtion mentions this agreement: "When Euktemon of Kydathenaion was archon (408/7), Megillos, Endios and Philocharidas came from Lakedaimon to Athens as envoys." And he adds, "They returned those left over (after an exchange of prisoners), accepting one *mna* for each." He had previously stated that this was the agreement about prisoners.

[Androtion, *FGrH* 324 F 44 = Scholiast on Aristotle *Nikomachean Ethics* 5, 10]

An ancient commentator, explaining a phrase used by Aristotle, quotes from the *Attic History* of Androtion (*c.* 410–340 BC). Hdt. 6.79.1 tells us that ransom amongst the Peloponnesians was usually set at two *mnas*. Endios and Philocharidas had also been to Athens as envoys in 421 (Thuc. 5.44, see also **E42** for Endios as a friend of Alkibiades.)

Battle of Notion, 407 BC: See E121–E124
Battle of Aigospotamoi, 405 BC: See E127, E128

H44   Sparta supports the Thirty Tyrants in Athens 404 BC
However, when the Thirty began to consider how they might get the power to do just as they pleased with the state, their first act was to send Aeschines and Aristoteles to Lakedaimon and persuade Lysander to support their request that a garrison be sent. They claimed that this should remain there until they rid themselves of the 'the criminals' and establish their government; and they promised to pay for this garrison themselves.

[Xenophon, *Hellenika* 2.3.13]

SPARTA'S HEGEMONY AND DECLINE, 404–362 BC: H45–H74

The entire period is covered by Xenophon's contemporary *Hellenika*, though not in such a way as always to allow us to be sure of the sequence of events, let alone of motives and causation. The period almost exactly encompasses the reign of Agesilaos, subject of an encomium by Xenophon, a *Life* by Plutarch, and a selection of 79 anecdotes (Plutarch, *Mor.* 208C–215A). The best account of the whole period is Cartledge, *Agesilaos and the Crisis of Sparta* (1987).

H45   Sparta as leaders of Greece, *c.* 403 BC

[1] In Greece, the Lakedaimonians having put an end to the Peloponnesian War were acknowledged by all as holding the leadership by both land and sea. Appointing Lysander as navarch, they ordered him to journey around the city-states, installing in each officials they called harmosts, since the Lakedaimonians objected to democracies and wished to control the city-states through oligarchies. [2] They imposed tributes on those they had beaten in war, and though they had not used coined money before this time, they now collected each year more than one thousand talents in tribute.

[Diodoros, *Library of History* 14.10.1–2]

Thucydides (1.96) tells us that the tribute received each year by Athens was 460 talents at the inception of the Delian League and 600 talents p.a. by 431 BC (Thuc. 2.13).

H46   Spartan hegemony, 405–394 BC

The Lakedaimonians spent a long time competing for hegemony over the Greeks, but after they gained it they maintained it without dispute for scarcely twelve years.

[Polybius, *Histories* 1.2]

In the introduction to his account of how Rome achieved domination over the whole Mediterranean, Polybius contrasts their hegemony with that of other powers. The twelve year period will be from Aigospotamoi in 405 BC to Knidos in 394 BC (Xen. *Hell.* 4.3.10–12 and 4.8.1–2).

Spartan involvement in Persia, 401–395: see E151–E156
Kinadon conspiracy *c.* 399 BC – see E53

H47   Athenian-Boiotian alliance, 395 BC

Alliance of the Boiotians and Athenians for all time.

If anyone goes against [Athens] for war, [either by] land or by [sea], Boiotia is to help in full strength as called upon by the Athenians, [as far] as possible. And if [anyone] goes against [Boiotia] for war either [by land or] by sea, Athens is to help [in full strength as] called upon by the [Boiotians, as far as poss]ible. [*A couple more very fragmentary lines seem to set up a procedure for mutual changes to the treaty before the rest of the text is completely lost.*]

[*IG* 2² 14 = Rhodes & Osborne 6]

Two fragments of a *stele* from Athens preserve the defensive alliance formed in 395 BC in the face of the dispute which developed into the Corinthian War. The start of the dispute is described in detail by the Oxyrhynchus Historian (18), while Xen. *Hell.* 3.5.1–17, gives a convincing version of the Theban case for the alliance. A very similar document also shows an Athenian alliance with Lokris (*IG* 22 15).

CORINTHIAN WAR AND THE KING'S PEACE, 395–387 BC: H48–H56
The Corinthian War, 395–387 BC was fought by Sparta against a combination of Athens, Thebes, Corinth, Persia and others, resisting the threat of Spartan expansion. Diodoros' *Universal History* gives more prominence to events in Sicily in the relevant years (14.85–117). Xenophon who himself fought on the Spartan side at Koroneia (394 BC) gives an account in book 4 of his *Hellenika* which confusingly separates the naval campaigns from the rest of the narrative (4.8). In 394 BC Sparta won a victory at the Nemea river against a coalition army of the Athenians, Thebans, Argives and Corinthians (Xenophon, *Hellenika* 4.2.16–23, Diodoros 14.86). Later in the year, Agesilaos on his return from Asia won a victory at Koroneia with his army which was mainly composed of emancipated helots and the mercenary veterans of the Ten Thousand (Xenophon, *Hellenika* 4.3.1–23, Plutarch, *Agesilaos* 18). But Spartan control of the seas was ended by defeat at Knidos in the same year (**H49–H50**), by a Persian fleet commanded by the Athenian exile, Konon, and Sparta was already seeking peace by 392 BC (**H51**).

H48   The Corinthian War
Since most of the serious fighting in the war took place around Corinth, the war was called the Corinthian War and lasted eight years.

[Diodoros, *Library of History* 14.86.6]

H49   Spartan defeat at Knidos in 394 BC
[10] When Agesilaos was just about to enter Boiotia, the sun seemed to appear shaped like a crescent and news was brought to him that the Lakedaimonans had been defeated in a naval battle and that the navarch, Peisander, had been killed. He was also given an account of the way the battle had been fought. [11] For it was near Knidos that the two fleets had sailed against one another. Pharnabazus was navarch of the Phoenician ships, and Konon with the Greek fleet was positioned in front of him. [12] Peisander formed his battle line opposite Konon, although his ships were fewer in number than the Greek ships under Konon. However, his allies on the left wing immediately fled. Peisander himself, after he engaged the enemy at close quarters, was driven ashore, rammed by the enemy's beaks. All the others who were driven ashore abandoned their ships and escaped to Knidos, but Peisander fell fighting aboard his ship.

[Xenophon, *Hellenika* 4.3.10–12]

Following Agesilaos' recall (see **E155**), the Spartan fleet also set out to return but was defeated by a Persian/Athenian fleet led by Konon and Pharnabazus at Knidos in 394 BC. Xenophon was with Agesilaos at the time so presents the battle as it was reported, giving few details, though allowing exact dating by his reference to the eclipse (14 August 394). The Oxyrhynchus Historian 19–20 gives considerable detail of the Athenian general, Konon's efforts to get Persian money to maintain his combined naval force, while Diodoros (14.83.4–7), following the Oxy. Historian's (lost) account of the battle shows that fifty Spartan triremes were captured.

H50   End of Spartan rule at sea after Knidos, 394
Pharnabazus and Konon, after the sea-battle, put out to sea with all their ships against the Lakedaimonian allies. First the made the people of Kos revolt, then Nisyros and Teios. Next the Chians expelled the garrison and went over to Konon's side. The peoples of Mytilene, Ephesos and Erythrai similarly changed sides. A similar drive for change fell upon the cities; some expelled their Lakedaimonian garrisons and maintained their liberty, while others went over to Konon's side. As for the Lakedaimonians, it was from this time that they lost their command at sea.

[Diodoros, *Library of History* 14.84.3–4]

H51   Sparta offers peace with Athens (392/1 BC?)

Some people say that it is now imperative that we should continue fighting. So let us consider firstly, Athenians, why it is that we should fight. I think that all mankind would agree that war is necessary in the following circumstances – when one is being wronged or when helping those being wronged. Well then, we *are* being wronged and are helping the Boiotians who are being wronged. But if there is then an assurance from the Lakedaimonians that they shall stop wronging us, and if the Boiotians have decided to make peace and to allow Orchomenos to be independent, then why should we continue fighting? [14] So that our city might be free? She already is. So that we might build ourselves walls? That is allowed for in the peace. To be able to build new ships and refit and keep our current ones? That too is provided for, since the treaty makes all states independent. Or to bring back the islands of Lemnos, Skyros and Imbros? It is explicitly written that they are to belong to Athens. [15] Well then, is it to recover the Chersonese, our colonies, our overseas territories and our debts? But neither the King nor our allies give their support which we need to get them back by war. Or must we actually continue fighting until we have crushed the Lakedaimonians and their allies? We do not seem to have the resources for this, but even if we achieved this, what do we think we would have to face from the Persians once we had done so? [16] Well then, even if it were right to wage war for these reasons, and we had sufficient money and manpower, we ought not to do so. So if we have no reason, no enemies, no resources for war, how can it not be imperative for us to use all means to make peace?

[17] Now consider this, Athenians, that you are acting on behalf of all Greeks for a common peace and freedom, and creating the opportunity for them all to share in everything. Consider how the greatest states are ceasing hostilities. First the Lakedaimonians: when they went to war with us and our allies, they ruled land and sea, but now the peace leaves them neither. [18] And they are giving this up so that all Greece may be free, not because we have forced them to. In fact they have already won three battles: firstly at Corinth when all Corinth's allies were there, leaving her no excuse except that even on their own, the Lakedaimonians were strongest; next in Boiotia, under Agesilaos, when they gained a similar victory; thirdly when they captured Lechaion, though all the Argives and Corinthians were there, as well as us and the Boiotians. [19] But after showing Greece their amazing achievements, they, the victors in battle, are ready to make peace, keeping their own land and allowing those they defeated to keep their cities independent and to share the seas. Yet what peace terms would they have had from us if they had lost just one battle? …

[33] Some of you have an excessive eagerness for peace to be made as soon as possible: they claim that the forty-day period for you to deliberate is not required and that we have been wrong since we were sent to Lakedaimon with executive powers precisely to avoid having to refer the matter back to the assembly. …

[38] We achieved successes over a period of eighty-five years. [39] Then we were defeated in war and lost many things, including our walls and our navy which the Lakedaimonians took as securities. They took our fleet and demolished our walls to prevent our having them as a basis for setting up Athenian power once more. Yet now, as a result of our persuasion, Lakedaimonian envoys are now here with full powers to give back our securities to us, to allow us to have walls and a fleet, and to recognise our ownership of the islands. …

[41] Athenians, the choice is entirely yours as to what you want to decide. Argives and Corinthians are here to show you that war is better; Lakedaimonians have come to persuade you to make peace. That the final decision rests with you, not with the Lakedaimonians, is down to us: we, as delegates, have made all of you delegates. Each of you about to raise your hand is a delegate, making peace or war, as he decides. Remember our words, Athenians, and vote for things that you will never regret.

[Andokides, *On the Peace with the Spartans* 13–19, 33, 38–39, 41]

Andokides was the son of Andron (one of the '400' of 411 BC), and an Athenian orator who was sent as an ambassador to Sparta to discuss peace. His speech 'On the Peace with the Spartans' was delivered to the Athenian assembly on his return, but failed to persuade the Athenians who exiled Andokides and the other ambassadors. Xenophon does not mention Sparta's attempt to make peace with Athens but only the Spartans suing for peace with Persia in 392 BC (*Hell.* 4.8.14).

H52   Athenian rejection of Spartan peace offer, 392/1 BC

Not only did the Athenians not accept this peace, but they also rejected it as an outrage, as Philochoros describes in the following words in his account of the year of the archonship of Philokles of Anaphlystas [392/1 BC]: 'And the King dispatched the peace of Antalkidas, which the Athenians did not accept because it was written that all the Greeks who lived in Asia would belong to the King. Instead the Athenians exiled the envoys who had agreed to the peace in Sparta. Kallistratos proposed the motion and the envoys did not await the verdict. They were Andokides of Kydathenaion [*and three others*].'

[Didymos, *Demosthenes* 10.34 = Philochoros, *FGrH* 328 F149a]

Didymos wrote learned commentaries on a huge range of authors in the 1st century BC. Here his note on a peace treaty mentioned by Demosthenes quotes the *Attic History* of Philochoros (*c.* 340–260). That Andokides' speech (**H51**) nowhere mentions the Greek cities of Asia does not prove that the treaty proposed by Sparta did not include acknowledgement that they were to belong to Persia. In fact such a clause would best explain the assembly's angry rejection of the treaty and the exile of the envoys.

H53   The Peace of Antalkidas, 387 BC: Diodoros

[2] After these men had taken up office [387 BC], the Lakedaimonians who were struggling in their war against both the Greeks and the Persians despatched their navarch Antalkidas to Artaxerxes to seek peace. [3] Antalkidas did the best he could in negotiating the terms of his mission and the King said that he would make peace on condition that the Greek cities of Asia would be subject to the King, but all the other Greeks would be independent; and that he would make war on those who did not obey and did not accept the terms with the assistance of those who did consent to them. [4] The Lakedaimonians consented without opposition, but the Athenians and Thebans and some other Greeks were very unhappy at the cities of Asia being left in the lurch. But since they were not strong enough to fight on their own, they were forced to yield and accepted the peace.

[Diodoros, *Library of History* 14.110.2–4]

There may well have been a more important reason for **Athenian** and **Theban** unhappiness than that mentioned by Diodoros: 'other Greeks being independent' meant that the hegemony organisations building up around Athens and Thebes would need to end (see **H55** – *Hell.* 5.1.36), while Sparta's own Peloponnesian League, a free and voluntary organisation, would be exempted. Xenophon gives his account at *Hellenika* 5.1.29–31 including a little more detail on why Athenians and Argives also wanted peace. His quotation of the terms of the Peace is also slightly different:

H54   The Peace of Antalkidas/King's Peace, 387 BC: Xenophon

As a result, when Tiribazus ordered those who wished to hear the peace terms which he was bringing to them from the King to be present, all quickly attended the meeting. And when they had gathered, Tiribazus showed them the King's seal on a document and then read it as follows: 'King Artaxerxes thinks that it is right that the cities in Asia, and the islands named Klazomenai and Cyprus, should belong to him. He believes that all the other Greek cities, both large and small, should be left to govern themselves, except for Lemnos, Imbros and Skyros, which should belong to the Athenians, as in the past. If either of the two parties chooses not to accept this peace, I will make war upon them, together with those who accept this peace, both by land and sea, with ships and with money.'

[Xenophon, *Hellenika* 5.1.30]

The Peace of Antalkidas or King's Peace was the first of a series of 'Common Peaces'. Previous treaties, such as the Thirty Years' Peace had been for a specific period and between two cities (and sometimes their allies). The King's Peace, in contrast, was a multilateral agreement.

H55   Sparta as 'guardians of the King's peace'

The Lakedaimonians were just about holding their own in the war but, as a result of this 'Peace of Antalkidas', they gained a much more distinguished position. For by having been one of the main supporters of the King's Peace and by insisting that all the cities govern themselves, they had gained an additional ally in Corinth and they had made the Boiotian cities independent of the Thebans, an outcome which they had long desired. They had also ended the Argives' plan of taking over Corinth, by threatening to invade Argos unless she left Corinth alone.

[Xenophon, *Hellenika* 5.1.36]

H56   Opposition to the King's Peace

However is it not right, on account of the treaty, to wait a while and not to press on and make the expedition too soon? The states which have gained their freedom through this treaty feel much gratitude towards to the King because they believe that they have gained their independence from him, while those states which have been handed over to the barbarians complain bitterly of the Lakedaimonians and, to only a slightly lesser extent, of the others who entered into the peace because they were forced into slavery by them. Is it not then right to cancel this agreement, from which these sentiment have arisen – the notion that it is the barbarian who cares for Greece and stands guard over her peace, while among ourselves are to be found those who abuse and mistreat her?

[Isokrates, *Panegyricus* 4.175]

Isokrates is believed to have written this speech during the 380s BC, completing it by the summer of 380 BC. The speech – which calls for the Athenians to reassert their supremacy against the Persians– may have been intended to be delivered at a panhellenic festival, such as the Olympic Games, or may instead have been simply sent out to the cities in Greece.

H57   Spartan aggression against Mantineia, 385 BC

[5.1] At the same time as these events, the Lakedaimonians decided to make an expedition against Mantineia, ignoring the treaties in force, for the following reasons. Amongst the Greeks, the common peace of Antalkidas was in effect, according to which all the cities had removed their garrisons and recovered their independence as agreed. It was the nature of the Lakedaimonians to love to command and their choice to enjoy fighting; they found peace a great burden which they could not abide, and longed for their former dominance over Greece and were straining at the leash for some new opening. [5.2] So they immediately made trouble in the cities, using their own friends to creating factions in several of them which would provide plausible grounds for them to create trouble. For the cities, after recovering their independence, wanted a reckoning with those put in charge during the Lakedaimonian supremacy: this process was harsh, because the populations bore grudges, resulting in many being exiled, and so the Lakedaimonians took it upon themselves to help the defeated factions. [5.3] They gave a welcome to these men and sent them back with armed forces to return them to their homes, and thus initially enslaved the weaker cities but then later made war on the more important cities, making them subject: so they did not even maintain the general peace for two years. Seeing that the city of Mantineia was right on their borders and full of valiant men, the Lakedaimonians were jealous of it growing as a result of the peace and keen to humble the pride of its citizens. [5.4] So they first despatched ambassadors to Mantineia to order them to take down their walls and all move to the original five villages from which they had long since come together to found Mantineia. Since no one obeyed, they sent a force to besiege the city. [5.5] The Mantineians send ambassadors to Athens to ask for help. Though the Athenians did not choose to break the common peace, the Mantineians withstood the siege on their own and bravely resisted the enemy.

[12.1] In Greece the Lakedaimonians were besieging Mantineia, but the Mantineians gallantly resisted the enemy for the whole summer. They were indeed thought superior to the other Arkadians in bravery, which is why the Lakedaimonians used previously to have them standing next to them in battle as the most reliable of their allies. But with the onset of winter, the river which runs by Mantineia was greatly swollen by the rains, and the Lakedaimonians diverted it with great banks, turning the river towards the city and flooding all the surrounding region. [12.2] Buildings began to fall and the Mantineians in desperation were forced to hand over their city to the Lakedaimonians. They received the surrender and inflicted no punishment on the Mantineians except to order them to move back to their former villages. So they were compelled to raze their own city to the ground and move back to their villages.

[Diodoros, *Library of History* 15.5, 15.12]

Diodoros' account can be compared with the markedly pro-Spartan one given by Xenophon, (*Hellenika* 5.2.1–7 = **H58** below). In addition, Agesilaos contrived to be exempted from the campaign, embarrassing his rival king Agesipolis with an unpopular campaign against some of his own family connections (Xen. *Hell.* 5.2.3), while those of Agesilaos' family were the aristocrats who most benefited.

H58   Mantineian land-owners benefit from Sparta's enforced changes

After this, the wall was demolished and Mantineia was split up into four separate villages, like those they had inhabited in ancient times. At first they were displeased since they had had to tear down their houses and build new ones. However the owners of landed property were delighted with what had happened, since now they not only lived nearer to their estates, which were around the villages, but also enjoyed an aristocratic government and were rid of the bothersome demagogues. The Lakedaimonians sent to them not just one army officer, but one for each village. Indeed, they came in from the villages to join the Lakedaimonian army far more eagerly than they had done when they lived under a democracy.

[Xenophon, *Hellenika* 5.2.7]

'In this paragraph Xenophon expounds the secret of Sparta power in the Peloponnese, *viz.* prevention of unbanization, and support from the landed aristocracy.' Cawkwell (1979) in note on the Penguin translation, endorsed by Cartledge, *Agesilaos* 260, with the rider that this 'natural' sixth-century policy was now being reintroduced as a reactionary one.

H59   Sparta seizes the Theban akropolis (Kadmeia), 382 BC

[1] When Evandros was archon at Athens, the Romans elected six military tribunes, Quintus Sulpicius [etc. 382 BC] ... [2] the Spartiates gave orders to their commanders in secret that they should seize the Kadmeia if they had the chance. In accordance with this instruction, Phoibidas the Spartiate, who had been given command of a force to take to Olynthos seized the Kadmeia. The enraged Thebans rallied under arms, but he engaged them in battle and defeated them. He exiled three hundred of the most prominent Thebans, terrorized the rest, and put a strong garrison in place before going off on his own business. This act disgraced the Lakedaimonians in the eyes of the Greeks: they fined Phoibidas but did not remove the garrison from Thebes. [3] This was how the Thebans lost their independence and were forced to obey the Lakedaimonians.

[Diodoros, *Library of History* 15.20]

Xenophon, *Hellenika* 5.2.25–36 gives considerably more details of the attack, and goes on to say (5.4.1) that it was *the* cause of Sparta's downfall. It aimed at putting in power the pro-Spartan faction in Theban politics and succeeded because the Spartan forces caught the women of Thebes celebrating the *Thesmophoria* (a women-only religious festival) on the akropolis (named the Kadmeia after Thebes' legendary founder Kadmos). The event and Sparta's reaction was notorious: Plutarch (*Pelopidas* 6.1) remarks that the inconsistency of the Spartans in fining Phoibidas but maintaining control of Thebes amazed the rest of Greece. Moreover Agesilaos, having presumably paid his enormous fine, later sent him back to Boiotia as harmost of Thespiai, where he was killed fighting the Thebans in 378 (Xen. *Hell.* 5.4.41–6, Plut. *Pelopidas* 15; Diod. 15.33.5–6).

H60   Spartan reaction to the capture of the Kadmeia

Leontiades set out at once for Sparta, where he found the ephors and most of the citizens were angry with Phoibidas because he had executed this task without the authorisation of the state. However Agesilaos said that if the action of Phoibidas was harmful to Lakedaimonia, then he deserved to be punished; but, on the other hand, if it were good for Lakedaimonia, then they should remember the established rule that a commander in such cases could act on his own initiative: 'This point only should be considered,' he said, 'whether what he has done has been good or bad for Lakedaimonia.'

[Xenophon, *Hellenika* 5.2.32]

H61   The height of Spartan power, 380 BC
Once the Olynthians had signed up to the Spartiates' alliance many other cities were
eager to enlist under the leadership of the Lakedaimonians. So the Lakedaimonians
reached their greatest power at this time and held the hegemony of Greece both by
land and sea. [4] For the Thebes was occupied by a garrison; the Corinthians and
Argives were humbled by previous wars; the Athenians had a bad reputation in
Greece because they had imposed settlers on occupied territory. The Lakedaimonians,
however, had paid a lot of attention to having a large population and to armed training,
and were feared by all because of the strength of their rule.

[Diodoros, *Library of History* 15.23.3–5]

Xenophon gives a very similar judgement at *Hellenika* 5.3.27.

H62   Popular revolt against pro-Spartan faction in Thebes, 379/8
When Nausinikos was archon at Athens, the Romans elected four military tribunes with
consular power, Marcus Cornelius [etc. 378/7 BC] … During their year of office a war
known as the Boiotian War broke out between Lakedaimonians and Boiotians for the
following reasons. The Lakedaimonians had unjustly garrisoned the Kadmeia and exiled
many leading citizens: so the exiles came together, supported by the Athenians and
returned to their country by night. [2] First they killed the Lakedaimonian sympathisers,
catching them asleep in their own homes; next they rallied the citizens to the cause of
freedom, getting all the Thebans on their side. The population quickly gathered under
arms, and at daybreak tried to storm the Kadmeia. [3] The Lakedaimonians guarding
the citadel, who together with their allies numbered no fewer than 1,500, sent men
to Sparta to announce the Theban uprising and to call for help as soon as possible;
they themselves used their superior position to fight off the attackers, killing many and
wounding others badly. [4] The Thebans, anticipating that a large force would come
from Greece to help the Lakedaimonians, sent ambassadors to Athens to remind them
that they had helped restore the democracy at Athens when the Athenians had been
enslaved by the Thirty Tyrants: so they asked the Athenians to help with all their forces
in storming the Kadmeia before the Lakedaimonians could arrive.

[Diodoros, *Library of History* 15.25]

Xenophon gives a detailed version of the popular Theban uprising against Leontiades and the pro-Spartans
who had taken control in Thebes, supported by the Spartan garrison (*Hell.* 5.4.2–9). The Thebans besieged
the Spartan garrison on the akropolis. Both sides called for reinforcements leading to an Athenian force
joining in the siege. Accounts differ as to whether this force was raised after a vote in the assembly (Diodoros
15.26.1; Deinarchos, *Against Demosthenes* 39) or consisted of volunteers (Xen. *Hell.* 5.4.19, stressing that
the two generals were sentenced to death for leading this unofficial action). Xenophon's dating to 379/8 BC
is preferable to that given by Diodoros.

H63   Athenians help Thebans to liberate the Kadmeia in 379/378 BC
[378/7 BC] Encouraged by their commanders, the garrison on the Kadmeia showed
courage in warding off the enemy attack, confident that the Lakedaimonians would
soon arrive with a large force. While they had sufficient food they were strong in the
face of danger, and killed or wounded many of those besieging them, helped by the
strength of the akropolis. But when the shortage of essential supplies began to worsen,
and the Lakedaimonians took some time in getting the relief force ready, they began to
argue amongst themselves. [2] The Lakedaimonians thought they should die fighting,

while those serving alongside them from the allied cities who were far more numerous came out for surrendering the Kadmeia. So even the men from Sparta itself, being few in number, were forced to withdraw from the akropolis. Therefore they came to terms and were allowed, as agreed, to return to the Peloponnese. [3] The Lakedaimonians, however, were approaching Thebes with a considerable force, but were just too late and their assault failed. They put the three commanders of the garrison on trial: two were condemned to death; the third was given such a heavy fine that his estate could not pay it.

[Diodoros, *Library of History* 15.27.1–3]

Sphodrias affair – see E50

H64   Prospectus of the Second Athenian League, 378/7

[1] When Nausinikos was archon [378/7] …

[7] Aristoteles proposed: For the good fortune of the Athenians and the allies of the Athenians. So that the Lakedaimonians shall allow the Greeks to be free and independent, and to live at peace occupying their own territory in security … be it decreed by the people:

> [lines 15–46: *various clauses follow, promising that Athens will not do some of the things which had turned the Delian League into the Athenian Empire.*]

[46] If anyone goes for war against those who have made the alliance, whether by land or by sea, the Athenians and the allies shall help them both by land and by sea with all their strength as far as possible.

> [*The decree continues with various clauses to ensure its permanency and a further decree giving names of the states which joined the league.*]

[Rhodes & Osborne 22, lines 1, 7–14, 46–51]

This decree, enacted in Spring 377, is a prospectus, inviting states to join an existing league as a defensive alliance to resist encroachments by Sparta on the freedom of Greeks. The league kept itself within the terms of the Peace of Antalkidas (see **H53, H54**) as being for Greek states other than those ceded to the Persian King, and a free alliance. It is not clear whether the league was a response to the Sphodrias affair or the other way round. Diodoros (**H65**) is certainly wrong to place the league in 377/6 and may be wrong in his relative dating. For full text, translation and discussion of this decree and other related ones, see Rhodes & Osborne, *Greek Historical Inscriptions 404–323 BC* no 22.

H65   The Rise of the Second Athenian Confederacy

[377/6 BC] Now that the Lakedaimonians had stumbled at Thebes, the Boiotians were encouraged to unite and having made an alliance, put together a significant force, anticipating that the Spartans would come to Boiotia in great force. [2] Meanwhile the Athenians sent their most highly respected ambassadors to the cities which were under the Lakedaimonians, urging them to stand up for their common freedom. For the Lakedaimonians, because of the size of their armed forces, ruled those under them with contempt and severity. So many of those under them defected to the Athenians. [3] The first to take heed and leave the Lakedaimonians were the Chians and Byzantines, and after them the people of Rhodes and Mytilene and some of the other islanders. As the rush of Greeks increased still further, many cities went over to the Athenians. The democracy, buoyed up by the favourable response of these cities formed a common council of all the allies and appointed council members from each city. [4] It was decided unanimously that the council should meet at Athens, that each city, whether great or small, should be equal and have a single vote, and that all should be independent, while treating the Athenians as leaders. The Lakedaimonians, seeing that the movement of the cities leaving them was irresistible, nevertheless worked hard, through embassies, friendly messages, and announcement of benefits to make up for having alienated those people.

[Diodoros, *Library of History* 15.28.1–4]

H66   Spartan defeat at Tegyra in 375 BC

At the same time [376/5 BC] the Thebans marched against Orchomenos with a select force of 500 men, and achieved a memorable result. For the Lakedaimonians kept many soldiers stationed at Orchomenos and drew them up against the Thebans: a significant fight took place in which the Thebans attacked and defeated the Lakedaimonians who outnumbered them two to one. Never had such an event happened previously – it had seemed enough if a large force defeated a small one.

[Diodoros, *Library of History* 15.37]

Kleombrotos (Xen. *Hell*. 5.4.14) and then Agesilaos (Diodoros 15.32) had enjoyed successful campaigns in Thebes following the loss of the Kadmeia, but prior to the defeat at Tegyra. Plutarch gives further details of this battle in his *Life of Pelopidas* (the Theban commander at Tegyra) 16.1–2, 17.1–4, including the fact that the Thebans were outnumbered two to one. Though both Spartan commanders were killed (*Pelopidas* 17.3) the main importance of the battle was psychological, as Diodoros implies, and as a 'prelude to Leuktra' (*Pelopidas* 16.1). Xenophon's *Hellenika* omits the battle entirely.

H67   Common Peaces, 375/4 and 371 BC

[27.4] Epaminondas … delivered a speech not just on behalf of the Thebans but also for the Greeks as a whole, demonstrating that war had strengthened Sparta and caused suffering for everyone else. He urged that a peace be made on equal and just terms, saying that it would only be a lasting one if all were on an equal footing. [28.1] Agesilaos noticed that all the other Greeks were listening carefully to Epaminondas and admired his sentiments, so he asked him whether he thought that it would be just and equal for the towns of Boiotia to govern themselves. Instantly Epaminondas replied boldly by asking him in return whether he thought it just and equal for the towns of Lakonia also to enjoy independence. Agesilaos leapt up from his seat in anger and ordered him to state clearly whether Boiotia should be independent. [28.2] And when Epaminondas repeated his own question on whether Lakonia should be independent, Agesilaos was so furious that he used this as a pretext to erase the name of the Thebans out of the peace treaty and to declare war on them. He made a peace with the rest of the Greeks and dismissed them, saying that what could be settled peaceably, should be; what could not be would be dealt with by war, since it had proven too difficult to resolve and remove all of their differences.

[Plutarch, *Life of Agesilaos* 27.4 – 28.2]

Pausanias also includes this, clearly well-known anecdote of Epaminondas and Agesilaos, though he confuses it with the Peace of Antalkidas. The point seems to have been a growing Greek awareness that Spartan claims to championing Greek liberty contrasted with their treatment of their own perioikic towns (not to mention the helots). For the Spartans, this was, of course, and extremely sensitive point, hence Agesilaos' reaction.

H68   A summary of Leuktra, 371 BC
[5] That this expedition was undertaken more from anger than from reason is shown by
the timings. For the peace treaty was made at Sparta on the fourteenth of Skirophorion
and the Spartans were defeated at Leuktra on the fifth of Hekatombaeion, only
twenty days later. In that battle, a thousand Spartans fell. [6] Among them were King
Kleombrotos and the bravest of the Spartan warriors. Among these, it is said that the
handsome youth Kleonymos, son of Sphodrias, was struck down three times at the
feet of the king but rose to his feet three times and died there fighting the Thebans.

[Plutarch, *Life of Agesilaos* 28.5–6]

For detailed accounts of the battle, see **E106–E112.** Plutarch here gives the dates of July 6th 371 BC for the
Battle of Leuktra and dates the peace conference at Sparta to around June 16th.

H69   Agesilaos breaks Lykourgos' 'third *rhetra*'
[5] Records exist of a third *rhetra* of Lykourgos forbidding frequent campaigns against
the same enemies, in case those enemies became used to defending themselves and
became too warlike as a result. [6] In later years they levelled precisely this criticism
against King Agesilaos in particular, because his lengthy and frequent invasions and
campaigns against the Boiotians made them a match for the Lakedaimonians. This was
what made Antalkidas remark to the king, when he saw that he had been wounded,
"Now you are getting a fat teacher's fee from the Thebans for instructing them how to
fight when they did not know how and didn't even want to learn."

[Plutarch, *Life of Lykourgos* 13.5–6]

Plutarch also includes this among his *Sayings of Spartans* (Antalkidas). For the 'Great *Rhetra*' see **D48.**

H70   Epaminondas founds Messene
Epaminondas' period in office as boiotarch (Boiotian leader) had expired and the death
penalty was laid down for anyone extending their term of office. So Epaminondas,
ignoring the law as obsolete, continued as boiotarch and reached Sparta with his army.
When Agesilaos did not come out to fight him he then went off to found Messene.
So Epaminondas is the founder of present-day Messene, and the founding I have
explained in my account of the Messenians themselves.

[Pausanias, *Description of Greece* 9.14.5]

Pausanias had described Epaminondas' founding of Messene at 4.27.5–7 and the city itself 4.31.3 – 33.2.

H71   The refounding of Messene by Epaminondas, 369 BC
Epaminondas' nature was to be ambitious and to seek everlasting fame, so he advised
the Arkadians and his other allies to refound Messene which for many years the
Lakedaimonians had kept uninhabited since it occupied a good position for operations
against Sparta. With their agreement, Epaminondas sought out the remnants of the
Messenians, and founded Messene, enrolling as citizens any others who wished to,
and creating a large population. He divided the land among them, rebuilt and restored
a sizable Greek city, and gained a great reputation among all men.

[Diodoros, *Library of History* 15.66.1]

Epaminondas' refounding of Messene enclosed the citadel of Mt Ithome and surrounding land within a wall 9 miles long complete with 30 towers and a covered walkway. The work was apparently carried on in the space of 85 days (Diodoros 15.67.1 & Plutarch, *Sayings of Spartans*: Epaminondas): Pausanias (4.31.3) described the walls as stronger than anywhere he had seen.

H72   Mantineia and Megalopolis founded in the Peloponnese 370–367?

Then Epaminondas immediately hastened to matters in the Peloponnese at the eager prompting of the Arkadians. On his arrival he gained the Argives as eager allies, and brought the Mantineians back again into their old city, after their dispersal into villages by Agesipolis. He persuaded the Arkadians to break up all their weak towns and to build a common homeland, which even in our day is still called Great City (Megalopolis).

[Pausanias, *Description of Greece* 9.14.4]

Mantineia (Paus 8.6–12) was refounded in 370 BC (for its dispersal by the Spartans into villages, see **H57, H58**). Megalopolis (Diod. 15.72; Paus 8.27) was built from scratch as a fortified city sometime between 370 and 367 BC (sources disagree). Both were intended as bulwarks against any future Spartan aggression.

H73   An inconclusive result to the Second Battle of Mantineia
(for the battle itself, see E114)

[26] The outcome of this battle was the opposite of what all men had believed would happen. For virtually the whole of Greece had taken part, on one side or the other, and everyone imagined that if a battle were fought, the winner would become the ruling power and those who lost would become their subjects. But the god ordered both parties to set up a trophy as though they had won, and neither side to hinder the other from doing so. Both sides gave back the dead under a truce as though they had won and both sides received back their dead under a truce as though they had been defeated. Both sides claimed to be victorious. [27] However neither side was any better off after the battle, in regards to additional territory, cities or influence, than before the battle had taken place. In fact, there was even more confusion and disorder in Greece after the battle than before. Let this, then, conclude my narrative. Perhaps another writer will deal with the events after this.

[Xenophon, *Hellenika* 7.5.26–7]

H74   Spartans refuse to acknowledge Messenia in 'Common Peace' 362 BC

After the battle the Greeks came to terms with one another, since the result was not clear, and they had proved equal in courage; furthemore they were exhausted by the continuous hazards. After putting together a common peace and alliance, they began to include the Messenians in the alliance. [2] But the Lakedaimonians, because of their unwavering hostility towards them chose not to join in the treaty and, alone of the Greeks, remained outside it.

[Diodoros, *Library of History* 15.89.1–2]

H75   Epitaph to Epaminondas, *c.* 362 BC

The verses on the statue of Epaninondas … go like this:

> By our counsel Sparta has been shorn of her glory,
> Holy Messene at long last receives her children:
> By Theban weapons, Megalopolis was crowned,
> All of Greece is autonomous and at liberty.

[Pausanias, *Description of Greece* 9.15.4]

SECTION K
SPARTA AND ENVIRONS

THE TOWN OF SPARTA

Spartans famously boasted that their town needed no walls to defend it, only men (**F52.6**). Thucydides commented presciently on how unimpressive Sparta might one day look compared to Athens (**H1**), though the situation was complicated greatly by the building of Hellenistic and Roman Sparta. Pausanias gives a description of the Sparta of his day (*c.* AD 150) at 3.11–18, and gives us some useful information on the classical town, But even with his help, only two classical sites, the sanctuary of Artemis Orthia and the temple of Athena on the acropolis have been identified for certain.

K1   Sparta or Lakedaimon

As one moves away from Thornax, there is the city (*polis*) which was initially called Sparta, but over time came also to be known as Lakedaimon which was previously the name of the land.

[Pausanias, *Description of Greece* 3.11.1]

K2   The Persian Stoa

The most impressive thing in the *agora* is what they call the Persian Stoa since it was made of spoils from the Persian Wars: over time they have altered it to its current size and splendour.

[Pausanias, *Description of Greece* 3.11.3]

K3   The Temple of Athena

The Lakedaimonians do not have an akropolis rising up to a prominent height, like the Kadmeia at Thebes or the Larisa at Argos. But there are hills in the city, and they call the tallest of these the akropolis. [2] The temple of Athena, known both as Poliouchos ('Holding the City') and Chalkioikos ('Of the Bronze House') has been built there. They say that Tyndareos began the building of the temple. When he died, his children wished to make a second attempt to finish the building, intending to use the spoils from the people of Aphidna. They too left it unfinished, and many years later the Lakedaimonians made Athena's temple and her statue both in bronze. Gitiadas a local architect oversaw the work. Gitiadas also wrote Dorian songs, including a hymn to the goddess. [3] Many of the Labours of Herakles are worked on the bronze …

[Pausanias, *Description of Greece* 3.17.1–3]

K4   The 'Marshes' at Sparta

Inland from Taygetos and below it lies Sparta and Amyklai, where there is the temple to Apollo, and Pharis, The *polis* is sited in something of a hollow, though mountains are included within its limits. No part of it is now marshy, though in ancient times the area in front of the city was marshy and was called Limnai ('Marshes'), and the temple of Dionysos in Limnai stood on wet ground.

[Strabo, *Geography* 8.5.1]

K5   Theban invasion of Lakonia, 370/369 BC

They made no attempt to cross the bridge to attack the town, since the hoplites could be seen in the sanctuary of Athena Alea ready to face them. Instead, keeping the Eurotas on their right, they went past the town, ransacking and burning houses which were full of many valuables. … The Spartiates, since their city had no walls, were stationed here and there to guard it – there seemed few of them and there were few.

[Xenophon, *Hellenika* 6.5.27]

K6   A stone quarry at Gytheion

Let no one dig anything out. If anyone or his slave digs anything out, let him be cursed. […] according to the law. Let him keep away.

[*IG* 5.1.1155]

Inscription of the 5th century, carved into the rock of Mount Larysion at Gytheion. See Cartledge *SL* p.154.

BIBLIOGRAPHY

Literary Texts, Translations and Commentaries

Asheri, D., *et al., A Commentary on Herodotus Books I–IV* (Oxford 2007)

Boedeker, D. & Sider, D., edd. *The New Simonides* (Oxford 2001)

Campbell, D.A., *Greek Lyric II* (Harvard 1988)

Flower, M.A. & Marincola, J., *Herodotus, Histories* Book IX (Cambridge 2002)

Gow, A.S.F. & Page, D.L., *The Greek Anthology – Hellenistic Epigrams* (Cambridge 1965)

Gow, A.S.F. & Page, D.L., *The Greek Anthology – The Garland of Philip* (Cambridge 1968)

Hornblower, S., *A Commentary on Thucydides* (3 volumes, Oxford, 1991, 1996, 2008)

McKechnie, P.J. & Kern, S.J., *Hellenika Oxyrhynchia* (Oxford 1988)

Page, D.L., *Further Greek Epigrams* (Cambridge 1981)

Sommerstein, A.H., ('Aris & Phillips' editions with text, translation, and commentary on each individual play of Aristophanes, with separate volume of Indexes) (Oxford 1994–2002)

Talbert, R.J.A., *Plutarch on Sparta* (translation with introduction and notes) (London 1988, 2nd ed., 2005)

West, M.L., *Greek Lyric Poetry* (translated with introduction and notes) (Oxford 1994)

Xenophon, *A History of My Times* (tr. R. Warner, introduction and notes by G. Cawkwell) (London 1979)

Epigraphic texts, translations and commentaries

Fornara, C.W., *Translated Documents of Greece & Rome 1: Archaic times to the end of the Peloponnesian War* (2nd ed. Cambridge 1983)

Loomis, W.T., *The Spartan War Fund, IG V 1,1 and a New Fragment* (Stuttgart 1992)

Meiggs, R. & Lewis, D.M., *Greek Historical Inscriptions to the End of the Fifth Century,* (Oxford 1988)

Osborne, R. & Rhodes, P.J., *Greek Historical Inscriptions* 478–404 BC (Oxford 2017 (or 2018))

Rhodes, P.J. & Osborne, R., *Greek Historical Inscriptions* 404–323 BC (Oxford 2003)

Rhodes, P.J., *The Greek City States, a sourcebook* (2nd ed. Cambridge 2007)

Books and Collections

Burkert, W., *Greek Religion* (Oxford 1985)

Cambridge Ancient History IV: Persia, Greece and the Western Mediterranean c.*525–479 BC* (2nd ed. Cambridge 1988)

Cambridge Ancient History V: The Fifth Century BC (2nd ed. Cambridge 1992)

Cartledge, P., *Sparta and Lakonia, a Regional History* 1300–362 BC (2nd edition, London 2002)

Cartledge, P., *The Spartans, an Epic History* (London 2003)

Cartledge, P., *Agesilaos and the Crisis of Sparta* (Baltimore 1987)

Cartledge, P., *Spartan Reflections* (Bristol 2013)

Cartledge, P. & Spawforth, A., *Hellenistic and Roman Sparta, a tale of two cities* (2nd edition, London 2002)

Christesen, P., *Olympic Victor Lists and Ancient Greek History*, Cambridge 2007

Coldstream, J.N., Geometric Greece: 900–700 BC (2nd edition, Routledge 2003)

Dawkins, R.M., *The Sanctuary of Artemis Orthia at Sparta* (London 1929)

Ducat, J., *Spartan Education*, (Classical Press of Wales 2006)

Forrest, W.G., *A History of Sparta 950–192 BC* (London 1980, 3rd ed., 1995)

Hodkinson, S., *Property and Wealth in Classical Sparta* (Classical Press of Wales 2000)

Hodkinson, S. & Powell, A. (edd.), *Sparta: New Perspectives* (Classical Press of Wales 1999)

Hodkinson, S. & Powell, A. (edd.), *Sparta and War* (Classical Press of Wales 2006)

Hornblower, S., *The Greek World 479–323 BC* (3rd ed. London 2002)

Kennell, N.M., *The Gymnasium of Virtue: Education and culture in ancient Sparta* (London 1995)

Kennell, N.M., *Spartans: a New History* (Chichester 2010)

Kuhrt, A., *The Persian Empire: a Corpus of Sources from the Achaemenid period* (550–330 BC) (Oxford 2007)

Lazenby, J.F., *The Spartan Army* (Oxford 1985)

Lazenby, J.F., *The Defence of Greece 490–479 BC* (Oxford 1993)

Lazenby, J.F., *The Peloponnesian War: A Military Study* (Oxford 2004)

Lewis, D.M., *Sparta and Persia* (Leiden 1977)

Lewis, D., *Greek Slave Systems and their Eastern Neighbours* (Oxford 2017)

Luraghi, N., *The Ancient Messenians: Constructions of Ethnicity and Memory* (Cambridge 2008)

Luraghi, N. & Alcock, S.E. (edd.), *Helots and Their Masters in Messenia and Laconia: Histories, Ideologies, Structures* (Harvard 2004)

Murray, O., *Early Greece* (2nd ed. London 1993)

Ollier, F., *Le Mirage spartiate* (2 vols., Lyon & Paris 1933 and 1943)

Osborne, R., *Greece in the Making 1200–479 BC* (London 1996, 2nd ed., 2009)

Osborne, R. (ed.), *The Short Oxford History of Europe: Classical Greece, 500–323 BC* (Oxford 2000)

Pomeroy, S.B., *Spartan Women* (Oxford 2002)

Poralla, P., & Bradford, A.S., *A Prosopography of the Lacedaminonians from the earliest times to the death of Alexander the Great (X – 323 BC),* (2nd ed., Chicago 1985)

Powell, A., (ed.) *Classical Sparta: Techniques Behind Her Success* (London 1989)

Powell, A. & Hodkinson, S. (edd.), *The Shadow of Sparta* (London 1994)

Powell, A. & Hodkinson, S. (edd.), *Sparta Beyond the Mirage* (Classical Press of Wales 2002)

Rawson, E., *The Spartan Tradition in European Thought* (Oxford 1969)

Rees, O., *Great Battles of the Classical World,* (Pen & Sword 2016).

Rhodes, P.J., *A Short History of Ancient Greece,* (London 2014)

Salapata, G., *Heroic offerings: the terracotta plaques from the Spartan sanctuary of Agamemnon and Kassandra.* (Ann Arbor 2014).

Shepherd, W., *Pylos and Sphacteria* 425 BC: Sparta's island of disaster (Osprey 2013)

Tod, M.N. & Wace A.J.B., *A Catalogue of the Sparta Museum* (Oxford 1906)

Whitby, M. (ed.), *Sparta* (London 2002)

Articles

Andrewes, A., 'Notion and Kyzikos: the sources compared' *Journal of Hellenic Studies* 102 (1982), 15–25.

Bauslaugh, R. A., "Messenian dialect and dedications of the 'Methanioi,'" in *Hesperia* 59 (1990), 661–8

Bolmarcich, 'The Date of the "Oath of the Peloponnesian League"' in *Historia* 57 (2008), 65–79

Braun, T., 'Khrestous poiein' in *Classical Quarterly* 44 (1994), 40–45

Cartledge, P., 'Sparta and Samos: A Special Relationship?' in *Classical Quarterly* 32 (1982), 243–265.

Catling, H.W., 'Excavations at the Menelaion, Sparta, 1973–1976' in *Archaeological Reports* No.23 (1976–1977), 24–42

Catling, H.W., 'A sanctuary of Zeus Messapeus: Excavations at Aphyssou, Tsakona, 1989', *Annual of the British School at Athens* 85 (1990) 15–35

Catling, H.W. & Shipley G., 'Messapian Zeus: an early sixth-century inscribed cup from Lakonia', *Annual of the British School at Athens* 84 (1989) 187–200

Christesen, P., 'Kings playing politics: the heroization of Chionis of Sparta', *Historia* 59, 2010, 26–73.

Christesen, P., 'A New Reading of the Damonon *Stele' (forthcoming)*

Connor, W.R., "Pausanias 3.14.1: A Sidelight on Spartan History *c.* 440 BC?" in *Transactions of the Americal Philological Association* 109, 21–27

de Carvalho Gomes, C.H., 'Xouthias son of Philakhaios' in *Zeitschrift für Papyrologie und Epigraphik* 108 (1995), 103–106 = http://www.uni-koeln.de/phil-fak/ifa/zpe/downloads/1995/108pdf/108103.pdf

Dillon, M., 'Were Spartan Women who died in childbirth honoured with inscriptions?' in *Hermes*, 135 (2007), 149–165

Ducat, J., 'The Spartan 'tremblers'' in Hodkinson & Powell (2006)

Figuera, T.J., 'The Spartan *hippeis*' in Hodkinson & Powell (2006)

Flower, M.A., in Powell & Hodkinson, *Sparta Beyond the Mirage,* ch. 7A.

Figueira, T.J., 'The Demography of the Spartan Helots' in Luraghi & Alcock, *Helots*

Flower, M., 'The Invention of Tradition in Classical and Hellenistic Sparta' in Powell & Hodkinson (2002)

Griffiths, A., 'Was Kleomenes Mad?' in Powell (1989).

Hodkinson, S., *Transforming Sparta: new approaches to the study of Spartan society' in* Ancient History: Resources for Teachers Vol 41–44 (2011–2014) Mauarie University, NSW, Australia, pages 1–43 = http://eprints.nottingham.ac.uk/32475/2/Hodkinson.%20Transforming%20Sparta%20Ancient%20History%20Resources%20for%20Teachers%2041-44%202011-2014.pdf

Hooker, J.T., 'Spartan Propaganda' in Powell (1989).

Hodkinson, S., 'An Agonistic Culture' in Hodkinson & Powell (1999)

Hornblower, S., 'Thucydides, Xenophon, and Lichas: Were the Spartans Excluded from the Olympic Games from 420 to 400 B. C.?' *Phoenix* 54, no.3/4 (2000), 212–225

Lamb, W.M., 'Bronzes from the Acropolis, 1924–27', in *Annual of the British School at Athens* 28 (1926/7), 82–95

Lane Fox, R., 'Thucydides and Documentary History' in *Classical Quarterly* 60 (2010), 11–29.

Lippman, M., Scahill, D. & Schultz, P., '*Knights* 843–59, the Nike Temple Bastion, and Cleon's Shields from Pylos' in *American Journal of Archaeology* 110 (2006) 551–563

Low, P., 'Commemorating the Spartan war-dead' in Hodkinson & Powell (2006)

Parker, R., 'Spartan Religion' in Powell (1989)

Parker, R., 'Religion in Public Life' in Whitby (2002)

Powell, A., 'Why did Sparta not destroy Athens in 404, or 403 BC?' in Hodkinson & Powell (2006)

Schütrumpf, E., "Aristotle on Sparta" in Powell & Hodkinson (1994)

de Ste Croix, 'Trials at Sparta' in Whitby (2002)

Woodward, A.M. 'The Inscriptions' in ed. Dawkins, *The Sanctuary of Artemis Orthia at Sparta,* 1929

INDEX OF LITERARY PASSAGES

CONCORDANCE
OF INSCRIPTIONS

Reference	Code		Reference	Code
BM 1909,0522.1	C17		5.1.1316	C24
DAI, *Archaeologischer Anzeiger*			5.1.1329	B38
1965, p.400	C38		5.1.1338	B44
FD			5.1.1345	C27
3.1.3	B33a		5.1.1562	B8
3.1.90	B11		5.1.1563	B3
3 1.573	B11		5.1.1564	B27
IG			5.1.1564a	C55
1³.522	B13		5.1.1590	B45
2².14	H47		5.1.1591	B49
2².1388	B26		5.2.159	E73
2².11678	B25b		7.2462	B30
5.1.1	C34		*IvO* 171	C59
5.1.213	C83		*IvO* 247	B9a
5.1.214	B39		*LSAG* Lakonia 16a	C16
5.1.215	C11		*LSAG* Messenia 3	B9b
5.1.222	C67		ML	
5.1.226	C8		22	B8
5.1.231	C25		27	B5
5.1.238	C78		36	B10a
5.1.252	C7		67 bis	B15
5.1.252b	C6		74	B14a
5.1.255	C86		OR (Osborne & Rhodes)	
5.1.257	C90		112	B10a
5.1.263	C88		151	B15
5.1.269	C87		164	B14a
5.1.274	C89		192	B23
5.1.290	C91		RO (Rhodes & Osborne)	
5.1.457	C36		3	B27
5.1.699	B37		6	H47
5.1.701	B40		22	H64
5.1.702	B41		30	B30
5.1.703	B36		SEG	
5.1.704	B50		10.325	B13
5.1.707	B42		11.653	C12
5.1.708	B53		11.655	C81
5.1.713	B54		11.662	C14
5.1.714	B55		11.664	C15
5.1.718	B48		11.689	C1
5.1.919	C28		11.697	C82
5.1.927	C4		11.905	C3
5.1.928	C5		11.953	C27
5.1.1107a	C9		11.955	C18
5.1.1125	B47		11.989	C2
5.1.1155	K6		11.1180a	B1
5.1.1116	C13		11.1214	C23
5.1.1119	C26		11.1227	C49
5.1.1120	C79		14.329	C67
5.1.1124	B43		22.460	B32
5.1.1128	C20		23.324b	B23b

INDEX OF PEOPLE

Gods & Goddesses

INDEX OF PLACES AND PEOPLES

INDEX OF THEMES

Wars:
    Corinthian War: H48–H56
    Messenian Wars: A1, A12, B8, B9, D26,
        D34, D44, E16, E60, E62–E64, E66,
        H3–H5, H22
    Persian Wars: A21, B5, B6, D26, E25,
        E84–E86, E116, F9–F26, H15–H19
    Peloponnesian War (First): H23–H35
    Peloponnesian War (431–404 BC): B12,
        B21, B22, E29–E32, E34, E35,
        E37, E39, E40, E43, E56, E68, E76,
        E87–E104, E117–E130, E140, E141,
        E144, E146–E148, E150, E157–
        E159, F4, G3, G4, H36–H43, H45
    'Sacred War': H29
    Other wars: B10, B30, D69, D101, E69,
        E106–E114, E151, E152, E155,
        E156, G2, H8, H10, H62, H67
War in general: A8–A10, B15, B16, B18,
    B35a–b, B36, B40–B43, B47, B50–B53,
    C85, D5, D27, D28, D84, D88, D90, E28,
    H47, H64
Wealth: A9, C57, D9, D28, D52–D59, D63,
    D69, E16, E28, E49, E61, E70–E76, E136,
    E155, F5, G3
Weapons: see Armour

Whippings: C52, C53, C72, C92–C94, C84,
    C85, D41, D50, D74, D78, D80
Wine: D8, D44, D60, D61, D63, D68, D71,
    E77, E92, E127, F30
Women (in general): A6, A7, A13, A16, A17,
    A20, B35b, D8, D10, D15, D54, D64–
    D73, D78, D80, D96, E6, E69, E95, E112,
    E113, F30, F32, F35; see also Girls
Women (individuals): A14, A16, B7, B54, B55,
    C11, C14, C15, C27, D73, E81
Women (royal family): C52, C55–C58, D2,
    D63, D70, E8, E16, E20, E78, E79, E82,
    F30, F31
Wresting: A9, C40, C41, C44, C47, C48, D68,
    D70, D74, D94
Writing-tablets: D15, E78, F26

Xenia (guest-friendship): E13, E42, F25

Young men: (eirens): D74, D78, D80;
    (ephebes): C72, C73, C93, D80, D81,
    D90, E64; (*hebontes*): D74, D78, E50,
    E73; (*koros*): C36; (*neanikoi*): C69,
    D63, D70; (*neoi*): A7–A9, D15, D20,
    D44, D49, D70, D71, D74, D75, D78,
    D90, E53a, E82